Enemy Literature

An entire forgotten corpus of US writing on the Nazi German enemy boomed in a matter of a few years, peaked during World War II, and collapsed within months of the war ending. For a fleeting moment in history, significant parts of the intellectual world in the United States converged to provide a cool-headed analysis of the Nazi threat and a clear identification of the enemy. Starting in 1944, these writers also offered an elaborate plan for a postwar reeducation that would transform the National Socialist German nation into a democratic ally. Readers alarmed by the current resurgence of authoritarianism will learn from the work of those activists who analyzed Nazi Germany during World War II. This book, the first monographic study of this literature, provides pointed introductions to the main intellectual projects, their unique collaborative spirit, and their epochal results.

Frederic Ponten is Assistant Professor of German studies at the University of Regensburg.

Enemy Literature

*How American Intellectuals and European Émigrés
Collaborated Against Nazi Germany*

FREDERIC PONTEN
Universität Regensburg, Germany

Shaftesbury Road, Cambridge CB2 8EA, United Kingdom

One Liberty Plaza, 20th Floor, New York, NY 10006, USA

477 Williamstown Road, Port Melbourne, VIC 3207, Australia

314–321, 3rd Floor, Plot 3, Splendor Forum, Jasola District Centre, New Delhi – 110025, India

103 Penang Road, #05–06/07, Visioncrest Commercial, Singapore 238467

Cambridge University Press is part of Cambridge University Press & Assessment, a department of the University of Cambridge.

We share the University's mission to contribute to society through the pursuit of education, learning and research at the highest international levels of excellence.

www.cambridge.org
Information on this title: www.cambridge.org/9781009335362

DOI: 10.1017/9781009335379

© Frederic Ponten 2026

This publication is in copyright. Subject to statutory exception and to the provisions of relevant collective licensing agreements, no reproduction of any part may take place without the written permission of Cambridge University Press & Assessment.

When citing this work, please include a reference to the
DOI 10.1017/9781009335379

First published 2026

Cover image: Javier Zayas Photography / Moment / Getty Images

A catalogue record for this publication is available from the British Library

Library of Congress Cataloging-in-Publication Data
NAMES: Ponten, Frederic author
TITLE: Enemy literature : how American intellectuals and European émigrés collaborated against Nazi Germany / Frederic Ponten.
DESCRIPTION: Cambridge, United Kingdom ; New York, NY : Cambridge University Press, 2026. | Includes bibliographical references and index.
IDENTIFIERS: LCCN 2025020433 (print) | LCCN 2025020434 (ebook) |
ISBN 9781009335386 hardback | ISBN 9781009335379 ebook
SUBJECTS: LCSH: Anti-Nazi movement – Europe – History | Anti-Nazi movement – United States – History | Political refugees – Germany – History – 20th century | Intellectuals – Political activity – Europe – History – 20th century | Intellectuals – Political activity – United States – History – 20th century
CLASSIFICATION: LCC DD256.3 .P65 2026 (print) | LCC DD256.3 (ebook)
LC record available at https://lccn.loc.gov/2025020433
LC ebook record available at https://lccn.loc.gov/2025020434

ISBN 978-1-009-33538-6 Hardback
ISBN 978-1-009-33536-2 Paperback

Cambridge University Press & Assessment has no responsibility for the persistence or accuracy of URLs for external or third-party internet websites referred to in this publication and does not guarantee that any content on such websites is, or will remain, accurate or appropriate.

For EU product safety concerns, contact us at Calle de José Abascal, 56, 1°, 28003 Madrid, Spain, or email eugpsr@cambridge.org

For Jonas and Lukas

Contents

List of Figures   *page* ix
Acknowledgments   xi

1 Introduction: The Rise of Gray Literature   1
  1.1 Entering the Memorandum Culture   6
  1.2 Émigré Collaborators   12
  1.3 National Literature: German Problems   17
  1.4 Include Me Out   22
  1.5 Exclude Me In   34

2 Cool Collaboration   41
  2.1 Riesman's *Lonely Crowd* and the Other-Direction of the Memorandum   43
  2.2 Creole Hypothermia   48
  2.3 Transatlantic Continuities   52
  2.4 Renaissance of Cool   58
  2.5 Fool's Game Theory   63

3 The Invention of the Intelligence Report   66
  3.1 The Materiality of Intelligence: Index Cards and Microfilm   68
  3.2 Administering Intelligence   73
  3.3 Understanding German Morale after Tunisia   79

4 Applied German Folklore   86
  4.1 *Doctor Faustus* as Gray Literature   88
  4.2 German Folklore   97
  4.3 Modernist Folklore   101
  4.4 Thomas Mann's Memorandum to the German People   106
  4.5 Faustian Breaching Experiments   110

5 Nazi German Media Theory 114
   5.1 Culture, Kultur, and Propaganda 115
   5.2 Bateson and Kracauer: Translation Assistance at the Film Library 116
   5.3 Media Education in *Hitlerjunge Quex* 122

6 Germany as a Conceptual Scheme 136
   6.1 How German Is It? 139
   6.2 Less-than-Ideal Conceptual Schemes 145
   6.3 Antisemitism as a Problem for a Sociologist 149
   6.4 Mutual Misapprehensions 159
   6.5 Parsons' Double Contingency: Tipping the Scales 165

7 The Identity of the Enemy 170
   7.1 Identifying Identity 172
   7.2 Father Comes Home 174
   7.3 German Fear of Loss of Identity 177
   7.4 Indian Reeducation 181
   7.5 Sioux Socialism, Yurok Capitalism 184
   7.6 Cold War Pacifism 186
   7.7 Jewish Identity 189
   7.8 Erikson's Contribution to Reeducation 192

8 Epilogue: To Whom It May Concern 196

Notes 201
Bibliography 267
Index 299

Figures

1.1 Sinclair Lewis, *Gideon Planish* (1943), page 216.   page 28
4.1 Pages from original mimeograph copy of Thomas Mann's *Doctor Faustus*, published in the United States with a print run of 50 copies. Courtesy of the Department of Rare Books and Special Collections at Firestone Library, Princeton University.   89
4.2 The diagram from Robert Petsch's introduction represents the theory of a Latin original (L) of Doctor Faustus, with two lost intermediate German versions (U), (X) leading to two surviving German language Faust-prints (W) and especially (H), which is the print by Johann Spies in 1587 on which Petsch's edition of the *Volksbuch* is based.   101
5.1 Kracauer's note of Bateson's translation (Von Caligari zu Hitler [Vorarbeiten], Kapitel 16–21, Ma 7 T1, Siegfried Kracauer Nachlass). Courtesy of Suhrkamp Verlag.   120
5.2 Quex conversion chart. The chart shows a schematic view of the plot of *Hitlerjunge Quex* (Margaret Mead Papers, box O6). Courtesy of Bateson Idea Group.   130
5.3 An indicative lapse in the notes for Bateson's film analysis – "Na[r]zissism" (Margaret Mead Papers, box O6). Courtesy of Bateson Idea Group.   131
5.4 Bateson's diagrammatic analysis of *Hitlerjunge Quex*: double father (4), triple mother (2, 3, 5).   134
6.1 A unique wartime collaboration, authored by the Committee of Correspondence of the Council for Democracy: *Nazi Poison* (1941).   154

Acknowledgments

This book would not be a book without Cecelia Cancellaro and her senior editorial assistant Victoria Phillips from Cambridge University Press. I want to express my gratitude and appreciation for their work and unwavering support of this project over the past years, guiding it through every step of the way. This gratitude also extends to the anonymous peer reviewers for their extremely helpful comments on my work.

While most of the writing appears in print for the first time, some parts of this book build on previous publications. Chapter 5 is a slightly revised version of the article "Tremor, Tick, and Trance: Siegfried Kracauer and Gregory Bateson in the Film Library of the Museum of Modern Art," which appeared in *New German Critique*, No. 139, 2020, 141–172. An earlier version of Chapter 7 was first published in German as "Die Identität des Feindes: Erik H. Erikson, Margaret Mead und die Erfindung der Reeducation," in *Zeitschrift für Kulturwissenschaften* (2), 2020, 67–95. I am grateful to these journals for allowing me to draw on these articles for this book.

I want to thank Nikolaus Wegmann, Michael Gordin, the late Anson Rabinbach, and Erhard Schüttpelz for giving me invaluable advice, backing, and professional guidance during the early stages of this project. The German Department and the Program in History of Science at Princeton University served as highly engaging institutional contexts, in which my first ideas for this book took shape, and I am grateful especially to Marcus Hahn for his support as I completed the book manuscript during my years of teaching German Literature at the University of Regensburg.

In the meanwhile, I have accumulated more intellectual debts to scholars, research groups, artists, activists, librarians, archivists, and academic institutions than may be listed here. It is impossible, however, not to mention my gratitude to Irene Albers, Andrea Albrecht, Katharina Boehm, John Borneman, Veena Das, Devin Fore, Bernard Geoghegan, Anthony Grafton, Katja Günther, Anke te Heesen, Jonas Hock, Hannah Hunter-Parker, Christian Jany, Michael Jennings, Tom Levin, Felix Lüttge, Barbara Nagel, Omar Nasim, John Durham Peters, Christian Reiß, Avraham Rot, Sandra Schell, Andreas Schmid, Susanne Schmidt, Céline Trautmann-Waller, Tilman Venzl, Matthew Vollgraff, Hent De Vries, and Annette Werberger. Philipp Goll, Alice Christensen, and Till Greite were there from beginning to end. Ultimately, this book could not have been written without the support of my family and especially without the advice, criticism, patience, and encouragement of Elena Fabietti.

I

Introduction

The Rise of Gray Literature

When did the famed German nation of poets and thinkers fall from grace? – What makes a fanatical Nazi tick? – Why did Hitler come into power? – How can we make Hans listen? – Is Germany incurable? In the early 1940s, these were no strange questions. They were not only reasonable, they were vital, a matter literally of life and death. In fact, these were the critical problems that, many were convinced, would determine the very fate of human existence and community and that required a new, just, and global kind of action, a war on National Socialism.

Yes, the harrowing battles between Allies and Axis during World War II were first and foremost fought with all available military powers, ending for Europe with Nazi Germany's unconditional surrender. Nonetheless, after the uncomfortable yet increasingly inevitable reckoning with the catastrophic failure to accomplish a lasting peace in Europe after World War I, it became clear that a new kind of war also needed to be fought with the support of a novel, paper-based arsenal. Somebody, anybody needed to find a solution, to grasp and address the fundamental problems that could not be shot at or bombed away. What exactly made the German nation the prime aggressor to sink the world into chaos yet again? Germany, the rogue state, urgently had to be stopped, once and for all. But how? The United States as the last defender of democracy needed to come up with answers, now.

Journalists, intellectuals, academics, government officials, and military officers, they all cranked out texts about Germany at an unprecedented scale, with rare intensity and at times with surprising intellectual depth. In fact, some of the most brilliant women and men of the time put their individual research projects on hold, along with several of their usual intellectual disagreements and their often-bitter ideological differences. Instead, they banded together and pragmatically employed their intellectual capacities in the common war effort against the Nazi enemy. They did so with a paper-based arsenal, with texts, analyses, letters, reviews, fiction writing, studies, statements, memoires, intelligence reports, and memoranda. One should note that printing sheets were short in supply and there was little time for thorough editing and elaborate rewrites. For the American analysis of Nazi Germany, print publications indeed were only the tip of the iceberg, as their engaged writing mostly circulated in cheap, inconspicuous, and volatile formats such as carbon copies, handwritten notes, and mimeographs. The astonishing extent and variety of these formal and informal writings leads me to speak of a Nazi German enemy literature, a briefly flourishing genre that created some of the most important literary innovations of the times.

As one immerses oneself in the various types of writings, correspondences, applied studies, reports, and memoranda, one slowly rediscovers this US-American wartime literature on the Nazi German enemy as a captivating corpus of writing that has largely sunk into oblivion. This study therefore attempts to excavate an entire forgotten literary culture that rapidly grew in a matter of years, peaked during World War II and largely collapsed within few months following Nazi Germany's unconditional surrender. For a fleeting moment in history, significant parts of the intellectual world in the United States converged to employ their resources for a coolheaded analysis of the Nazi threat, the clear identification of the enemy, and starting in 1944, for the elaborate planning for a postwar reeducation of the fascist, imperialist, militaristic, racist, antisemitic, xenophobic, chauvinist National Socialist German nation into a democratic ally.

In the following, I want to present this highly productive moment in the history of the United States, when Americans and European émigrés, several of which held the precarious legal status "friendly enemy alien," worked together in the collaborative study of Nazi Germany. These collaborations first of all addressed the epochal crisis of the twentieth century, but they also created the mostly unacknowledged grounds for the intellectual revolutions of the mid-century and the rendering of modern American culture as a "model" for the rest of the world in the cultural politics of the Cold War. Nazi German Studies served as the murky, locally entangled test case and launch pad for US-American theories and practices of universalism during the Cold War such as Cold War modernism, identity politics, or the theory of social systems.

1 Introduction: The Rise of Gray Literature

For a topic of such thrust, significance, and renewed present-day urgency, our knowledge of this historical moment is extremely fragmented.[1] While several of the historical actors, that is, individuals, but also media technologies, institutions, and schools of thought, have received significant attention within their respective disciplines and fields, there is still a demand for synthetic studies of the wartime analyses of Nazi Germany that both leave room for the historical complexities of those collaborative projects situated in the 1940s US-America and yet also strive to draw these various stories together into a coherent narrative.

The American contemporary study of Nazi Germany had four distinct phases: It was first motivated by a growing, yet diffuse sense of danger starting in 1930 and then between 1933 and 1938, until the Nazi pogrom on November 9, a highly publicized media event in the United States, alarmed the American public to the violence of the Nazi regime. The period between the events of late 1938, the German attack on Polish territory on September 1, 1939, the attack on Britain after the fall of France in the summer of 1940 and the attack on the Soviet Union in June 1941 up until December 7, 1941, and the German declaration of war against the United States four days later was defined by intellectual attempts to reinforce the American public against National Socialist propaganda latching on domestic fascist tendencies, balanced on the razor-thin edge in the political struggle to keep the United States out of the war, ultimately leading to the recognition of Nazi Germany as the enemy. Between December 1941 and the summer of 1943, the analysis of Nazi Germany in the United States reached its peak with a spring tide of texts concerned with German problems. In its final phase, spanning from 1943 to early 1945, when it became clear that the Allies would win the war against the Nazi enemy, texts on the planning of a German reeducation rose to fleeting prominence, before the epoch-making genre of Nazi German literature collapsed in a matter of months.[2]

Two unexpected protagonists, who rose to the challenge of the moment during World War II were Librarian of Congress Archibald MacLeish and cultural anthropologist Margaret Mead. MacLeish, who was a promising lawyer turned modernist poet, playwright, and journalist, took on the physical task to organize the intellectual struggle against Nazi Germany. How so? MacLeish reorganized the Library of Congress from an allegedly dysfunctional institution into a national research library, that is, as a legislative tool preparing to fight Nazi Germany in the approaching war. He also made sure that intellectuals could gain access to the most recent German materials in newspapers, journals, and books. He helped to create the newly emerging Office of Strategic Services (OSS), arguably the predecessor of the CIA, in the complex world of federal departments and agencies with their own stakes in the analysis of Nazi Germany and he was instrumental in coordinating the intellectual life of Washington's power elite, for example, by hiring the Nobel Prize–winning German author in exile Thomas Mann as an advisor to the Library of Congress. MacLeish, both thanks to his artistic reputation and his strong ties to the highest ranks of the establishment, went on to function as a magnetic pole. This magnetic pole, the power pole, organized the American study of Nazi Germany especially with regard to two aspects: politics and art. The opposite – yet closely coupled – pole, the pole of knowledge, produced the invisible but tangible magnetic field that helped orient large parts of the intellectual scene. Close to the imagined center of these various informal and institutional networks stood Margaret Mead. Mead, who had first risen to public prominence at a young age as the author of the provocative study *Coming of Age in Samoa* (1928), was one – if not the – major intellectual force in the collaborative study of Nazi Germany. She commuted regularly between New York and Washington, DC, where she started working in 1942 in a an inconspicuous but extremely well-connected position as executive secretary for the National Research Council's Committee on Food Habits. She wrote, solicited, and edited reports, letters, and memoranda; she organized committees, group discussions, film screenings, interdisciplinary academic conferences, exhibitions; and she conducted interviews, linked her contacts, met with émigrés, pressed for political action, held lectures, and traveled throughout the United States and to England. Mead connected the various worlds of private institutions, New York's philanthropic circles, foundations such as the Rockefeller Foundation, the Carnegie Foundation, the Guggenheim Foundation, East Coast and West Coast Universities, and medical and psychological institutions and played a key role in the early consolidation of the idea of a German reeducation. Mead's was the pole of knowledge that attracted scholarship, as well as credit, as in appreciation and acknowledgment or in the form of stipends and fellowships. To think of MacLeish and Mead as the two poles organizing the study of Nazi Germany during World War II helps to structure an unruly field full of rank growth, opportunism, failed projects, vested interests, institutional constraints, and unexpected consequences. It should, however, not give the false impression that a higher rationality guided them. While I find it useful to personalize these two intellectual poles, I want to put strong emphasis on the fact that they both had powerful institutions, intellectual infrastructures, and energetic networks working for them, which served as the volatile and improvised base of the collaborations between European émigrés and American intellectuals. Indeed, what follows is not a hagiographic account of these two (truly exceptional) individuals. Instead, I will focus on the magnificent group effort of the 1940s and for this reason, I draw on their collective literature – and media production – as object of inquiry.

In order to understand the far-ranging effects of this great convergence, I trace in a history of entanglement the very nature of the intellectual collaboration between European émigrés and American scholars who worked together in government institutions, universities, philanthropic circles, but also informally in circles of friends and families. The common ground of their undertaking, however, was neither personal nor intellectual. Instead, they shared a common practice of communication. They enthusiastically embraced bureaucratic genres and ultimately formed a specific sociality, in which their writings circulated. I will call this the American "memorandum culture" of the 1940s which is at the center of a literary phenomenon that despite its undisputed significance so far has not been considered, the rise of "gray literature."

The memorandum culture started to blossom in the era of the New Deal, when the enlistment of intellectuals and scientists as government experts gained a new quality, the fruits of which came to full bloom during World War II. The fragile alliances between European and American lawyers, political theorists, geographers, librarians, physicians, cultural anthropologists, artists, film historians, journalists, military officers, sociologists, philosophers, psychoanalysts, government officials, fiction writers, and historians formed in this memorandum culture served as a ferment for a particularly productive moment in the history of the humanities and social sciences, and had a transformative effect on the postwar US-American academic culture, initiating some of the great intellectual projects in American history.

Approaching the intellectual history of this unruly, yet transformational encounter, each of my book's chapters aims in various ways at a classic publication defining the postwar era and situates the story of its making in collaborative project environments and vis-à-vis other prominent but also lesser known wartime publications as well as unpublished materials. I focus on American publications by both American intellectuals and

European émigrés for this study of the memorandum culture, and I try to do justice to its breadth as well as depth, but also its idiosyncratic nature. The selected publications include David Riesman's *Lonely Crowd* (1950), Franz Neumann's *Behemoth* (1944), Thomas Mann's *Doctor Faustus* (1947), Siegfried Kracauer's *From Caligari to Hitler* (1947), Talcott Parsons' *Social System* (1951), and Erik H. Erikson's *Childhood and Society* (1950), all classics in their respective fields in sociology, political science, legal and economic history, modernist fiction, film studies, systems theory, and developmental psychology.

The book's basic plot is nothing more, but also nothing less than to trace – in various ways – the heterogenous entanglements of such canonic works in the temporarily forged intellectual networks of the wartime memorandum culture. Chapters 2 and 3 will ground the intellectual history of the American memorandum culture and lay out the social theoretical as well as the material basis of collaboration and communication in the study of Nazi Germany. Chapter 4 then turns to the problem of representing German culture, which is followed by Chapters 5–7 with groundbreaking analyses of German media, society, and psychology. The book thus tells the story of how Nazi Germany captured and transformed the imagination of intellectuals in the United States.

1.1 ENTERING THE MEMORANDUM CULTURE

On January 17, 1943, Gregory Bateson sent a friendly letter with an urgent request for a memorandum addressed to the Institute of Child Guidance at Berkeley, California:

Dear Erik: In connection with our studies of German character structure, the problem of what data could be obtained from the study of German prisoners, now in the hands of the United Nations, inevitably suggests itself. It occurs to me that it might be well for us to have in our hands a confidential memorandum on the possibilities for such a study, which could be submitted from time to time to such government authorities as may be interested. I know that you have given this matter some thought, and this is a formal request to prepare such a memorandum for the Council's use. Sincerely yours, Gregory Bateson[3]

Bateson, a prewar social anthropologist and postwar communication theorist, started in 1939/40 to work in response to the Nazi threat, not as a professor, journalist, freelance writer, political activist, civil servant, or functionary. Rather, he joined various action groups such as the Council on Intercultural Relations, the Committee for National Morale – as a "secretary." A portion of the most important wartime analyses of foreign nations first passed through "Bateson's busy mimeograph machine,"[4] and entered the surging mail circulation among New York action committees, Washington, DC, government agencies, and East Coast universities thanks to the Manhattan secretary and his tedious crank-handle Xerox. Bateson's brief request for a confidential memorandum on the methods of study of German war prisoners for the Council on Intercultural Relations' use, sent to psychoanalyst Erik Homburger Erikson, therefore lays out paradigmatically the operational character of the quickly growing amount of applied research memoranda employed in the intellectual fight against the Axis powers. Wartime memoranda were not primarily written for the consumption by a general public but rather to produce special interest. Under the label of "to whom it may concern," they addressed authorities and institutions and created various exclusive but overlapping readerships that partook in the circulation of those texts.

The brisk pace and intensity of the emergence of US-American analyses of Nazi Germany cannot be fully accounted for unless one comes to terms with the unprecedented enthusiasm of scholars and intellectuals for writing in bureaucratic genres, adopted from their use in establishment communication: to prepare forms, create protocols, record minutes, keep attendance sheets, file notes, compile dossiers, reference index cards, revise documents, transcribe recordings, generate reports, bring forward joint motions, phrase official letters, submit applications, request funds, acquire expertise, draw organizational charts, enhance procedures, refer to style sheets and follow guidelines – all of which flourished in what I call a memorandum culture.

By the early 1940s, the booming production of literature on Nazi Germany had reached such a level of volume and interconnectedness that people started considering it a topic worthy of its own review journal. Between 1941 and 1944, the "American Friends of German Freedom" grouped around the theologian and "high priest of Protestantism's young intellectuals"[5] Reinhold Niebuhr published a monthly journal that collected and reviewed exclusively writings on Nazi Germany, a journal called *In RE: Germany*.[6] The programmatic title of the journal, the subject line of a memorandum on Germany, indicates that the historical actors studying Nazi Germany perceived themselves as part of a culture producing and consuming gray literature. The journal reviewed an impressive range of published texts, but also of pamphlets and memoranda available beyond the traditional publishing channels, providing a major opening into the study of Nazi Germany – that serves today as an invaluable source for the study of wartime literature on the topic. The journal also came with a heavy intellectual bias, and despite its enormous range, with serious limitations due to the restricted availability of texts. After all, significant parts of the gray literature circulated in small institutions, some of them semiprivate, some of them semipublic, and some of them secret – and never reached the reviewers of *In RE: Germany* who had to rely on the publication networks they were able to access. Nevertheless, the texts that were reviewed, but also those that should have or could have been reviewed in this journal, are the topic of this book.

Arguably, the studies of the history of World War II literature conducted in intellectual history, cultural history, media studies, the history of the social sciences, and not least German Studies – they all exhibit a certain tendency to feel naturally attracted by published works. Indeed, refocusing the attention on the proliferation of gray literature challenges several well-established concepts and practices of reading. Gray literature, one of the most inconspicuous, operative, and menial literary formats, often produced within and between institutions, leads to several problems regarding physical access and basic understandings of authorship, publishing practices, and readership. My main methodological intervention here lies in the attempt to introduce a mode of reading works of "Nazi" gray literature not only individually and "as if published," but also in their interrelationship, following their movements and transformations on institutional infrastructures. For this purpose, it has proven highly productive to shift the focus from the study of individual authors to collaborations, under the social historical conditions of warfare, migration and the contact between European émigrés and American intellectuals. The American-European encounter, part of a larger pattern of intellectual migration – "Hitler's gift"[7] to the world – has in fact already spurred a wealth of studies with an emphasis on (auto-)biography, influence, and the development of academic disciplines, initially conducted by wartime intellectuals and their students.[8] This was followed by a second generation of scholarship that reflected on the work and experiences resulting from this encounter with a focus on issues such as power, ethnicity, gender, diplomacy, epistemology, and the "alchemy of exile."[9] While there has been in the last decades a strong emphasis on the latter, dismissing as methodically naïve the first, the enormous amount of work of the two generations needs to be equally appreciated for their indispensable insights and, in fact, this book could not have been written without both of them.[10]

Following the ideal of an "anthropological gaze," I attempt to defamiliarize the reader's view of gray literature, which, after its great success in the twentieth century, most people are now accustomed to encountering on a daily basis, but which hardly anyone attempts to understand beyond its immediate purpose. The term "gray literature," after all, was coined by information scientists who registered, with a certain delay, a new development in print culture.[11] Libraries and special libraries were managing an increasing amount of paper that did not arrive from commercial publishers and did not fit into the established categories of books, journals, and newspapers, and accordingly, into the filing systems of library stacks and shelves. Common to all attempts to define the elusive category of gray literature is the recognition that it is produced and distributed outside of the channels of commercial publishing. The rise of gray literature is in fact often dated around World War II and is related to the new types of "classified" texts produced in Allied communications, such as intelligence reports.[12] In many cases, however, the exclusivity of gray literature does not come with the full force of the American legal system, which is reserved, for example, for the protection of nuclear secrets, but can also be found in the daily routines of institutional communication "From:" – "To:" – "In Re:" and so on. The library sciences are right to point out that gray literature is largely written out of the public eye, but it must be added that the texts certainly show an awareness of it, and in some cases may even be composed to negotiate the precarious boundary between private, institutional, and public communication. Some may also avoid using established publishing channels because of their contested status, as did mail-order brochures or pamphlets and broadcasts using new media such as radio and cinema, to deliver propaganda messages to some of those citizens, who were not part of the general reading public, and to influence their morale.

The anthropological gaze in fact needs to ignore these categorizations to some extent and focus its attention on the various types of agency and interests involved. "Following the actors" – another guiding anthropological ideal of this work – thus leads directly into the memorandum culture and its social practices of collaboration, cooperative meaning making, negotiation of conflicts, clarification of misunderstandings, as well as the work of maintenance and repair, all of which are often rendered in surprisingly creative ways in the case of the gray literature produced during World War II. Gray literature hence becomes a privileged object of study for the wartime work of intellectuals, as a central means of their imagination, a social medium that coordinates the material flow of communication, a socio-technical mediator between old and new media infrastructures, a tool that guides the movement and transformation of concepts and practices.

The history of science and science and technology studies, in their highly innovative phase toward the end of the twentieth century, have developed several methodological and conceptual innovations that help observing the intricate forms of human and nonhuman agency exhibited in the interaction between various actors and cultural artifacts using institutional or other types of infrastructures. At first sight, in the fast-moving academic world of theory and discursive fashions, these innovations may seem a bit aged by now. Quite to the contrary, I would like to contend, however, that most fields of research, including intellectual history, have been slow to come to terms with these innovations, and therefore have not even really started to draw the far-reaching consequences that also might help to reorient the study of the literature originating from the American-European encounter during the 1940s.

Following Édouard Glissant's prominent use of "creolization" to approach American cultural history from a "Caribbean" point of view,[13] but also Peter Galison in his study of microphysics, I understand the various places of encounter and cultural exchange such as the OSS, action committees, research projects, roundtable discussions, as well as the intense informal or semiformal meetings of intellectual circles in apartments as "trading zones" in which an unforeseen creolization of knowledge happened.[14] Neither the American intellectuals nor the European émigrés fully understood what they were in for, and neither side could fully agree on the basic terms and motivations for their intellectual exchange, and, in consequence, neither side could have created individually the conceptual innovations and penetrating analyses found in the gray literature on Nazi Germany. The concept of creolization therefore helps moving beyond monodirectional concepts of influence, of individual or group-assimilation, of cultural appropriation, taking the unequally distributed agency of both sides into account. I follow here, again, an anthropological ideal of reconstructing symmetrically a "reciprocity of perspectives." Thinking of creolization hardly allows for a rational, guided development, but rather emphasizes the haphazard, unclear, highly local, minute details of exchange and the processes of their mediation in the nitty-gritty questions of translation, corrections of first drafts, note taking and copying quotes, use of preliminary outlines, diagrams, and visual aids, team meetings, transcription of interviews, conception of questionnaires, common authorities and side readings, support by spouses and children, trips and visits, project pitches, sharing of notes, materials, and access, day jobs, hands of invisible technicians, during which some of the most fundamental theoretical questions were collaboratively answered, "from tools to theories."[15] It is therefore always necessary to highlight the contradictory impulses and vested interests resulting in a high degree of improbability predicating all collaborations that produced or failed to produce gray literature.

The interplay of coincidence, unclear situation and momentous decisions can be seen, for example, in the disappointing letter arriving at the Institute of Social Research, at the time located in New York. The historian Eugene N. Anderson at the American University in Washington, DC, responds on December 19, 1940, to an offer to collaborate on a new project within the memorandum culture as follows:

> Dear Dr. Horkheimer – I learned a few days ago that the Rockefeller Foundation has assumed charge of the furtherance of studies in this country of Nazi Germany. It is now deciding on the next steps to be taken. I feel very grateful to you for offering the position of collaborator on your project of study of Nazi Germany [sic]. But I still think that you would be much more advised to find someone in New York, and I really do not see my way clear to attempting the work. I must finish a book [...].[16]

Anderson, briefly after, changed his mind and offered his collaboration, but the Institute's project proposal to the Rockefeller Foundation failed. Instead, Anderson went on to work for the OSS as section chief of the "Central European Section," mainly responsible for Nazi Germany. Anderson, like many other actors in the memorandum culture navigated within and in-between institutions, crossing the distinction between scholarship and activism, between private and public, and secret.

Sponsored by universities, by philanthropies, but also with government money, the collaboration between European émigrés and American intellectuals heterogeneously applied concepts available to the various contributors from their previous work – often formed and solidified over several decades. They generated texts that created – in a joint effort – shimmering projections of the enemy nation. The wartime collaborations in the memorandum culture worked less, however, toward a shared image of the enemy. Instead, the various collaborators rather shared a practice of "imagination,"[17] absorbed in the German enemy. They all did take fascists very seriously – which means in turn for a work on the study of National Socialism that they all should be taken equally seriously as well. Accordingly, the central method to examine the intellectual – sociological, political, fictional, etc. – imagination of Germany in this study is to systematically ignore the failure and success of individual projects as the only measure of historical significance, and, using the same modes of explanation for both, to reconstruct the specific sociality emerging in the collaboration between the various actors, as a history of projects and projectors.[18] In order to grasp these projects, special attention is, again "following the actors," directed toward professional careers as point of access to the collaborative, project-based writing practices.

Rendering the research into gray literature operational, the two main points of departure for my reconstruction of wartime collaboration are, as stated earlier, concepts and practices. I draw accordingly on the history of concepts[19] on the one hand, and the theory of practice[20] on the other – both, however, from the point of view of literature, reading examples of Nazi gray literature both esoterically, as well as exoterically.

1.2 ÉMIGRÉ COLLABORATORS

The dictum to "follow the actors" poses special methodical problems and leads to unexpected places, when studying wartime collaborations due to the high mobility of some of the intellectuals undergoing voluntary and forced migration. This is obviously true for the European Hitler refugees and exiles of the late 1930s and early 1940s, but it is also true for the distinct group of German language émigrés of the 1920s and early 1930s, who often took on prominent roles within the memorandum culture. Despite the Immigration Act of 1924 following the first major restrictions in 1917, as well as violent anti-German sentiments in parts of the US-American population during and after World War I, which put an end to the long history of free-flowing economically, politically, and religiously motivated migration from Germany, they still encountered much more beneficial conditions to launch their American careers than those fleeing Nazi German aggression after 1938. Often in collaboration with Germanophile American academics, who had fond memories of European tours and who in some cases even held German PhDs, they were able to resettle and establish their professional career in the United States under vastly different circumstances. Especially these earlier arrivals from Europe played key roles in the formation phase of the memorandum culture studying Nazi Germany. Among them were highly influential reformers of administrative techniques and practices such as the German legal scholar Arnold Brecht.[21] Brecht arrived in New York in 1933 as one of the transatlantic Nazi refugees to take up one of the few sought-after positions at the newly founded "University in Exile" at the New School for Social Research, initially funded by a Rockefeller Foundation Grant. This position enabled him to publish *The Art and Technique of Administration in German Ministries* (1940), coauthored with his student Comstock Glaser, as well as his pioneering study on the collapse of the Weimar Republic *Prelude to Silence: The End of the German Republic* (1944), and to work in the memorandum culture, for example, for the Council for Democracy, as advisor to the War Department, the Office of War Information, as chairperson of a special committee for comparative international administration created by the Social Science Research Council,[22] and as teacher at the School of Overseas Administration at Harvard University.[23] The Jewish-Austrian Paul F. Lazarsfeld, one of the founders of empirical social research and the academic study of propaganda in the United States in the Princeton Radio Research Project, arrived with the help of a similar grant in the same year.[24] One of the most prominent members of the memorandum culture, Hans Kohn, the nestor of the American study of nationalism is a particularly interesting case in point, as his career in the decades before his arrival in 1934 both represents the irreducible complexities American intellectuals faced when collaborating with émigrés, as well as the intellectual potential of their encounter.

When Kohn, professor for Modern European and Asiatic History at Smith College in Northampton, MA, published his study *The Idea of Nationalism* in 1944, in which he historicizes the idea of nationalism, he acknowledges in his preface in sufficiently clear terms – for anybody who cares to know – his membership in the memorandum culture. He states that "[d]uring the years of collecting and organizing the material the author has been generously helped at various times by grants-in-aid from the Social Science Research Council and the Bureau of International Research of Harvard University and by a fellowship from the John Simon Guggenheim Memorial Foundation, to all of which he feels greatly indebted."[25] Both the Social Science Research Council and the Bureau of International Research of Harvard University were financed by funds dispersed through the Laura Spelman Rockefeller Memorial Fund, closely connected to the Rockefeller Foundation, one of the largest philanthropic sponsors of group projects and individual collaborators in the memorandum culture, acting besides the Guggenheim Foundation, mentioned in the above quote, the Carnegie Foundation and others.

To get a better grasp of how, in the case of Kohn, nationalism and memorandum culture come together, a detailed look at Kohn's career seems warranted, before proceeding with the brief outline of his argument on the concept of nationalism as a historical practice of imagination. Furthermore, Kohn's work provides rich materials for the literary historical interest of this study. His distinct life story also offers some clues regarding the unavoidable misunderstandings and the general imponderability of the political and intellectual background of the individual European émigrés entering the memorandum culture. Several of the émigrés, which were loosely identified as German or European, in fact originated from a highly mobile class of academics that makes it necessary, to put on, as David Blackbourn has shown in his history of *Germany in the World*, a lense of global history to understand the trajectories of German emigration during the 1930s.[26] The esoteric and exoteric readings of gray literature therefore not only zoom in on minute details, but they also zoom out to grasp the various actors' interconnectedness in world-spanning chains of operation.

Kohn[27] was born in Prague in 1891 to a secular Jewish upper middle-class family and attended school at the same institution as did authors Franz Kafka and Hugo Bergmann about ten years earlier. Even before reaching the age to attend university, he joined the Zionist student club *Bar Kochba*, intensely discussing a Jewish nationalism. He then began, still in Prague, at the time part of the multiethnic and multilingual Austro-Hungarian Empire ruled by the Habsburg Monarchy, to study law, while also engaging in Zionist publication projects like editing the anthology *Vom Judentum*.[28] In 1914, at the onset of World War I, Kohn's initial enthusiasm led him to join an Officer Candidate School in Salzburg. He eagerly volunteered for a mission in the Carpathian Mountains in February 1915. After less than two months in action, the Imperial Russian army captured Kohn, and brought him as prisoner of war (POW) to the "Oriental Russian Colony" Samarkand. Thus began a five-year-long involuntary yet formative journey. After attempting to escape toward Afghanistan, Kohn was deported further eastward to Gultscha in the Pamir Mountains of Turkestan. Toward the end of 1916, he underwent a 32-day transfer, first to Samara on the Volga, then again eastward to a prisoner camp for officers in Khabarovsk. After the Bolshevik revolution in March 1917, Kohn was relocated even farther east to Novosibirsk and the Krasnoyarsk camp. It was during this period that he dedicated himself to self-education, immersing himself in a wide range of subjects. In addition, he assumed the role of chairman in the Siberian POWs' largest Zionist organization, engaging in both political and cultural pursuits that involved delivering biweekly public speeches. When Kohn was eventually released from the POW camp in 1919, he decided to remain in Siberia, likely influenced by his political involvement with the local Jewish population.[29] He moved to Irkutsk where he assumed the role of secretary at the Zionist central office of

Siberia. Simultaneously, he applied for Czechoslovakian citizenship to serve as a cultural administrator for the newly established Czechoslovak Republic. In the winter of early 1920, he started his long way back home, traveling through Khabarovsk, Yokohama, Tokyo, the Indian Ocean, and the Suez Canal to Marseille. Passing through Switzerland and southern Germany, he eventually arrived in Prague, where he wasted no time in publishing various manuscripts he had written during his time as a POW. Notably, he translated Joseph Klausner's history of "Neo-Hebrew" literature into German[30] and produced an affirmative book on nationalism.[31] These publications marked the resurgence of his lifelong dedication to writing and publishing. Soon after his arrival, he left Prague for Paris – and for good. In Paris, he took up a short-term position with the *Comité des Délégations Juives* before relocating to London in 1921. In London, he became an active participant in the World Zionist Organisation and assumed membership in the socialist Fabian Society. Additionally, he devoted himself to propagating the cause of *Keren Hajessod*, a Zionist organization dedicated to financing settlements in Palestine. In this function, he moved in the mid-1920s to Palestine. Furthermore, in 1925, Kohn played a pivotal role as one of the founding members of *Brit(h) Shalom*. This organization advocated for the establishment of a binational state in which Jewish and Arab citizens would enjoy equal rights. However, after a conflict emerged in 1928 over the Wailing Wall of Jerusalem, resulting in violent clashes, Kohn's faith in the Zionist cause began to wane. He decided to publicly recognize the legitimacy of claims of an Arabic nationalism, which led – after 20 years of Zionist engagement – to his incremental resignation from his several functions in 1929/30. Before stepping down, though, he obtained Palestinian citizenship in 1929. In 1931, faced with perpetual financial instability, Kohn embarked on a venture, with assistance from the Institute of International Education, to deliver paid lectures in both Europe and the United States. Following a successful series of lectures at the New School for Social Research in New York, Kohn secured a position at Smith College in the autumn of 1934. At the age of 42, he obtained a stable academic position for the first time. Consequently, he relocated from Palestine to Northampton, MA, to assume his role as a highly popular teacher at Smith College. In the new position, Kohn indeed not only thrived as a prolifically publishing professor, but also emerged as a prominent public intellectual, who toured the lecture circuit throughout the United States. He quickly built an impressive network of contacts on the East Coast, continuing his highly mobile existence with weekly trips to New York, and after starting to teach at Harvard Summer School in 1936, to Cambridge, MA. He maintained at his home together with his wife a busy social life. Beyond the circles at Smith College associated with William A. Neilson, the college's president, and contacts to the colleagues at nearby colleges and universities in Massachusetts, such as to Carl J. Friedrich at Harvard University, he gravitated around New York institutions, especially the aforementioned Institute of International Education, the New School for Social Research, but also the Asia Institute and the American Association for Adult Education. He could rely on close contacts to the émigré circles around the Mann family, the scholarly community of the East coast, especially including experts on Asia, as well as Black intellectuals such as Alain Locke and W. E. B. Du Bois interested in his ideas on Jewish nationalism reverberating with discussions about Black nationalism. Not least thanks to his head start and his early involvement in American institutions already during the New Deal era, he became one of the most influential émigrés in American intellectual life during World War II. In this capacity, he participated in various groups and committees, for example, in 1939/40 together with, among others, Thomas Mann, Lewis Mumford, Giuseppe Borgese, and Hermann Broch on the publication of a conservative, humanist, and anti-isolationist manifesto *City of Man*. A "First memorandum" was attached to this publication, presenting the argument of my work in historical plain text: "The collaboration of what is best in American culture with what is best in European intellectual immigration might be the source of incalculable benefits for the active intelligence of tomorrow."[32]

To sum up: When the "German émigré" Kohn became naturalized as US-American citizen in 1940, he was or had been fluent in six languages from four language families and held his fourth citizenship. Over the course of his lifetime, the young Zionist went on to experience several political reorientations, transitioning from a monarchist Zionist to a socialist Zionist, then evolving into an anti-Zionist liberal pacifist and humanist. Eventually, he emerged as a vocal anti-fascist, before identifying as a conservative anti-communist. His numerous ideological shifts were so profound and diverse that it is entirely appropriate to describe his journey as driven by "multiple metamorphoses."[33]

Kohn's exceptional experiences granted him a singular authority to speak about a multitude of phenomena, particularly nationalism. His shifting perspectives throughout his career contributed to his nuanced understanding, while his dedicated study of both "Western" and

"Eastern" nationalisms continued over several decades. His firsthand observations of the utopian rise of nationalism among Czech Jews circa 1900, coupled with his active involvement in the early twentieth-century Zionist endeavor in Palestine, provided him with invaluable insights into the complex political realities associated with nation-building. He had also learned from an early age to exercise his practice of imagination in the context of his collaborative work in clubs, committees, and institutions in multilingual and multiethnic alliances. Like many of his contemporaries in Europe who had lived through the tumultuous events of the early twentieth century, Kohn was well versed in a crucial "biographical" technique that was integral to the figure of the collaborator – conversion.[34] The practice of conversion involves renouncing one's outdated beliefs, undergoing a radical change of perspective, and embracing the new creed. This is quickly followed by the unwavering adoption of a disciplined state of mind – and body. This state, as I will argue in the following chapters, is strongly associated during the 1940s with the concept of "objectivity." Especially for the European émigrés, but also for American intellectuals, conversion was a crucial skill to adapt to the new political scene of the memorandum culture, and to use their existing intellectual resources in a new, sometimes contradictory environment, to find common ground with other European and American intellectuals of various backgrounds, to please sponsors, while at the same time pursuing their long-developed projects and reasserting their agency.

1.3 NATIONAL LITERATURE: GERMAN PROBLEMS

After outlining Kohn's biography and the complex political practices of imagination of European émigrés entangled in patterns of global migration, the crucial conceptual question may be tackled. What is, after all, in 1944, nationalism – and correspondingly national literature – according to Kohn?

- Nationalism is a historical phenomenon: "Nationalism as we understand it is not older than the second half of the eighteenth century."[35]
- Nationalism is bound to the rise of the bourgeoisie: "Nationalism is inconceivable without the ideas of popular sovereignty."[36]
- Nationalism is not bound to the state: "Among these peoples, at the beginning it was not so much the nation-state as the *Volksgeist* and its manifestations in literature and folklore, in the mother tongue, and in history, which became the center of the attention of nationalism."[37]

- Nationalism is a feeling: "For its composite texture, nationalism used in its growth some of the oldest and most primitive feelings of man, found throughout history as important factors in the formation of social groups."[38]
- Nationalism is anonymous and deterritorialized: "Nationalism – our identification with the life and aspirations of uncounted millions whom we shall never know, with a territory which we shall never visit in its entirety [...]."[39]
- Nationalism is a practice of imagination: "Nationalism is first and foremost a state of mind, an act of consciousness, which since the French Revolution has become more and more common to mankind."[40]
- Nationalism is international and symmetrical: "[The] very growth of nationalism all over the earth, with its awakening of the masses to participation in political and cultural life, prepared the way for the closer cultural contacts of all the civilization of mankind (now for the first time brought into a common denominator), at the same time separating and uniting them."[41]
- Nationalism is arbitrary: "Although some of these objective factors are of great importance for the formation of nationalities, the most essential element is a living and active corporate will. Nationality is formed by the decision to form a nationality."[42]
- Nationalism is traditional: "Nationalities are created out of ethnographic and political elements when nationalism breathes life into the form built by preceding centuries."[43]
- The ultimate limit of nationalism is fascism:

Nationality, which is nothing but a fragment of humanity, tends to set itself up as the whole. Generally this ultimate conclusion is not drawn [...]. Only fascism, the uncompromising enemy of Western civilization, has pushed nationalism to its very limit, to a totalitarian nationalism, in which humanity and the individual disappear and nothing remains but the nationality, which has become one and the whole.[44]

The last point deserves special attention. "Fascism" becomes in an otherwise largely historicist display of humanist erudition the contemporary extreme and breaking point of Kohn's argument. The relativism between absolute parts coexisting in a whole disappears in the moment that one part takes on the role of the whole for all other parts which it does not recognize as such. In other words, Kohn's well-balanced theory and historical narrative becomes subject to what may be called Nazi Germany's "hostile takeover" of nationalism. This appropriation of the analysis

1.3 National Literature: German Problems

by one object of Kohn's work in particular – and of significant parts of US-American imagination in general – needs further explanation. At some point in the 1930s, Nazi Germany in all its shapes, forms, and conceptualizations as "Nazism," "Fascism," "National Socialism," "totalitarianism," and "Hitlerism" started to take on a topical role as extreme point, hyperbole, negative example, litmus test, Rorschach test, as the place of chaos, terror, evil, darkness, anomie, pathology, irrationality, perversion, or as the figure of the mentally ill, villain, criminal, gangster, perpetrator, barbarian, liar, charlatan, terrorist, false prophet, demon, Antichrist, devil – and to invade sociological, anthropological, psychological, linguistic, political, legal, economic, philosophical, pedagogical, and aesthetic theories.

For the idea of nationalism, the hostile takeover during World War II – in the case of Kohn long prepared by four preceding books (as well as several articles, speeches, and lectures) published between 1936 and 1942[45] – has been irreversible. All further books on the topic are haunted or respectively remotely controlled by the undeniable nationalism of National Socialism, even after the reassessment of nationalism in the global light of the extra-European and postcolonial foundation of nations.[46]

Looking back at Kohn's life work, it appears as if one might just add to his later historicization of nationalism Kohn's early Zionist engagement, his publication of *Vom Judentum*, his participation in the revival of Hebrew as a national language, as well as his translation of a history of Hebrew national literature, *Geschichte der Neuhebräischen Literatur*, to arrive at a novel concept of national literature in 1944, not in theory, but in practice. The memorandum culture formed by American intellectuals and European émigrés studying German problems apparently produced a short-lived imagined community that participated intellectually, passionately, and largely anonymously in the production, distribution, and consumption of national literature, in both fact and fiction, as well as several genres in between, imagining the distant German nation. Dealing with the pathologies of nationalism, Nazi German "enemy literature" was, following Kohn's reflections and literary practice, the truest of national literatures, and it also served the purpose of concrete nation building as it fundamentally shaped the imagination of what a new German nation without National Socialism might look like. In this sense, this book on the memorandum culture of World War II and its collaboratively produced gray literature is in its broadest definition a study of German national literature.

In the manner of an umbrella study of American Nazi literature as national literature, I follow several of the murky roads traveled by the various actors. Indeed, these often lead to rather unexpected places, discursive formations, and specialized literatures, which might come as a surprise to some readers, such as business history, the development of microphotography, the edition of Early Modern prints, Balinese dance, Calvinism, and the Pine Ridge Reservation of the Oglala Sioux. I introduce relevant aspects of these and several other contexts not primarily because they are curious, but more importantly since this is where some of the most striking and historically important features of the American imagination of Germany were shaped. As such, they are crucial to foster a better understanding of German national literature during World War II. Accordingly, the chapters of this book may be read individually by those with a special interest in specific topics such as "intelligence" (Chapter 3), "exile literature" (Chapter 4), "propaganda" (Chapter 5), or "reeducation" (Chapter 7). Taken together, however, the reader will find in the succession of these chapters on the study of Germany the outline of a hidden intellectual history of the 1940s.

Enemy Literature starts with a meditation on David Riesman's concept of "other-direction," laid out in his classic study *The Lonely Crowd* as a theoretical baseline for my book (Chapter 2), moving from other-direction to émigré-direction to enemy-direction. I consider various paradigmatic experiences of transatlantic migration and their consequences for American sociality, with a special focus on conceptions theorized by Black intellectuals, such as Zora Neale Hurston and Alain Locke, and their consequences for a symmetrical approach to the intellectual history of American–European collaborations in World War II. The chapter provides a theoretical outline for understanding the sources and aspirations of the cool-headedness observed in these collaborations.

The first historical case study of the encounter between American lawyers and German-Jewish Marxists focuses on collaborative writing practices (Chapter 3). It traces the invention of the intelligence report during World War II and describes this genre's characteristics as paradigmatic for the bureaucratic style of the memorandum culture. Franz Neumann (the intellectual head of the OSS's Research and Analysis branch) and his grand analysis of Nazi Germany in *Behemoth* is thus considered in close relationship to his work as intelligence analyst collaborating with his European and American colleagues. In this chapter, I describe the medial infrastructures that were used to analyze the distant enemy, and I ask in a reading of the intelligence report "German Morale after Tunisia" what it meant to "understand" the Nazi enemy in 1943.

The next chapter (Chapter 4) plays mainly between Washington, DC, and Pacific Palisades, CA. I present the writer Thomas Mann as part of the memorandum culture fighting against Nazi Germany and I demonstrate, what a literary-critical analysis of his work looks like, if one takes his job situation in the early 1940s into account: Consultant to the Library of Congress, appointed by MacLeish. For this purpose, I highlight the central role of Mann's collaborations – on various scales and levels of intensity – with folklorist Gustave O. Arlt and scholar Joseph Campbell, critical theorist Theodor W. Adorno and journalist Agnes E. Meyer in the making of *Doctor Faustus*.

Chapter 5 moves from Washington, DC, to New York and details the brief collaboration between Siegfried Kracauer and Gregory Bateson, the husband of Margaret Mead, in the Film Library of the Museum of Modern Art as an intriguing encounter in American intellectual history, the history of film and media studies, and the history of German Studies. I look at the Frankfurt School as part of the 1940s memorandum culture and thereby reconsider the historiography of critical theory during this formative period within a broader intellectual landscape, that is, in dialogue and institutional competition with further projects to study the Nazi German enemy, in this case, the Culture and Personality School. My argument takes Bateson's and Kracauer's analyses of a song in the Nazi movie *Hitlerjunge Quex* as a case in point and develops some of Kracauer's and Bateson's most important methodical innovations and insights into Nazi German propaganda that underlie Kracauer's famous film historical study *From Caligari to Hitler*.

The Harvard sociologist Talcott Parsons is one of the prime intellectual actors of World War II producing applied studies of Nazi Germany and providing training to members of the military government entering the occupied areas in Germany. Chapter 6 revisits his collaboration with Carl J. Friedrich, especially on a pamphlet on *Nazi Poison*, his momentous meeting with social philosopher Alfred Schuetz and political theorist Eric Voegelin. I argue that the insights that he gained into the supposed "anomie," that is, the chaotic nature of Nazi Germany starting in 1938 and throughout World War II, significantly shaped – by means of inversion and contrast – his positive design of a functioning social system in his postwar study *The Social System*, at first for the United States, but then also globally, as a scheme for the organization of modern society as such.

Erik H. Erikson's book *Childhood and Society*, started, as I show in Chapter 7, with his "remote" psychoanalysis of Adolf Hitler. I present the transatlantic history of the concepts "identity" and "reeducation," which may serve as a prime example for the impact of the study of Nazi Germany's alterity on postwar intellectual discourse. Chapter 7 traces the use of the two concepts in a microhistorical account in order to arrive at macrohistorical revisions. I show how the conception of reeducation migrated from Native American reservations to the wartime pathologization of the Nazi German enemy. Only then – in collaboration with Margaret Mead – it became the name of the policy according to which the United States planned and initially attempted to subject, as Occupation power, the postwar German society in order to reintegrate the outcast nation back into the family of man.

The individual chapters do not intend to serve as critical commentary, as text genetic accounts, or as comprehensive interpretations of major postwar publications according to the respective author's image of Nazi Germany, even though a reader attentive to these questions might find in this book several lines of argument, observations, and framings of interest. Rather, each chapter forges a distinct pathway of imagination, traces a chain of translations, draws an intellectual trajectory, sequences a creative process, and thereby shows how central aspects of the conception, production, or reception of these works moved in and out of the memorandum culture. In this way, exploring the rise of gray literature, I attempt to establish the principles of generation and administration of collaborative wartime literature, its concepts and practices that – often with little or no reference to the circumstances of their emergence – are synthesized in these famous postwar book publications.

1.4 INCLUDE ME OUT

Since the phenomenon – a distinct memorandum culture producing gray literature for the study of Nazi Germany – has never been fully recognized in research, it is fair to ask, whether I am dealing with a hallucination rather than with a serious object of study, or, if real, rather with a marginal aspect, or, if central, rather with a fuzzy problem that fails to capture the imagination? Indeed, there are substantial problems in pinpointing the phenomenon – largely stemming from the high mobility and diversity of the actors – to be considered along the way. In the second part of this introduction, I would like therefore to create a more concrete picture of the American memorandum culture, necessarily including some serious flaws and distortions, and yet, answer most affirmatively that it was real, central, and certainly did capture the imagination during the 1940s.

There was at least one author, who, however, seriously suffered from hallucinations on several occasions during episodes of delirium tremens stemming from his alcoholic disease, who was an outsider to both the literary establishment and the bohemian avantgarde and who made it his literary project to situate fuzzy problems in the milieu of their making. Almost as forgotten as the culture that produced the gray literature on Nazi Germany is its most important immediate – albeit satirical – imaginative representation in a major work of fiction, Sinclair Lewis' *Gideon Planish* (1943).[47]

Lewis, who won in 1930, one year after Thomas Mann, as the first US-American author the Nobel Prize in literature, had become famous for his satires, highly critical of American professional culture. His portrayals of frauds, misguided idealists, and middle-class conformism, as well as of surprisingly strong female characters, were partly based on his experiences of growing up in the semi-periphery of the mid-West in Sauk Centre, a small town in Minnesota, but they were also based on social scientific as well as journalistic practices of qualitative research. These included participant observation, expert interviews, oral history, as well as investigative journalism, digging for scandals, and a long series of road trips into the country. After collecting "dope,"[48] that is, raw material for his novels, the highly prolific writer created in his fiction a world that gained a representative quality for contemporary developments in American culture and were read as a "social document of a higher order."[49] He thus straddled the line between fact and fiction in various genres, ranging, among others, from magazine serials, to poetry, plays, short stories, and major novels – a career sustained largely by New York's growing world of publishing, hungry for authentic material to reach audiences beyond the city's bubble.[50]

During World War I, along with several socialist intellectuals, he took a pacifist and "non-anti-German" position, as in his unpublished story "He Loved His Country,"[51] before ultimately supporting American intervention. Lewis wrote his first bestselling novel *Main Street* (1920) on a wave of what his publisher Alfred Harcourt picked up as the "zeitgeist" of the post-war moment, a "questioning of standards," which meant that "non-fiction on urgent topics would have bestseller potential, along with iconoclastic, realistic fiction," such that his novel was published in the same spirit – and by the same editor – as British economist J. Maynard Keynes' *Economic Consequences of the Peace* (1919), "a timely demolition of the Versailles Treaty."[52] The novel was followed by *Babbitt* (1922), satirically depicting George Babbitt, a businessman, who arguably represents the "prototype of the 'other-directed' personality later analyzed by David Riesman in *The Lonely Crowd*."[53] For *Arrowsmith* (1925), Lewis developed a technique of literary collaboration with Paul de Kruif, a trained microbiologist, to work with an expert as informant and (uncredited but paid) coauthor, to write a novel about a bacteriologist.[54] Lewis shared with de Kruif an iconoclastic spirit of "debunking," as well as a habit of excessive drinking under the conditions of the Prohibition era. They also both held a strong skepticism toward American philanthropies, evidently built in large parts on the money of "robber barons," such as John D. Rockefeller, whom Lewis despised after the infamous Ludlow Massacre of 1914,[55] carried out one year after the establishment of the Rockefeller Foundation. Before turning into a freelance writer, de Kruif had in fact been working for the Rockefeller Institute for Medical Research, but was fired after being identified as the anonymous author of a piece that "charged the institute with commercialism and flawed science,"[56] an affront possibly aggravated by his apparent antisemitic sentiments toward Simon Flexner, director of the Institute and brother of the educational reformer Abraham Flexner.[57] *Arrowsmith* directly – yet largely implicitly – targets these changes in what de Kruif and Lewis perceived as an increasingly impersonal and profit-driven American medical culture taught in standardized "scientific" programs at medical schools, resulting from the highly influential (Abraham-)Flexner Report, originally written for the Carnegie Foundation in 1910.

As Lewis suffered more and more from an alcoholic disease during the 1920s, which he spent mostly traveling between the United States and Europe, in close vicinity but ignored by the avantgarde circles in Paris, he repeated this model of collaboration with the Unitarian minister Leon M. Birkhead in *Elmer Gantry* (1927), a novel on religious hypocrisy, commercialization, and corruption in the evangelical movement. The publication created, even more than *Main Street* and *Babbitt*, a scandal, which successfully translated for the PR-savvy author into publicity that in turn boosted the sales. He failed, however, in these years, despite several research trips, concepts, and promises to his editor to realize his long-held plan of a *mangnum opus*, a novel about the American labor movement.[58] While the Nobel Prize cemented his literary reputation, it was his relationship with activist journalist and author Dorothy Thompson starting in 1927, then chief European correspondent in Berlin for the *Philadelphia Public Ledger* and the *New York Evening Post*, which gave his flagging work during the 1930s a new direction. Thompson, who interviewed Adolf Hitler in 1931, quickly became one of the most vocal public critics of National Socialist Germany, and for Lewis a new collaborator with expert knowledge, literary skill and – unlike de Kruif – a public persona in her own right.[59] Lewis' novel *It Can't Happen Here* (1935) is an early literary response to the debates on fascism, depicting the rise of an American dictator Berzelius "Buzz" Windrip, who is modeled after Huey Long, a populist Democratic governor and then senator from Louisiana, whom Thompson interviewed in early 1935 – before his assassination in September[60] – as he considered mounting a third-party bid for the 1936 presidential election. As one of Lewis' biographers lays out the disquieting political map of American fascism and national socialist tendencies in 1935 in front of Lewis:

> The real threat came from a weird mélange of quasi populist movements, each founded by a charismatic leader: Huey Long's "Share our Wealth" movement; Father Coughlin's Union of Social Justice; Dr. Francis E. Townsend's Old Age Revolving Pensions Plan; and Upton Sinclair's more or less socialist End Poverty in California (EPIC) Party. If they could unite and attract disaffected Democrats like Al Smith and Jeffersonian Democrats, they could conceivably elect their man president. To the seething cauldron be added native fascist groups like the Silver Shirts, the German-American Bund, and the Black Legion, which preached a hate litany of anti-Semitism, anti-Catholicism, and anti-immigrantism and extolled Hitler and the Nazis.[61]

Thompson, while not directly involved in the writing process, provided Lewis with the necessary "impetus," served as "one of his advisors on the subject of Nazism,"[62] as well as his "researcher"[63] on domestic politics, giving the novel much of its poignancy.[64] Lewis' genuine addition to the imagination of an American public facilitating a dictatorship is already present as a topic throughout his work of the 1920s and the early 1930s, albeit in different contexts – the social role of clubs, associations, councils, committees, unions, leagues, and societies in American middle-class culture.[65] The subversive cell of American fascism in *It Couldn't Happen Here* provides the setting for the book's opening sentence: "The handsome dining room of the Hotel Wessex, with its gilded plaster shields and the mural depicting the Green Mountains, had been reserved for the Ladies' Night Dinner of the Fort Beulah Rotary Club."[66] Lewis puts a philanthropic circle at the beginning of his novel, in which the retired Brigadier General Herbert Y. Edgeways and Mrs. Adelaide Tarr Gimmitch spread fascist propaganda.[67] The setup leads journalist Doremus Jessup, the liberal counterpart to the dictator Windrip, later to the novel's key statement: "This is revolution in terms of Rotary."[68] American fascism, according to Lewis' pungent pun, is mediated in social clubs, spreading the upper class principle of philanthropy in middle-class settings.[69]

By the late 1930s, after Lewis' and Thompson's separation, he turned his attention to writing and producing plays. Apparently with some spite toward Thompson's strong public positioning and advocacy for American aid to Britain after the start of World War II, Lewis again fell back on his early World War I isolationist attitudes and joined the emerging memorandum culture from the extreme right, through the short-lived, yet infamous America First Committee. As several other public figures and intellectuals, Lewis picked up on a popular noninterventionist sentiment and coalesced with people such as the world-famous aviator Charles Lindbergh, who spread his antisemitic views and publicly praised the achievements of Hitler and National Socialism, but also retired Brigadier General Robert E. Wood, chair of the retail chain Sears Roebuck. Lewis in effect joined "in terms of Rotary" the proto-fascist coalition between charismatic populist leaders and Republican extremist capitalists he had warned of only a few years earlier.[70] However, briefly after the attack on Pearl Harbor and the end of American noninterventionism as well as after finalizing his divorce with Thompson in January 1942, he started pursuing the plan to return to a critical satire about the "Great Leaders who stand up on platforms and lead noble causes – any damned kind of causes." In his view, they were constituting "a new crop of Saviours of Democracy"[71] found in the world of philanthropy, the nucleus of *Gideon Planish*.

Gideon Planish is a reinstatement of Lewis' literary innovations of the 1920s, but applied to his political development alongside Dorothy Thompson in the 1930s, followed by a recent move away from narrative prose toward dramatic and oral forms of expression. About fifteen years after *Elmer Gantry*, Lewis again contacted Birkhead, this time because of his role as president of the political organization Friends of Democracy, founded in Kansas City in 1937, and then moved to New York in 1939. He also hired James Hart, a former journalist, to investigate potential scandals in the world of charitable foundations as material for his novel. Another line of research came through his renewed experience of American university culture, more than thirty years after graduating from Yale University, on occasion of teaching a creative writing course at the University of Minnesota. Most importantly, however, he draws on his participant observations of Dorothy Thompson and her circle's engagement in the emerging memorandum culture.

Lewis tells in his novel the story of the social climber Gideon Planish, starting with his childhood in the fictional mid-western state of Winnemac, his college education and participation in the "Adelbert College Socialist League,"[72] where he starts training his debating skills, including the ability to influence people's opinions, but also to drastically change his own political positions, before he is hired as a "Professor of Rhetoric and Speech in Kinnikinick College, Iowa"[73] at age 29. As professor, he becomes infatuated with one of his first-year students: "He thought, this Peony Jackson is so fresh and jolly and *cool*."[74] They quickly marry and become an ever-indebted 1920s wannabe power-couple, dysfunctional but highly ambitious, pursuing half-baked ideas, as they enter the world of clubs, religious charities, and private philanthropies, among them, notably, the Kinnikinick Rotary Club.[75] Lewis picks up the theme of philanthropy largely implicit in *Arrowsmith* and explicit in *It Can't Happen Here*, and throws the married couple into the world of the memorandum culture, which takes them from Ohio and Iowa eastward to the suburbs of New York, Washington, DC, and finally New York City. Always more imposter than scholar, Planish quits his university position and becomes editor for Rural Adult Education, where he further develops his art of using commonplaces and learns his most important lesson in public speech, to respect "taboos and libel laws. He must invariably speak reverently of mothers, duck-hunting, the Y.M.C.A., the Salvation Army, the Catholic Church, Rabbi Wise, the American flag, cornbread, Robert E. Lee, carburetors and children up to the age of eleven."[76] As no job ever pays enough, the protagonist of *Gideon Planish* – a screwball comedy with institutional rather than romantic entanglements – moves through various odd jobs provided by his connections to "organizators"[77] and wealthy donors such as ghost-writing an autobiography. "Planish had been honored by his first invitation to become a 'national director' of a great organization with its office in New York: The Sympathizers with the Pacifistic Purposes of the New Democratic Turkey." The organizations acronym "S.P.P.N.D.T."[78] is the first in a series of increasingly absurd abbreviations, such as the "Heskett Rural School Foundation [...] H.R.S.F.,"[79] whose activities remain a mystery to the protagonist even after he joins the National Directorship of the foundation: "Before the annual conference of the Heskett Foundation, Dr. Planish had learned everything about it except why it existed at all."[80] In his new role, "managing secretary," he is responsible for the publication of speeches by among others H. Sanderson Sanderson-Smith, in "flat little gray pamphlets."[81] He also sends out elaborate fundraising schemes to supporters of the foundation, possibly one of the first graphic depictions of a memorandum in literary fiction (Figure 1.1). Lewis turns on this occasion to the aforementioned "nucleus" of the novel, giving a detailed description of the circular logics underlying Gideon Planish's bureaucratic work in philanthropy.

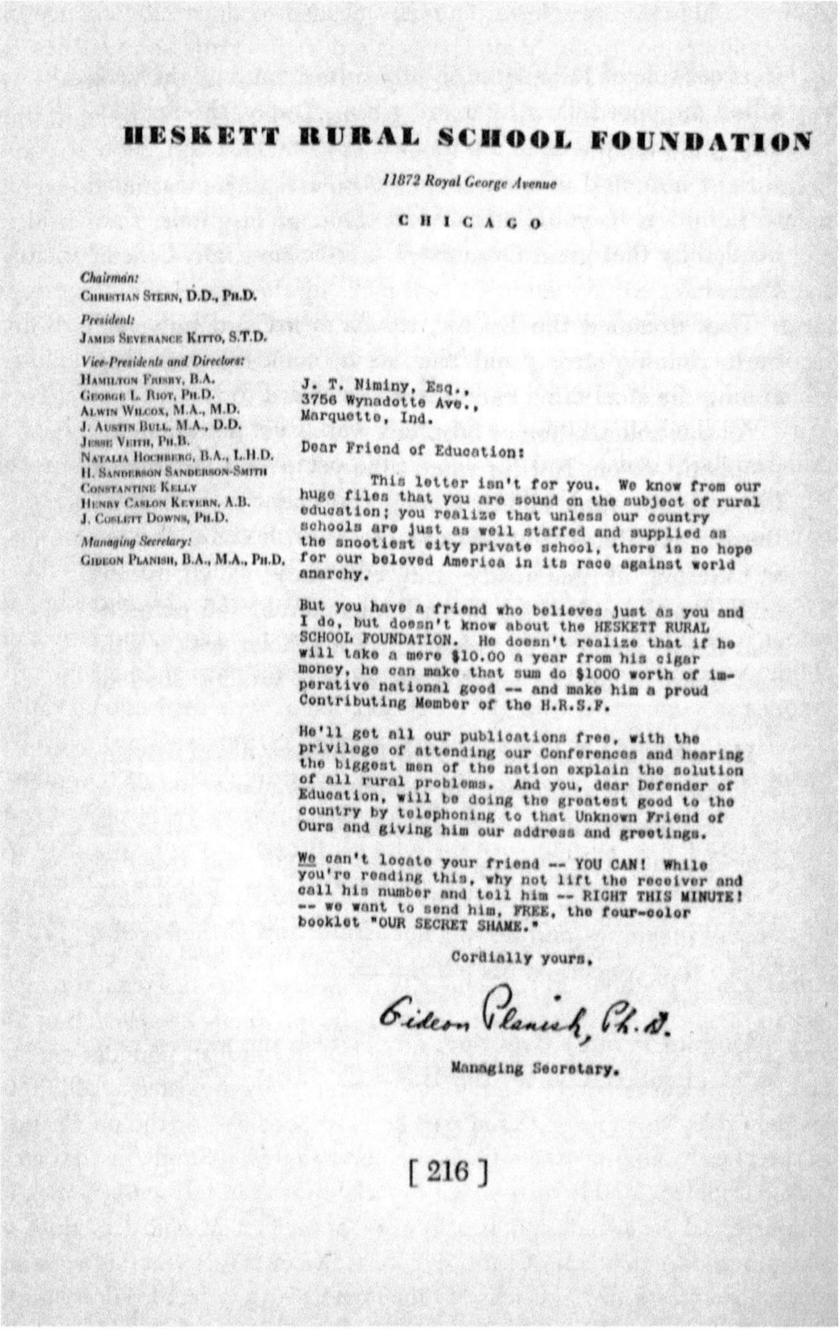

HESKETT RURAL SCHOOL FOUNDATION

11872 Royal George Avenue

CHICAGO

Chairman:
CHRISTIAN STERN, D.D., PH.D.

President:
JAMES SEVERANCE KITTO, S.T.D.

Vice-Presidents and Directors:
HAMILTON FRISBY, B.A.
GEORGE L. RIOT, PH.D.
ALWIN WILCOX, M.A., M.D.
J. AUSTIN BULL, M.A., D.D.
JESSE VEITH, PH.B.
NATALIA HOCHBERG, B.A., L.H.D.
H. SANDERSON SANDERSON-SMITH
CONSTANTINE KELLY
HENRY CASLON KEVERN, A.B.
J. CORLETT DOWNS, PH.D.

Managing Secretary:
GIDEON PLANISH, B.A., M.A., PH.D.

J. T. Niminy, Esq.,
3756 Wynadotte Ave.,
Marquette, Ind.

Dear Friend of Education:

    This letter isn't for you. We know from our huge files that you are sound on the subject of rural education; you realize that unless our country schools are just as well staffed and supplied as the snootiest city private school, there is no hope for our beloved America in its race against world anarchy.

But you have a friend who believes just as you and I do, but doesn't know about the HESKETT RURAL SCHOOL FOUNDATION. He doesn't realize that if he will take a mere $10.00 a year from his cigar money, he can make that sum do $1000 worth of imperative national good -- and make him a proud Contributing Member of the H.R.S.F.

He'll get all our publications free, with the privilege of attending our Conferences and hearing the biggest men of the nation explain the solution of all rural problems. And you, dear Defender of Education, will be doing the greatest good to the country by telephoning to that Unknown Friend of Ours and giving him our address and greetings.

We can't locate your friend -- YOU CAN! While you're reading this, why not lift the receiver and call his number and tell him -- RIGHT THIS MINUTE! -- we want to send him, FREE, the four-color booklet "OUR SECRET SHAME."

                      Cordially yours,

                      Gideon Planish, Ph.D.

                      Managing Secretary.

[216]

FIGURE 1.1 Sinclair Lewis, *Gideon Planish* (1943), page 216.

With the passion for exactitude and flapping charts which is part of the New Scientific Philanthropy, Dr. Planish calculated that it cost ten cents to send out a letter, including stationary, postage, mimeographing, filling in, the booklet, overhead, and purchasing lists of persons known to have been philanthropic – which were rather coarsely known as "sucker lists," and which were sold commercially, like fly-paper. As the professional saviors put it, "If one per cent of the prospects on the sucker list kick through, the cost of the campaign is covered."[82]

Gideon Planish joins, with the help of H. Sanderson Sanderson-Smith, a declared opponent of democracy, who later in the novel gets jailed as a Nazi agent, the CCCCC (Citizens' Conference on Constitutional Crises in the Commonwealth, also known as Cizkon), based in Washington, DC. He then becomes "Directive Secretary of the DDD – the Dynamos of Democratic Direction,"[83] serving again in an administrative role as the largely invisible, yet most important agent behind each such group.[84] In the meanwhile, Gideon Planish had also come to be considered – without the slightest insight – an "expert on Eskimos,"[85] thanks to his work for the Association to Promote Eskimo Culture. A "quiet man" listening, toward the end of the novel, to one of Gideon Planish's final speeches for the DDD again connects Lewis' 1943-novel also explicitly to his earlier political critique of philanthropy: "[T]he one thing that might break down American Democracy was the hysterical efficiency with which these pressure groups crusaded to seize all the benefits of that Democracy for themselves."[86] The quiet man, in a climactic monologue, goes on to formulate a blistering assessment of the "private armies led by devout fanatics," and ends his thoughts in a patriotic prayer:

God save poor America, this quiet man thought, from all the zealous and the professionally idealistic, from eloquent women and generous sponsors and administrative ex-preachers and natural-born Leaders and Napoleonic newspaper executives and all the people who like to make long telephone calls and write inspirational memoranda.[87]

The last, pivotal, and truly brilliant part of the novel plays mostly in New York, satirically depicting the standoff between Isolationists and Internationalists, non-Interventionists and Interventionists, in the days leading toward December 7, 1941 and the attack on Pearl Harbor, after which the DDD collapses and the story of Gideon Planish ends. The author himself, in 1943 apparently had radically changed course once more, jumping from a position of pacifist isolationism toward blunt interventionism. At least in his novel, Lewis shows clear sympathies for the character of Gideon Planish's daughter Carrie and a character from the Midwest called Mr. Johnson, who are in favor of effective military action instead of wasting time with further memoranda.[88] The head of the DDD Colonel Marduc, instead immediately starts plotting to produce even more gray literature, ordering Gideon Planish to work out "[t]he Marduc Plan, [...] reduce 'em [Germany] to the small separate kingdoms and duchies that they were before 1870 – a lot of small weak states. [...] Send 'em all [the powerhouses] a mimeographed bulletin tomorrow and remind 'em that we warned 'em about this Pearl Harbor danger months ago. Months!"[89]

The novel stands and falls with its ability to satirically depict and to provocatively debunk the world of charities and philanthropies. The novel achieves this most elegantly, when Gideon Planish himself, after the breakdown of the DDD, in an attempt to consolidate the swirling mass of organizations, exploits the schematic nature of their names:

Now [...] he began to list all the national welfare and educational organizations with headquarters in New York City. He stopped when he had listed two thousand of them, mostly with titles containing the words American, National, Committee, Institution, Guild, Forum, League or Council.[90]

In terms of popular reception reflected in sales numbers – more than 150.000 copies – the novel was an unexpected success – and indeed seems to have captured the imagination of the American reading public in 1943. In terms of scandal, however, the novel did not measure up to his earlier work, as Lewis' editor's initial prediction failed to come true: "It's going to stir up the animals, all the way from the Carnegie Foundation up and down."[91] No one in the world of philanthropy seems to have contradicted, or even taken offense – at least publicly. A simple answer to this conundrum might be that Lewis did enough work to fictionalize his characters – a literary strategy he had developed early on, first of all to avoid lawsuits – so that no one could feel personally attacked, or respectively, some of those who could reasonably feel offended, such as the imprisoned George S. Viereck, were in 1943 in no position to respond.[92] The publicly highly active Thompson on the other hand was apparently a big enough person, after their divorce, to ignore her unfavorable portrayal as Winnifred Marduc Homeward, the overly talkative and at the same time ruthless daughter of media mogul Colonel Charles B. Marduc. Some readers apparently took the novel in fact as Lewis' revenge after the breakup. They failed to suspect, maybe not least for this reason, that the novel still contained large amounts of insider knowledge, "dope," which Lewis received from Thompson over the years.

In an inscription to one copy of the book, he wrote – apparently in response to this problem: "My most serious book – therefore, naturally, not taken too seriously."[93] To the detriment of the novel's long-term reception, the DDD complex has not received the attention that it deserves, neither for its satirical bravura, nor for its analytical insight, both of which are intimately connected. The DDD is headed by "Colonel Charles B. Marduc, the big New York advertising man and publisher,"[94] and ambitiously pursued plans to have chapters throughout the United States. Colonel Marduc, evidently a composite character built on more than one model, has nevertheless received significant traits from Henry R. Luce, the magazine magnate and publisher of *Time*, *Life*, and *Fortune*, among others, some of which were publicly known, but some of which were also most likely passed on in private and not meant to be published.[95]

Colonel Marduc tries to set up the Governor Thomas Blizzard as a challenger to the sitting President, as arguably did Luce with Republican candidate Wendell Willkie, the failed contender of Roosevelt in the 1940 presidential election, supported by Thompson as well. The fictional Colonel Marduc has, despite his apparent support for American democracy and interventionist politics a history of sympathizing with fascist leaders such as the Spanish dictator Franco, as well as for Mussolini and Hitler and, in America, "Defense First":

The Colonel had been fidgety about Milo Samphire's [and his interventionist Call to Arms League's] demand that the American dislike for Fascism extend to war. Indeed, for a time, the Colonel had nearly slipped into the Isolationist faction. Secretly, he rather liked the way of Hitler and Mussolini in dealing briefly with anyone who opposed the Rule of the Strongest – the Colonel considering himself quite a good candidate for the Strongest in America. He had even spoken a few noncommittal words at a Defense First anti-war meeting, a few months ago. But when he saw the newspaper editorials about the meeting, he publicly explained that he hadn't said what he meant and, most decidedly, he hadn't meant what he said. He called up Dr. Planish and told him that from that moment on, the DDD would have nothing to do with the Isolationists.[96]

While Luce allowed the Italian "Duce" Mussolini to be lauded as a strong leader in *Fortune* as late as 1934, winning him at his Times Inc. the – at least grammatically incorrect – nickname "il Luce,"[97] and while he did not order his magazines to take a clear editorial line against the Spanish leader Franco of the fascist Falange during the first years of the Spanish Civil War in 1936/37, he in fact orchestrated in 1941 in his magazines a domestic campaign against the America First Committee and its members, rather than secretly sympathizing with it.[98]

Even if an early reader in a letter to Lewis suspected behind Colonel Marduc the controversial media mogul William R. Hearst, who notoriously provided in his magazines a platform for texts by German National Socialists in the 1930s and who is today largely remembered as one of the models for the protagonist of *Citizen Kane* (1941), there are several aspects to Marduc that tie him more directly to Luce, if one starts looking closely at the world of committees forming part of the memorandum culture of the 1940s. First of all, Luce was an initiator – not of the DDD but – of the interventionist Fight for Freedom Committee, the FFF, started in 1941, against the more established internationalist but noninterventionist Committee to Defend America by Aiding the Allies, the CDAAA, founded by progressive Republican William A. White one year earlier in 1940.[99] For this study, however, one of the most important similarities that appears during a critical moment in the overall narrative, is the depiction of the aforementioned Librarian of Congress MacLeish as Otis Canari, "the poet-orator,"[100] originally "one of Marduc's Bright Young Men"[101] – as was MacLeish, though not quite as young anymore, to Luce. Lewis' introduces Otis Canari in a "regular quarterly meeting of the DDD directors,"[102] in which the "basic spiritual aspects of that monumental coming American Century"[103] were supposed to be laid out, as chairman of a committee: "Sherry went on, 'The first thing on our agenda today is the report of the Committee for the Determination of a Definition of the Word 'Democracy' for Propaganda, of which committee Otis Canary has been our invaluable chairman. Come on Ote, let's hear your report.'"[104] While Otis Canary is able to play the role of chairman to perfection, he fails in his basic intellectual task and provides an elusive non-definition with flowery metaphors, which is, however, met with enthusiasm, except for the Midwesterner Mr. Johnson, and Gideon Planish, who is bored, before receiving a phone call that provides a stark contrast to the useless proceedings of the committee. The protagonist receives the news of a Japanese bombing of American ships in Pearl Harbor.[105]

As mentioned previously, the satirical portrayal of MacLeish's work for Luce was not accurately deciphered at the time, and accordingly, to Lewis' disfavor, its achievement was not fully perceived. The historical reception of the book instead is divided between highly critical reviews lamenting the outdatedness of Lewis' prose – indeed most of its literary techniques were from the 1920s, fully developed eighteen years earlier in *Arrowsmith* – and a considerable popular success in the American reading public.

Lewis' well-worn social documentary style is particularly befitting for the depiction of the newly emerging memorandum culture, which itself heavily relied on practices of documentation. *Gideon Planish* reads in fact like a protocol, in which several episodes, observations, and lose threads are put together in chronological order without being synthesized, a flaw only at first sight that leads to comic effects and artistic moments of *mise en abyme*. The true shortcoming of *Gideon Planish*, written largely after returning from isolationism to physical isolation in what Lewis considered a provincial setting during the summer and fall of 1942 in Minnesota lies in his view on the world of philanthropy as an isolated bubble that bursts after Pearl Harbor.[106] Put another way, Lewis' ethnographic work stopped precisely at the moment, when the memorandum culture was being supercharged by the new urgency of America's entry into the military conflict; and relatedly, the encounter of American intellectuals with the recent wave of European émigrés, many of which arrived only between 1938 and 1941, and only started to collaborate in the memorandum culture after significant barriers – legal and otherwise – had been lowered sufficiently. While it is true that parts of the supporting institutions feared financial strain in 1941/42, as significant portions of the American war economy were diverted to the military, this development did not stop the production of gray literature, which, in fact, only intensified.

Lewis' novel, after all published, clearly does not take too seriously the intellectual value of any text circulated as a memorandum, which makes him miss the very point I am trying to ascertain. Nevertheless, thanks to his deep commitment to social scientific and journalistic techniques of research, he is able to perceive some of the crucial dynamics of the memorandum culture and records the various underlying entanglements and infrastructures of the fleeting gray literature of World War II, and in fact presents with a unique clarity of vision, even if satirically exaggerated, in Gideon Planish the social figure of the academic-turned-secretary, who administrates gray literature.[107] He also profiles the paradoxical dynamics and the enormous range of internationalist actors resulting from the highly confusing political alliances and ruptures of the late 1930s and early 1940s. Already in 1943, Lewis' *Gideon Planish* provides an analysis of the social world of committees, that historians only in recent decades have started to make sense of – the processes of imitation, division, proliferation, and amalgamation within and in between the short-lived committees.[108] More recently, historian Andrew Johnstone has pointed out with regard especially to the biggest organization of them all, the massive

Committee to Defend America by Aiding the Allies, the CDAAA also known as the White-committee with more than 800 local chapters by December 1941, that these organizations, founded with strong noninterventionist sentiments, were indeed able to bridge a wide spectrum of opinions.[109] Even more crucially, their noninterventionist infrastructures could be transformed in a matter of days into platforms for the production of interventionist literature, so much so that in retrospect, the distinction between isolationist or respectively noninterventionist versus interventionist clearly emerges as insufficient to understand the memorandum culture of the 1940s. It rather appears, as the example of Lewis' has shown, to be a strategic historical categorization of American foreign politics, which in turn was, for a long time, uncritically accepted at face value in research.

1.5 EXCLUDE ME IN

For the purposes of this study, the image of the memorandum culture in *Gideon Planish* is at best partial, as it reduces the consequential encounter with European émigrés to minor confusions, and therefore stops, when it really gets interesting. Yet, Lewis' novel is a unique work of fiction in that it mediates a crucial moment in the history of literature – the rise of gray literature – that most authors and researchers otherwise have largely shunned for several decades. Let me therefore tackle, once more, the same point from the other direction, moving on from the fictional characters Otis Canari and Colonel Marduc, to starting with their historical models MacLeish and Luce, essentially asking the question: Why is there no *Gideon Planish* – or any comparable work of prose, poetry, drama – by the writer MacLeish?

In a letter from May 15, 1939, the lawyer, modernist poet, popular playwright, and journalist MacLeish politely refuses a prestigious but daunting job offer:

> If I were the distinguished person to whom your memorandum of May eleventh was addressed, I should immediately [...] appoint your candidate: a more persuasive brief I have never read. Being merely your candidate I can only tell you, first, how proud I am [...] and how troubled I am that I cannot feel as you do about the end result. [...][110]

Replying to his friend and former teacher Felix Frankfurter, who had been recently appointed as associate justice of the Supreme Court, MacLeish, with a lengthy autobiographical explanation, expresses his unwillingness to become the new Librarian of Congress, a position that for the last 40 years had been held by the librarian Herbert Putnam:

> From the beginning of my more or less adult life I have been plagued by the fact that I seem to be able to do more or less well things which don't commonly go together. [...] I first decided leaving the school not to go into practice, and when later I left [law] practice to write verse. [...] I think I was made to suffer as acutely over my decision to quit the law for poetry as it is possible to make a man suffer over any decision in his own life. [...] The most recent of the many crises of this type presented itself about a year ago, when, as I think I told you, Harry Luce wanted to make me Editor of *Fortune* in complete charge of editorial content of the magazine. [...] What you will perhaps not understand – because it is so easy for you to do many things together – is that the practice of my art requires, in my practice at least, long periods of completely free time. [...] This, it seems to me, the directorship of the Congressional Library could not give.[111]

It turns out that Frankfurter's was a recommendation that MacLeish could not simply decline. Two weeks later, on May 28, he feels compelled to directly address the person responsible for the job offer, President Franklin D. Roosevelt, expressing his indisposition in even starker terms:

> [...] I attempted to argue myself into a contrary opinion. I argue so successfully that I wrote you two letters, each of which I later destroyed. When it came down to it I could not believe that the job of Librarian of Congress was a job a man with an art to practice could fairly undertake. Either the art or the library would suffer, and either result would be disastrous to the man. [...] I can only thank you with all my heart for thinking of me and for the great honor you have done me and tell you with what regret I feel I must decline.[112]

The crisis was resolved only four days later on June 1, when MacLeish wrote a second letter to the President, expressing an abrupt reversal of attitude:

> The question which troubled me when you first told me what you had in mind – the question, that is, of time in which to continue my own writing – touched me even more as I realized more clearly the great responsibility of the position of which you spoke & the great importance of the work which might be done in it. I am assured, however, by those in whose judgment I trust that time undoubtedly could be found. I am therefore writing you now to say that I should be very proud indeed to serve as director of the Congressional Library should you wish to name me.[113]

Announcing the appointment, on June 6, "the President told newsmen that the post had been difficult to fill because of its many requirements [but that] he had found what he wanted in MacLeish 'a gentleman and a scholar' ... 'who, in every nation of the world, would be known as such.'"[114]

After the hiccup that accompanied his passage from poetry into civil service, MacLeish went on to fulfill his assignment all the more vigorously, reorganizing the Library of Congress from an allegedly dysfunctional institution into a national research library, that is, as a legislative tool preparing to fight Nazi Germany in the approaching war.

> They [librarians] must think of their libraries as organizations of intelligent and well-trained men and women qualified to select from the record in their keeping such materials as are relevant to the decisions the people must make and able to provide those materials to the people in a useful form. They must think of their libraries, in other words, not as books and catalogues with the men to serve them, but as expert men to whom the books and catalogues are tools for the performance of a duty.[115]

Making the passage from the private world into his position as the Librarian of Congress, MacLeish realized quickly that he was put in a unique position of power: the highest-ranking administrator of knowledge in the political center of his nation, orienting the memorandum culture analyzing Nazi Germany toward his office.[116] Among the many initiatives not necessarily to be entailed in the job description of a librarian, MacLeish, as mentioned earlier, started to house the first US-American foreign intelligence service in the Library of Congress in 1941[117] and appointed the prime national author of the "Other Germany," Thomas Mann, as a "Consultant to the Library of Congress." Moreover, his own wartime speeches and writing to follow his "strategy of truth" – despite its flawed implementation in the failed Office Facts and Figures – played a central role in drumming up the American public and its intellectuals and scholars against the Nazi enemy.[118] For the moment, however, to understand the sociality of the memorandum culture with and beyond Lewis, I want to go back in time to late spring of 1939 and approach MacLeish's work at the Library of Congress from the moot moment of MacLeish's objection to playing along.[119]

How was the crisis solved? Two statements stand out. MacLeish directs the responsibility to others: "I am assured, however, by those in whose judgment I trust that time undoubtedly could be found." And Roosevelt answers: "he had found what he wanted in MacLeish 'a gentleman and a scholar.'"[120] MacLeish was not convinced through recurrence to his inner, poetic self but through trust in external judgment. Looking at Roosevelt's precise choice of words, it becomes clear whose judgment this was: he found in MacLeish a "gentleman." MacLeish's reference to "those" points to his social circle of gentlemen, his "Old Boys Network,"[121] whose collective pressure apparently facilitated his radical change of status, namely to give up his dream of being a poet, for which he had abandoned earlier in his life an extremely promising legal career. These strategies of "adaptation to failure" are described in one of the classics of mid-century sociology as "cooling out," in which the "mark" is asked to see things objectively. In the moment that the person dealing with failure agrees to the regimen of the "cooler,"[122] they submit to a "trial of strength"[123] that provides a para-legal procedure according to which – all facts considered[124] – the "sucker's" loss appears reasonable. Their subjective feelings are hurt, but they are objectively doing the right thing by playing along. And as already mentioned, this cooling strategy was in MacLeish's case extremely effective. He fulfilled his role to the best of his abilities as he shrunk his silent protest to the bare minimum, renouncing to write – besides one known piece – any poetry at all during the years of his service as Librarian of Congress.[125]

Instead, MacLeish turned against his own caste and took on the role to strike – to great effect[126] – against his generation of American intellectuals, scholars, and writers who failed "to oppose [the destructive forces in Europe] with the arms of scholarship and writing"[127] – coincidentally the actual reason for Lewis' grudge against MacLeish. "History," MacLeish argues, would judge the intellectuals' engagement in stopping the Nazi danger, on the basis of, as he aptly points out, their work in the memorandum culture: "It will be asked of books we have written, the carbon copies of our correspondence, the photographs of our faces, the minutes of our meetings in the famous rooms before the portraits of our spiritual begetters."[128]

This statement counted for more than florid metaphor. Only a few months later, MacLeish did indeed play a vital role in actively transferring the subject of history to America. On February 17, 1941, MacLeish's former boss, the editor Luce,[129] first published his epoch-making address "The American Century" in one of his magazines, *Life*. It met instant success.[130] Luce's famous essay – in light of the memorandum culture – is as important for its genesis as for its contents. Reading through the reasonably sized editorial of five magazine pages, it is easy to forget that "The American Century" was not thought out by a single mind in a day's work, but that it constituted an elaborately designed product of intense intellectual collaboration. It did not merely receive additional polishing but in fact was, from beginning to end, generated through formal and informal state of the art literary techniques, journalistic methods, and social scientific procedures in order to target American public opinion. Luce invested months of intermittent work in developing this short piece of writing.

Moving backward: In arriving at the final version for *Life*, the text had gone through various stages of testing and tailoring: before its final redaction by *Life*'s managing editor, John Shaw Billings, for the magazine's readership,[131] both form and content had been confronted with polling numbers.[132] In early 1941, Luce had "audience tested" the text in speeches to powerful professional associations in Pasadena, CA, Tulsa, OK, and Pittsburgh, PA.[133] Between July and November 1940, Luce had discussed his ideas in his immediate political circle in New York, the members of the "Century Group,"[134] named after the Century Association, a private social club. And in the earliest conceptions of "The American Century" in the summer of 1940, Luce had initially relied on and, to a certain extent, appropriated ideas and style from memoranda composed by two of his most prominent writers, the journalist Walter Lippmann[135] and MacLeish, now the Librarian of Congress, two of his Ivy League-trained "Bright Young Men."[136] In many ways, "The American Century" originated from, developed, and started to circulate as gray literature, before it was published for a general audience.

To be sure, Luce, the son of a missionary, may have skillfully contributed to the address's florid, sermonizing sound full of implicit and explicit religious references. This sound carried his slowly moving meditation on "The American Century" and clearly helped connect with a wide array of readers. It seems just, however, to point out, that Luce's involvement of others' expertise for his editorial granted its immediate and long-standing effect. This is true for MacLeish's "historic" contribution through gray literature, and it also applies to Luce's engagement in the Century Group as well as his substantial financial support of parts of the memorandum culture such as the Fight for Freedom Committee and the Council for Democracy, which go hand in hand with his most important public political statement in "The American Century."

The best point of view from which to look at the argument of Luce's intricate address lies at a rather early stage, before its publication: Election Day in November 1940, when Luce's ill-fated support of the internationalist Republican candidate Wendell Willkie against the second-term incumbent Roosevelt failed. Win or lose, Luce's message did not depend on the outcome of the election. What did change was the form: the seizure of power in "American Century" needed to be delivered as a concession speech. Luce performs in his intervention two acts of displacement in order to redirect the inward aggressive potential of American noninterventionists, at the time largely represented by the Republican Party, outward. Act one: Fishing an argument from the extreme right,[137] Luce identifies the inner adversary, Roosevelt, with the National Socialist enemy of the outer friend, England.[138] This identification enables Luce to redirect Republican resentment and outrage by means of a pact with the inner American devil – against the outer Nazi hell. Roosevelt has shown his ability to win, so the American people best oppose him domestically by supporting his effort to defeat the outer enemy. Once Luce has brought the American people to consider themselves as directed toward the enemy, and therefore as being perceived by the outer enemy,[139] he can broaden this sense of being perceived by others: to America's "environment," "the entire human family," "our world" – all of whom call for America's world leadership and for an "internationalism of the people, by the people and for the people."[140]

Then, Luce offers a list of American cultural export goods appreciated by the rest of the world that defines America in the world. It starts, truthfully – and this is the second act of displacement – with "American jazz," a complex that parts of the population he addresses at the time domestically would only have referred to with racial slurs, not as part of their national culture.[141] "American jazz, Hollywood movies, American slang, American machines and patented products, are in fact the only things that every community in the world, from Zanzibar to Hamburg, recognizes in common."[142] It is, according to Luce, exactly this universal "prestige"[143] that stands as the unmistakable sign of America's calling to world leadership.

To sum up: the case for American hegemony in "The American Century" starts with self-contempt and then gets its outward direction in the face of Nazi Germany, a move based on the often-unacknowledged transitions between American noninterventionism and internationalism, evidenced by the case of Lewis' *Gideon Planish*. This in turn leads America to acknowledge its internationalism that, once the Nazi German enemy has disappeared, should guide America's world-historical peace mission.

The examination of textual genesis and argument of Luce's epochal and epoch-making essay vis-à-vis the memorandum culture studying Nazi Germany shows, how the historic shift of American foreign policy heralding the "American Century" depended both on the collaborative practice of its making and on its theoretical underpinning with an emphasis on the perception of others leading to a new conceptualization of sociality. The indispensable ingredient for this sociality puts, as will be argued in the next chapter, "American jazz" front and center. Despite supposedly irreconcilable intellectual disagreements, as well as the economical, psychological, and social difficulties in which almost all émigrés arrived in the United States after traumatic experiences of displacement, fear, and loss, several of them managed to join the memorandum culture. American-European collaborations were facilitated by a belief in objectivity, specifically in an emotional style of coolness. The successful collaboration leading to the rise of gray literature, I want to argue in the following, was based on a process of mutual misapprehension and mimesis of each other's coolness, a collaboration of the cool. Since the next chapter's relevance to the argument is largely theoretical, readers, who are primarily interested in history may wish to skip directly to Chapter 3 and perhaps return to it later.

2

Cool Collaboration

Social interactions between intellectuals can be awkward for many reasons. Studying social interactions between intellectuals can be awkward for just as many. And after all, what is scholarship more than receiving and sending out a series of letters to colleagues, students, and friends, to friendly readers, to whom it may concern, that is again, social interaction between intellectuals? In approaching a historical study of the collaborative work of intellectuals in the USA around World War II, it seems prudent to guard against the imponderability of these encounters with the help of a theory of social interaction. And where better to start searching than with the theories provided by the historical actors themselves?

The book market of the mid-century found that the US-American reading public was keenly interested in the social theories of wartime intellectuals and indeed motivated to absorb thick paperbacks filled with rather complicated and technical arguments that helped especially the upper middle class come to terms with their new situation in American society, which had undergone tectonic shifts in the previous decades, but also with America's hegemonic role on the world stage. Arguably as the most prominent among these publications figures one book that provides a striking assessment of a new type of sociality. Namely, "other-direction" served as the central notion in David Riesman's canonical study of the American Character, the collaboratively published *Lonely Crowd* (1950). Largely based on community studies, character studies of individuals, group interviews of teenagers, but apparently also drawing on his experience working as a trained lawyer in various office jobs, Riesman strings together a long succession of vignette analyses describing, with reference to social psychological theories, a new American sociability originating in white-collar culture: "The type of character I shall describe as other-directed seems to be emerging in very recent years in the upper middle-class of our larger cities. [...] Yet in some respects this type is strikingly similar to *the* American."[1] According to Riesman, the rules for the other-directeds'[2] conduct do not correspond to an internalized morality, but they come from their social environment. The behavior of the "other-directed man [...] will depend on the situation created for him by the others who set the expectations to which he responds."[3] The other-directed indeed turns any situation into a social situation, they "perceive it only *in terms of the others* – to see not a landscape with figures but figures with a landscape."[4] While most of the immediate historical reception regarded Riesman's description of the other-directed type as a social critique of alienation and conformism, the – at the last minute – tendentiously titled *Lonely Crowd* has actually some positive things to say particularly about their relationship to others. Among those, I want to point out a main tenet of middle class – or rather bourgeois – morality, the appreciation of empathy. The type of empathy, however, performed by the other-directed, is not based on a moral code, but on imitation: "His ability to assimilate issues in terms of people induces him to see issues as others see them and, with seeing, to pardon rather than to moralize."[5] Alas, the lack of essential ethical values, of an inner compass protected from outside influences – the lack of a "gyroscope"[6] – potentially leads to a blunted moral relativism. Unfortunately, the "virtue of tolerance [...] turns to a vice when it serves to lower his own emotional tone by the constant demand he puts on himself to be objective."[7] Riesman registers a certain coolness in the other-directeds' behavior in order to achieve objectivity, that is, to accept the social order in which a common-sense perception of the facts of a social situation precedes a subjective point of view that may not agree.

In some fundamental ways, it has become more and more difficult to accept the universalizing claim of Riesman's other-directed type, primarily for the swift mode in which Riesman feels comfortable to move in one passage from the experience of twentieth century White upper middle class males to "the American,"[8] a point of view, for which the most enigmatic, but also most precise historical US-American term might indeed be that of the "establishment."[9] Historically, nevertheless, I find other-direction still useful: to some limited degree as a diagnostic or rather heuristic tool, more so as revealing of actor's categories related to the larger complex of "othering,"[10] but especially for its limitations, its contradictions, its unintended consequences, and what they tell us about the awkwardness of the social interactions between intellectuals.

2.1 RIESMAN'S *LONELY CROWD* AND THE OTHER-DIRECTION OF THE MEMORANDUM

To be clear, Riesman's *Lonely Crowd* was a Cold War-era collaborative project, researched, written, and published after 1945 without a precise intellectual trajectory tying its origins to the "Nazi German" gray literature produced by the memorandum culture of World War II. Therefore, it falls – as a historical piece of literature – out of the immediate object range considered in my study. There is, however, one striking connection that is generic, in the literary sense of the word. Riesman's discussion of "other-direction" in his book, the very text of *Lonely Crowd* was – literally – a memorandum before it became a book.

In a draft, a hybrid between report and chapter, dated April 19, 1949, and entitled "XI. Inner-Direction and Other-Direction: Changes in the Agents of Character Formation," Riesman commences with a one-page summary:

> The memorandum distributed to the Committee on National Policy herewith is a revised version of "The Genesis of Marketers: Some Observations," a memorandum written in July and August, 1948, for the use of my collaborators. When further revised, it is intended as a chapter in our forthcoming publication, which will follow directly upon the chapter on "Some Types of Character and Society" (Memorandum #X) [...].[11]

I want to point out, how strange the first page of this memorandum really is, especially considering the future of the "forthcoming publication." Riesman explains here that he worked on *The Lonely Crowd* in a series of memoranda, which were distributed in various draft versions to specific recipients and for specifically designated purposes, first shared to facilitate the collaborative research for the book, then filed to satisfy his sponsor, the Committee on National Policy at Yale University. He moves in his writing effortlessly to address various bureaucratic demands, with the ease of an expert in gray literature. The future publication appears almost as an afterthought to this work of careful administration, and, in effect, consists of a series of numbered memoranda.

In the late 1940s, the memorandum apparently was quite naturally able to bridge the boundaries between letter, report, outline, instruction, work sample, and academic study. Little, however, seems to be predictive of the triumphant success of the *Lonely Crowd* during the paperback revolution as the number one best-selling American sociological study in the twentieth century, with more than 1.4 million sold copies, as reported by Riesman's collaborator Nathan Glazer in 1995.[12] Clearly, planning the book as a series of targeted memoranda did not hurt its universal reception. On the contrary, it seems that the reading public was ready, or even primed, for this new kind of book publication. One might therefore be inclined to ask: What had happened to the genre of the memorandum to gain center stage in the mid-century since its inconspicuous beginnings in the Early Modern communication techniques of the "ars tradiendi," that is, of the art to transmit information?[13] And what did Riesman exactly mean in 1949, when he called his draft a memorandum?

Literary critic John Guillory points to the late nineteenth century as the pivotal moment in the history of the memorandum as a genre of writing, when the anti-rhetorical movement in the footsteps of Francis Bacon's *Of the Proficiency and Advancement of Learning* (1605) and of Adam Smith's *Lectures on Rhetoric and Belles Lettres* (1762–1763) had led to the "collapse of the rhetorical empire."[14] The reign of classical training in the United States received its death blow "when Harvard president Charles William Eliot established the elective system of the 1870s that effectively ended the curriculum in Greek and Latin,"[15] and instead was quickly replaced by the introduction of new style guides such as *The Elements of Style* (1918) by William Strunk, propagating a clear, concise, and information-oriented prose in college education.[16] These new style guides, one might conjecture, trained a new type of readership that by mid-century was ready to appreciate a book based on inconspicuous memoranda.

According to JoAnne Yates, historian of organizational communication in the United States, the meaning of "memorandum" evolved in the late nineteenth century from "note to oneself"[17] to "internal correspondence"[18] within growing and increasingly departmentalized companies[19] and in the context of a new philosophy of systematic management.[20] Working primarily with the archives of two manufacturing companies and with historical textbooks, Yates concludes that "the innovations most relevant to the memo genre occurred in the creation and storage of written documents,"[21] particularly with the typewriter and vertical filing. The memo as a distinct genre, however, only gained its lasting prominence when external (outgoing and incoming) and internal correspondence were all written on the same machines and stored in a single filing system.[22] Ironically, it was thus the standardization of internal correspondence around 1920 that introduced some of the most consequential innovations for twentieth-century (external) letter writing, particularly in the "memo heading with 'To,' 'From,' and 'Subject' lines at the top [...]."[23] In attempts to make correspondence more "efficient" and consistent, preprinted forms more and more replaced elaborate formulas to communicate hierarchy, while the contents of one letter were supposed to survey in utmost brevity only one subject matter.[24] Yates shows in a 1923 report of the New York City Board of Education, how this new focus changed the very classification of the genre formerly associated with the letter, now grouped with the report. "Both the report and the memo, the New York City Board report noted, were characterized by their 'logical arrangement' and their 'explicitness, literalness, and cool impersonality of statement.'"[25] She concludes therefore with an insistence on the communicative function of the memo: "Thus the reclassification of the memo as a form of report rather than an off-shoot of the letter reflects actual similarities (though similarities to the letter remain as well), but ignores the genre's origin."[26] The new constellation becomes even clearer, if one puts it in Riesman's terms. The memorandum switched from inner-direction (note to oneself) to other-direction (report), after which it became "the humblest yet perhaps the most ubiquitous genre of writing in the modern world."[27] To Riesman, one may conclude, the memorandum is particularly attractive, because it carries a complex history of institutional communication that helps him address the multiple demands in one, supposedly neutral and universally legible genre. His book, considered in a history of reading, makes the case for Riesman's central thesis, the memorandum mediates other-direction.

Other-direction therefore opens up a nexus between social and literary theories that draws renewed and sustained attention to gray literature. The concept of other-direction entails – and at least in parts of its immense twentieth-century reception conceals – complexities that I want to reveal once again with regard to the awkwardness of social interactions of wartime intellectuals studying Nazi Germany.

For now, let us playfully turn the tables on other-direction and further develop Riesman's theory, applying a method of exaggeration and then substitution. Riesman's inquiry into other-direction may be continued in the following manner: What is other-direction from the point of view of the other? To the other of other-direction, other-direction signals a standing offer for collaboration. But who can count as the other of other-direction? Anybody, if you are willing to collaborate "as" the other's other, and as one other among other others. And if the other-directeds acknowledge you as another other, what exactly are the terms that the pact with the other-directeds has to offer? Whatever the answer, in the moment of collaboration, these terms need to be invisible so that one can signal, again, other-direction to yet different others. And what about those others to whom one is the other of other-directeds? The objective is to develop a new answer to this theoretical q&a, informed by the intellectual history of transatlantic migration and war, when other-direction has to be considered even beyond its official limits as an abstraction of 1940s émigré-direction and enemy-direction. Indeed, it transforms beyond the supposedly private or professional sphere of the office and turns into a problem of domestic and foreign politics. What does other-direction look like during World War II?

Curiously, in *The Lonely Crowd*, Riesman does not shy away from this problem and sets up himself this reversibility of substitution between "other," "émigré," and "enemy," without however taking seriously its consequences. Exchanging the "other" for the "enemy," Riesman describes the American wartime President Franklin D. Roosevelt as follows:

> We are accustomed to thinking of him as a man of great power. Yet his role in leading the country into war was very different from that of McKinley or even of Wilson. Think of McKinley pacing the floor of his study, deciding whether or not to ask for a declaration of war on Spain – when he already knew that Spain would capitulate. McKinley felt it was up to him; so did Wilson. Roosevelt felt he could only maneuver within very narrow limits, limits which came close to leaving the decision to the enemy.[28]

The Commander in Chief Roosevelt and his allegedly new type of military leadership shows that the new conception of sociality in *Lonely Crowd* reaches from white-collar culture to the higher strata of society and even to the most powerful office. Roosevelt, Riesman argues, is "other-directed" toward the "enemy." According to the same logics, following a proposal by émigré playwright and rogue Sinologist Karl A. Wittfogel, Riesman also calls the other-directed type the "radar-type,"[29] referring to a central military technology developed to perceive "enemies" as "others." Tellingly, the radar-type serves as the central metaphor of the other-directed.

Equally, the "émigré" as "other" plays a significant role for Riesman's analysis. Explicitly so, one may find an abundance of materials of second-generation immigrants in *Faces in the Crowd* (1952), in which Riesman published – two years after the success of *Lonely Crowd* – some of the underlying ethnographic materials, questionnaires and interviews he had collaboratively produced in 1948/49.[30] Beyond that, the encounter and professional collaboration with émigrés as his peers and immediate "others" has fundamentally shaped Riesman's work. Consequently, he reflects in one of his later autobiographical writings on his own "direction" that guided him on a "quixotic" path from a legal career to a social scientific best seller:

If one recalls that my parents were Francophile and Italophile in culture and Anglophile in manner, then my interest in contemporary German – that is, Weimar – culture was a way of finding *my own direction* [emphasis added] as distinct from theirs – a direction facilitated not only by Friedrich and Fromm but also by the many refugees I met through both those men and through my own concerns.[31]

Riesman, the son of an upper middle-class secular Jewish Philadelphia family and educated at Harvard University and Harvard Law School, clerk to the first Jewish-American Supreme Court Justice Louis Brandeis and professor of law at age 27, refers here to an initiative that he started with his early mentor Carl J. Friedrich[32] to support German-speaking refugees after the November Pogrom in 1938. In December 1938, Riesman started working as a secretary of the "American Committee for the Guidance of Professional Personnel" where he took on a crucial intermediary role in "providing fellowships to refugee lawyers seeking retraining in American law schools,"[33] offering advice and letters of recommendation.[34] This collaboration continued and intensified throughout World War II, when he served as one of the frequent contributors of memoranda to Friedrich's "Council for Democracy," initially financed in significant parts by Henry Luce.[35] The second émigré, mentioned in Riesman's autobiographical reflection quoted above, Erich Fromm, the Jewish-German psychoanalyst associated with the early critical theory developed in the Frankfurt school, is largely credited to be the one who actually brought about the concept of other-direction. As Riesman himself acknowledges in *Lonely Crowd*, Fromm first advanced in *Man for Himself* (1947) the idea of a "marketing orientation" that Riesman picked up and developed.[36] Like many other encounters within and around the memorandum culture, the personal relationship between the two formed beyond – and to some degree against – the control of strict institutional codes of conduct which for example medical or academic institutions would provide. Fromm worked since 1939 as Riesman's psychotherapist and quickly took on the role of his mentor, a relationship that since has been if anything overemphasized in historical accounts, but has never led to a substantial revision of "other-direction" as product of a creolization between Weimar German *kulturkritische* mass psychology and Main Street American social psychology, while problematizing the other as émigré or enemy.

2.2 CREOLE HYPOTHERMIA

Theorizing other-direction as a tool for understanding the American-European encounter, there is particular relevance in two prominent readings of Riesman's *Lonely Crowd* that converge on a theme that is not explicit in the original book. Peter Stearns' *American Cool* proposes a history of a twentieth-century "Emotional Style," in which he credits Riesman's other-direction as the first prominent articulation of the cultural phenomena he is interested in: American Cool as an inversion, starting in the 1920s, of Victorian Cool – from low intensity sexuality and high intensity emotional expression to low intensity emotional expression and high intensity sexuality that he finds in WASP America.[37] The second adoption of Riesman's other-direction appears in Helmut Lethen's *Cool Conduct*, his ground-breaking study not of 1920s America but of Weimar German literature of the same decade, in which he credits Riesman for first describing a new social type that unites other-direction and autonomy.[38] Lethen's argument – that Riesman's description of American cool and the cool persona depicted in the German literature of New Objectivity ("Neue Sachlichkeit") are essentially the same – rests on the wartime influence of Weimar émigré intellectuals like Fromm, a point Riesman readily acknowledges in his book – but which is in need of further inquiry. The notion of "influence," as in the direct "transmission" of an idea is, strictly speaking, rather misleading at least when it comes to the collaborative study of Nazi Germany. It seems more appropriate to point out that the collaborators working in the memorandum culture gained confidence and trust by constructing a local procedural basis for successful interaction, while largely disagreeing on major conceptual questions. The crucial question regarding the theory of social interaction between American and European intellectuals during World War II may thus be put in the following manner: How can we understand the "trading zone"[39] of 1940s collaborations, in which the meeting particularly of two national styles of other-direction, that is, of American Cool and Weimar Cool, in which American objectivity and Weimar New Objectivity were fused and made productive in the production of gray literature?[40] The aspired attitude of sociality was neither truly Anglo-American nor entirely German.[41] Instead, I want to propose in the following, it was based on a misunderstanding and facilitated by the copresence of a marginal third element, often neglected by intellectual historians, an "Aesthetic of the Cool"[42] that is best understood as originating from West African, mostly Yoruba diasporas, in the creole communities of the

"Greater Caribbean."[43] I do not argue for a direct intervention or even conscious appropriation of Yoruba cool in large parts of the memorandum culture of the early 1940s. Theoretically, however, highlighting the transatlantic histories of cool and bringing them in a speculative conceptual dialogue adds crucial aspects to the understanding of American collaborations in asymmetric relationships.

The concept of cool offers access to the history of an attitude that rests at the intersection between aesthetics, emotion and sexuality, sociality, and epistemology. So far, studies of the American-European encounter have not sufficiently considered the largely African-American[44] eponymous "birth of cool" during the 1930s and its powerful spell on twentieth-century concepts of White coolness, on which at least Stearns and Lethen rely.

Ships, telegraphic messages, and, beginning in 1939, commercial airplanes transporting airmail on three routes between North America and Europe make it easy to forget that, also in the 1940s, the Atlantic Ocean whirled between the United States and Europe, dominated by Nazi German violence. Consequentially, any attempt at writing about their relationship turns out to be a travelogue of a passage of the latter.[45] The particular historical agency of this enormous "intermediary"[46] that both divided and connected the two as world powers is best marked by the introduction of an adjective. The Atlantic Ocean, as a historical agent, needs to be reconsidered – by intellectual historians as well – as "Black," as in *Black Atlantic*.[47] The unavoidably smattering historical exposition of this complex will show the heuristic value and the conceptual gain of situating the Black Atlantic between the United States and Nazi Germany by further laying out a social theory of coolness.

In the following, I will trace one line in the global history of Black coolness, as its conception and cultural practices forcibly migrated from West Africa westward over the Atlantic to North America, where it was rediscovered and reappropriated as part of a subaltern African cultural heritage in the context of activist and artistic research based on folklore studies during and after the Harlem Renaissance in the 1920s and 1930s. I then theorize this attitude of coolness in dialogue with Riesman's mid-century vocabulary, and further develop the notion of other-direction as a tool for approaching the asymmetries of collaboration in the memorandum culture.

I do not claim that White European émigrés took on the same role or subject position as did Black American intellectuals in their collaborations reaching across the color line. I also do not claim that Black coolness significantly influenced the attitudes of coolness held by White Americans or European émigrés analyzing Nazi Germany in gray literature, even though certain cultural practices underlying the aesthetics of cool developed in Black American culture were almost immediately mimetically reproduced, and eclectically appropriated by White intellectuals and artists in Europe and the United States. Instead, I want to show that the experience of Black American intellectuals collaborating in the memorandum culture helps the reader to better understand the entire spectrum of other-direction, most poignantly expressed in the term invented for the precarious political status of German émigrés who embraced American social ideals, "Friendly Enemy Aliens." Other-direction during World War II stretches from close community all the way to enmity and ultimately to the violent exclusion from the role of the other. I will highlight some of these differences adding to other-direction the terms émigré-direction and enemy-direction. Considering Black coolness, one may conclude that White American and Weimar cool looked more alike and, in this sense, helped facilitate the asymmetric collaboration between Anglo-American and European émigré others, who often took on a crucial but also vulnerable position in between status roles, as they mediated between "other" and "enemy."

The Black aesthetic of the cool was formalized, mediated, and popularized in various manifestations in quick progression during the first decades of the twentieth century, following the start of the "Great Migration" of African-Americans, that reinvented around World War I a highly mobile Black culture in the United States.[48] This Black culture successfully traveled from the United States over the Black Atlantic to Europe as part of modern "entertainment," and got picked up and was further transformed through forms of "minstrelsy," "slumming," and other racist practices which today are subsumed under the larger notion of "cultural appropriation," most prominently in the complex of "American jazz."[49] In fact, most intellectual historians would depart from this point. Famously, the marred understanding of jazz as "entertainment" among European intellectuals was expressed in the critical writings of Jewish-German émigré Theodor W. Adorno. Based on his experience of American popular culture, he reflected in a series of essays on the topic of jazz music and popular dances like the jitterbug as a phenomenon of American sociality.[50] Adorno struggled at the time with problems first developed in his earlier work on composer Richard Wagner and, as intellectual historian Martin Jay points out, with the relationship of folk-art and propaganda, that is, in the influential

2.2 Creole Hypothermia

coinage of Horkheimer and Adorno's *Dialectic of Enlightenment*, the "culture industry," mixing a critique of capitalism with that of National Socialism. "All of jazz's claims to express liberation Adorno scornfully rejected. Its primary social function, he contended, was to lessen the distance between the alienated individual and his affirmative culture, but in the repressive manner of *völkisch* ideology."[51] Adorno's neo-Marxist critique of jazz as minstrelsy was primarily informed by his disappointing German experience of the ideological malleability of large parts of popular arts. Adorno's views on jazz nevertheless have far more in common than one might expect with, for example, that of one of his contemporaries, who was incomparably better versed in jazz culture, African-American writer Ralph Ellison.[52] Within intellectual history, however, Adorno's inhibiting distance to the social realties of African-American "folk culture," and accordingly to the social history of Black coolness is less of analytic than of symptomatic significance, that is, for the complicated relationship between academically trained elites and popular culture full of unacknowledged inversions, projections, and misrepresentations.

Instead, I want to propose that the analytic value of cool as a model of sociality may best be retrieved "in motion,"[53] a transatlantic motion that started in West Africa, not with European or American social styles of coolness, but with "Yoruba cool." Unfortunately, understanding Yoruba cool's forced movement through the violent "Middle Passage" of the Black Atlantic, lacking the well-preserved documentation to produce a seventeenth-century intellectual history like Edmund S. Morgan's classic transatlantic study of Puritan sociality in *Visible Saints*,[54] remains highly circumstantial and speculative.[55] In the case of Yoruba coolness, the best available historical attempt to bridge the largely erased archive of the intellectual history of enslaved people started during the transition from colonial to postcolonial anthropology with field research conducted in West Africa around 1968. Anthropologists began to study contemporary cultures to access their history and to reconstruct from that ambiguous perspective an "original" Yoruba cosmology, as it may have started to travel to the Caribbean and the Americas over several decades and centuries, reaching early twentieth-century New York City. According to this Yoruba cosmology, the continuity of this transatlantic African-American tradition of cool coincides with the travel of one particular god, Eshu Elegba, the divine trickster, a problem which already has received sustained treatment in scholarship tracing the history of the Black Atlantic.

2.3 TRANSATLANTIC CONTINUITIES

For academic purposes, so far, the coolness of the Black Atlantic, which is neither a "keeping cool" in the face of danger nor a desirable character-trait for conversing with appropriate restraint of either sexuality or sentiment on social occasions, is tied up in the pioneering lifework of the art historian Robert Farris Thompson. Among the various Atlantic passages through which Thompson has traced the aesthetic of the cool, I will primarily follow his *Flash of the Spirit* (1983) and his essay "Black Saints Go Marching In," in which he analyzes "Yoruba Art and Culture in the Americas," since West African artistic objects, as will be shown later, took on a particular role for the aesthetics of cool. In Thompson's analysis of the creolization of African gods and Catholic saints in the Caribbean, one "Black Saint," the trickster-god Eshu-Elegba, stands out as closely allied with coolness, or more precisely "mystic coolness (itutu)"[56] as a central part of Yoruba religion. In order to understand Yoruba cool as it arrived in the United States, the characterization of *itutu* in some detail is necessary, summed up here in nine steps. As supplement, I provide the reader with some of the interview material, observations and reflections by Thompson, on which his theoretical and conceptual work is based. After going through this list, I will further summarize Thompson's conception of *itutu*.

1) According to a description by one of Thompson's collaborators in Nigeria, J. K. Adejumo in Ipokia, the capital of the Anago Yoruba, in 1968, coolness in the Yoruba universe is at the basis of sociality. "Coolness or gentleness of character is so important in our lives. *Coolness is the correct way you represent yourself to a human being.* [...] It is *itutu*, answering past *itutu*, you made to me."[57]
2) Coolness toward others is articulated through posture, gesture and facial expression.

   "If you want to talk to an elder, you do not stand, you kneel. [...] *Kneel* and give with both hands [...]" Giving with both hands, in a gesture of submission, emphasizes in traditional terms the act of giving as an embodiment of character and perfect composure, a point given further focus, in both art and life, by the firmness of the facial expression that accompanies the noble act. "Constant smiling is not a Yoruba characteristic."[58]
3) Being cool is a self-technique that garners prestige.

   "Like character, coolness ought to be internalized as a governing principle for a person to merit the high praise 'His heart is cool' [...]."[59] In its most sophisticated form, exerting coolness becomes a form of cooling the gods practiced by means of "(1) direct sacrifice [...] of cherished objects [...] and (2) propitiation, the utterance of conciliatory words or acts [...]."[60]

4) In this way, cool conduct extends to elements of artistic beauty involved in the process of cooling that Thompson feels compelled to speak of an "aesthetic" of the cool.

The notion of coolness in Yoruba art extends beyond representations of the act of sacrifice and acts or gestures of propitiation. So heavily charged is this concept with ideas of beauty and correctness that a fine carnelian bead or a passage of exciting drumming may be praised as "cool."[61]

5) In his improvisation on Yoruba cool, Thompson then comes to a moment of mystic redemption, when this pursuit of beauty turns into grace.

As we become noble, fully realizing the spark of creative goodness God endowed us with – the shining *ororo* bird of thought and aspiration – we find the confidence to cope with all kinds of situations. This is *àshe*. This is character. This is mystic coolness. All one. Paradise is regained, for Yoruba art returns the idea of heaven to mankind wherever the ancient ideal attitudes are genuinely manifested.[62]

6) And it is precisely this redemptive mysticism that is at the heart of Thompson's art-historical argument regarding the passage of Yoruba cool over the Atlantic.

The Yoruba remain the Yoruba precisely because their culture provides them with ample philosophic means for comprehending, and ultimately transcending, the powers that periodically threaten to dissolve them. That their religion and their art withstood the horrors of the Middle Passage and firmly established themselves in the Americas (New York City, Miami, Havana, Matanzas, Recife, Bahia, Rio de Janeiro) as the slave trade effected a Yoruba diaspora – reflects a triumph of an inexorable communal will.[63]

7) Yoruba coolness has been, according to Thompson, a central technique to keep up a community even under the gravest and most violent pressures of disintegration in slavery. The continuity was maintained through cunning transformation: "[E]specially in Cuba and Brazil, New World Yoruba were introduced to the cult of Roman Catholic saints, learned their attributes, and worked out a series of parallelisms linking Christian figures and powers to the forces of their ancient deities."[64]

8) In the violent creolization of these communities of the Greater Caribbean, the cunning trickster god took on his central role.

Eshu-Elegba became one of the most important images in the black Atlantic world. Blacks honor him in Cuba, for example, where "men or women of African descent pour cool water at crossroads – unobtrusively if white strangers be about – in honor of Eshu." Cuban blacks associate Eshu with change: "favorable, he modifies the worst of fates; hostile, he darkens the most brilliant of happenings."[65]

9) Eshu-Elegba, the god of the crossroads and the messenger of the gods, is, however, – because of his trickster nature – often misunderstood according to the moral dualism of Christian observers. He has been characterized by missionaries and Western-minded alike as 'the Devil.'[66] This is, however, only half the truth.

> His role is dual and paradoxical – both social and anti-social. He is not only the symbol, but also the solution of man's conflict between instinctive desires and social demands. In accepting the blame he keeps the peace, while still offering escape from the rigidity of social laws.[67]

In brief: Coolness, as the basis of Yoruba sociality, is enacted through posture, gesture, and facial expression in order to garner prestige. More abstractly, it means beauty, so much that Thompson speaks regarding Yoruba culture of an aesthetic of the cool. Thus, coolness, in the sense of grace, provides access to mystic redemption in moments of hardship. During the forced transatlantic passage of Yoruba enslaved people, this coolness helped to hold together the diaspora community, thanks to its ability for abstraction that provided continuity through cunning transformation during the history of violent African-European creolization. This process of social transformation gave special prominence to the social and anti-social trickster god Eshu-Elegba, identified with coolness.

Clearly, twentieth-century cool is inextricably tied to the history of transatlantic migration and serves as one of the most glaring forms of proof that cultural and intellectual historians can no longer afford to ignore African and Caribbean history without missing the point entirely. But how may one render this history theoretically useful to conceptualize the sociality of collaboration in a history of gray literature?

If the Greek god Hermes, the "divine trickster," has been able to serve – through a folk etymology – as an agent for modern theories of communication such as Hans-Georg Gadamer's project of hermeneutics or Michel Serres' *Hermes* pentalogy (1969–1980), why not the trickster god Eshu-Elegba? This idea, in fact, is not new but has a history of its own. Literary critic and historian Henry L. Gates, Jr. followed exactly this path from Greek gods to Yoruba gods in his classic study of the "black vernacular tradition" in *The Signifying Monkey* (1988) and spelled out its implications in terms of post-structuralist literary theory.[68] The resulting critical project is called "*Esu-'tufunaalo*, literally 'one who unravels the knots of Esu.'"[69] What happens to the coolness of Riesman's other-directeds, one may ask, if one unravels the knots tied by Eshu?

Among the mythemes surrounding Eshu-Elegba, one in particular stands out to deal with the problem of writing an intellectual history from Yoruba Africa to twentieth-century America.

Similarly, tales of his [Eshu Elegba's] birth seem to contradict each other, and he is described both as first born and as last born; as old man and as child. But in both the old man and the child there is privileged freedom from some of the demands of the social code. These extremes have, therefore, a binding principle. His age is reflected in his cunning and the wisdom concealed in his trickery; his extreme youth in his wantonness and caprice and in his impulsive behaviour. Whether old man or child there is a disregard for the normal code; he enjoys the natural licence of the innocent and the privileged licence of the aged. As a child he is the experimenter who breaks rules; as an old man he enjoys the wisdom that takes him beyond rules. Thus when the Yoruba say he is the youngest of the orisha, but the father of them all, they are aware that he contains this paradox.[70]

Eshu-Elegba, the irritable god of communication, guarding the continuity of his community of the cool by means of constant disruption, challenges the order of linear time and history with his confusion of birth and age. In order to date the African-American "birth of cool" accordingly, one would have to look for such a paradoxical event. The closest Thompson comes – in 1973 – in one of his studies of cool aesthetics to dating the first occurrence of cool as an American term is the year 1935. He rediscovers "African" cool in a Floridian expression used to charm a woman: "Being charming is also being cool, as suggested by the following interlude among black folk in Florida: 'I wouldn't let you fix me no breakfast. I get up and fix my own and then, what make it so *cool*, I'd fix *you* some and set it on the back of the cook stove…' This man was flirting."[71] Thompson goes on to explain the peculiar idiom as a citation of "the cool in an African sense, a diagram of continuity."[72] The man, according to Thompson "had promised to assume the role of another person in order to earn her love. He had promised to dissolve a difference which lay between them."[73] The trickster-like behavior, turning the man into a relatable other of the woman's other-direction, granting continuity through cunning transformation, is no chance event, but based on a well-kept traditional knowledge of mystic coolness: "The charm of what 'made it so cool' in these senses suggests he knew, in Zen-like simplicity, the divine source of the power to heal, love.

He had thereby identified the center from which all harmony comes."[74] This knowledge serves for Thompson as evidence for a direct connection to the man's West African ancestry: "This highly cultivated, yet deceptively simple, idiom of social symmetrization clearly seems ancestral."[75]

Equally, the source of this Floridian interlude itself is "deceptively simple." As the unassuming reference in the footnote shows, Thompson quotes here Zora Neale Hurston, virtually forgotten in 1973,[76] and her literary treatment of her seminal collection of Black folklore in *Mules and Men* (1935) she conducted – like Sinclair Lewis – by car in the US-American South, starting from her hometown in Florida.[77] Thompson in fact normalizes the quotation from Hurston that is phonetically much more oriented toward the spoken word, possibly to avoid association with the widespread stereotypical use of slang in racist caricatures of "shuckin' and jiving'" based on the nonstandard English dialect spoken in the South. Unfortunately, he thereby undercuts the seminal transregional literary project of the Black ethnographer. The quote from Hurston reads in the original: "'Now me, Ah wouldn't let you fix me no breakfus.' Ah git up and fix mah own and den, whut make it so cool, Ah'd fix *you* some and set it on de back of de cook-stove so you could git it when you wake up."[78] Thompsons lack of philological rigor here, implicitly assuming an "oral birth of the cool," came at a price. The expression "whut" or "what make it so cool" appears not only once, but four times in "Part 1" of the book, entitled "Folk Tales." In addition, Hurston uses the same expression almost simultaneously in an artistic context, in her 1935-play *Spunk*, an adaptation of her breakthrough-short story from 1925, as the main character Spunk utters the idiom regarding his son.[79] A bit earlier in August 1933, the expression also appears in her short story "The Gilded Six-Bits" about a young marriage soon to be troubled by an act of adultery, but ending in forgiveness.[80] The repeated use in various contexts shows that "what make it so cool" is a set phrase in Hurston's literary vocabulary. In fact, it is possible to date the "birth of cool" in Hurston's writing with surprising precision, on May 26, 1932. After her first ethnographic work in Harlem, she most likely found the phrase in her notes from her field research in the Gulf Coast-states starting in 1927, first with a small research grant organized by her teacher Franz Boas and then under the patronage of philanthropist Charlotte O. Mason, intermittently continued until 1932. While pursuing a teaching job in Florida, she wrote a letter to "Grandmother," as the young Black artists of the Harlem Renaissance addressed Mason, about her progress on *Mules and Men*, as well as "The Gilded Six-Bits" and appended five curious phrases together with her own translations. Among them, this time indeed grammatically standardized for her patron: "'And what makes it so cool' = furthermore."[81] Unlike the other phrases in the appendix, this translation seems odd, as there is no obvious relationship in content or form between the two expressions. But Hurston's laconic translation is spot on, and it clearly reverberates with Thompson's interpretation. "What makes it so cool" is an expression of continuity, "furthermore," granting through cunning transformation – from *itutu* to cool – the continuity of cool from West Africa to the United States, the literary "birth of cool."

Looking at Hurston, the study of the American-European encounter and the intellectual migration of German scholars therefore needs to extend beyond the history of transatlantic (and transpacific) migration and should also consider domestic movements of migration such as the "Great Migration" from the southern rural areas to the northern urban centers starting in the 1910s, not only as national US-history, but in the context of the Greater Caribbean. Thompson's intuition about the "birth of cool" therefore is right, although slightly misleading. Hurston, one of the most important African-American authors of her generation – trained in anthropology as a student of the Jewish-German founder of American cultural anthropology Franz Boas and later assistant to Melville Herskovits – did not act only as a folklorist passively recording a Floridian sociolect, but she actively contributed as a mediator between the various culturally distinct African-American creole heritage groups, not only Yoruba Americans but also the Gullah-Geechee culture, Igbo and Fula Americans, to the emergence of the term herself, as a lively member of the social scene in Harlem, New York City.[82] As far as the common use of the term in "hip" language has been reconstructed in oral history interviews, the Harlem-based jazz musician Lester Young was responsible for the initial popularization of "cool" in the late 1930s,[83] followed by Bebop musicians such as Charlie Parker; Miles Davis then famously used the term in the era of the Cold War for his 1957 album *Birth of the Cool*. It is important and correct to point out again, following similar methodical problems in historical linguistics studying the history for example of Wolof-speaking communities that these types of conceptual histories are highly speculative. Young had no direct access to the "nomenclature of hot and cool modes from West African performance beyond an untraceable continuity of African retentions in the musical culture of the Mississippi Delta and New Orleans."[84] This problem in the academic study of forced migration and communities of enslaved people should not be used to discount their contributions to

American intellectual history altogether, especially, when one starts to find clear traces and a heightened interest in these problems of genealogy among the historical actors themselves.

2.4 RENAISSANCE OF COOL

Putting the question slightly differently, one may ask: When does Thompson's historical account of a continuous tradition of the "cool" – and the reinvention of cool based on African sources – become conceivable? Eshu-Elegba's mytheme, quoted above, again helps to point to the right decade: the 1920s, the decade of the Harlem Renaissance,[85] the birth of *young* African-American art – as a rebirth of *old* Yoruba cool, presented in one of its central documents, *The New Negro*.[86] The genealogical conflict presented in *The New Negro* between the Harvard educated African-American philosopher Alain Locke,[87] editor and author of multiple essays in the volume, and the anthropologist Melville J. Herskovits, son of Jewish immigrants and influential anthropologist, finds its standard interpretation as a curious inversion in Herskovits's approach.[88] In Locke's edited volume, young Herskovits defined Harlem's "New Negro" in a strategic move against the predominant racism as an inherently American phenomenon: "And finally, after a time, it occurred to me that what I was seeing [in Harlem] was a community just like any other American community. The same pattern, only a different shade!"[89] Only later – and arguably convinced by discussions with African-American intellectuals, such as Locke, tracing their ancestry geographically to the African continent – starting in 1928/29, Herskovits went on to conduct field studies of African-American communities outside of the United States, in Surinam, from where he developed his theory that regards Caribbean cultures as strongly related to their "origins" in Africa and Europe and as exerting their genealogical influence in the United States. This discovery coincidentally also brought to prominence the technical term that Herskovits appropriated for the cultural anthropological analysis of this phenomenon: creole.

At least equal attention needs to be paid to the intricacies of Alain Locke's side of the argument and the context of its making. Locke was clearly thinking in terms of migration and creolization, as he lays it out in his essay "The New Negro," the programmatic first piece of his volume. Here he describes the blossoming of a new African-American culture as a direct result of recent migration in an enthusiastic description of 1920s Harlem:

Take Harlem as an instance of this. Here in Manhattan is not merely the largest Negro community in the world, but the first concentration in history of so many diverse elements of Negro life. It has attracted the African, the West Indian [Caribbean], the Negro American; has brought together the Negro of the North and the Negro of the South; the man of the city and the man from the town and village; the peasant, the student, the business man, the professional man, artist, poet, musician, adventurer and worker, preacher and criminal, exploiter and social outcast.[90]

For Locke, Harlem is a place of cultural and linguistic encounter and creolization, coincidentally the source for a new Black cosmopolitan nationalism created by New York's printing culture: "Harlem [...] is the home of the Negro's 'Zionism.' [...] A Negro newspaper carrying news material in English, French and Spanish, gathered from all quarters of America, the West Indies and Africa has maintained itself in Harlem for over five years. [...] As with the Jew, persecution is making the Negro international."[91] This motive of a Black culture, stretching throughout the world will become even more prominent in his wartime work. For the moment, "[w]ith the American Negro, his new internationalism is primarily an effort to recapture contact with the scattered peoples of African derivation, [even if] Garveyism [referring to the pan-African Black nationalism developed by Jamaican activist Marcus Garvey] may be a transient, if spectacular, phenomenon [...]."[92]

Finally, with Locke's description of 1920s Harlem in mind, one may also return to and further develop Riesman's notion. In artistic and intellectual collaborations during the Harlem Renaissance built on an influx of migrants during the Great Migration, coming from the Southern States, the Caribbean, as well as from the African continent, other-direction always meant émigré-direction.[93]

As Locke established a new relationship between African, Caribbean, and African-American culture, Locke was looking at West African objects, masks and sculptures collected in the Barnes Foundation Collection, the same kind of objects that Thompson about 35 years later starts describing with the fashionable term "cool." As Locke writes in "The Legacy of the Ancestral Arts," another of his contributions published in *The New Negro*:

There was in this more than a change of art-forms and an exchange of cultural patterns; there was a curious reversal of emotional temper and attitude. The characteristic African art expressions are rigid, controlled, disciplined, abstract, heavily conventionalized; those of the Aframerican, – free, exuberant, emotional, sentimental and human. Only by the misinterpretation of the African spirit, can one claim any emotional kinship between them – for the spirit of African expression, by and large, is disciplined, sophisticated, laconic and fatalistic. The emotional temper of the American Negro is exactly the opposite. What we have thought primitive in the American Negro – his naïveté, his sentimentalism, his exuberance and his improvising spontaneity are then neither characteristically African nor to be explained as an ancestral heritage. They are all result of his peculiar experience in America and the emotional upheaval of its trials and ordeals.[94]

The "curious reversal of emotional temper and attitude" from cool to hot – and possibly back – is the starting point for Locke's highly influential artistic manifesto and stands out indeed as an "aesthetic" of the cool. Locke does not, however, propose a straightforward African-American primitivism. Instead he urges young African-American artists to follow the lead of Albert Barnes and the Barnes Foundation Collection[95] "in the battle royale over who would introduce America to the power of African art,"[96] where African objects were collected alongside European avantgarde art, influenced by them – and to join the modernist art movement's approach to African objects.[97] Locke proposes to develop a new form of objectivity:

The Negro physiognomy must be freshly and objectively conceived on its own patterns if it is ever to be seriously and importantly interpreted. [...] In idiom, technical treatment and objective social angle, it is a bold iconoclastic break with the current traditions that have grown up about the Negro subject in American art.[98]

By joining forces with the avantgarde in 1925, Locke hopes, finally, to enable African-American culture to enter into a symmetrical relation by submitting to the "trial of strength" of objectivity. Locke's emphasis on objectivity[99] in *The New Negro* is striking, as he clearly has identified the "white lie"[100] that regulates the authorization to play along in the world of Riesman's other-direction. This birth of cool, it turns out, however, can only be had in form of a utopian diagram: through a (European) inversion of American objectivity meeting West African objects to African objectivity meeting American objects.[101]

To understand Locke's project better, another mytheme involving Eshu-Elegba might prove helpful. The myth of "The Two Friends," "probably the most well known of the Esu canon [...], one of the canonical narratives that survived the Middle Passage and is as familiar among the Yoruba cultures of Brazil and Cuba as it is in Nigeria."[102] Here, especially one mytheme is of particular interest: the two-colored hat that undermines any objectivity.

The myth most often repeated tells how Elegba broke up the life-long friendship of two men whose farms were adjoining. Their friendship was so great that they were always seen together and always dressed alike. Elegba decided to walk down the path which divided their farms wearing a hat which was black on one side and white on the other; he put his pipe at the back of his head, and hooked his club over his shoulder so that it hung down his back. After he had passed, the two friends quarrelled about the direction the old man had taken and over the colour of his cap-one asserting he went one way and wore a black cap, the other insisting he went in the opposite direction and wore a white cap. The quarrel grew to such proportions that it was brought to the attention of the king. While each of the friends was still hotly accusing the other of lying, Elegba told the king that neither of them was a liar, but that both were fools, and then confessed to his mischief. [...][103]

For the Harlem Renaissance in relation to other-direction, the black and white hat now has a special effect. Both American and European cultures had created a liminal position for African-American artists, who were invited within the looser social boundaries of entertainment to play along in one group of "Black" and "White" artists crossing the "color line" in both directions. In turn-of-the-century African-American culture at least, artistic collaboration was well established. As literary critic Frances Smith Foster points out, the African-American artistic tradition Post-Bellum and Pre-Harlem was emphatically collaborative and often based on mutual aid. Preceding Locke's New Negro, there is an entire "New Negro Movement at the end of the nineteenth century."[104] But the crossing of the "color line" came at a cost. Best exemplified in musical collaborations, playing together[105] in bands could not abolish the social asymmetry between Black and White artists – the hat remains two colored.

It was in these liminal spaces of collaboration such as those created in American Jazz, however, that the attitude of "cool" was formalized, when African-Americans were authorized to be part of the community as the other of other-direction,[106] under the condition that they agree to keep the asymmetry of this collaboration invisible, under an entertaining, yet impenetrable, "mask."[107] The curious result of the protective character of this mask was the development of a distinct, African-American cool. In the most powerful rendition of this asymmetry of collaboration enabled by the Harlem Renaissance around Locke, a new attitude became possible to let this inner cool come to the fore. From the point of view of the Anglo-American and German other-directed, the new African-American cool amusingly mimicked the (post-Victorian)-American cool or Weimar cool, while this "other" actually outmatched them with an original and artistically superior avant-garde/African cool. This attitude worked both to motivate "primitivist" patrons like philanthropist Charlotte O. Mason, and it also enabled collaboration in the memorandum culture of World War II for Black intellectuals like Locke. Locke, in fact, was particularly well versed and used to writing in precarious situations of unevenly distributed agency, pursuing his projects in contradictory environments, where financial support and racist attitudes often came from the same source, as was the case with the Barnes Foundation. In collaborations across the "color line," Locke, as virtually all Black intellectuals and artists therefore had to be on guard not to become a target. Other-direction in these settings therefore often coincided with enemy-direction. Locke was a gifted diplomat in the world of philanthropic bureaucracy, for example, when he came to Hurston's rescue after an incident, in which she had offended Mason's – that is, the White patron's – "racial sensitivities."[108] He was also an early expert in various types of gray literature, in composing institutional letters, reports, and memoranda. These addressed both local and domestic issues, but also foreign policy questions such as his memorandum for the Foreign Policy Association regarding the future of African colonies formerly held by Germany, written in 1927 after a trip to the League of Nations headquarters in Geneva, Switzerland, observing the deliberations about this question.[109] Particularly Locke's "invisible"[110] engagement in the world of Communist Front organizations such as the American Committee for the Protection of Foreign Born[111] constitutes the context for his important review of Katherine Garrison Chapin and William Grant Still's choral ballad *And They Lynched Him on a Tree* in "Ballad for Democracy" published in 1940, the year "he was at his collaborative best."[112] The same is true for his coedited volume, funded by the Progressive Education Association and the General Education Board, endowed by John D. Rockefeller, *When Peoples Meet* (1942). The world of the memorandum culture branched out from philanthropic patronage not only to the right but also to left radicalism. Communist activities provided with its organizations, conferences, and publications a rare opening for African-American intellectuals to address the general public, and Locke made exceptional use of it. During World War II, several Black intellectuals joined the intellectual fight against Nazi Germany, using the conceptual mechanism to switch between other-direction and enemy-direction, in Locke's case, to transform his domestic project into a global critique of racism. The volume *When Peoples Meet* spanned 15 introductory chapters, 95 short pieces, mostly excerpts, by 76 authors on 756 pages in its first edition. In the process of publishing this tome,

Locke skillfully used his mastery of producing gray literature to move the project despite significant hurdles forward. Especially his abilities as an editor to acquire, excerpt, and compile essays turned the work into an invaluable source book, impressive in range, presenting the state of the art of the social sciences, with special attention to cultural anthropology, starting with the introduction to Ruth Benedict's *Patterns of Culture* (1934) and to Franz Boas' foundational work of antiracism *The Mind of Primitive Man* (1911), but also including texts by Margaret Mead and Hans Kohn among many other scholars, activists and artists engaged in the memorandum culture. Locke connects them in the marginal genre of the "interchapter"[113] to outline his vision of a global analysis of race and culture. The interchapters "display Locke's thought at its most polymathic,"[114] moving over the entire world map and deep into world history. In these short texts, his analysis of the problem of domestic racism is connected to a world-wide examination of oppression of minorities, with Nazi Germany as the quintessence of imperialism and racism. The volume is particularly fascinating for its intermediary position, a document of the largely Anglo-American intellectual transition from a colonial to a postcolonial world order that replaces oppression with "reciprocity."[115] The term goes back to Locke's Black cosmopolitanism mentioned earlier in the *New Negro*, first introduced into his vocabulary in the same year in a 1925-article, in "Internationalism – Friend or Foe of Art."[116] Reciprocity is Locke' answer to the domestic problem of the indeterminacy of other-direction, émigré-direction, and enemy-direction, now conceptualized on the scale of foreign politics and cultural migration. Locke's social philosophy accordingly has been called – and sometimes criticized as – "cultural pluralism," defined as "the right to be different."[117] Reciprocity also provides the conditions for cool collaboration. This is coincidentally in line with the interpretation of Eshu-Elegba: "Esu as the figure of indeterminacy extends directly from his lordship over the concept of plurality."[118]

2.5 FOOL'S GAME THEORY

Historically, the transatlantic process of creolization between Weimar, Anglo-American, and Black cool started after World War I, continued throughout the interwar period and started to produce new forms and syntheses during World War II. Again, to be clear, I do not pursue the claim that Black attitudes of cool started to dominate or even replace all other forms of cool before or during World War II, and I do not argue that European émigrés fleeing National Socialism took on the social role shaped by Black intellectuals such as Alain Locke or Zora Neale Hurston in the decades before their arrival or during the war by Black intellectuals and artists such as Ralph Bunche and Georg Olden, working for the Office of Strategic Services.[119] Rather, my aim was to describe one important element, missing in most intellectual histories of the 1930s and 1940s so far to theorize the sociality of collaboration. Black cool, and an understanding of its conceptual history, helps to appreciate the hybrid composition of the – at least in retrospect – stunning attitude of objectivity facilitating wartime collaborations between intellectuals with apparently extremely different social, professional, and gender roles as well as linguistic, economic, cultural, and political backgrounds.

Looking now at the end of this long transatlantic journey of cool back to Lethen's Weimar cool and Stearns's American cool, the same mytheme of "The Two Friends," but in a different version, helps theorize the creolization of their cool in the 1940s – a creolization that works only in relation to the African-American cool.

There were two friends who always wore the same dress and who went everywhere together. They had sworn that they would remain friends to the end of their lives. Ifa [a practice of divination] had advised them to sacrifice to Eshu, but they refused. So Eshu decided to disrupt their friendship. One day they were working on the farm, a little distance from each other, when Eshu passed between them. He was wearing a cap that was red on the one side and white on the other. One friend asked the other: "Who was that man who passed by in the red cap?" The other replied: "His cap was not red, it was white!" "What, are you blind?" said the other, "I saw distinctly that it was red!" So they argued for a while. A little while later, Eshu returned from the other direction. The first friend saw him and said: "I am sorry my friend: I now see that this cap was indeed white and not red. I don't know how I could make such a stupid mistake." But the other one grew furious: "Are you trying to make a fool of me? Do you think I have no eyes in my head, not to see that this cap is red?" And they came to blows, wounding each other seriously. When they recovered, they followed Ifa's advice and sacrificed to Eshu. From then on they remained close friends for the rest of their lives.[120]

After being fooled for the second time by Eshu-Elegba, returning after a while from the other direction, the object of contention is no longer only the red and white hat,[121] but also the objectivity of the relationship between the two friends, that is, the other's supposed intention to hold up for ridicule the respective friend's earlier misperception. Or put differently, the friends are faced with two equivalent (mis-)perceptions, of the "other's" intentions and of the "other other's" hat color. The conundrum may be solved in the following manner of a fool's game theory: The American and the Weimar émigré still regarded the African-American, that is, the "other other's" cool as an imitation of their respective cool. Rather than admitting their ever-failing objective perception of the African-American cool in relation to their own, they decided to agree on the primacy of each other's other-direction, the "objectivity" of the relation of imitation and original, the identity of "Western man" and therefore – to the benefit of their collaboration – on the fundamental identity of their respective cool conduct. This was other-direction in the memorandum culture at the core of creolization of coolness, which facilitated the collaboration between European émigrés and American intellectuals to produce gray literature on Nazi Germany.

In my account of the American-European encounter in wartime collaborations, I want to bring these contradictory dynamics into play and render them visible by reducing the findings of this chapter to a heuristic formula that may serve as a backdrop for the theoretical approach of this book. My interest lies in discerning the process of *mutual misapprehension* and *mimesis*, mistaking awkwardly each other's cool as one's own, that the respective collaborator – in an ill-conceived narcissism – admired and then mimicked the other's conduct. In this way, either side played along with the white lie of "objectivity," achieving a balanced, symmetrical relationship in an asymmetrical situation, a process that indeed closely resembles Thompson's description of the original Yoruba "itutu." In order to theorize these asymmetric forms of social interactions in the memorandum culture, the interventions of Black intellectuals during and after the Harlem Renaissance and not least their participation in collaborations with European émigrés have been crucial to develop Riesman's conception of other-direction to include émigré-direction and enemy-direction during World War II. After proposing a revision of Riesman's influential mid-century social theory presented in *The Lonely Crowd* to point out the fundamental role of objectivity in the memorandum culture, I will turn in the next chapter to a few central aspects of the material conditions of the rise of gray literature.

3

The Invention of the Intelligence Report

Franz L. Neumann's monumental *Behemoth* stands out today as the single most important book to get a sense of the astonishingly comprehensive knowledge about Nazi Germany publicly available in the United States in 1942.[1] In *Behemoth*, the Jewish-German émigré Neumann skillfully analyzes the structure and practice of National Socialism, its political, bureaucratic, economic, military, and ideological foundations as a polycratic system. He also gives a realistic sense of the self-contradictory yet highly explosive nature of its aggressive development leading to its pursuit of a "total" war of annihilation.[2]

In its first edition, the more than 500-page-tome clearly shows the massive amount of academically processed knowledge available to the historical actors, but – in the thick of it – what should be made of such a clunky publication amid a raging World War? A scholarly reading of the book according to the assumption of an "orderly" writing period, a prestigious publication process in a University Press leading to a broad reception, in the beginning of which fellow experts review and possibly certify the quality of the book, followed by an audience with a general interest in the topic, seems to be out of place.[3] Instead, I am going to relocate *Behemoth* in the memorandum culture of the 1940s, the place of its production and immediate reception. In this chapter, *Behemoth* mainly receives the treatment it received in the historical context of its origin as I employ the methods usually reserved for the approach to oversized contributions to gray literature – as the memorandum culture did – ultimately disregarding the publication apart from a one line summary and the prestige it bestowed on its author letting him get a job for the government. This provocative if not defiant approach, to look

3 The Invention of the Intelligence Report 67

at the gray literature of the memorandum culture from the historical actors' perspective, however, leads to the discussion of a fundamental question. If "the" standard work on the topic – which was even contemporaneously available in print – cannot necessarily provide an appropriate answer – what did it actually mean to "understand" Nazi Germany in wartime studies?

For the purpose of answering this question, it will be necessary to take a closer look at the actual collaborative work conducted in the memorandum culture. This requires dwelling on the media history of library administration and especially microphotography, which lays bare one of the central material conditions of gray literature, before looking at the institutionally regulated bureaucratic practices that determined its writing procedures. The literature produced by the memorandum culture in and in between philanthropies and government institutions can historically be understood only as a literary project shaped in a nation of lawyers – and can be interpreted appropriately only with special attention to bureaucratic communication,[4] theorized in the previous chapter. In the United States, the central, officially sanctioned genre of gray literature emerging in this moment of danger, that is, the genre in which national security is conceived of was the "intelligence report." I argue that without explaining the thrust of this exemplary literary invention originating in the United States during the early 1940s as a means to defend national security against outside danger, and without rendering this form of "classified writing" legible, as this chapter does, any attempts at understanding the immediate intervention and long-term relevance of the American study of Nazi Germany will be in vain.[5]

The odd wartime institution that paradigmatically shaped several of these usually invisible but consequential contexts surrounding the invention of the intelligence report was the Office of Strategic Services (OSS). The OSS is steeped in legend for its various spying activities in Europe and around the world; adventurous stories recount hazardous trips behind enemy lines to gather valuable intelligence or to conduct acts of sabotage, the use of the newest spying technology and alleged truth serums, the ingenious production of black (i.e. false flag) propaganda to deceive enemy populations, and attempts at organizing local resistance movements. Less remembered, but equally fascinating and arguably even more momentous figures the OSS, and especially its Research and Analysis (R&A) Branch (where Neumann worked as an intelligence analyst during these years), initially hosted in the Library of Congress, as one of the most prominent sites of the rise of gray literature.

3 The Invention of the Intelligence Report

3.1 THE MATERIALITY OF INTELLIGENCE: INDEX CARDS AND MICROFILM

The first centralized US-American intelligence service started on July 11, 1941 as an administrative reform of rivaling departments and agencies, organized around a newly invented concept: "national security."

> There is hereby established the position of Coordinator of Information, with *authority to collect and analyze all information and data, which may bear upon national security* [emphasis added]; to correlate such information and data, and to make such information and data available to the President and to such departments and officials of the Government as the President may determine; and to carry out, when requested by the President, such supplementary activities as may facilitate the securing of information important for national security not now available to the Government.[6]

In the early 1940s, the former military officer, trust and antitrust lawyer, and part-time spy William J. Donovan was one of the most important transatlantic mediators, particularly between the United States and the United Kingdom,[7] and it was delegates of the latter who provided the blueprint Donovan used to create the first US-American intelligence service, against strong resistance within the complicated political landscape of Washington, DC. Taking on the position of Coordinator of information (COI) and facing the President's large-scale hermeneutic assignment, nothing less than the administration of national security, Donovan quickly built an entire institution around himself, partly in the pragmatic spirit of the many New Deal agencies founded throughout the last decade, but also relying on his expertise stemming from his New York corporate law firm Donovan Leisure Newton & Lumbard. As a historical institution, the COI participated in the – from an outsider's point of view, largely unfathomable – three-letter games of the Roosevelt administration and developed within the capital's hazardous political process, which however largely determined the agency's shape and parts, and, accordingly, its text production. After only one year of its existence, in 1942, Donovan had to give up the COI and split it into two uneven parts, leaving behind a smaller domestic propaganda ministry, the Office of War Information (OWI), while focusing on the OSS. Within the OSS, Donovan kept the largest administrative unit, the R&A Branch, the site of the invention of the intelligence report.

Herbert Marcuse, the German-Jewish émigré, student of Martin Heidegger and member of the Frankfurt School of late fame during the student protests of 1968, who worked for both the OWI and then the

3.1 The Materiality of Intelligence

R&A-Branch of the OSS, compares in a letter to his former employer Max Horkheimer, head of the exiled Institute of Social Research, the two workplaces[8] with a pointed remark that may appear trivial at first sight but reveals a key mechanism of intelligence work: "I have seen that the OSS has infinitely *better material* [emphasis added] [...]."[9] – The obsession with access to "better material"[10] needs to be considered not simply as an expression of one of the ideals of scholarly pursuit – to work from a *copia*, an abundance of material – but inherently tied to institutional thresholds of the COI and its successors. The "clearance"[11] process required for members to enter the institution marked the first boundary, which Marcuse had initially ridiculed in front of his previous "closed community"[12] but then, once being initiated[13] into the new system of classified writing, ostensibly affirmed with a new sense of being in an insider-position of superior access to the distant reality of Nazi Germany.

In order to gain perspective on the apparently novel quality of the OSS and its R&A Branch obsessed with material, which several important historical accounts have painstakingly outlined in its hybrid constitution and complicated development,[14] one may start with a question pointing in the opposite direction: to whom does this odd institution look most familiar? Searching for an answer to this question, one may point to a short paper from 2006 by Trevor J. Barnes, a geographer, whose historical interest in the OSS lies not so much in its intelligence report writing but rather in its collective practices of map- and atlas-production. Accordingly, he regards "R&A as a center of calculation,"[15] and thereby manages to give with the least effort one of the best accounts of that institution:

First, it [R&A] was to bring the rest of the world as it bore on military intelligence to the centre, in this case, to the R&A Branch at the South Building at 23rd Street and East, Washington DC. The world came to R&A in the form of various kinds of paper inscriptions and representations such as maps, photos, on-the-ground reports, census information, regional monographs, academic articles, newspaper clippings, statistical tables, line drawings, foreign encyclopaedia entries, and more. Second, R&A's task, as in all centres, was then to join such heterogeneous sources, to "paper shuffle," to engage in "nth degree inscriptions," that is, to effect translations in order to produce yet more inscriptions. Finally, if completed successfully, R&A by virtue of the knowledge it accumulated possessed the potential to dominate other sites, to "act at a distance on many other points."[16]

All these "paper inscriptions and representations"[17] were evaluated and processed in the OSS's Central Information Division (CID).[18] By 1945,

R&A had collected "300,000 captioned photos, 300,000 classified intelligence documents, over 2 million assorted types of maps, 350,000 foreign serial publications, 50,000 books, thousands of biographical files."[19] To render this collection useful, the CID's librarian Lewis had taken on the excruciating task to reference this collection on "1 million 3 × 5 index cards organized by subject, cross-indexed, and containing pictorial material."[20]

With Barnes's account in mind, one may begin to appreciate Robin W. Wink's classical statement, so far largely inconsequential in OSS research, about the "most powerful weapon in the OSS arsenal"[21] designed to organize these massive amounts of material. The index card,[22] the main tool of R&A's collaborative writing practices – and a central product of Donovan's collaboration with Archibald MacLeish –, was the subject of a major debate in the 1940s. When MacLeish arrived as the new Librarian of Congress in 1939, one of the main challenges he encountered as a librarian was to deal with an enormous backlog of uncatalogued books, "1,670,161 volumes out of a total estimated collection of 5,800,000 volumes. Furthermore, this backlog was increasing at a rate of thirty thousand volumes a year."[23] MacLeish oversaw the restructuring and centralization of the various procedures of cataloging ("card, accessions, descriptive cataloging, subject cataloging, and catalog preparation and maintenance")[24] into one "processing department," conflating tasks that formerly were assigned to library administrators on the one hand and specialized catalogers on the other. Disregarding the elaborate system developed in the past half century to deal with the philological intricacies in adequately representing the respective publication in the library's catalog,[25] the focus shifted to a slip of paper, the inconspicuous but central tool of the library, the index card. This meant, instead of regarding the index card mainly as a tool of truthful representation, catalogers started to create a mode of "administrative reference" that foregrounded the card's quality as a signpost within the drawer of a filing cabinet, to facilitate "access" to materials. The innovations for "short cataloging,"[26] which was the term coined for the new method, conceptualized the Library of Congress no longer as an institution that collected books and expressed its reverence of scholarship and scientific knowledge with an equally scientific cataloging system, but instead as a place that was organized around its own documents and their inherent incoherence and messiness, which would need to be met with tacit knowledge and good "judgment,"[27] instead of mechanically applying a "fully developed body of definitions, rules, decisions, and precedent."[28]

3.1 The Materiality of Intelligence

Amid the debate surrounding this fundamental reorganization of the cataloging procedures in the Library of Congress, Donovan asked MacLeish to help him in his search for a librarian that might take on the task to build a filing and indexing system suitable for the demands of the OSS. After a failed attempt to hire former Archivist of the United States R. D. W. Connor,[29] they managed to recruit librarian Wilmarth S. Lewis, a friend of MacLeish's, as the first head of the CID. As a result, the OSS filing system developed as one of the most effective among Washington's administrations – which was indeed a direct result of the debates surrounding the reorganization of the Library of Congress's processing procedure, and particularly the new techniques to create administrative reference: "A report issued after this examination [of the CID] cited the reference section as 'the backbone of the division.'"[30]

From a transatlantic point of view, besides the index card, a second bureaucratic medium has so far received even less scrutiny – Barnes for example barely mentions it – but it was equally important for the analytic work at the OSS, and decisive for the invention of intelligence report writing: the "microfilm." When the shipping of enemy publications across the Atlantic became under the conditions of war more and more difficult, microfilm was the prime "immutable mobile" to transfer large amounts of enemy-knowledge across the Atlantic. The librarian Robert C. Binkley had introduced microfilm in the United States on a large scale, particularly on occasion of the microphotographic publication of nonconfidential records by the National Recovery Administration (NRA) and the Agricultural Adjustment Administration (AAA) during the 1930s, when "the cost of publishing all 315,000 pages would have been prohibitive."[31] With a significant grant coming from John D. Rockefeller, micropublishing started to gain steam: "Known only as 'Project A,' this massive effort supervised by historian Samuel Flagg Bemis, resulted in the copying of some two and a half million pages in Europe, Canada, and Mexico of materials relating to America which eventually were placed in the Library of Congress."[32]

It was precisely through micropublishing that it became both politically relevant and economically feasible to import America's foreign national literature, that is, "materials relating to America," which was already only one step away from Donovan's job description: the import of "literature relating to America's national security." To put it in slightly stronger terms: from a "material" point of view, *Project A* needs to be considered one of the largely forgotten immediate predecessors of the OSS.[33]

This perspective brings a little remembered heroine of World War II into the spotlight: the émigré Lucia Moholy, Bauhaus photographer and among other things uncredited coauthor of László Moholy-Nagy's famous avant-garde manifesto "Produktion – Reproduktion,"[34] who had been working for a further Rockefeller funded project at Cambridge University,[35] started in 1942 to organize in London the "ASLIB Microfilm Service." Her photographic service processed the majority of time-sensitive materials, such as journals and newspapers published by the enemy – the prime source material for political intelligence reports – and distributed it, among other institutions, to the OSS. "By late 1945, its [ASLIB Microfilm Service] total production of microfilms photographed, copied, recorded and indexed was five-and-a-half-million pages."[36] The story, however, comes with an important twist. As Moholy writes in 1946 in her report reviewing ASLIB's wartime activities, Eugene Powers came from Ann Arbor, Michigan to England in April 1942, "to arrange for the supply of microfilms of scientific and technical periodicals from enemy and enemy-occupied countries of government departments, research institutions, and university libraries in the United States."[37] The new arrangement was of critical importance, "for the United States, more even than Britain, was completely cut off from all supplies of enemy publications."[38]

The major institution for the transport of time-sensitive publications – microfilming of scientific and technical periodicals needed to be completed in 48 hours, newspapers in 24 hours[39] – was in fact established and financed for the transfer of scientific knowledge that was in the hands of the "Office of Scientific Research and Development" (OSRD),[40] while the R&A branch's interest in enemy publications was merely an afterthought. If anything, the ASLIB wartime activities were triggered by chemist Otto Hahn and his associates, who published in 1939 in *Naturwissenschaften*, a publicly available German scientific journal, papers on atomic fission that may have helped, besides other factors, to convince the US-American government of the strategic importance of creating a new ad-hoc infrastructure to bring enemy publications to the United States.[41] Identifying and tapping latent infrastructures with political relevance was the common denominator that unified seemingly disconnected wartime activities of the OSS, be it enemy publications, conservative opposition and opportunists within the Nazi Party organs, shady business contacts originating from the Dawes commission, clerical underground networks, or dormant allegiances within the abdicated central European aristocracy.

Moholy's political work to document cultures on microfilm, from the USA to Nazi Germany found its immediate continuation in her postwar engagement for UNESCO, first as a tool for Germany's "re-education"[42] and then as a postcolonial tool to reform[43] societies, all in the utopian spirit of "Produktion – Reproduktion." The anthropological argument for historicizing human sensory perception by means of media of reproduction, present in the early text of 1922, finds its continuation in a series of texts dealing with the further development of data processing, in particular Moholy's reception of the Belgian modernist bibliographer Paul Otlet.[44] More directly, however, in an essay on "The Co-Ordination of Scientific Information" from 1948, Moholy deals with the director of the just-mentioned OSRD, Vannevar Bush, who published his famous essay "As We May Think"[45] at the end of World War II. From today's perspective, the text is a visionary draft that anticipates various developments in computer history; in particular, the "Memex," the name of a device presented here, is seen as a precursor to the personal computer, already using hypertext and functions that anticipate the Internet, and indeed, the text historically also played a role for the early developers of the darpa or arpa-net, such as J. C. R. Licklider. The central vision of Bush's "As We May Think" from 1945, it should be noted here, is the miniaturization of knowledge not by means of digital data storage, but through analog microphotography. The Memex has no real computational functions whatsoever, but is based on indexing documentation, much like the CID's "3 by 5 index cards" in the OSS. For Lucia Moholy, who in "The Co-Ordination of Scientific Information" from 1948 still represents the World War–perspective on "As We May Think," Bush's text is actually merely addressing the efficient use of microphotography.[46]

3.2 ADMINISTERING INTELLIGENCE

Microfilm was, more than any other foreign intelligence material, the source of US-American national security's "enemy," crucial for the collaborative creation – between Americans and European émigrés – of the intelligence report.[47]

Anderson: Well, it began with the sources, which came from newspapers, other reports and from wherever, especially German newspapers – first they needed to be compiled and interpreted. We were sitting in a large L-shaped room, and we had a large round table in the middle, where we discussed. We came to an understanding about a certain object, be it for an individual report, be it for the "weekly report," as it was called, always reacting to the newest events in Germany.[48]

The brief interview with Eugene N. Anderson,[49] important administrator and in 1943 section chief of the "Central European Section," conducted 40 years later in 1983 and published only in German translation, needs to be considered with some philological caution toward documents of oral history.[50] It is nevertheless the best available firsthand account of the collaborative studies conducted among émigrés and Americans in the OSS and deserves extensive quotation to experience the invaluable historical "sound" of the "Collaboration of the Cool," analyzed in the previous chapter, now at work in a concrete setting.

Anderson: Among the émigrés, Neumann was the most important man, he guided the research, but he did it in a cooperative manner, like all the others. I participated in the round-table-discussions, but I left the research in his hands, although I was of course always informed. Franz took the initiative, but he was open to what people had to say, he could listen. What mattered was not simply to follow Franz, but it was the collective thought process of a whole group. My god, these people discussed without interruption, at lunch or at night, they were obsessed with their object [Gegenstand], they lived it. I have to tell you, I would not have suspected that there might be a group of émigrés that keeps on their task in such an objective, such a cool [original in English], such a passionless manner. Please get me right. I personally often got much more enraged, I have to admit, about what happened in Germany; they however did not succumb to their emotions. Their ideas were as erudite, as scientific as one could only wish for. This work process was an expression of an entirely new mentality. It had been practiced at the Institute of Social Research before, but now in America they saw that there really was something like *the* social sciences.[51]

What stands out in this quote is indeed the description of the specific "coolness" of the "friendly enemy alien"[52] Neumann,[53] his focus, the extreme form of single-minded – almost submissive – concentration on their object of study, the Nazi enemy, which finds its literary equivalent in the intelligence report. This specific form of objectivity is at the core of Neumann's unique qualification as an analyst at the OSS as he possessed "at the time unrivaled command of evidence culled from German newspapers, periodicals, and official publications,"[54] the decisive literary skill underlying both *Behemoth* and his intelligence work. This perception of Neumann's objectivity was certainly grounded in his social scientific ethos of axiological neutrality most prominently formulated by German sociologist Max Weber one generation earlier.[55] But as such, it remains too abstract to fully explain cultural similarities and differences.

The émigré John H. Herz, who was born in 1908 in Düsseldorf as Hans Hermann Herz, and who was before and after his employment by the OSS a colleague of Alain Locke – treated in the previous chapter – at

Howard University,[56] emphasizes with regard to collaboration in the R&A Branch:

> The work of individuals merged, accordingly, the results were of a collective nature. But there was a different reason for this: when we generated a text, this was not the final product. Even in the R&A Branch we had so called editors as superiors – one of them for example was the today renowned Arthur Schlesinger Jr. –, and they did not only make linguistic corrections, but also occasionally with regard to the object [Sache], of course in agreement with us.[57]

Even in Herz's oral history interview, which ostensibly draws a harsh distinction between the émigrés and US-American collaborators, arguing for an asymmetrical relationship between the two groups, one can find the same admiration of the others' coolness:

> We had two assignments to accomplish: to collect and interpret information, that is, research proper; furthermore, to make policy recommendations and to give recommendations for action. The second assignment opened a rift between the different agencies. It was a rift typical probably not only for American, but for all government agencies. They wanted to be realistic, they were "hard nosed" [original in English], as they say here. I remember a statement by an American who said: we enormously respect the intelligence of a Franz Neumann, but he is, after all, not really "American" – a typical attitude that illustrates the collision of two worlds. We appeared always as somewhat uncanny to the Americans, they called us "ideologues," they didn't know what to do with our insistence on theories, because it contradicted their pragmatism. We were not belittled, on the contrary: people held this sharp intellect in high regard, but somehow, we were uncanny to them: too idealistic, not realistic, as the buzzwords always went. Privately, we were on good terms with them, we were often together, officially and unofficially. But people always let us understand that they had only grudgingly taken us on in the R&A Branch – that they didn't really want us.[58]

Herz's account of his "hard-nosed" colleagues therefore is equally striking in its consequence: if there really was, as outlined earlier in theory, a process of mutual misapprehension and mimesis, the repeated statement "we were uncanny to them" would be the best description one side could give. The concern with the indeed striking ideological differences of the various collaborators, especially in the context of both earlier New Deal-era fights and the Red Scare of the later McCarthy-era, has accordingly defined most of secondary literature written about the R&A Branch.

Alfons Söllner, Anderson's and Herz's interviewer, holds on to the "primacy of politics" in World War II collaboration, too, as he regards Neumann's, Marcuse's, and Kirchheimer's work at the OSS as part of the history of critical theory.[59] Along the way, however, he hints in his interpretation at how to put these two divergent perspectives together and arrives at a conception of the OSS that comes surprisingly close to that of a trading zone, in which an unlikely local compromise between a former Republican lawyer and a former Social Democratic lawyer facilitated collaboration:

> The transitional mechanism which connected the American war politician with the Marxist theorist of society becomes discernible. There is no need for great interpretative efforts in order to figure out the parallels between the function that Donovan assigns to the social sciences for the practice of intelligence work and the theoretical approach of the Neumann-group. The ideologue-in-chief of total information [Donovan] demands – certainly without being aware of the implications for the theory of science – no less than a social science that analyzes the totality of society as primarily defined by the economy. And Neumann succeeded, starting from his Marxist analysis of National Socialism, in coming to conclusions for political and psychological warfare.[60]

If one nevertheless takes this form of creolization seriously and puts it, indeed, into the center of analysis, one might arrive at a slightly different trajectory of the OSS's role within intellectual history.[61] To the first creolization, the local agreement on "political and psychological warfare," one would need to add, following Söllner's characterization of Donovan and Neumann, a second creolization. As lawyers, both American and émigré could agree that in intelligence report writing of the OSS, the Nazi German "monopoly capitalism" could be approached with the methods of an American "anti-trust case."[62] Thus, slowly the agreement on a local common understanding of the Nazi German enemy happened within the trading zone of the OSS and was negotiated within the genre of the intelligence report, for example, through technical discussions of "fact-finding"[63] methods and how these facts may be referenced in footnotes of intelligence reports,[64] or through the establishment of a hermeneutic part-whole relationship that makes it possible to interpret single reports with the "big picture" in mind,[65] instead of treating them as unsystematic "'spot' reports."[66]

Looking back from the OSS at Riesman's *Lonely Crowd* treated in further detail in the previous chapter, other-directedness, émigré-directedness and enemy-directedness come together in the problem of "objectivity." Cool collaboration, objective representation, cool manner, New Objectivity, political neutrality, and scientific objectivity: all these divergent conceptions and misunderstandings of "being objective" converged temporarily in the OSS and were considered by all collaborators, US-Americans and émigrés, as one. Historian Barry Katz draws together several of these elements while giving an account of the "epistemology of intelligence."⁶⁷ Although it is not entirely wrong to explain the problem of objectivity with regard to positivism and the history of rhetoric, I claim that the intelligence report was indeed in its genesis defined as a genre by the rules of administration and bureaucratic communication. This can be shown in a reading of the "manual" on how to write an intelligence report, a memorandum from geographer and "guardian of objectivity" Richard Hartshorne.⁶⁸

The main document that all accounts of objectivity in the R&A Branch of the OSS rely on is a memorandum⁶⁹ – and one has to be precise now – not "by" but "from" Richard Hartshorne, sent "to" "Division and subdivision chiefs for preparation of political reports," with the "subject"-line – not the "title": "Draft of proposed guide to preparation of political reports." This heading is followed by a note in brackets that further complicates the memorandum's authorization:

(This draft, prepared by a subcommittee, will be considered by the special committees studying the problem. Comments are requested and should be delivered to division chiefs or the writer. If desired, copies may be distributed to section chiefs in the political subdivisions.)

The draft for a guide comes from Richard Hartshorne, but it is prepared by an anonymous subcommittee that in turn requests comments to be delivered to division chiefs (part of "to:") or the "writer," in the singular. All in all, there are four positions explicitly referenced and distinguished in the text "From:", "To:", "prepared by," and "writer," which all fall under the immediate responsibility of "authorship." One might be inclined to interpret this redefinition of authorship as an attempt at providing an example for the consequences of objective report writing, as the memorandum outlines them, but the rest of the memorandum actively contradicts this interpretation. In the short list below, I indicate in italics some of those unruly and highly subjective acts performed by the memorandum, followed by examples in quotation marks.

The memorandum entices: "There is an urgent need [...]."
The memorandum threatens: "There is [...] no future for R&A as a pressure group [...]."
The memorandum empathizes: "no matter how strongly we may believe we are 'right' [...]"
The memorandum commands: "A rigid distinction is to be drawn [...]."
The memorandum warns: "[...] is particularly dangerous [...]"

The memorandum corrupts: "If the writer is describing effects of American actions or policies that are clearly unfavorable to American interests, he must avoid either the statement or the implication that those actions or policies were unwise."

The memorandum moralizes: "Generally speaking, 'should,' 'ought' – not to mention 'must' are taboo."

The memorandum wisecracks: "Proust, Jouce [sic], or Gertrude Stein would all be equally out of place in R & A."

The memorandum inverts: "The contents of the paper should serve simply to amplify and demonstrate the summary."

The memorandum imposes: "The staff will therefore understand that studies of this type must be subjected to the most careful and painstaking editing before presentation to the Director."

And how could it be different? The memorandum to establish the rules of objectivity needs to fulfill a paradoxical purpose. It is supposed to create with all institutional authority available – domesticating all kinds of benign and malign affects, threats and subversive urges – a policy in intelligence report writing to precisely avoid any involvement in domestic politics through political intelligence report writing. In this sense, the R&A-Branch's supposed function is to write intelligence reports about foreign materials and particularly the enemy that in fact are not essays with an author and an anonymous readership mediated through a publisher, but classified texts that may circulate From: – To: as "internal communication" in the thorny political environment of Washington, DC.

The dissolution of authorship is therefore not primarily an anonymization in favor of scientific or stylistic objectivity, but it is a performance of the same manipulation that the memorandum as a whole attempts, to create, bureaucratically, an impression of agreement while compelling its recipients into facilitating a common "understanding." Here lies the power of the memorandum, uniquely expressed in written form in the shape of the style guide underlying the invention of the intelligence report. The memorandum turns its elusive author into a trickster-like figure, who submits to the rules of the (intelligence) community in order to be able to manipulate it, with the enemy material as the only ally in the fight against their collaborators – all under the disguise of cool objectivity.

The rigorous pressure on the intelligence community to stay out of domestic politics thereby creates a bureaucratic collegiality between enemy, R&A Branch, and its addressees. Writing political reports about state, statistics, and statics of the enemy nation generates an inverse picture of US-American national security, a world in which domestic politics appear as a "black hole" in the center of the foreign politics-universe. In effect, national security becomes, through intelligence reports, an absolute value without any clear meaning in itself, and ironically, subject to bureaucratic other-directedness, controlled by the enemy. The opposite consequence, however, is more important for the case of Nazi Germany. The detached, objective picture of nations as structural enemies invites – other-directedness turning into enemy-directedness – attempts to manipulate these structures, or to attack the state structure as a whole, with a *coup d'état*. The *coup d'état*, this chapter argues, is the ultimate consequence of intelligence report writing that Franz Neumann's *Behemoth* as a book could never achieve, if not broken down and repurposed for an intelligence report.

3.3 UNDERSTANDING GERMAN MORALE AFTER TUNISIA

The reading of one intelligence report, "German Morale after Tunisia,"[70] filed on June 25, 1943, concludes this chapter, and will show how the descriptions of the intelligence report outlined above find their immediate reflection in the historical record. The academic standard procedure, to describe, explain, and maybe interpret a three-page document, written in plain English, is, as should have become clear by now, anything but trivial when it comes to intelligence reports. As the OSS was built as a large-scale hermeneutic project, reading a single report always presupposes an understanding of the OSS as a whole. Beyond that, the extreme dependence of intelligence reports on historically specific para- and contextual information – the reports are literally about "everything under the sun" – renders immanent readings virtually impossible. Beyond the historical actors involved, there are maybe a half dozen people in the world who can or could at a point in time legitimately claim, after year-long archival research on the topic, to have found a way through the multilayered hermetic seal of R&A's writing on Nazi Germany and to have gained, through some extremely messy "reverse engineering" of R&A's hermeneutical machine, after-the-fact-"clearance" to achieve some sort of insider status themselves. Instead of making yet another attempt to pursue a deeper understanding of the OSS and intelligence reports, this final analysis continues to limit itself to answering the question brought up initially: what did it "mean" to understand the Nazi enemy in 1943?

3 The Invention of the Intelligence Report

Raffaele Laudani, the editor of a collection of R&A intelligence reports, gives the following introduction to his edition of "German Morale after Tunisia," with abbreviations referring to the filing system of the National Archives, where the R&A reports are available on microfiche, stored in large drawers:

> Editor's note: R&A 933. This was an OSS report published in the form of a pamphlet for internal use. An introductory note points out that the text is "based on a memorandum from the Research and Analysis Branch." Most probably, this was the memo titled "The Nazi Defeat in Tunisia, the Coming Invasion of Europe, and Our PW [Political Warfare]," sent by William Langer to General Donovan on 17 May 1943, because in his opinion it was "particularly interesting" (which would also explain the reason for its redrafting, unlike most of the reports R&A produced, into the form of an essay). Neumann's authorship is indicated in Political Intelligence Report (R&A 1113.6–8, section I.A.I), and in a letter, dated May 14, 1943, from H. Deutsch to William Langer (RG 226, entry 38, box 5). Classification: Secret[71]

Accordingly, the report edited by Laudani has lost many of the attributes that qualify most of the intelligence reports circulating as administrative texts, so much that Laudani calls the text an "essay." One must acknowledge that it was ultimately the archivist's act to preserve this late version of the report rather than any prior rendition. Instead of reconstructing a supposed "urtext," according to a principle of misunderstood philological purity, it is better to keep in mind that intelligence reports are, as long as they are administratively relevant, constantly evolving, to the point that even the same copy is not the "same" on the desks of two different people. All an archivist may preserve are arbitrary and incomplete snapshots of something that the historical actors considered "one" report, often starting with a preprinted form for proposals to which, if approved, a number was assigned.

Among all intelligence reports, "German Morale after Tunisia" has received, implicitly or explicitly, most of the scholarly attention, to the point that by now, one may make the foolhardy claim that it is indeed "the" intelligence report of World War II. A brief redescription of the report will take up some of the arguments made in the secondary literature and put them in the context of cool collaboration between European émigrés and Americans in the genre of the intelligence report.

"German Morale after Tunisia" records, for the R&A Branch, the world historical turn of tides in World War II, the moment of triumph against the enemy following the "German defeats at Stalingrad and in Tunisia."[72] Instead of joining the predominant enthusiasm, the report

3.3 Understanding German Morale after Tunisia 81

coolly reassesses the victory's consequences according to the intelligence report's inherent other-directedness, drawing technical conclusions for the rules of the genre. According to report no. 933, the military turning point coincides with the moment that the central object of R&A's focus in "psychological" warfare, German "morale," needs to be entirely reinterpreted in terms of "political" warfare.[73] In the past, German attacks and resulting military victories built the fundament of Nazi Germany – which one may call in the logics outlined above the "enemy's enemy-directedness" – in propaganda, an argument clearly taken from Franz Neumann's *Behemoth* regarding Nazi Germany's aggressive foreign policy.[74] Nevertheless, according to the report, their collapse would not lead to psychological collapse among the German people. Intelligence from Germany about changing morale and unrest, while "probably basically correct,"[75] has to be "disregarded" for the interpretation of the Nazi enemy in intelligence reports, because of Nazi German "totalitarianism."[76] This major change, proposed for the genre rules of the intelligence report's other-directedness – the question what may be regarded as a genuine expression of the enemy – away from field intelligence and toward official statements printed in newspapers, first of all strengthens the hermeneutic authority of the center of R&A against its periphery. It also has immediate infrastructural implications, for example, which intelligence material needs to be granted priority for trans-Atlantic delivery.[77] The report argues that one needs to get a clear picture of the "functionalist"[78] mechanism of Nazism, through which Nazi social theory becomes unmediated social practice: "The sum of Nazi institutional and social arrangements is designed to render individual feelings negligible – to force the industrialist to produce, the worker to work, the soldier to fight, no matter how much they may hate the regime and desire to end the war. Morale is thus a Nazi expendable."[79] The reversibility of social theory and practice in National Socialist totalitarianism works through a complicity that forces individuals into choosing between being either friend or enemy.

> From the start, the Nazis have understood that their system of control rested on keeping people in a perpetual state of tension. Their essential governing technique has been to give people the choice between submitting themselves to the system or rebelling against it; to make that the only choice; and constantly to confront them with that choice, so that a succession of decisions results in moral and psychological commitments of ever mounting strength.[80]

In this way, the "German people" have no choice but being enemies, either of the violent Nazi state or of the Nazis' enemies. Accordingly, any "bad morale" that may be used to trigger a *coup d'état* is bound within the system: "The only way in which this discontent may be released in a form which will exert pressure on the state is by destroying physically the system whose controls have so successfully eliminated morale as a crucial factor."[81]

Circling back to the memorandum culture and its approach to texts – what sense would a reading of *Behemoth* make after receiving report no. 933? It should have become clear by now that for a historical reading, it is better to look at Franz Neumann's *Behemoth* not as the magisterial analysis of Nazi Germany that anticipates decades of historical research, but as a further document in a pile of gray literature, potentially browsed, for example, by one of the many graduate students working in the administration of the OSS,[82] trying to figure out their émigré bosses' attitude with regard to the newest intelligence coming in from the ASLIB Microfilm Service. Indeed, a cursory reading of *Behemoth* presents in relation to intelligence report writing in general, and "German Morale after Tunisia" in particular, the problem of what exactly – in the absence of direct interaction and communication with the enemy during wartime – is the material from which one may develop an understanding of the enemy, their plans and their actions. Among the various historical conjectures, the interpretation of statutes, decrees, edicts and legislation, analyses of propaganda and newspaper articles, the long genealogies of National Socialist ideologies and policies, Neumann arrives in *Behemoth* time and again at an impasse about how to deal with his sources regarding the Nazi state and its "irrational rationality" – most poignantly expressed in a passage toward the end of the book: "National Socialism has no rational political theory. [...] It may not be exaggerated to say that National Socialism acts according to a most rational plan, that each and every pronouncement by its leaders is calculated, and its effect on the masses and the surrounding world is carefully weighed in advance."[83]

Such a reading in a bureaucratic institution, browsing with little free time to spare through *Behemoth*, however "catapults" a contemporary reader, who some time ago may have overheard some gossip about scholarly rivalries among émigrés immediately out of the monumental book again and leads to the next one. Ernst Fraenkel, Neumann's former colleague in their Berlin law firm, had conceptualized the very problem outlined in *Behemoth* one year earlier in his *Dual State*, where he developed the distinction between rational "normative state" and irrational "prerogative state."[84] Now, one might as well be enticed to get to the bottom of this conundrum. It is worth pointing out that Fraenkel's analysis pivots on a critique of Carl Schmitt – to whom both were in close contact until

3.3 Understanding German Morale after Tunisia

1933 – and his concept of a "concrete theory of order" whose bearer is supposed to be a "community."[85] In *Behemoth*, Neumann picks up the problem of Nazi rationality from Carl Schmitt's *On the Three Types of Juristic Thought*,[86] and, tied up in a garbled mix of quote, paraphrase and translation, provides a groundbreaking reinterpretation: "They prefer 'juristic order and structure [or community] thought,' or *Sachgestaltungsdenken*, that is to say, thought that is shaped by the needs of the concrete situation."[87] According to Neumann, it is the term "*Sachgestaltungsdenken*" that comes closest to describe the irrational rationality of *Behemoth*.[88] The turn to "*Sachgestaltungsdenken*" in 1934 in fact is often considered an opportunistic conceptual break with Schmitt's prior theory of decisionism, on which his famous definition of politics according to the enemy/friend-distinction relied.[89] It is not, however, Schmitt who draws the full consequences of this turn in "thought." The closest *Behemoth* comes to spelling out the implications of this shift is in an analysis of the political theory of the Nazi lawyer and theoretician Werner Best,[90] which accordingly marks in Neumann's description the boundary line between rationality and irrationality. According to Neumann, Best envisions – engaging with Schmitt's writings[91] – a spatial theory ("Großraum") based on the concept of race that therefore ceases to be a "political" theory, and lays out the "legal" fundament for German imperialism:

(1) By denying that states are subjects of international law, it denies the equality of all states and allows differentiation among them. (2) By denying that states have sovereignty, it destroys the last elements of rationality in international relations. The spatial and functional limits inherent in the notion of state sovereignty disappear. (3) By proclaiming the sovereignty of the race, it subjects all racial Germans, whatever their nationality, to the law of the Germanic race. (4) By denying that international law exists among rival empires, it rejects any legal frontier to aggression, while at the same time it defends its own empire by a perverted Monroe Doctrine. (5) By applying the term international law to the relations between the folk groups within its empire, it destroys the last remnants of minority protection, and invests minority oppression with the sanctity of international law.[92]

As Werner Best's biographer Ulrich Herbert remarks, Neumann omits in his description of Best's argument exactly those passages that would need to be understood as an essential expression of Nazi antisemitism.[93] This is true and hints to a larger question surrounding Neumann's understanding of antisemitism, but it is also beside the point of this chapter less interested in "what" but "how" the American memorandum culture was able to study Nazi Germany.[94] Best indeed reappears in the appendix of the 1944 edition of *Behemoth*, in the role of a functional analyst of anti-Semitism – as someone who "understands" – a passage that is practically a literal appropriation from intelligence report R&A 1113.9:

[...] Dr. Werner Best, in 1942, clearly defined the function of Anti-Semitism for consumption abroad. A country, he said, that surrenders to Anti-Semitism has thereby already surrendered its liberal tradition. It has abandoned its bulwark against totalitarianism and is on its way to becoming a totalitarian society.[95]

Despite the inherent problem of irrational rationality and Neumann's harsh dismissal of all Nazi publications, one finds in Neumann's argument with Schmitt and Best at least two Nazi enemy theoreticians that gained an "understanding" of the irrational rationality, the "*Sachgestaltungsdenken*" of their own state.[96] Schmitt's and Best's is an understanding of Nazi Germany on "friendly terms" that Neumann, in his double role as friendly enemy alien was able to access and understand – referring again to Riesman's concept – by virtue of his other-directedness.[97] But, "betraying" his former colleagues, he could in collaboration with his American and émigré colleagues in turn mobilize this understanding as "objective" and make it accessible for the OSS. At least for the intelligence report, the analysis of wartime cool collaboration in the previous chapter needs to be slightly qualified: the genesis of the intelligence report spans all the way from American Cool to objectivity to cold persona, New Objectivity ("Neue Sachlichkeit") and "Völkische Sachlichkeit."[98]

As I have shown, the OSS took on a paradigmatic role in the bureaucratic reorganization of access to enemy publications that facilitated the study of Nazi Germany during World War II. This work is based on the virtuosity of those processing these materials, such as Lucia Moholy. Thus, the monstrosity of *Behemoth* – often explained theoretically with Neumann's affiliation to the critical theory developed at the Neomarxist Institute of Social Research – may be considered first of all practically, as the work of another virtuoso in processing German material, best exemplified in his work for the R&A Branch of the OSS. A crucial role in the interpretation of these materials to gain an understanding is played by the European émigrés collaborating with Americans and relying – apparently without ever mentioning the fact – on their personal acquaintance to and intimate knowledge of enemy theoreticians who indeed were – or easily could have been – their former colleagues and fellow paper pushers. It was thus possible, with the help of the power of the memorandum best exemplified in the intelligence report, to come to an "understanding" of Nazi Germany.

3.3 Understanding German Morale after Tunisia

The transatlantic transfer between Nazi Germany and the United States depended in this sense on émigrés with first-hand experience to interpret German materials. Especially Thomas Mann as arguably the most important German public intellectual during World War II brought this problem to the extreme, acting – not primarily based on intelligence, but on his very persona – as a mediator between German culture and American public, carrying, so to speak, the German letters in his body.

4

Applied German Folklore

Thomas Mann's novel *Doctor Faustus* along with Max Horkheimer and Theodor W. Adorno's *Dialectic of Enlightenment* is widely regarded as a canonical work of German exile literature for its seminal treatment of the "German catastrophe." Since its publication in 1947, the story of the two protagonists of the novel has provided for many readers a striking narrative rapprochement to the German nation's fall from grace. On the one hand, Mann created the character of the high school teacher Serenus Zeitblom, who was seen as representative of those Germans who, although quietly opposed to the Nazi regime, did not leave their country but instead went into "Inner Emigration." On the other hand, Mann introduced the composer Adrian Leverkühn, who was regarded as representative of Germany's decadent artistic avant-garde. In order to achieve his artistic breakthrough, Adrian Leverkühn makes a Faustian pact with the devil, which he has to pay for with his mental health and ultimately with his life. The conventionally realist, if unusually encapsulated, narrative full of detailed musical discussions is also reputed to be Mann's most difficult work. The plot follows the life of an emphatically German composer, as unmistakably specified in the novel's subtitle – *The Life of the German Composer Adrian Leverkühn as Told by a Friend* – and is indeed told by Leverkühn's friend Serenus Zeitblom in first-person voice. Zeitblom gives his account in a frame narrative during the last years of World War II from within the confines of "Fortress Europe," adding a catastrophic portent to the fictional biography. The account starts with their early childhood, recounts Leverkühn's formative experiences during his school years and interweaves his studies in theology and music at the university with the early beginnings of German racist nationalism. Leverkühn's career as a composer, his European travels, as well as his reclusive life in the periphery of Munich are told against the backdrop of the ideological run-up to World War I, followed by the surge of irrationalist thought in the Weimar Republic, staged in proto-National Socialist intellectual debates in the apartment of Sixtus Kridwiss, a designer in Munich. The story ends with Leverkühn's mental collapse at the peak of his creative work in 1930, which has been often interpreted in relation to the National Socialist Party's ascent to power in 1933.

Of particular importance for the novel's status in postwar Germany has been its composition in the United States as a work of exile literature. It is therefore striking that Mann's text has only recently been considered within the local sociohistorical context of its creation between Los Angeles, CA, and Washington, DC – without, however, sufficiently addressing its entanglements in the American memorandum culture grappling with the problem of Nazi Germany.[1] This continued neglect has long skewed the perception of *Doctor Faustus*, hindering the path to a balanced interpretation. Reexamining the making of *Doctor Faustus* allows to gain a new understanding of Thomas Mann's position as perhaps the most important representative and "mediator"[2] of German culture in the United States during World War II.

In the years following Mann's arrival in the United States, "millions of Americans were desperately seeking answers to such questions as, What were the origins of Nazism? Were the Germans inherently evil? Could peace ever be made with Hitler?"[3] The American public was desperate for answers to questions regarding Nazi Germany from an authoritative source. "Thomas Mann provided them with answers in speeches, essays, and interviews,"[4] as Tobias Boes has recently suggested. Thinking of Mann as a mediator of German culture in the United States, however, one still must elaborate further on the unique circumstances that put him in this position – and the people working in the background guiding his path. After all, there was a plethora of exiled German authors and intellectuals, starting with his immediate family, his older brother Heinrich Mann, his children Klaus and Erika Mann, who could have and indeed tried to appear as mediators, albeit with limited support and consequently with limited success. Arguably, Thomas Mann was uniquely qualified for this new public role, and he played it with great insight, care, and nuance. Yet, he could have never achieved his eminent status in the US-American public sphere solely based on his reputation generated as a German author and public intellectual. Mann needed massive institutional support, private patronage, and intellectual input, while navigating the entangled networks of American intellectuals and European émigrés.

This chapter attempts to extend this American perspective on Mann's writing to encompass one of his major literary accomplishments in *Doctor Faustus*. The merits of the novel can only be fully appreciated, as I intend to demonstrate, when one considers Mann's collaborative work on *Doctor Faustus*, and takes seriously the novel's suggestive title, named after the protagonist of a classical legend, as a piece of German folklore. Mann's wartime engagement with folklore is closely linked to his appointment as "Consultant in German Literature"[5] at the Library of Congress, starting in 1941. Archibald MacLeish, arguably the central organizer of the memorandum culture in Washington, DC, effectively served as "a kind of national caretaker of culture,"[6] when he employed the German Nobel Prize–winning author to work in direct contact with the American power elite. Despite his physical distance, residing in California at the time, and scant evidence that his work had any significant impact on the collection of German holdings, Mann took his job seriously – albeit in his own idiosyncratic reinterpretation of his role as mediator between American and German cultures. He committed substantial literary and intellectual resources to his addresses delivered at the Library of Congress from 1942 to 1949. In 1943, he rendered the connection to the institution most visible, when he made the symbolic decision to draft the manuscript of his novella *The Tables of the Law* on the library's stationery.[7] The most profound consequence of his fellowship at the Library of Congress, however, unfolded in the same year, when he ventured into a contemporary project of "national literature" and to write his new novel, *Doctor Faustus*, after devoting seventeen years to his Biblical *Joseph*-tetralogy, on the topic of Germany. Only by viewing Mann's novel as a product of his work under the auspices of the Library of Congress and MacLeish but also of his collaborations – on various scales and levels of intensity – with folklorist Gustave O. Arlt and scholar Joseph Campbell, critical theorist Theodor W. Adorno and journalist Agnes E. Meyer, can one gain access to some of the well-hidden secrets of this famous novel.

4.1 DOCTOR FAUSTUS AS GRAY LITERATURE

Little known, and if known, considered to be no more than a historical curiosity, the first publication of *Doctor Faustus* was not the oft-cited Stockholm edition issued by Mann's editor Gottfried Bermann Fischer, printed in Winterthur, Switzerland. Instead, the novel was first

4.1 Doctor Faustus *as Gray Literature*

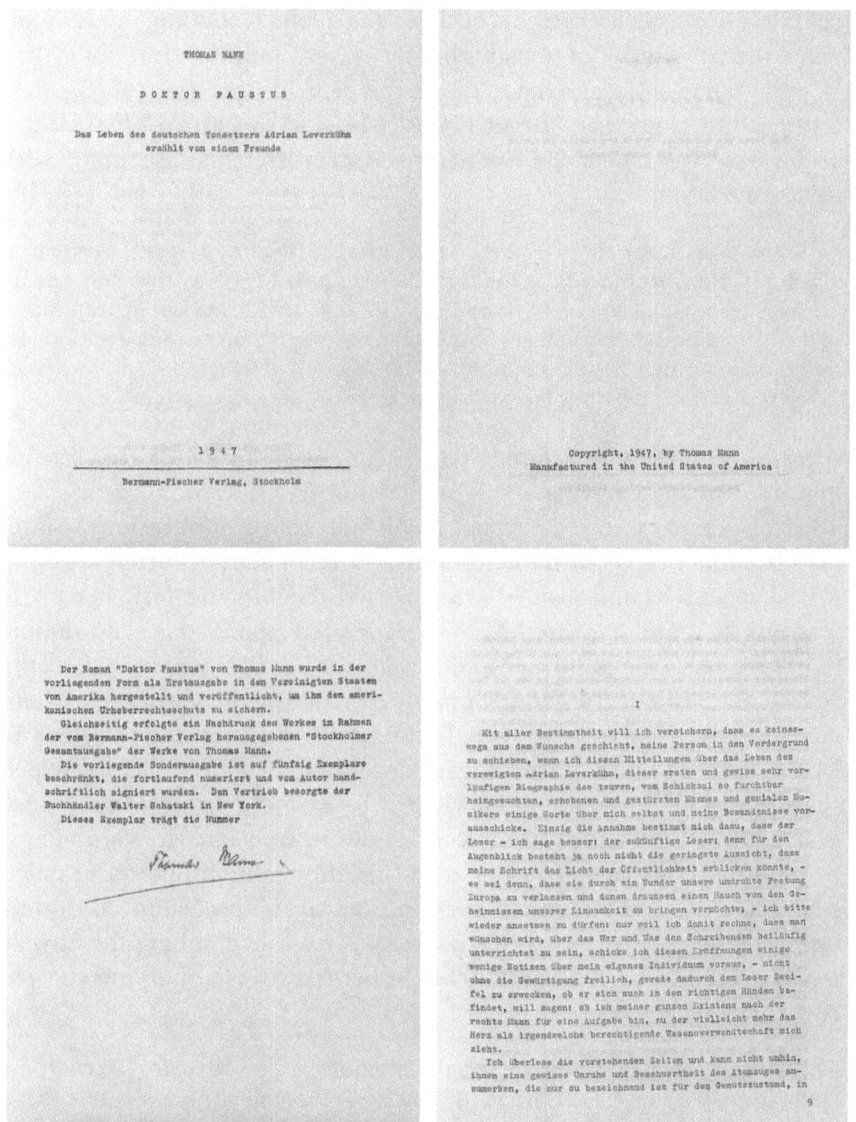

FIGURE 4.1 Pages from original mimeograph copy of Thomas Mann's *Doctor Faustus*, published in the United States with a print run of 50 copies. Courtesy of the Department of Rare Books and Special Collections at Firestone Library, Princeton University.

published on American soil as a mimeograph print (Figure 4.1) with a run of 50 copies.[8] *Doctor Faustus* was printed, or "manufactured," as the rare first edition's peritext states, outside the traditional publication channels – as gray literature – utilizing the media technology that dominated the circulation of texts within the memorandum culture of World War II. What had happened? In a letter sent in June 1947 to the new Librarian of Congress, Luther Evans, who had succeeded MacLeish in 1945, Mann explains the situation and expresses his discontent with it in some detail:

> Early this year, I completed a new novel, entitled "*Doctor Faustus*" – a story on which I worked for more than three and a half years. I may say that never in my life have I been engaged more passionately in any literary work. The translation of this voluminous book will yet be a matter of several months. Since, moreover, the manufacturing of books continues to be slow in the States, the publication of "*Doctor Faustus*" may not be expected before the summer of 1948.[9]

After his arrival in the United States, Mann was faced with the difficult question, how to navigate the publication of his German writing on a literary market geared toward English language publications. Mann mainly collaborated with the translator Helen T. Lowe-Porter, working for Alfred A. Knopf. Lowe-Porter proved reliable and fast, her prose was polished and captured Mann's venerated ironic style, and importantly for both the publisher and Mann, her English copies sold on the American market.[10] When it came to *Doctor Faustus*, however, Mann had initially tried to win over the journalist and translator Agnes E. Meyer to work on the English translation of his *Doctor Faustus*, which she declined.[11] Instead, Mann yielded to Knopf's proposal that once more, Lowe-Porter take over, who set out to translate the voluminous novel at a brisk pace. The English translation was published in quick succession after the German version, appearing, as Mann accurately estimates in his letter, with Knopf in 1948. While planning the novel's launch with his German editor, Mann became aware of an unexpected copyright issue:

> The German original, however, could be published by Bermann-Fischer, my German publishers in Stockholm by August or September of this year – ahead of the American edition, as were all my previous books as long as I was but a resident of the United States. But the legal situation has changed in so far as I am now a U.S. citizen and there exists a law according to which any American author who permits a book to be manufactured abroad, prior to its publications at home, forfeits the American copyright for the work in question. Evidently, this law is meant to protect the American book trade against foreign competition and would not logically apply to foreign language editions which, for obvious reasons, have never been prepared in the United States and the manufacturing of which abroad will never constitute a threat to American

interests. It appears, though, that cases such as mine were not taken into consideration when the law was passed and that, technically at least, the latter also embraces works written in any language other than English. Hence, if I permitted *"Doctor Faustus"* to be published at Stockholm this year, I would run the risk of losing the American copyright, a risk which I can hardly afford to take. [...][12]

Since his last book publication, Mann had become a US citizen – a change in legal status that introduced an unexpected complication, which would lead to forfeiting his intellectual ownership rights over his work in his new home country and consequentially a significant portion of the royalties. Due to the ongoing paper shortage in the United States, Mann's publisher was not able to print his book in his new home country immediately. Yet, he had the opportunity to publish the novel promptly after the completion of the manuscript for the German language market in Europe. Mann first introduces a linguistic argument that the American copyright for books should only apply to English language texts, on the grounds that the original intent of the law was to protect the financial interests of American publishers, who would in his case not stand to lose any money.

He then makes a second point about the timeliness and urgency of the German subject matter of his book contending that while American copyright law discourages European first prints, the publication of his novel might well be in alignment with pressing American foreign policy interests, as his book could help the military government in the American-occupied zone of Germany with its reeducation policies – a consideration of national security taking precedence over any copyright concerns.

I might add that *"Doctor Faustus"* deals with some of the most crucial problems of our time in that it tells – in a way – the story of the German character and destiny. [...] [T]here can be no doubt that my European and above all my German readers are waiting impatiently for the book to appear; more, its early publication in German might actually assist in the re-education of at least some of my former countrymen. [...] I understand that during the war all sorts of technical difficulties and impossibilities caused the American copyright laws to be far less rigidly applied. We are not at peace yet and I trust that prevailing conditions (abnormally slow production, etc.) may lead the authorities even now to take a lenient view. Happily, dear Mr. Evans, you are part of these "authorities."[13]

To Mann's chagrin, Evans did not adopt a "lenient view" on the copyright situation regarding *Doctor Faustus*.[14] Despite being written in German and on Germany, the novel by Mann, the citizen naturalized in 1944, was legally classified as a work of American literature.[15] Consequently, the aforementioned handcrafted mimeograph print run had to be improvised and filed for the records kept in the Library of Congress, in order to claim the copyright for the novel.[16] Evans was judicious in his decision to prioritize the American copyright law over foreign politics. By 1949, 15,000 copies of the German original of *Doctor Faustus* had sold, a decent achievement considering the difficult circumstances in Europe, but these numbers paled in comparison with the novel's success on the American market. At the same time, the English translation, published in 1948, had already sold 223,000 copies. It would undoubtedly be a false revisionism to claim, echoing some of the vilest attacks against Mann in the German postwar controversy over the status of exile literature, that Mann's American prose no longer belongs to the German literary tradition. Nevertheless, by the end of the war, Mann, the American, had been embraced by the American reading public, and it is hard to deny that *Doctor Faustus*, in its postwar reception, proved to be indeed American literature.[17] Instead of dismissing this instance as a minor blip during the chaotic post-war years in the long publishing history of Mann's works, this chapter argues that the original *Faustus*, the mimeograph-*Faustus*, the *Faustus* issued as gray literature, is in fact central to a new understanding of the novel's entanglements in the American memorandum culture.

It is helpful to briefly reconsider Mann's professional path in the United States. In 1937, Mann met Meyer during a lecture tour to the United States, one year before his celebrated arrival in New York together with his wife Katia Mann in 1938, stepping off the "Queen Mary," which marked the onset of his American exile. As literary critic Hans R. Vaget points out in his edition of the Mann-Meyer letters, Meyer generously supported – both indirectly and directly – Mann and his family's subsistence during their initial years in the United States. In fact, in Mann's profession as a writer, which depended on a fragile infrastructure of patrons, literary institutions, and reading public, there were only a handful of authors, whose move to the United States allowed them to continue their work without interruption, both due to lack of funding and lack of access.[18] For Mann, it was Meyer, who, mostly operating in the background, helped steer his career through the intricate American system of philanthropies, universities, the publishing industry, and politics. Her patronage, more than anything else, allowed Mann to continue his work as an author and to augment his American image as a representative and mediator of German culture. In return,

4.1 Doctor Faustus *as Gray Literature*

Mann expressed his gratitude to Meyer through extensive personal letters, inducting her into some of the hermetic aspects of his writing, and sharing readings of his unpublished materials. Arguably he also portrayed her, among others, as the marginal character of Frau von Tolna in *Doctor Faustus*, an invisible but ever-present admirer and supporter of the Faustian protagonist's work.[19]

With an acute sense of the rules of upper-class decorum and literary celebrity, Meyer assisted Mann in financing his journal *Mass und Wert* and secured for him his first prestigious appointment as "Lecturer in the Humanities" at Princeton University. Silently, she also funded his appointment at the Library of Congress. After six years, her sustained support aided in the selection of his fourth Joseph novel *Joseph the Provider* for the "Book-of-the-Month Club" in 1944. The influx of royalties ensuing from this exposure to a wide American readership provided Mann for the next few years with the means to live a financially independent life on the West Coast in Pacific Palisades, California, in a house built three years earlier with a loan vouched for by Meyer as a guarantor.[20] Following Mann's sometimes dismissive attitude, some literary critics tend to reduce Meyer and her support of Mann to her presumed romantic infatuation with him. This misguided view casts her primarily as Mrs. Eugene Meyer, the wealthy but lonely wife of the former chairman of the Federal Reserve and publisher of the *Washington Post*. It ignores the fact that Meyer produced important "national literature" in her own right, especially during World War II. Despite being barred from combat and facing great obstacles, she consistently carved out a space for herself to join the war effort, serving as one of the most important female political activists, who visited various often marginalized places throughout the country. She wrote influential social commentary and reportages about race, class, and gender issues that also informed Mann's view on the domestic situation of the United States during the war.[21] Mann learned, for example, about the background of the Zoot Suit Riots, referenced previously in Chapter 1, from Meyer's writing.[22] Her support of Mann accordingly hinged upon the usefulness of his public presence as a mediator at the "Humanist Front,"[23] in-as-much as it aligned with her ongoing project on the US-American "Home Front," and Mann was keenly aware of this interdependence. Indeed, during his 14 years in the United States, in terms of sheer time, his occupation with *Doctor Faustus* and subsequently *The Story of a Novel. The Genesis of Doctor Faustus* spanning about four years ranks only second. The first place takes, by far exceeding this period, his appointment at the Library of Congress in Washington, DC, beginning in late 1941, which remained active, even after he left the United States in 1952, until his death in 1955. His monthly propaganda[24] speeches rank a close third. From late 1940 to 1945 (with interruption), these speeches were radio-transmitted by the British Broadcasting Corporation (BBC)[25] to Nazi-Germany and published as *Listen, Germany! (Deutsche Hörer!)*. Both of his institutional affiliations, with the Library of Congress and the BBC, positioned him – as evidenced by a cursory glance at the heavy mail traffic, diligently recorded in his diaries of the war years – in the innermost circles of the memorandum culture.[26]

Although it is still necessary to qualify the depth and intensity of Mann's investment in the various roles he assumed under Meyer's patronage, this quantitative perspective helps remember that Mann's aforementioned letter to the Librarian of Congress, despite its apparent jovial cordiality, was not a private message to a friend but rather an official communication to his direct superior. Following this logic, quite a different understanding of "Mann, the American,"[27] and his work on *Doctor Faustus* emerges. This begins, for example, with a reconsideration of a detail such as the very name of the Faustus character and protagonist of *Doctor Faustus*. Both Adrian and Leverkühn have been meticulously analyzed for their meaning, the twelve letters from A[28] to L, which numerically mirror Leverkühn's musical "invention" of the dodecaphonic composition technique, the semantic interpretation largely based on Mann's own repeated statements linking the surname to Nietzsche and his concept of "living dangerously" ("gefährlich leben") – a phrase that had been appropriated by the Italian Prime Minister Benito Mussolini as a fascist slogan. It has also been established that Mann stumbled upon the protagonist's surname through his American patron. Shortly before the outbreak of war, in August 1939, during a diplomatic trip to Berlin, Meyer met the banker Paul Leverkuehn, who introduced himself as the son of August Otto Leverkühn, the executor of Mann's sizeable inheritance, which had sustained Mann financially during his transition into adulthood after his father's early death. Mann falsely shrugged off Leverkuehn's claim as "megalomaniac,"[29] but apparently kept the name in mind. As most scholarship now points to the executor of estate and "poet jurist"[30] August Otto Leverkühn as the protagonist's namesake, the immediate and much more intriguing connection is overlooked. It is evident that Paul Leverkuehn, the son, was not a random German banker whom Meyer casually encountered by mere chance. After World War I, Paul Leverkuehn spent several years in the United States and served as a member of the Dawes Commission, which negotiated Weimar Germany's war debt. Following this engagement, he started spying as one of the highest profile members of the *Abwehr*, the National Socialist intelligence service of the German *Wehrmacht*, whose head Hitler rightly suspected of collaborating with the enemy. In the late 1930s, Leverkuehn served in fact as the principal conduit to the United States, thanks to his personal acquaintance with William J. Donovan, founder of the OSS.[31] After the war, while Mann was still engrossed in *Doctor Faustus*, Leverkuehn again played a significant role as a German collaborator and lawyer in the first Nuremberg Trials. It remains unclear to what extent Mann was made aware of Paul Leverkuehn's covert identity[32] by Meyer, his "'trusted contact' in Washington"[33] who frequently spilled insider knowledge and secrets to Mann behind closed doors and occasionally even over the phone. In any case, the story should be told as follows: Through his collaboration with Meyer, Mann appropriated for his protagonist, the megalomaniac artist Adrian Leverkühn, the name of a Nazi German double agent. This, in turn, provides the 12 syllables tied to the general 12 tone row of Adrian Leverkühn's final composition "Lamentation of Dr. Faustus" in *Doctor Faustus* "For I die as both a wicked and good Christian"[34] ("Denn ich sterbe als ein böser und guter Christ"), the quintessential result of Leverkühn's Faustian pact, in the context of the collaborative memorandum culture with a concrete contemporary allegorical meaning.

However, what is at stake is not only important details, but the very genesis of the novel. To elucidate this point, I shall start by highlighting the intricate philological problem of tracing the authorship of the line, "For I die as both a wicked and good Christian." Mann borrows this central quote, as several further phrasings and musical inventions, from one of his Californian collaborators, critical theorist, classically trained musician, and avid writer of wartime memoranda Theodor W. Adorno. Indeed, the fact that Mann felt the need to write a "making-of" for his own novel, in which he acknowledges his help and that of others in *The Story of a Novel. The Genesis of Doctor Faustus*, is often viewed as a reaction to the lavish praise some critics unduly heaped upon Mann's supposed musical expertise in *Doctor Faustus*. It gave him the opportunity to publicly credit[35] "Dr. Adorno" for his role as a collaborator, that is, as "helper, adviser and sympathetic instructor,"[36] after all, he had copied some passages word by word from Adorno's "drafts," including passages that were originally planned as an excursus for *Dialectic of Enlightenment* and later became part of his *Philosophy of New Music*. Adorno, in turn, discovered the line in a 1911 (second) edition of a sixteenth century print of Faust-stories, *Das Volksbuch vom Doctor Faust*, prepared by Robert Petsch. Both Adorno and the *Volksbuch* are bound by what Mann terms his "montage principle."[37] Once more, if one seeks to understand, philologically but also conceptually, how Faustus ended up in California, the answer leads back to the Library of Congress.

In 1941, Meyer writes in a letter to the Librarian of Congress, MacLeish about the job that provided Mann with his monthly income from December 1941 to end of 1944:

I am sending Dr. Mann a letter outlining the points you made: 1. That you should feel free to send him letters concerning important *inquiries in the field of German culture and literature* [emphasis added]. 2. That he ought to try to be in residence at least two weeks every year. 3. That he should deliver one lecture at the Library of Congress to a date to be arranged between you and him. [...] I know that he [Mann] is very happy to have an official connection with the Library and to be of some use to this country, and I hope that the arrangement will turn out to be a source of satisfaction to you.[38]

It is true that MacLeish did not issue any known inquiries to Mann, which he would have been obliged to answer first as a "Consultant in German Literature" and then as a "Fellow." Nevertheless, his special appointment contributed more than anything else to his respectability in the United States, which was of paramount importance to the bourgeois writer. It is therefore a matter of stringent choice that the subject of Mann's new book-project for the first time since his *Reflections of a Nonpolitical Man*, written during World War I, dealt explicitly with Germany. Mann did indeed work squarely "in the field of German culture and literature." Institutionally, *Doctor Faustus* fit right into his professional environment. Mann's folklorization of Germany was not just a result of his German cultivation, but also part of a broader cultural project of American folklore administrated by the Library of Congress. The institution had collected American folklore since 1928; and under the direction of MacLeish, especially resulting from his engagement in the Federal Writers' Project (FWP) financed by the New Deal Works Progress Administration (WPA), it gained prominence during World War II.[39] Alongside the musical collection efforts by John A. Lomax and Allan Lomax, it was folklorist Benjamin A. Botkin, who aimed through "applied folklore,"[40] to generate a new national literature at the Library of Congress. Regarding Mann's "infrastructure," the situation is clear. His work on *Doctor Faustus* started with two letters, one sent to folklorist Gustave O. Arlt,[41] one of his Californian interlocutors, the other to the Librarian of Congress MacLeish, requesting two books, the *Volksbuch* on Faust from Arlt and a collection of correspondence by composer

Hugo Wolf from the Library of Congress.[42] Intriguingly, the two letters reenacted and, ultimately, brought to fruition, the idea formulated in an old note that Mann had held onto for almost 40 years.

4.2 GERMAN FOLKLORE

> Old note: Figure of the syphilitic artist: as Doctor Faustus and beholden to the devil. The poison acts as intoxication, stimulant, inspiration; he may create genial, wonderful works in rapturous enthusiasm, the devil guides his hand. But finally, the devil takes him: paralysis. (The matter with the pure young girl, with whom he proceeds until marriage, as episode.)[43]

The "old note" transcribed on the top of page 2 in the collection of handwritten preparatory work[44] – Lieselotte Voss aptly calls it the "germ cell"[45] of Mann's *Doctor Faustus* – was an idea for a novella jotted down early in his career in 1904 or 1905.[46] Mann planned to combine the narrative of the Faustian pact with the "pathography"[47] of "syphilitic artist[s]," initially of the composers Hugo Wolf and Robert Schumann, but ultimately focusing on the pathography of German philosopher Friedrich Nietzsche. In 1943, according to his *Story of a Novel*, Mann finally put it to use for his "late work."[48] For Mann's initial plotting of the novel, the entire timeline is predicated on the effort to map the 24-year Faustian pact with the devil physiologically onto Nietzsche's biography and his supposed infection with syphilis at a brothel in Cologne,[49] 22 years before his "collapse in 1888."[50] The technical intricacies of synchronizing Faustus and the syphilitic artist have been well analyzed and have provided a crucial framework if not the definitive blueprint for critical interpretations of *Doctor Faustus* as an allegory[51] for the German catastrophe. This is no easy task, as there are a lot of moving parts. Allegorical readings have to reconcile Faustus and Nietzsche with twentieth-century German political history, Mann's biography, the time passing-by as Mann worked on the novel, and the narrator's time of writing the biography of the protagonist Adrian Leverkühn (born in 1885; syphilitic infection in 1906; confirmation of pact with the devil in 1911; collapse in 1930; death in 1940). Even for Mann, this led to serious problems and occasional failings, most visibly marked on the first page of the novel with the changing starting date May 23/May 27 1943 across different editions.[52]

As Mann revisited the biography of the "original" Faustus, he may also have got distracted. When he started to reconstruct the life of Faustus in the modern edition of one of the classics of German folklore, trying to connect it to contemporary artistry, the impact of that reading extended far beyond biographical problems. The reading of the *Volksbuch* affected, and arguably radicalized, Mann's modernist writing practices – as well as the conception of the novel's two protagonists, thus providing them with a covert, shared philological origin. Both Adrian Leverkühn, the Faustian artist, and the first-person narrator Serenus Zeitblom, a bourgeois Catholic humanist and high school teacher of Latin, Greek and History received Faustian traits from the *Volksbuch*.

As the scholar of Early Modern literature Marguerite de Huszar Allen has shown, Mann's montage technique[53] in *Doctor Faustus* results from rereading in Spring 1943[54] a prestige object of German folklore studies – Robert Petsch's aforementioned second edition[55] of *Das Volksbuch vom Doctor Faust*. De Huszar Allen readily acknowledges that thanks to previous Mann-scholarship, especially Hans Wysling's archival studies of Mann's use of source materials and Hans Meyer's *Poetics of Quotation*, certain, if not most, practices of quotation connected to Mann's montage can be traced to his earlier work: "The montage technique in *Doktor Faustus* does not seem, then, to represent a radical departure from the montage technique that generally typifies Mann's late novels beginning with the Joseph tetralogy."[56] One might add that, in his letter to Adorno from 1945, referenced earlier, in which he spells out his concept of montage, Mann himself traces the first use of this technique back to the onset of his career. In his letter, he mentions the description of Hanno Buddenbrook's typhoid fever, which he transcribed from an encyclopedia into his debut novel *Buddenbrooks*. De Huszar Allen, nevertheless, argues that Mann's radicalized use of the montage technique indeed took on a novel quality in *Doctor Faustus*: "What is perhaps not so readily apparent is how the *Faustbuch* might have influenced the fact that the extreme use of montage came to belong intrinsically in Mann's thinking to the conception, to the very idea of *Doktor Faustus*."[57] In this conception, Faustus is a figure of mythical reenactment and a result "of the coming of the printing-press"[58]. In one of his Princeton lectures as "Lecturer in the Humanities" in 1938 – mostly funded by the Rockefeller Foundation – Mann outlined his interpretation of the Faustus myth in the *Volksbuch* as follows: the assumed historical Faustus-model in the sixteenth century, the charlatan Georg Helmstätter started to call himself "Magus II, Faustus Junior," after reading the "fashionable" *Recognitiones*, an account supposedly from the second century prepared for print in 1526, in which the "religious con artist [religiöser Hochstapler]" Simon Magus, the "first" Christian heretic, receives the epithet Faustus, the "fortunate one." Mann therefore concludes that the relationship between the various conmen taking on the role of Faustus up to the 1587 printing of the German language *Volksbuch*, to which all subsequent Faustus versions refer, "was not about succession, but about identity, mythic recurrence, reincarnation, sublation of individuality into a type."[59] As de Huszar Allen adeptly summarizes with maximum parsimony: "Fifty years after his [Faustus Junior's] death, all the magic stories associated with him and his life were set to paper and the written legend of Faustus was born."[60] As much as especially Goethe's *Faust* is a rich source of quotations that entered the German language,[61] what matters to Mann even more is that the "original" German Faustus is himself a quotation taken from the print culture in which he is generated through reenactment and literary montage. From this point of view, it is plausible that Mann found in Petsch's descriptions of the *Volksbuch*'s composition not just linguistic materials to work with, but a manual for his own authorship in *Doctor Faustus*:

> Thus, for example, the following styles and stylistic elements are all juxtaposed: Luther's pithy humour, earthy expressions, and Biblical style, the sermonizing of the narrator, Latin expressions and syntactical constructions, rhymes from Sebastian Brant, the popular mode of the disputation, the travelogue style of the *Weltchronik*, the dry pedantry of encyclopedias and dictionaries, folksy proverbs, together with spicy jokes and coarse ribaldry characteristic of popular folklore. Mann, of course, would have been highly sensitive to the peculiar qualities of the *Faustbuch*'s mixture of styles.[62]

In *Doctor Faustus*, this literary primitivism comes to underly Adrian Leverkühn's musical practice, through which he attempts to overcome "culture" and return to the "cult" origins of art.[63]

Especially when considering Serenus Zeitblom as a first-person narrator, it is worth following up on one of the points that de Huszar Allen mentions only in passing, namely the question of editor Petsch's point of view on the *Volksbuch*'s authorship. The trained folklorist Robert Petsch[64] pursues in his polemical examination of the theologically and stylistically incoherent earliest German version of the *Volksbuch* the assumption of a lost coherent text, the "theory of a Latin original,"[65] as the ultimate point of reference for his argument. In fact, he religiously disapproved of the Early Modern writing practices that led to the creation of the texts underlying his edition. His edition therefore contains an appendix of about 120 pages – virtually matching the length of the

Volksbuch-text – in which he dissolves the edited text into its diverse parts and sources. The little coherence that remains of the past harmony in the *Volksbuch* for Petsch stems from the attempt to act as an "interpreter [Dolmetsch]"[66] from Latin. It is the quest for this assumed Latin original that incites the philological fervor of Petsch's meticulous description of various text versions. In sum, Petsch's theory requires no less than three lost earlier versions in two languages to support his assumption of a coherent Early Modern Faustian text:

> And this is the point, according to which one needs to understand the manifold extensions of the text from German original sources […]: U [the presumed first version of the *Volksbuch* in German] steals, wherever he finds anything, and even the most hackneyed, outdated content by Elucidarius is most welcome, in order to flaunt erudition in the sciences that is "out of the ordinary"; thus Schedel's World History of 1494 [sic] served for instruction […], and in case of emergency he made do with the word lists of Dasybodius. […] What follows […], is […] added based on loose associations […]. In short, everything gets mixed up here, the editor [Bearbeiter] combined components from L [original version in Latin], gravely lacking in comprehension, with all sorts of textual witnesses, and X [second version in German] probably excerpted the *rudis indigestaque moles* [Original in Latin; raw, undigested mass] of his predecessor with little more understanding than Schedel's report of the genesis.[67]

L, the putative Latin original appears as the source of a past harmony. It is first corrupted by U, the equally hypothetical first German translation, which is then followed by an assumed second German version, labeled X, which further corrupts the Latin original. Only the version X led to two surviving German language Faust-prints W and especially H, the latter being the print by Johann Spies in 1587 on which Petsch's edition of the *Volksbuch* is based.

One needs therefore not only de Huszar Allen's reading "*contre cœur*" of Petsch, but also his zealous reconstruction of a Latin past as a source of harmony (Figure 4.2) in order to fully comprehend the impact of Early Modern printing culture and the *Volksbuch* on Mann's writing practices in *Doctor Faustus*. Both contradictory impulses are intertwined in the first-person narrator, whose voice mediates the literary text formed by means of radical literary montage, all the while standing in as a philistine representative longing for a past classical world harmony, Serenus Zeitblom. The "old note" quoted above apparently led Mann down a rabbit hole, from which he emerged with a reappraisal of German folklore in the light of Early Modern print culture. But this was only half of the equation; Mann also came to a reevaluation of Modern folklore.

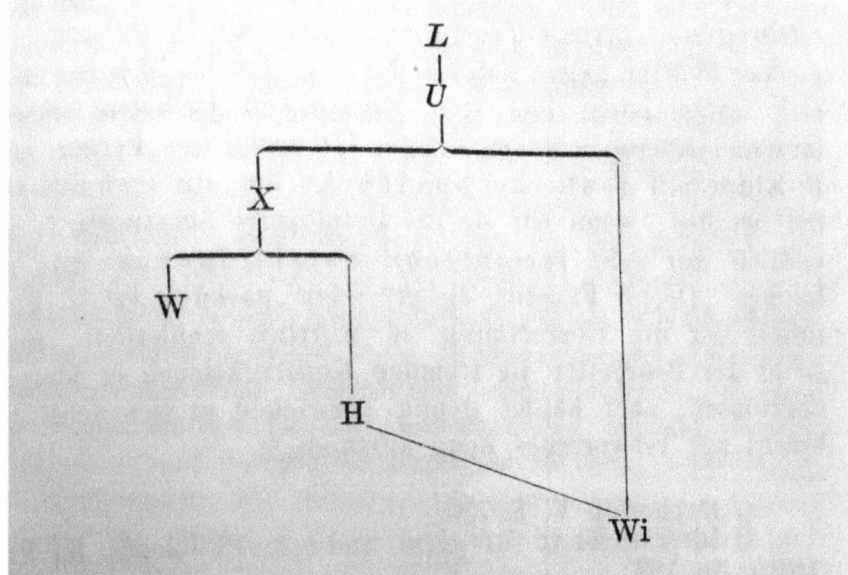

FIGURE 4.2 The diagram from Robert Petsch's introduction represents the theory of a Latin original (L) of Doctor Faustus, with two lost intermediate German versions (U), (X) leading to two surviving German language Faust-prints (W) and especially (H), which is the print by Johann Spies in 1587 on which Petsch's edition of the *Volksbuch* is based.

4.3 MODERNIST FOLKLORE

> When I began to write, that Sunday morning, my notes were scanty and there was no actual written outline. Yet the book, insofar as the sequence of events was concerned, must have lain plainly before my eyes; I must have had a fairly good over-all view of it to be able at once to take up its entire complex of motifs to give the beginning the perspective in depth of the whole [...].[68]

In his *Story of a Novel*, Mann identifies the technique of motivation as key to the creation of his novel. But what moves the motifs through the novel? Mann himself justifies the equation syphilitic artist = Doctor Faust, the combination of (Nietzsche's) patho-biography and *Volksbuch* with a premise that resonates with his views on the Faustus myth as interpreted earlier by de Huszar Allen. The premise is "to look upon all life as a cultural product taking the form of mythic clichés, and to prefer quotation to independent invention."[69] In order to get a better understanding of this view, it may be helpful to introduce folklore as a new term not only for his research on the Faustus legend but for Mann's general access to and processing of his material as "cultural product"[70] (rather than individual literary invention) which, as literary critic Bernd Hamacher points out, needs to be considered as mediated by ever changing "masks."[71] Mann, who classifies his own writing as "traditionalism" and as having "a link with tradition,"[72] works not only with the *Volksbuch*. Using the same literary practices, he also draws on a popular tale from Nietzsche's legendary biography with a dubious tradition,[73] indeed on *folk-lore*. In this sense, Mann draws on a corpus of German folklore, both Early Modern and Modern,[74] – with Modern folklore as the standard case and Early Modern textual tradition in need of meticulous reconstruction as folklore, starting with the revisionist invention of the genre of the supposed Early Modern *Volksbuch* (translated in English as "chapbook") in the early nineteenth century.[75] Consequentially, if one views Mann's novel from the perspective of folklore studies, the discipline largely responsible for the study of traditional masks and masquerade, the initially perplexing picture of its hybrid constitution becomes clear, arguably for the first time. "One has to take the *myth* away from intellectual fascism,"[76] Mann famously writes in 1941 in a letter to Hungarian mythologist Karl Kerényi, while working on the last volume of the Joseph tetralogy, *Joseph the Provider*. Mann means this literally, that is, with regard to literature. During World War II, he realizes that his literary contribution is vital to the US-American "provincialization" of Europe. His new *Doctor Faustus* does not only mimic, but "is" German folklore. As he records in his diary in March 1943:

> Read with pleasure stories in "Gesta Romanorum," further in "Nietzsche u. die Frauen" by Braun/ and / Stevenson's masterpiece "Dr. Jeckyls [sic] u. Mr. Hyde," thoughts focused on Faust-material, which is still far from taking shape. Even though the pathological should be elevated into the fairy-tale-like, connected to the legendary, it emits a certain worry, the difficulties appear unsurmountable.[77]

Mann scholarship has meticulously traced the sources from which Mann got his ideas and materials to write the novel: *Gesta Romanorum* (the highly influential fourteenth-century Latin collection of medieval tales and folk legends), *Hammer of Witches* (a historical witch-hunting manual), Luther's *Letters*, Grimmelshausen's *Simplicissimus*, Scheible's *The Cloister* (which includes a sizable collection of "apocryphal" Faustus legends), Andersen's *The Little Mermaid* and various fairy tales, folk tales, puppet shows, droll stories, children's rhymes, canons, commercium songs, proverbs, prayers, curses, spells, puns, but also Shakespeare poems and pieces, Romantic poetry, realistic novels; Mann uses Dürer-prints as models for character descriptions; moreover

4.3 Modernist Folklore

a selection as rich as eclectic of popular turn of the century biographies of musicians, philosophers and "great men" (including the earlier mentioned pathographies by and after Paul Julius Möbius), popular science articles, *Meyers Kleines Lexikon*, German national character studies, his own propaganda speeches addressing the German *Volk* – folklore,[78] literature of the German folk, all woven together into a new *Volksbuch*.[79] Facing the prospect of a "physical" end of German culture in World War II and seeking after the salvation of German history, Mann repatriates German national literature back into its vernacular. In doing so, he inadvertently joins the American project of salvage ethnography, initiated in the late nineteenth century by Jewish-German cultural anthropologist Franz Boas with the purpose of preserving the "folklore" of perishing cultures for the benefit of "traditional humanistic scholarship."[80]

Mann's explicit use of the term folklore remains largely bound to the class-distinction between German peasantry on the one hand and the bourgeoisie and aristocracy on the other. This class distinction was enshrined by German "Volkskunde" (folk-studies) of the 1920s[81] and most prominently conceptualized in Hans Naumann's elitist "trickle-down" theory of folk-art as "gesunkenes Kulturgut" (sunken cultural goods),[82] serving in this sense as a blunt tool to culturally affirm the hierarchy of power in Weimar Germany.

This classist notion can be also found in *Doctor Faustus*, when, after sealing his pact with the devil, Adrian Leverkühn settles in the bucolic Pfeiffering situated in the periphery of Munich for the composition of his main works.[83] Here he lives on a family farm primarily in the company of a peasant woman, Else Schweigestill, who takes care of his subsistence.[84] However, folklore – with and against Mann – is not only a central notion for interpreting the plot of *Doctor Faustus*, nor merely a technical term[85] for describing Mann's writing practices, but indeed his major American literary achievement, largely defining his heritage in world literature. It turns out that those literary-critical categories used for interpreting Mann's oevre, latently suspect for their intellectual value, such as Mann's humor,[86] his ironic distance,[87] his use of tradition,[88] of myth,[89] were all codenames for the same complex – the continuation of the enormous late nineteenth-century literary project under the conditions of Wilhelminian nationbuilding, the invention of tradition[90] through folklore. These very same materials contribute to Mann's self-folklorization in California, a process that allowed him to become by the end of World War II part of the emerging American – humanist – world mythology. For a US-American reader in the late 1940s, Mann's *Doctor Faustus* is the German continuation of his preceding "ethnographic" work on "foreign" cultures, the "Egyptian" tetralogy of the biblical *Joseph and his Brothers*, as well as his novella *The Tables of the Law* on Moses and *The Transposed Heads. A Legend of India*.

The German émigré Indologist Henry R. Zimmer, who taught at Columbia University in New York and upon whose work Mann heavily relied for the latter novella,[91] prophesizes in a 1943 letter to the US-philanthropist Mary Mellon, right before the inaugural publication of the first volume of the famous *Bollingen Series* in émigré Kurt Wolff's newly established publishing house Pantheon Books:

> There will be quite a wave, a high tide of symbolism and mythology in the next years. Wherever I look I see symptoms of this turn. The Mellon Foundation could not come in more timely. It will command an increasing audience from the very beginning and make many people aware of things they were looking for all the while without knowing it.[92]

Rather than Zimmer, who died of pneumonia not long after writing this letter at age 52 on March 20, 1943, it was rather the independent scholar and late protégé of Zimmer Joseph Campbell, who, while "on an extended Bollingen fellowship"[93] funded by the Mellons, shaped the project of world folklore as "comparative mythology."[94] Especially Campbell's postwar work *The Hero with a Thousand Faces*[95] would become famous for its lasting influence on Hollywood, starting with George Lucas' *Star Wars* trilogy. Campbell, who first met Mann thanks to the introduction by Meyer in 1939, emerged as one of Mann's most influential US-American readers – and collaborators – thanks to his and Henry Morton Robinson's book[96] on Joyce's *Finnegans Wake*, generated as "Work in Progress" between 1923 and 1939. Campbell had gifted Mann his coauthored book, while the latter was writing *Doctor Faustus* in August 1944. "After lunch in Campbell's book on 'Finnigans [sic] Wake.' Perhaps, it is *the* ingenious literary work of the epoch. Mine should seem like tenuous traditionalism. But Mr. C. [Campbell] admires it [Mann's work] as well and sees kinship."[97] Mann's knowledge of Joyce, until then, had been largely mediated through a monograph by Harry Levin, imbued with comparative remarks to Mann's work.[98] Levin's interpretation of Joyce emphasizes the need for *keys* (map and myth in the case of *Ulysses*), "The keys to,"[99] as Levin quotes from *Finnegans Wake*. Levin's book is also a strong contender for being the model of Mann's appropriation[100] of the term "montage."

The international psychoanalytic movement, under the direction of Jung, had its headquarters in Zurich during the war years while Joyce was writing *Ulysses*, and he could scarcely have resisted its influence. And, although philosophy could not have offered him much in the way of immediate data, it is suggestive to note that Bergson, Whitehead, and others – by reducing things-in-themselves to a series of organic relations – were thinking in the same direction. Thus the very form of Joyce's book is an elusive and eclectic *Summa* of its age: the *montage* of the cinema, impressionism in painting, *leit-motif* in music, the free association of psychoanalysis, and vitalism in philosophy.[101]

Campbell's response to Levin's method of interpretation – the "skeleton" key – instead transforms Joyce's book into a reader's digest.[102] It states that – as Mann probably noticed – "[t]he first page and a half of *Finnegans Wake* hold in suspension the seed energies of all the characters and plot motifs of the book."[103] In fact, Campbell had learned the first page and a half by heart[104] and commented on them in a popular lecture, held for example at a meeting of the James Joyce Society in 1951.[105] It was precisely this humanist public lecture mode of delivery, dissolving the novel through and into liberal arts,[106] that allowed for the recognition of the aforementioned kinship between the two authors – especially in their manner of recognizing kinship. Even if Mann found no direct access to Joyce's book – and even less had been able to identify a supposed germ cell or "seed energy," he might have found already on the second page of Campbell and Robinson's *Skeleton Key* a description of "Finnegan" that resonated with his "old note" on Doctor Faustus:

> The first clue to the method and mystery of the book is found in its title, *Finnegans Wake*. Tim Finnegan of the old vaudeville song is an Irish hod carrier who gets drunk, falls off the ladder, and is apparently killed. His friends hold a deathwatch over his coffin; during the festivities someone splashes him with whisky, at which Finnegan comes to life again and joins in the general dance. On this comedy-song foundation, Joyce bases the title of his work. But there is more, much more, to the story. Finnegan the hod carrier is identifiable with Finn MacCool, captain for two hundred years of Ireland's warrior-heroes, and most famous of Dublin's early giants. Finn typifies *all* heroes – Thor, Prometheus, Osiris, Christ, the Buddha – in whose life and through whose inspiration the race lives. It is by Finn's coming again (Finn-again) – in other words, by the reappearance of the hero – that strength and hope are provided for mankind.[107]

It is useful to point once more to the philological groundwork creating the condition of possibility for recognizing the "mythic recurrence" of Finnegan = Finn-again, for Joyce, Mann, and Campbell as well. It is the result of decades of recording, collecting, cataloging, and editing of oral and written "folk literature." These efforts were most prominently synthesized in one of the great achievements of folklore studies, the *Motif-Index of Folk-Literature*.[108] First published simultaneously in Scandinavia and the United States between 1932 and 1936 as a collaboration between the Finnish School of folklore and the Harvard based[109] enterprise of American folklore study, this publication represents the first coherent turn of the century North-Atlantic literary system.[110] Its influential classificatory scheme, the "Aarne-Thompson-Index," though criticized for its regional imbalances, provided for the first time a global analysis of folk-literature, creating a synoptic arrangement that indeed suggested to reveal a universal kinship of world mythology arising from the very movement of motifs as a literary medium common to all humanity.[111] In this specific sense and at that historical juncture, the (folklorist) medium became the (social) message in *Doctor Faustus*.

4.4 THOMAS MANN'S MEMORANDUM TO THE GERMAN PEOPLE

Concluding three months of preparatory work in which he delved into German folklore and its literary fabrics, the onset of the writing process finally confirmed that Mann's association with the Library of Congress not only provided the financial, material, and conceptual means to support his writing, but indeed generated the novel itself. As Mann received more books from the Library of Congress – to point out some little-noticed biographical fragments in the plethora of notes in his diaries – Meyer, who was a staunch opponent of Roosevelt and his New Deal, returned from her journey through the working-class districts of the United States as a "socialist,"[112] thereby providing Mann with new political latitude. Mann had firsthand experience with intoxication as he took heroin to alleviate a severe cough.[113] His son Klaus Mann trained as an intelligence officer to join the US war effort on the ground to break through into the "Fortress Europe."[114] Thomas Mann maintained regular contact with literal mediumism through the person of Eva Hermann, one of his émigré neighbors in Pacific Palisades, for example, by having lunch with her on the day he started to write *Doctor Faustus*.[115] Furthermore, a member of the musical avant-garde residing in his vicinity in the Greater Los Angeles Area, composer Arnold Schoenberg, told Mann that since about 1940, "modern music, including 12 tone music, was approved of, in a certain sense favored"[116] in Nazi Germany. Then, on May 20, following a conflict with Meyer, Mann started to compose a "Letter of Divorce,"[117] both breaking up his intimate friendship with Meyer and announcing the resignation from his position at the Library of Congress – at the time still the Mann family business's only reliable source of income. Two days later, Mann drafted a corresponding letter to MacLeish, but still held off sending either one. Although Mann later accused Meyer of distracting him from his work, it was precisely from this imagined artistic outsider position that he began to write *Doctor Faustus* the next day, on May 23. Not only started Mann working with a ready complex of motifs, as quoted above, but also, freed from the social constraints of his bourgeois life, as a bohemian: "Began to write 'Dr. Faust' in the morning./ (Introduction Zeitblom)."[118] After diligently preparing one of his propaganda messages for the BBC over the next days, he finally sent his letter to Meyer on May 26.[119] Owing to MacLeish's prompt intervention and Meyer's capitulation, Mann and Meyer quickly made amends. Nevertheless, Mann's – temporary and largely virtual – enactment of bohemian defiance and a-sociality, this time eluding not Lübeck's bourgeois narrowness, Munich's charismatic intellectual circles,[120] or neutral Switzerland's "demand for tact,"[121] but the cool collaborative objectivity of the US memorandum culture, conditioned the composition of his late work, first outwardly, and later also inwardly in the genre of an American social novel.

Already in 1935, two years after leaving Germany for Switzerland and one year after his first visit to the United States,[122] Mann had started to sense and ruminate on the formatting that would suit best his speech and allow him to "address" Nazi Germany. As he wrote in his diary on Good Friday:

Since a few days, I've been deliberating besides the novel-problems the thought of a newly planned political piece [Politikum], a missive or *memorandum to the German people* [emphasis added], in which the feelings of the world towards them are elucidated and in which they should be warned of the fate of an inimicus generis humani [enemy of the human race] in a warm, truthful manner. Once again, I am dealing with the political salvation of the soul, for which I am constantly searching the proper and appropriate form, – but also the proper and appropriate occasion and situation [...].[123]

Mann only started his public addresses in 1936, after a long period of silence. In his first *memorandum to the German people* then, he staked his continued claim, as an émigré, on the concept of "German national literature."[124] It was this entanglement between German national literature and memorandum, forged on the 'ground floor' of the *Neue Zürcher Zeitung* as part of a local scuffle, that became Mann's (Swiss[125]) tool to enter as a mediator into the US-American memorandum culture. This holds true for his previously mentioned propaganda speeches, *Listen Germany! (Deutsche Hörer!)*,[126] produced for the BBC, in which he perfected his art of addressing, from: Thomas Mann to: the German nation, based again on a memorandum by the BBC,[127] but also for his speeches from: Thomas Mann to: the US-American nation.

Mann delivered five addresses at the Library of Congress, "The Theme of the Joseph Novels" (1942), "The War and the Future" (1943), "Germany and the Germans" (1945), "Nietzsche's Philosophy in the Light of Contemporary Events" (1947), "Goethe and Democracy" (1949),[128] showcasing his insights in the field of German culture and literature during and after World War II. A sixth address planned for 1950 was canceled amid the peak of McCarthyism. Among these evening lectures, held in front of Washington's "power elite"[129] in the Coolidge Auditorium of the Library of Congress, three fall directly into the phase of Mann's conception and writing of *Doctor Faustus* from 1943 to 1947. In particular, "Germany and the Germans," delivered on May 29, 1945, under the impression of Nazi Germany's unconditional surrender, played a crucial role early on as a key to a political reading of *Doctor Faustus*.[130] After "That Man Is My Brother"[131] ("Bruder Hitler"), an essay in which Mann argued six years earlier[132] for a German kin liability and his own moral self-implication,[133] "Germany and the Germans" embraces a strict cultural relativist perspective on the enemy, "from the Romantics to Hitler." "German *Romanticism*, what is it but an expression of this finest German quality, German inwardness [Innerlichkeit]? [...]"[134] German inwardness, according to Mann, is the source of Germany's greatest national accomplishments, but it is equally at the root of National Socialism: "[R]educed to a miserable mass level, the level of a Hitler, German Romanticism broke out into hysterical barbarism [...], which now finds its horrible end in a national catastrophe, a physical and psychic collapse without parallel. [...]" He therefore concludes, as "an American citizen" who speaks in "English" and as "an official member of the American state institution," where his "type of Germanism is most suitably at home [...], the racial and national universe called America"[135]:

[T]he story of German "inwardness" [...] should convince us of one thing: that there are *not* two Germanys, a good one and a bad one, but only one, whose best turned into evil through devilish cunning. Wicked Germany is merely good Germany gone astray, good Germany in misfortune, in guilt, in ruin. [...] Not a word of all that I have just told you about Germany or tried to indicate to you, came out of alien, cool, objective knowledge, it is all within me, I have been through it all. In other words, what I have tried to give you here within the limits of time, was a piece of German self-criticism; and truly, nothing could have been more faithful to German tradition."[136]

After declining an offer in November 1943 by an initiative of the Free-Germany movement, later organized in the "Council for a Democratic Germany" to take on the role of president of a German government in exile,[137] Mann represents Germany at the moment of its defeat as a mediator between German culture and the USA, proclaiming his vision for Germany's future – and the social program for his novel: "Should it not be possible after all that the liquidation of Nazism may pave the way for a *social world reform* [emphasis added] which would offer the greatest prospect of happiness to Germany's very inclinations and needs."[138] If inwardness was at the root of the problem, the new national literature for Germany needs to be a social (world reform) novel.

In the course of arguably his most powerful enactment as mediator, Mann subtly reintroduces the theme of folklore: "[Romanticism] raised the treasures of song and story from the depths of folk culture of the past; Romanticism was the genial patroness of the science of folklore [...]."[139] Two years earlier, in his address "The War and the Future," which was predicated on his indirect reception of Franz Neumann's *Behemoth*,[140] Mann suggested that the new German national literature needed to reestablish sociality as such. "[N]ational socialism means: 'I do not want the social at all. I want the folk fairy-tale.'"[141] Conversely, one is lead to think that for Mann, social reform would have to start with the folk fairy tale. Especially when uttered at the Library of Congress and with regard to *Doctor Faustus*, his statement on National Socialism is anything but an innocent claim. Indeed, in line with Botkin's concept mentioned earlier, Mann proposes in his 1945 address – a proposal that distinguishes his study of the German national character from virtually all others –, the approach of "applied folklore" in order to deal with Germany and the Germans, starting with an amendment of German folklore, performed in *Doctor Faustus*: "It is a grave error on the part of legend and story not to connect Faustus with music. He should have been musical, he should have been a musician."[142] Put differently: At the end of World War II, and from a Library-of-Congress-point-of-view, Mann created *Doctor Faustus* as "applied folklore" to "assist in the re-education"[143] of Nazi Germany. According to him, this reeducation of Germany, however, is also a task of universal importance to humanity: "In the end the German misfortune is only the paradigm of the tragedy of human life. And the grace that Germany so sorely needs, my friends, all of us need it."[144]

4.5 FAUSTIAN BREACHING EXPERIMENTS

Around the same time that Mann started writing his speech "Germany and the Germans" in February 1945, he had just finished the central chapter 25 of his novel – Adrian Leverkühn's manuscript, which records his dialogue with the devil. In this dialogue, the Christological parallel between German catastrophe and human tragedy is brought to a theological extreme, spurring some of the most important contemporary interpretations in the post-war years.[145] Social world reform of inwardness in *Doctor Faustus*, however, was still in need of a literary device – a new genre in a new setting:

> At present, Faustus has entered in a phase of the social novel [Gesellschaftsroman]. It plays now in Munich, and I am digging in my memories of the social life in Munich in 1910. Adrian of course hardly fits into the atmosphere of this plain Capua [allusion to a famous poem by Viennese playwright Franz Grillparzer, FP], which then should become the "cradle of the [National Socialist] movement."[146]

Mann had started to introduce Munich[147] and the "Kridwiss circle" right before the "climax," in chapter 23, as the main intellectual point of reference, underlying the sociality of the rest of the novel. On the level of writing practices "digging in his memories" meant for Mann to revert to and process an old convolute of his materials, the "Maja-project,"[148] which included love letters and biographical notes. The material originated from Mann's time in Munich in the early 1900s, contemporaneous to the imagined time of Leverkühn's "infection" in *Doctor Faustus*. Mann held on to this material throughout his emigration and, lacking direct access to Nazi Germany, he now treated it as an invaluable source for his "humaniora,"[149] Mann's folklore studies. The social novel of Munich brought along its own social psychological baggage – apparently inescapable for Mann – the narrative of degeneration (of Adrian Leverkühn). This narrative had become – related to syphiliphobia – a popular structure also in Nazi German antisemitic literature. The highly problematic translation from Munich to Nazi Germany and to humanity produced, thanks to its radical application, arguably the most important aesthetic insight in *Doctor Faustus*. In the longest chapter of his novel, in which, after thorough preparation for this moment in the preceding chapters, Mann's literary artistry fully culminates, he inconspicuously introduces in the devil's speech the new turn of phrase: to "break through [Durchbruch]."[150] In the further course of *Doctor Faustus*, mostly in the speech of the protagonist Adrian Leverkühn, the meaning of "breakthrough" shifts in various contexts, ultimately relying on the formative war experience of Mann's generation: to break through the enemy front lines in World War I, Germany's attempt to break through to world power, to break through to a new political life form, to break through from culture back to cult,[151] to break through artistic isolation into the world, to reach a breakthrough in artistic production. The term breakthrough aptly denotes the intrinsic involvement of modern art in political and religious struggles, struggles in which Mann also participated and without which his work cannot be understood. By allowing these extremely heteronomous conceptions to coincide, Mann provides a striking reformulation of what the French military term "avantgarde" arguably also expresses in relation to artistic aesthetics: the reversibility and mutual intensification between "devil ecstasy," "enemy ecstasy," and "artistic ecstasy," which is also displayed in the climactic structure of the novel. The narrative pinnacles toward the "middle" chapter about the artist's pact with the devil, instigated by the protagonist's earlier conscious infection with syphilis through sexual intercourse with a woman called Esmeralda by Adrian Leverkühn in Poszony, Hungary.[152]

Generation and degeneration of the novel coincide in the final chapter, with which I want shall conclude my reconstruction of Mann's novel's entanglements in the American memorandum culture. Here, a reading of Mann's *Doctor Faustus* as applied German folklore comes full circle. Adrian Leverkühn's parting speech marks his final artistic performance – a rigorous conclusion to Mann's initial bohemian a-sociality[153] – presented as an early example of Californian social scientific methodology, of an "expectancy breaching procedure."[154] On the occasion of his final breakthrough, Adrian Leverkühn had gathered and set up his social circle from Munich around himself in Pfeiffering for a breaching experiment, not only by reenacting Doctor Faustus, but – approaching a trancelike state – turning into him.

- As Adrian Leverkühn addresses the people with obsolete expressions, they first laugh and grin amusedly. As this continues, however, the crowd becomes more and more confused –

From here and there again came some polite laughter [...], though with some embarrassment.[155]

- Then he starts indirectly to talk about the presence of the devil –

Here once again there were scattered snorts of laughter, but there were also several people who clicked their tongues, and shook their heads, too, as if at some tactless indiscretion, and some eyes took on a darkly probing look.[156]

– The references to the devil turn explicit –

An embarrassed, tense silence now reigned in the room. A few people were still listening comfortably, but one also saw a good many raised eyebrows and faces in which one read the question: What is he getting at, what is this all about? If just once he had smiled or winked by way of marking his words as artistic mystification, it would have set things halfway right again. But he did not, and instead sat there in ashen earnest. [...]¹⁵⁷

– He explains his pact with the devil –

I [Serenus Zeitblom] flinched, for at this point a voice from the audience interrupted – that of the poet Daniel Zur Höhe in his clerical garb, who struck a blow with his foot and pronounced his hammering judgment, "It is beautiful. It has beauty. Indeed, indeed, one can say that!" [...] [A] relieved "Ah, yes!" passed through the assembly, and one lady, the wife of Radbruch the publisher, felt encouraged by Zur Höhe's words to say, "One feels one is listening to poetry."¹⁵⁸

– He gets explicit about his sexual encounter with the prostitute, sent by the devil –

At these words there was a stir in the audience and someone made to leave. [...] But the other guests showed no discernible inclination to follow this example. They sat as if spellbound, and when the sounds of departure had died away outside, Zur Höhe was once again heard to utter his peremptory, "Beautiful! No doubt whatever, it is beautiful!"¹⁵⁹

– He declares that he murdered the people that he loved –

At this point another group of guests left the room [...].¹⁶⁰

– He speaks of children playing music in his room, showing signs of putrefaction –

These words were once again the signal for several listeners to leave the room [...]. Sixtus Kridwiss, however, at whose home they held their disputations, remained in his seat, but with a very agitated look-along with some twenty others who still remained after these departures, though many of them were standing now, evidently ready to flee. Leo Zink held his eyebrows raised in malicious expectation, repeating his "Jesus!" the way he used to do when passing judgment on someone's painting. As if to protect him, a few women had collected around Leverkühn [...].¹⁶¹

– He declares his own damnation and announces that he is going to play now the music of the devil –

"This man," we heard the clearly articulated, if asthmatic voice of Dr. Kranich say in the silence, "this man is mad. Of that there can no longer be any doubt, and it is regrettable that no one representing psychiatric science is part of our circle. I, as a numismatist, consider myself completely incompetent here." And with that he left.[162]

– He attempts to sing, but collapses. It is at this point that Frau Schweigestill, the representative of the German folk, intervenes and separates Adrian Leverkühn from his audience –

Clear out, all of you! You haven't the least understanding, you city folk, and there's need of understanding here. He talked a lot about eternal grace, the poor man, and I don't know if it reaches that far. But real human understanding, believe me, that reaches far enough for all![163]

The artistic impersonation of German inwardness has imploded, and for the sake of future social world reform, Doctor Faustus returns into folklore.

The ending of Mann's novel on the German catastrophe remains enigmatic, but possibly, its interpretation as a breaching experiment opens up a new line of inquiry that I will pursue in the next chapter. How does one study and possibly reform such a culture of inwardness that actively declares to be incomprehensible for non-Germans? One possible route lies in social scientific studies of its popular self-expressions, for which particularly Nazi German film propaganda provides rich materials.

5

Nazi German Media Theory

In the early 1940s the world's biggest center for film studies was the Film Library of the New York Museum of Modern Art.[1] Founded in 1935, the Film Library formed part of a large-scale initiative directed by John Marshall, a Rockefeller Foundation officer and patron of early US-American media studies,[2] who distributed large sums of money to acquire film reels and employ specialized staff. By 1942, one year after Siegfried Kracauer and one year before Gregory Bateson arrived as in-house film analysts,[3] the library personnel had reviewed 3.8 million feet of film not for academic purposes but as a service to government agencies.[4] When hiring Kracauer, but also Bateson's British friend Geoffrey Gorer three years earlier, Marshall pursued the ambitious plan of creating a "new sort of film research" that would "make film scholarship part of the humanities."[5]

The task of this chapter is to tell the story of this encounter between Kracauer and Bateson, two unorthodox members of the Frankfurt School and the Culture and Personality School, working in 1943 at that busy Film Library, analyzing the Nazi propaganda film *Hitlerjunge Quex*. The Frankfurt School as well as the Culture and Personality school formed part of the 1940s memorandum culture and produced a wealth of gray literature as they pursued collaborative projects on the study the Nazi German enemy.

With a focus on Kracauer's related writings, among others his memorandum "Propaganda and the Nazi War Film" as well as his classical study of Weimar cinema, *From Caligari to Hitler*, and Bateson's 1943 memorandum "An Analysis of the Nazi Film, Hitlerjunge Quex, (1933)," I approach this collaboration within the US-American memorandum culture in two steps.⁶ First, I lay out the improvised social scientific common ground between Kracauer and Bateson to explain their interest in *Hitlerjunge Quex*.⁷ I discuss the conceptual connection between propaganda and culture, and the shared concern with phenomena related to hypnosis and trance, through a microanalysis of Kracauer's and Bateson's interpretation of billowing flags in *Hitlerjunge Quex*. Second, I situate the collaboration in Bateson's adventurous professional path from social anthropologist to film analyst to cybernetic communication theorist. Here I identify an inconspicuous but recurring problem in Bateson's work: his conceptualization of a specific form of rhythmic muscular tremor called "clonus." I relate Bateson's interpretation of clonus to all the previously mentioned aspects of culture and propaganda, as well as hypnosis and trance. This fosters a better understanding of Bateson's curious "media theory" at work in his analysis of *Hitlerjunge Quex* and how it considers trance media and mass media within a single conceptual framework. Finally, this is a chapter about the mystifying, troubling, and eerily mesmerizing lyrics of a song.

5.1 CULTURE, KULTUR, AND PROPAGANDA

At the brink of World War II, few could rival the critical knowledge of Weimar cinema than Kracauer.⁸ During the later years of his exile in Paris, he turned to the problem of propaganda. Together with his wife, Elisabeth Kracauer,⁹ and with the support of Max Horkheimer's exiled Institute of Social Research in New York, he wrote between 1936 and 1938 an extensive study on totalitarian propaganda. This work, Kracauer hoped, would open doors and secure him and his wife a transatlantic passage to the United States. To his dismay, however, the first review of the text by the thirty-four-year-old Theodor W. Adorno was extremely unfavorable. In his report on his early mentor's text for Horkheimer and the institute,[10] Adorno remarked that "the work is neither of actual theoretical value, nor is it sufficiently based on empirical material, but expresses at times in most useful literary phrases particular experiences and observations, which carry prevalence beyond the outsider [English in original] position of the author."[11] Adorno rigorously revised the text for publication in the institute's journal *Studies in Philosophy and Sociology*, but Kracauer declined the publication offer, since he found his text "defaced beyond all recognition."[12] In 1940 Adorno recycled his abridged version for a project that had come to occupy the staff of the institute and would continue to do so for most of the coming year, the German Project[13]:

"[Leo] Löwenthal related to you my suggestion to limit the new German Project to the 'infrastructure' [Unterbau] and to replace the section on culture with propaganda. I would prepare the draft of the propaganda section following Kracauer's article, which might after all prove useful for us."[14]

In the introduction from February 24, 1941, the institute's German Project makes the case for a problem-oriented group study "to provide an understanding of National Socialism by placing the movement in its cultural setting [...]. The economic problems of totalitarianism are covered by other studies now in progress, but the cultural problems have not yet been treated on the basis of an integrative method. They will form the subject matter of this project."[15] Pitting the "culture of the Thirties" against German Kultur,[16] this brief outline describes large parts of wartime German studies conducted in the United States. The study of the Nazi German "cultural setting" through propaganda thus gained momentum: Kracauer's work on totalitarian propaganda, even if it deviated from the institute's orthodoxy, brought the German Project (which would be rejected in May–June 1941) to the Film Library. It was there that Bateson adopted the sequence *Kultur into propaganda into culture*.[17]

5.2 BATESON AND KRACAUER: TRANSLATION ASSISTANCE AT THE FILM LIBRARY

In 1942 the anthropologists Margaret Mead, central organizer of the memorandum culture, and Gregory Bateson, her husband, decided to put all new projects on hold and deal exclusively with America's enemies and especially with the threat of Nazi Germany. Within their academic circle, the Culture and Personality School sought to develop a comparative grid of culturally relativistic sociologies and psychologies,[18] and Mead and Bateson had started in 1940 to create research projects that dealt with the impossibility of conducting fieldwork in enemy nations. In the rush of events dictated by the war, they quickly wrote up and published first articles on "morale" and improvised a research program later called "the study of culture at a distance." They entered the memorandum culture of the 1940s: they worked in various private institutions and circles (Mead mainly operated from the Museum of Natural History in New York and commuted to Washington, DC), participated prominently in political action committees (Bateson held, among others, a position at the Council on Intercultural Relations and functioned as secretary of the Committee for National Morale), and formed panels for interdisciplinary conferences on the war. They interviewed German émigrés in New York, psychoanalysts and sociologists with expert knowledge of the current situation in Europe. Furthermore, they collected and analyzed cultural artifacts, audio recordings, photographs, and films. They designed an exhibition on Germany, created a card game for children to promote democracy, organized film screenings, and produced in the process vast amounts of gray literature.[19] In 1942–1943 Bateson, supported by the Film Library's Rockefeller Foundation Funds, assumed a position as a film analyst in the MoMA Film Library.[20] There he spent most of his time preparing a detailed study of the "Nazi German character" in the propaganda movie *Hitlerjunge Quex (Hitler Youth Quex)*, a "martyr film"[21] produced by the Universum-Film AG in 1933,[22] one of the recent additions to the library's European films collection.[23] *Hitlerjunge Quex* shows the conversion of a twelve-year-old boy, Heini Völker, into a Hitler Youth member and, in the terms of Eric Rentschler's classic study of Nazi cinema, into a "political medium."[24] The film is loosely based on the 1932 murder of Herbert Norkus.[25] As a martyr of the Nazi movement, he turned into the mythical "standard-bearer of the youthful Immortals, and his blood drenched the magical Blood Flag of the Hitler Youth."[26]

Before leaving the United States to conduct intelligence work and create "black propaganda" for the Office of Strategic Services,[27] Bateson circulated versions of the resulting text as a mimeographed memorandum in 1943 and again in 1945,[28] but it remained, in its entirety, unpublished until 1980 and has gone – with few exceptions – largely unnoticed.[29] Instead, shorter versions of his analysis have been much more influential in the critical reception of *Hitlerjunge Quex*. It would be wrong to speak of mere prepublications, as each of them has its own emphasis and reception history. The first publication originating from Bateson's analysis of *Hitlerjunge Quex*, "Cultural and Thematic Analysis of Fictional Films," published in 1943, had the most immediate impact on the analysis of Nazi Germany during World War II. Its main takeaway was that a Jekyll-and-Hyde-style split constitutes the Nazi personality: "In fact the problem of Germany is in part a problem of preventing a pendulum from swinging too far into aggressive purity in good times and into degenerate self-contempt in bad."[30] Further parts of the analysis were published in 1953 as "An Analysis of the Nazi Film *Hitlerjunge Quex*," a composite text edited from elements of the 1943 publication and the unpublished memorandum. The 1953 summary, brilliantly reworked by Mead in *The Study of Culture at a Distance* and in the context of the Cold War, recapitulates the memorandum's most important aspects, however, with a strong bias toward an analysis of totalitarianism. It focuses on how in *Hitlerjunge Quex* communism appears as the "systematic opposite" of Nazism. Indeed, in representing the communists, "the Nazis are merely describing the worst side of their own nature"[31] – Bateson's lasting contribution to film studies.[32] A third, rather unusual, and rarely quoted but extremely influential mode of publication was a didactic version of the film *Hitlerjunge Quex* with analytic title links, including short summaries and translations, prepared for the Museum of Modern Art. Most US film scholars of the second half of the twentieth century viewed *Hitlerjunge Quex* interrupted during the film's first forty minutes time and again by Bateson's comments, an idiosyncratic but suggestive mix of political and psychological analysis of German family life, starting with a new title sequence:

In its heyday, in 1933, Nazism offered the glamor of Perpetual Youth and/or Heroic Death. And these two themes were played up to the full. The first chapter of "Mein Kampf" tells us how Hitler won the struggle against his father and became a leader of Youth, instead of growing up into a responsible bureaucrat and father of a family. If we want to know what makes a fanatical Nazi tick, we must look at how the Nazi propagandists represented the German family – how they made it appear that Youth was infinitely desirable, and what sort of "love" they took as their model when they set out to build a population of boys in love with Death. The film represents the conversion to Nazism of Heini, a 12-year-old boy. Partly he is converted by an idealized picture of "Nazism," set against a caricature of "Communism" – but, more significantly, his conversion is woven into a stock picture of German family life. Our analysis will deal with this question: How are the loves and hates in the stereotyped German family invoked and rearranged by the propagandist to make them support Nazism?

Bateson's didactic title links are structured toward his diagrammatic analysis of the film's plot, with special attention to family and sexual relations, including Quex's and National Socialism's homoerotic inclinations. Taken together, these three publications contain several of the main ideas relevant for the following analysis.

Bateson's full memorandum, however, first published in 1980, is the most comprehensive and nuanced account of his film-analytic work. "An Analysis of 'Hitlerjunge Quex'" attempts a cultural analysis through propaganda analysis. In a virtuoso composition, Bateson sees two major "cycles" toward the protagonist's death, "first his incomplete death when his mother turns on the gas and second, his final death at the hands of the Communist."[33] He scrutinizes the film's family structure, its representation of political affiliation, and its quasi-religious motives, interweaving these themes into one of the great intellectual achievements of the memorandum culture. It should therefore serve as the most important source

5.2 Translation Assistance at the Film Library

for further studies of Bateson's analysis of the culture of Nazi Germany in *Hitlerjunge Quex* and, as this chapter intends to show, his collaboration with Kracauer at the Film Library.

When Bateson arrived at the library, Kracauer had already established himself as the institution's *spiritus rector*, even if he lacked a steady position due to his legal status as friendly enemy alien.[34] Especially his publication of "Propaganda and the Nazi War Film" in 1942 distinguished Kracauer within the library and beyond. The collaboration between Kracauer and Bateson during their overlapping tenure in the first months of 1943, as far as one can reconstruct it, was based on translation assistance. Bateson, who rated his German-language skills in a CV of the early 1940s as "read with difficulty," asked Kracauer for help in translating German idiomatic expressions like *Schinkenkloppen* (a game of spanking in *Hitlerjunge Quex*). It is likely that these discussions of cultural concepts led Kracauer to lecture the eager ad hoc film analyst Bateson about German film history – *From Caligari to Hitler* in 1943 – as one must assume from Bateson's confident references to Weimar and Nazi cinema at the time he wrote his study later that year.[35] Kracauer's historical claim that Weimar cinema prefigured the monstrous characters and events that then became real clearly informs Bateson's argument.[36] Beyond that, Bateson's notes leading to "An Analysis of 'Hitlerjunge Quex'" show that he adopted and developed Kracauer's vocabulary and method of "Structural Analysis,"[37] as presented in appendix 1 of "Propaganda and the Nazi War Film." In particular, Bateson's analysis is inspired by the interpretation of one of Kracauer's observations that associates the advancement of German soldiers with the waving of flags.[38]

> The soldiers eat on the march and sleep in airplanes, on travelling tanks, guns and trucks [...]. This eternal restlessness is synonymous with impetuous advance, as the Nazi films never fail to point out through moving maps and marching infantry columns [...]. Their appearance on the screen is particularly well suited to conveying the idea of advance, and that is obviously the effect strived for. It is obtained, too, by repeated closeups of waving Swastika banners, which, by the way, serve the additional purpose of hypnotizing audiences.[39]

Bateson's influence on Kracauer, on the other hand, surfaces in a single detail, an inconspicuous question of translation. This detail, however, is crucial and warrants more careful attention, namely, the rendering of the word flattern in the Hitler Youth song "Vorwärts! Vorwärts! Schmettern die hellen Fanfaren" (Forward! Forward! Blare the bright fanfares), written by Youth leader Baldur von Schirach on the occasion of the film production of Hitlerjunge Quex (Figure 5.1).

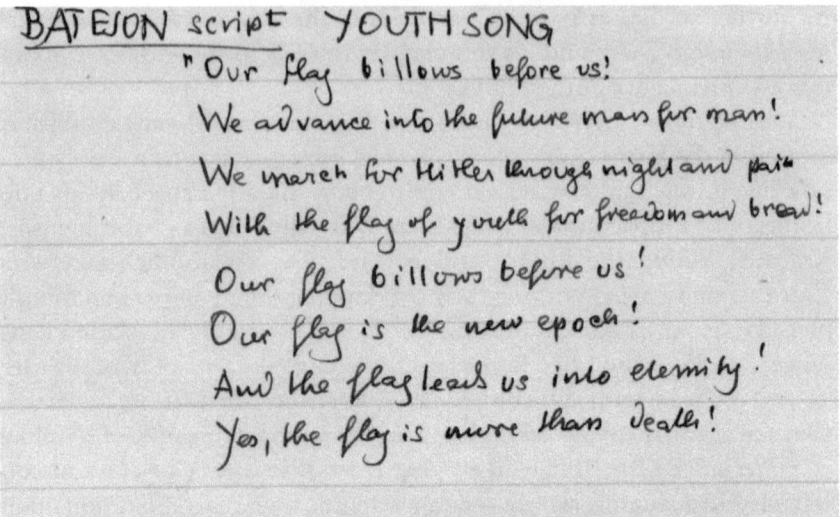

FIGURE 5.1 Kracauer's note of Bateson's translation (Von Caligari zu Hitler [Vorarbeiten], Kapitel 16–21, Ma 7 T1, Siegfried Kracauer Nachlass). Courtesy of Suhrkamp Verlag.

In the concluding chapter of *From Caligari to Hitler*, "National Epic," Kracauer tries to capture the Nazi tendencies of "mountain films" produced in the early 1930s, especially in their relation to more explicitly political "national films." In particular, Kracauer characterizes Luis Trenker, a South Tyrolean alpinist, filmmaker, and actor, as a "rebel" and argues that the use of a "flag" serves as proof for the proto–Nazi character of Trenker's movies. To establish a strict connection between rebel and flag, he first makes a reference to Erik Homburger Erikson's psychoanalysis of Adolf Hitler.[40] The paraphrase,[41] however, is so obscure that Kracauer must have assumed a general knowledge that no longer exists. Erikson, affiliated to the academic circle around Mead and Bateson, interpreted the Nazi appeal to the German people based on his analysis of Hitler as a figure that "asks both fathers and sons to identify with the Führer; *an adolescent who never gave in.*"[42]

Kracauer then moves from the Nazi adolescent rebel to the flag: "To enhance national passion, elaborate use is made of close-ups of flags, a device common with the Nazis."[43] He explains the role of the flag in the final scene of Trenker's *Rebel* and then describes a similar use of the flag in *Hitlerjunge Quex*, one of the first propaganda movies to employ adolescents as its protagonists: "This apotheosis of rebellious ardor is all but duplicated in *Hitlerjunge Quex*."[44] Kracauer refers to the Hitler Youth song "Vorwärts! Vorwärts!" and its chorus, which pervades *Hitlerjunge Quex*. At this point Kracauer might be expected to quote his own translation of the first line of the chorus "Uns're Fahne flattert uns voran," etymologically close to the original, "Our banner flutters before us."[45] Instead, he chose Bateson's version: "Our flag billows before ... "[46] The wavelike quality of "to billow" that is lost in "to flutter" (and, arguably, in the German *flattert*) guided Bateson's seminal analysis of *Hitlerjunge Quex*, I argue, "for the light which [it throws] on what makes Nazis tick."[47] And apparently, by giving preference to the verb *to billow*, Kracauer adopted Bateson's line of interpretation.[48]

In a footnote, Bateson adds to his text a lengthy explanation about why he preferred *billow* instead of *flutter* to describe the flag's waving. This choice seems to have resulted from extensive discussions about the term with several people, most likely including Kracauer:

> In translating the "Nazi Youth Song," the word *flattern* has been rendered as "billow." The dictionary meaning of this word is "flutter," and the German word is certainly sometimes used in this sense (e.g. in referring to birds.) A small experiment shows, however, that Americans, when asked to visualize a flag fluttering, usually see a small flag moving rapidly or a large flag rather far away, whereas the image called up in Germans by the words *Fahne* and *flattern* is of a large flag close up. In Nazi films, the flags are usually photographed to fill the frame, so that the emphasis falls not to the changing outline of the flag, but rather on the wave motion in the middle of the fabric. This billowing motion is clearly intended to have a fascination similar to that of waves in water.[49]

To understand the impact of this minor difference in word choice, *flattern* – "to flutter" – "to billow"[50] – Bateson's work in the Film Library on Nazi Germany needs to be situated within several of the many spheres of his work before and after, that is, as the "missing link" in Bateson's biography between his fieldwork as a British social anthropologist studying the Iatmul of the Sepik River region of New Guinea, as well as the people of Bajoeng Gede in Bali,[51] and his later work as a communication theorist within the cybernetic circles established through the conferences organized by the Josiah Macy Jr. Foundation. In short, the hypnotic quality of the billowing flag, its endless waving, connects Bateson's and Mead's anthropological analysis of schizophrenia in "primitive" people, particularly expressed in Balinese trance rituals, to what Bateson later called "psychology," contemporary neurophysiological research conducted on clonus, a specific form of rhythmic muscular tremor.[52]

Or even shorter, expressed in a scheme: clonus (trance) – to billow (propaganda) – clonus (cybernetics).

5.3 MEDIA EDUCATION IN *HITLERJUNGE QUEX*

To reevaluate Bateson's work on cybernetics, propaganda, and trance, it proves helpful to put Bateson's work into perspective from the moment of his own retrospective, during which his full memorandum was first published in 1980, the year of his death. Only in 1977, more than three decades after his work in the Film Library, in an address delivered to a conference in New York, did Bateson refer explicitly to the connection between clonus and cybernetics:

> To this "law" [of sensory perception] Norbert Wiener added a second part which I think he never published fully, though *I consider it to be the most important item in "psychology" after the original Weber-Fechner-Law* [emphasis added]. Wiener was working on the formal structure of that cybernetic oscillation of muscle called *clonus* [emphasis added] and found that the tension of an isometric muscle is proportional to the logarithm of the frequency of neural impulses reaching the muscle. A most elegant finding, which shows that (expectably, though it took one hundred years to get there) the efferent side of the brain works by the same epistemological limits as the afferent.[53]

The rhythmic muscular tremor called clonus came to be one of the classical examples that contributed to the shaping of cybernetics.[54] However, Bateson's offhand remark about "the formal structure of that cybernetic oscillation of muscle called clonus" was more than a footnote to Wiener's research. It came about two years after a more thorough reinterpretation of his own early work in his essay "Some Components of Socialization for Trance," without directly quoting Wiener's research but specifically discussing muscular clonus. Clonus is central to Bateson's work, I argue, because it helps us to understand the relationship between his studies of "mind" and body,[55] as well as between his studies of Balinese and German culture, that is, in the terms of his intellectual circle between culture and personality.

In 1975 Bateson looked at his and Mead's book of 1942, *Balinese Character*, which includes a photographic analysis of Balinese culture and personality, a work completed at the same time that they analyzed the "German Character." The volume was the first major publication of materials from their fieldwork in Bali in the late 1930s, which was funded by a grant from the "Committee for Research in Dementia Praecox."[56] Bateson had employed photography and film to document a foreign culture, taking stills and film at the same time, with one camera in his hand and the other around his neck.[57]

5.3 Media Education in Hitlerjunge Quex

In *Balinese Character* the photographic representations of Balinese culture were Bateson and Mead's main analytic tool, while writing was reserved for the introduction and the descriptive notes to the book's hundred plates. Already in 1942 and contemporaneously with their New Yorker "Cerebral Inhibition Meeting" discussing "hypnosis" and "conditioned reflex,"[58] clonus had caught his and Mead's attention in "plate 18," as they had used psychological terminology to characterize "dementia praecox," or schizophrenia. The plate depicts the arrangement created for the purpose of transitioning two young girls into a trance state while four men are holding strings to which dolls are attached. These men's arms perform involuntary jerking movements and therefore appear to turn into independent limbs. Mead and Bateson interpret this phenomenon in relation to dementia praecox, as a disintegration of the men's psychological and bodily coherence.[59]

"After a few minutes, trembling or changes in tension of the string set up *clonic contractions* [emphasis added] in the arms of the two men, and the dolls begin to 'dance.' [...] Rhythmic clonic contraction is an example of a part of the body taking its own independent integration."[60] In his 1975 reinterpretation Bateson commented on the same phenomenon, replacing the cultural specificity of the Balinese case with the universalizing terms of cybernetics. "This oscillation is called *clonus* in neurophysiology and is a recurrent series of patellar reflexes, generated in a feedback circuit. The effect of each contraction is fed back as a modification of tension to the calf muscle. This change of tension triggers the next patellar reflex."[61] The same sequential paradox, Bateson argues, is generated "in, for example, a buzzer circuit."[62] Although the brain has no direct control over the involuntary contractions of antagonizing muscles, it may serve, according to Bateson, as a higher authority that can regulate or stop the oscillations with "meta-injunctions."[63]

Bateson's essay "Some Components of Socialization for Trance" (1975) could be understood as such a "meta-injunction." It exposed the poor interpretative work that the photo book on Bali had received since its publication, despite its status as founding document for what would become visual anthropology. Taking the task into his own hands and with the help of clonus, Bateson reconsidered a Balinese model of trance and used it as a basis for a theory of socialization.[64]

This theory of socialization has three key components or "teleologies."[65] These procedural patterns describe modes of experiencing alterity in Balinese trance: an inner force, leaving the body, *Outwards*; an outer force, entering the body, *Inwards*; a transformative force that creates a remotely controlled body, *New Self*. Bateson's modelization of trance in Bali deserves further analysis, all the more since his interpretation of Nazi Germany, especially in regard to trance states, is directly linked to his work on Balinese culture. Accordingly, Bateson's work on Balinese trance is crucial to a full appreciation of his collaboration with Kracauer on Nazi film propaganda. As shown in the following, Bateson's film analysis relates to his own use of media as research tools, and both relate to his media theory. A conception of media exists in Bateson's work that continues a legacy of the nineteenth century in which technical means of communication were theorized according to religious and quasi-religious modes of communication with other worlds and higher beings, for instance, grasped in the term "spiritist medium."[66] Only with this tradition in mind does it become possible to comprehend the close connection between trance and media in Bateson's work, one so close that it is fair to assume that he asked himself: What sort of trance medium is *Hitlerjunge Quex*?[67] To assess Bateson's media theory, one should employ a descriptive use of the term "media" rather than a normative one. A common misunderstanding of this method originates from the suspicion that in this way everything turns into media and that such an approach reduces the term *media* to a catchall and thus renders it meaningless. Instead, the limitation proposed here functions differently and arguably methodically even more soundly: only those few things and people that the actors in question take to be media are considered media. In the case of Bateson, then, this means the media of a certain, Balinese or Nazi German, culture.

Outwards (Bali): Bateson describes the – effortlessly achievable – induction of clonus to an academic readership, supposedly bent into chairs, as follows:

> While sitting, place the leg with thigh horizontal and foot supported on the floor. Move the foot inwards towards you so that the heel is off the floor and the ball of the foot supports the weight of the leg. When the weights and angles are correctly adjusted, an oscillation will start in the muscle of the calf with a frequency of about six to eight per second and an amplitude of about half an inch at the knee.[68]

The rhythmically shaking limb, presented as a universal experience of uncontrollable inner force, "outwards," is then, as cited earlier, recognized in the pictures in *Balinese Character*. It is the same tremor, generated in the biceps of the Balinese men during the *sanghyang déling* dance, discussed in the following.

Inwards (Bali): Bateson describes a scene of trance induction through rhythmic clonus, referring to the aforementioned plate 18 that depicts the physical education of Balinese children – although Bateson's photo camera actually could not capture the clonus. The clonus, in the first example experienced as an outward manifestation of an internal force, now becomes an outward force with an internal manifestation.

In plate 18, two little girls are put into the trance state in which they will dance. The procedure is a little complicated: two dolls, weighted with bells, are threaded on a string about fifteen feet long which is strung between two vertical bamboo sticks. The sticks are held by two men in such a way that clonus in their biceps will change the tension in the string causing the dolls or *dedari* (angels) to dance up and down, while the weighted dolls provide a feedback promoting the clonus in the men's arms. When the *dedari* are dancing fast, the girl who is to go into trance takes hold of the shaking stick so that she is violently shaken by the man's clonus. Meanwhile the crowd around is singing songs about *dedari*. The girl's action in holding the stick breaks the rhythm of the clonus and she takes control of the stick beating with its end upon the wooden stand that supports it. She beats out a few bars of the song that the crowd is singing and then falls backward into trance. She is then dressed up by the crowd and will dance as *dedari*.[69]

The two Balinese girls, I Renoe and I Misi, each experience the clonus as part of a larger, in fact, "totalizing" arrangement of various media surrounding them: doll, singing, clonus.[70] These media, however, take hold of their bodies, "inwards," and lead to the induction of a trance.

New Self (Bali): Through the mimetic identification of the *dedari* doll, dancing up and down in a self-repeating and therefore potentially endless feedback mechanism with clonic contractions, to which the respective girl is first subjected, then breaks in, only to perpetuate this "dance," the girl herself becomes a trance medium. This identification with a member of the Balinese cosmology, the angel, its public appearance in front of the crowd, perfectly captured in a photograph, marks the moment of socialization, of "self-evidence,"[71] and, with regard to critical theory, one might add, a bodily experience of "nonidentity": even after the trance has subsided, the clonus keeps on ticking. Bateson describes this process of socialization through trance as an experience of gaining a new, socialized, remotely controlled self.

"I" see my leg move but "I" did not move it. The detachment of the object [that is, the involuntary movement of a clonus as object of perception] proposes then two lines of development: (1) the possibility of "out of body experience," and (2) the possibility of integrating to perceive the body as an autonomous ego-alien entity. Either the detached "I" or the detached "body" can become the focus of elaboration. Of these paths, it is the second that Balinese follow so that, by a curious inversion, the word "raga," which seems to have the primary meaning of "body" comes to mean "self."[72]

Accordingly, one finds in Balinese arts representations of individual limbs and body parts with their own faces, representing their independent selves.[73] The clonus has traveled outward and inward and has helped create a detached new self, the Balinese trance medium.

This, in a nutshell, is Bateson's implicit media theory of socialization through trance in Bali; it also frames his analysis of *Hitlerjunge Quex*. To be sure, Bateson offers only a few hints in this direction. In a letter from January 1943, he writes that he analyzes Nazi German movies, "for the light which they throw on *what makes Nazis tick* [emphasis added] [...] – It's really all the same sort of work that we used to do in New Guinea and Bali – rather more hectic – and rather less thorough – using the best hunches that we can think of instead of waiting for complete documentation – but we still hope a good deal better than lay intuition."[74] Bateson attempted in his improvised analysis of German propaganda movies to find the functional equivalent of the Balinese clonus, "what makes Nazis tick." As such, a comparative analysis of Balinese character and Nazi German character in Bateson's sense first needs to find a common model that, as it turns out, appears in his propaganda analysis as a variation of the Balinese teleologies of trance.

Inwards (Nazi Germany): The common ground for the comparability between Nazi German tic and Balinese clonus lies in Bateson's media theory. It might be helpful for the reader's understanding to preface the citation of the respective passage in his film analysis again with a reference to his postwar work. Bateson later often evoked the epistemological underpinnings of this media theory with an elliptic reference to Alfred Korzybski's aphorism, "The map is not the territory."[75] With this reference, he highlights the distinction between different levels of abstraction in representation. The negative proposition of "the map is not the territory" needs to be emphasized because, according to Bateson, the meaning of medial presentation and representations (i.e., as explained earlier, of trance media and of technical media) tends to acquire "self-evidence" within the respective culture, thereby becoming inaccessible to immanent understanding. In both cases, Nazi Germany and Bali, Bateson attempts to work through the logical problem posed by self-evidence – and begins this process with the help of media as privileged object of inquiry.

With this in mind, one may turn now to Bateson's propaganda analysis. For Nazi German propaganda movies, Bateson assumes that "the camera [...] can lie freely about whatever passes in front of the lens, but inasmuch as the film was made by Nazis and used to make Nazis, we believe that at a certain level of abstraction the film must tell us the truth about Nazism."[76] This introductory remark to "An Analysis of 'Hitlerjunge Quex'" is significant both in the media theoretical context of his work on Bali and for his collaboration at the Film Library. The quote serves as the justification and methodological opening for his propaganda analysis, connecting it to his media theory. At the same time, it needs to be read as nothing less than Bateson's inheritance of the institute's orthodoxy for the German Project, mediated through Kracauer and his decisive impact on US propaganda studies. Propaganda analysis could be used for the anthropological study of cultures at a distance, inasmuch as Nazi ideology conveyed in propaganda was in fact an appropriate stand-in for Nazi culture. Adorno states, parallel to Bateson's study, in 1943: "Fascist hypnotism may be characterized as being essentially self-hypnotism."[77] With *Hitlerjunge Quex* Bateson takes for his analysis of Nazi German culture the film that the Nazis had chosen to make their political movement appear self-evident. Modeled according to Bateson's conception of trance, this means in analogy to the dolls dancing in front of the girls: in fact, he chose the film that was shown in ritually repeated screenings to the Hitler Youth that its members could admire themselves, without the control of their will moving in a motion picture, an outer force entering the body, "inwards."

Outwards (Nazi Germany): While it is his media theory that frames the problem of static self-evidence, Bateson also presumes a dynamic element in his understanding of the relationship between culture and personality – the process of socialization. "The most direct approach is that of looking at sequences of interchange between parents and other teachers and children in which the former are 'socializing' the latter."[78] Bateson later explained how proto- and deuterolearning,[79] that is, learning and learning to learn, need to be distinguished and – like map and territory – kept in separate categories. However, in his work on national character, he arrives at an analysis of what today would be called "media education." Here Bateson crosses the boundaries of his own theory: the process of media education is identical with the education of people as media. In the moment of socialization, the map *is* the territory, the medium is the represented, a case of false "abstraction" and confusion of "logical types,"[80] of nonidentity. This means, however, that the represented and the representation (territory and map, Balinese trance medium and angel, Hitler Youth and *Hitlerjunge Quex*) are and are not identical. Socialization is a process of creating self-evidence via transformation. It is only media education that makes self-evidence appear natural; the act of trance induction is identical with the act of socialization. Assessing *Hitlerjunge Quex* as an educational medium for young Nazis, Bateson searched for hints to locate a transition between medial education and trance induction that functions analogously to Balinese education of trance media. Indeed – finally the riddle of "to billow" may be solved – he might have located it.

Six years after the first sound film *Jazz Singer*, the soundtrack of *Hitlerjunge Quex* provides a central device that Bateson uses as starting point for his film analysis, namely, the aforementioned song of the Hitler Youth, "Vorwärts! Vorwärts!" The song describes the relation between a waving motion of the flag, endless marching and what Bateson calls, following émigré psychologist Kurt Lewin and social scientist Lawrence K. Frank, "time-perspective."

Our flag billows [*flattert*] before us! / We advance [*ziehn*] into the future man for man! We march for Hitler through night and pain [*Not*] / With the flag of youth for freedom and bread! / Our flag billows before us! / Our flag is the new epoch [*Zeit*]! / And the flag loads us into eternity [*Ewigkeit*]! / Yes, the flag is more than death![81]

Bateson finds that the Nazi time-perspective – perhaps best understood as an "applied" philosophy of history – is in parts reminiscent of the millennialism that is also present in the philosophy of history of German communists: "through chaos to Elysium."[82] The difference lies, however, in the Hitler Youth's "cult of the dead," its passage "through death to a millennium."[83] Interpreting the Hitler Youth song, Bateson describes this complex on that "certain level of abstraction" that allows one to see a transfer between film medium and Hitler Youth.

Particularly if one keeps Kracauer and the circles of the Frankfurt School in mind, the conception of Bateson's interpretation is less implausible than it might appear at first glance, as it constitutes a significant yet largely overlooked instance connecting photography and film to the philosophy of history and salvation history. Put differently, Bateson closely follows early Weimar film theory and practice modeled on hypnotic suggestion, somnambulism, and trance.[84] He points here to the "dizziness symbols" that explicitly link *Hitlerjunge Quex* to the Weimar cinema, in keeping with Kracauer's transition *From Caligari to Hitler*.[85]

Kracauer indeed revisited the same complex – with brief reference to *Hitlerjunge Quex* – in a coeval study of "Nazi Newsreels," the less prominent but in the context of Bateson's film studies highly instructive follow-up to "Propaganda and the Nazi War Film." First, Kracauer considers Nazi marching in the history of German Youth movements, "following the idealistic conception that the world is in eternal movement

5.3 Media Education in Hitlerjunge Quex

toward eternal ideals, [...] the young idealists revered movement as a goal in itself, and as they wandered aimlessly they all had the gratifying feeling of expressing a metaphysical creed."[86] In those newsreels, the marchers are, according to Kracauer, dismembered: "The former long shot picturing [the marching column] as a unit has now changed into a close shot that singles out several individual soldiers or even mere fragments of them: their heads, their torsos, their marching legs. Thus the whole gives way to the puzzling movements of its parts."[87] Later, in "Nazi Newsreels" Kracauer describes, with attention to similar details as Bateson, flags, albeit unwaveringly in Frankfurt School critical terms:[88] "Flags [...] are the accessories of the grandiose show [...]. The camera approaches them closely, with the result that the screen is alternately covered by waving flags and a forest of standards [...]. The spell of that forest reinforces the lulling effect of the flags' undulations. These pictures are an opiate, making spectators submit more readily to the image of the mass."[89] Bateson, instructed by his experience with Balinese trance, inverts the interpretation of the "lulling effect of the flags' undulations." He observes that most of these dizziness symbols situated at a fair in *Hitlerjunge Quex* are connected to communism. They exhibit, however, a communality that is employed in the film's plot of Nazi conversion.

There is clearly a rather close relationship between the hypnotic fascination that comes from staring at waves and that which comes from looking at spinning objects [noted by Bateson in the Nazi characterization of communism] [...]. There is, however, an important difference between waves and spinning objects. Waves contain an illusion of progress, of forward movements, but spinning objects evidently get nowhere. It is possible that the waves used to characterize Nazism are related to the endless marching which has such great fascination for Nazis and which appears in almost every Nazi film.[90]

Depicting communist German trance, the Nazis, again, "are merely describing the worst side of their own nature" and employ the representation of their enemy as a systematic opposite for their own trance induction.[91] It is only in this sense that Bateson's translation of the Hitler Youth song, and especially his preference for "to billow" becomes plausible and, indeed, striking. "Endless marching," following a flag that billows ahead – a German practice developed during Romanticism[92] and, as Bateson also points out,[93] central to early Youth Movements like the *Wandervögel* – plays a central role for the socialization of Hitler Youth members, an inner force, leaving the body "outwards." This practice of marching behind a billowing flag is potentially transformative: "Each death is represented on the screen by a sort of billowing or waving

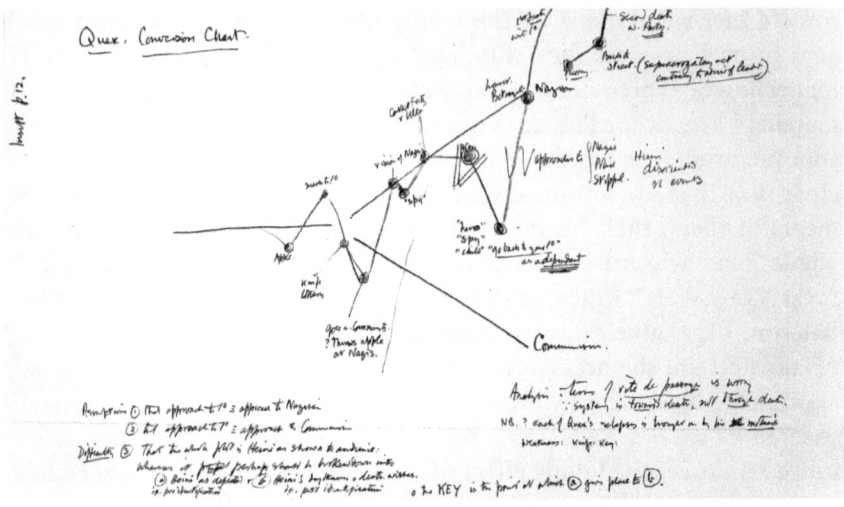

FIGURE 5.2 Quex conversion chart. The chart shows a schematic view of the plot of *Hitlerjunge Quex* (Margaret Mead Papers, box O6). Courtesy of Bateson Idea Group.

motion. In the case of the gas death, we see the fumes fill the screen and move like heaving waves. In the final death, it is the Nazi flag itself which fills the frame and billows before us."[94]

New Self (Nazi Germany): But who is this new self, emerging through the billowing of the Nazi flag? While Bateson does not speak about *Hitlerjunge Quex* in terms of media or trance, it is finally possible to fully reconstruct "Some Components of Socialization for Trance" in German propaganda film: The "Quex Conversion Chart" is a preliminary plot scheme that underlies Bateson's film analysis (Figure 5.2). Here Bateson considers Heini Völker's conversion into a Hitler Youth member as a "rite of passage," arguably the most influential anthropological concept of socialization.[95] After mapping the protagonist's developmental stages between communism and Nazism, Bateson comments on his own chart with a drawing pencil: "Heini dissociates [i]n events" or "Heini dissociates [in] n events." Even though this dissociation is not made explicit as such in Bateson's final analysis, it results in one of his central diagnoses of Nazi German culture, here presented as a lapsus (Figure 5.3). The pathology of "Nazism" in *Hitlerjunge Quex* needs to be understood as "narcissism," expressed in the movie where the protagonist admires himself at key moments before a mirror, especially when wearing a uniform.

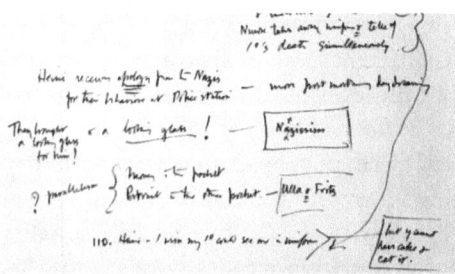

FIGURE 5.3 An indicative lapse in the notes for Bateson's film analysis – "Na[r]zissism" (Margaret Mead Papers, box O6). Courtesy of Bateson Idea Group.

Both the self-alienation in the mirror and becoming somebody else in a costume are analogous to Balinese practices. In fact, Bateson describes this narcissism explicitly as a perversion of the Balinese model – the only time that Bali is mentioned in his film analysis: "Some of the most peaceful people in the world are the most narcissistic, the Balinese, for example, are among the most peaceful and the most narcissistic. Warfare and personal aggression are virtually unknown among them, and internationally speaking, they would be ideal neighbors [...]. The important factor is what is admired in the self."[96] The aspect admired in the Hitler Youth self, or better the aspect that has to be displayed by the initiated male Hitler Youth member as his "self," is a "heel-clicking exhibitionism" of obedience and discipline,[97] continuously practiced in the Hitler Youth's physical education: "Discipline as imagined in the Nazi ideal depends upon extreme passivity – almost an impassivity – in the face of sudden, barked commands [...]. Discipline is not so much a toadying to authority as a controlled steadying in the face of sudden shock, *whether this shock be a sudden command or an enemy attack* [emphasis added]."[98] The education of Hitler Youth members finally reveals in Bateson's analysis a structure equivalent to the Balinese trance media education through clonus. Two contrary impulses, "sudden barked commands" and "enemy attack," induce one and the same physical state of trance, a remotely controlled "controlled steadying,"[99] that is, of being in cold blood in the face of terror.[100]

"There is an *a priori* case to be made out for the propagandic effectiveness of themes which are not explicit," claims Bateson in his conclusion. "The audience is rewarded by enjoyment of the film for accepting these as implicit premises and is, in a sense, punished for refusing to accept them."[101] By linking Bateson's two analyses of Bali and Germany, one may understand this distinction between implicit and explicit meaning not as opposites but as different levels of abstraction. As Bateson initially points out, it is that "certain level of abstraction" that throws light on "what makes Nazis tick." Bateson brings to the collaboration with Kracauer on the analysis of Nazi German propaganda a highly idiosyncratic methodology that is not only abstract but intends to scrutinize abstraction itself as a problem. In keeping with the Culture and Personality School's attempt to create a comparative grid of culturally relativistic sociologies and psychologies, and strongly influenced by behaviorist psychology, he finds a common matter of debate with Kracauer on the basis of the universal and universally transgressive experience of trance, hypnosis, awayness, somnambulism, extreme concentration, suggestion, controlled steadying.

Bateson ends his *Quex* memorandum with a rather obscure parable, comparing a finding from behaviorist learning experiments on rats with Nazi learning. One can read it as an application of his theory of media education – as well as a direct answer to Adorno's German Project:

> This case is based, however, upon the structure of simple learning experiments, and it is a very long step from these experiments – from the rat which learns that the sound of a buzzer is the precursor of an electric shock that can only be avoided by lifting the right foreleg – to the more complex learning phenomena with which we are here concerned. The Nazi convert learns to remodel his *Weltanschauung*, his interpretation of the universe in which he lives, and his interpretation of his own behavior. To compare him with the experimental rat, we should have to suppose that the rat learned not merely to lift his leg whenever he hears the buzzer, but also to expect future sequences to be patterned like the experimental setting: that pain would always be preceded by some warning; and that, for him, the problem of life consisted in trying to guess what magical behavior would avert these pains. Such a rat might be said to have learned not only the connection between a buzzer, lifting the leg, and pain, but also to have learned a *Weltanschauung* or ideology.[102]

Ideology (right foreleg-lifting) is experienced as the appearance of an infrastructure (electric shock), and propaganda (buzzer) sustains it. In fact, socialization into an ideology identifies infrastructure with its propaganda, to the point that the originally pain-induced trance via a buzzing sound works without reference to the infrastructure. Only when the trance is constant, that is, when it has found its media, in Bali, in Germany, and in behavioral experiments, is the permanent closing of the buzzer circuit no longer experienced as a paradox, for the socialization is complete and the ideology self-evident.

The jarring discovery of Bateson's analysis is therefore not the Nazi trance per se but its cold-bloodedness. The cult of Nazi trance is made explicit in the last verse of the chorus: "The flag is more than death!"[103] The cult of Nazi trance celebrated in *Hitlerjunge Quex* is a cult of the dead. In the film's martyr death scene (which is of a piece with the earlier symbolic death by gas), as the protagonist expires in the arms of a Hitler Youth member, the boy utters the beginning of the Hitler Youth song's chorus.[104] The camera fades to a billowing flag and the superimposed marching members of the "racial corpus."[105] "Thus, in giving Heini two deaths, the propagandist has epitomized a whole social system and a time perspective that envisages repeated symbolic deaths."[106] The Nazi movement is an imagined community of the dead and the living. Regarding the plot as a whole, Bateson himself infers: "The beginning of the cycle, through suffering and effort to individual death, is comparatively common in fanatical cults, but the final goal toward which the Nazi nominally strives is a rather unusual one. It appears to be a sort of multiple reincarnation in this world." In death, the Hitler Youth member not only arrives through death to a millennium but also becomes part of a self-multiplying collective, of a community of the dead and the living crowding the world. Indeed, *Hitlerjunge Quex* is a filmic variation of the death march on November 9, one of the most important rituals in the Nazi Party's liturgical calendar:[107]

A similar promise of multiple reincarnation is still more explicit in another Nazi film, *Fuer uns* (1937). This is a documentary account of a Nazi party ceremony in which we see the dedication of sixteen concrete blocks to the memory of the sixteen martyrs of early Nazism. Each block has on it the name of a hero (Hans [sic] Schlageter, Horst Wessel, etc.) and the words "On call" (*Zum Appel*) [sic]. Each block supports a great urn in which flames billow. As a wreath is laid at the foot of each block, the name of the hero is called, and a thousand men somewhere in the stadium answer "HERE." The procession goes on to the next hero, and again the answer comes back from another section of the stadium.[108]

Bateson finds in *Hitlerjunge Quex* an "applied" Nazi social science at work that engineers a new social psychology or "culture pattern."[109] He captures the design of this social engineering in five diagrams, the methodical innovation of his memorandum and, in regard to abstraction, his outstanding accomplishment. He first developed the idea for these diagrams while editing the aforementioned didactic version of *Hitlerjunge Quex* prior to writing the final version of his analysis, cutting up individual sequences and adding analytic title links.[110] Bateson condenses the story of *Hitlerjunge Quex* to its artificial core, with a special effect; the "culture pattern" engineered by the propagandists in the film and the social scientific model of analysis look very much

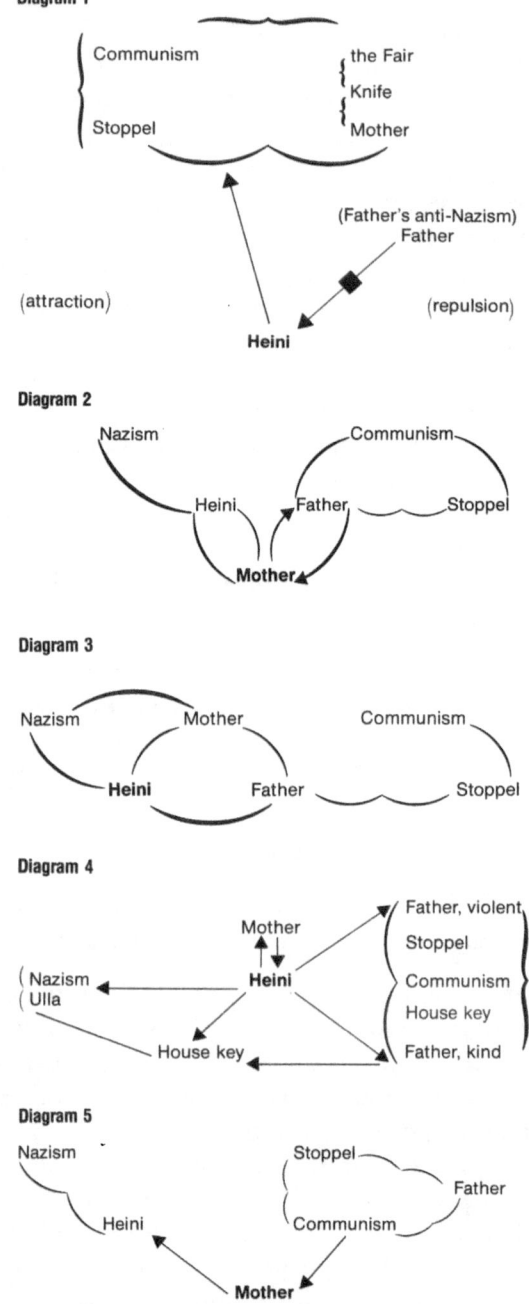

FIGURE 5.4 Bateson's diagrammatic analysis of *Hitlerjunge Quex*: double father (4), triple mother (2, 3, 5).

5.3 Media Education in Hitlerjunge Quex

alike (Figure 5.4). This uncanny resemblance recalls Adorno's observation of 1943 that "fascist propaganda is profoundly interconnected with basic trends of modern cultural anthropology."[111] Indeed, a year before writing his analysis of *Hitlerjunge Quex*, Bateson had remarked that "it is hardly an exaggeration to say that this war is ideologically about just this – the role of the social sciences."[112] And Talcott Parsons, the Harvard sociologist discussed in the following would have certainly agreed.

This must well have been the impression that Kracauer gained from this exchange. For him, Bateson was a propaganda analyst, who, despite his idiosyncratic methodology, surprisingly conformed to the orthodoxy of Horkheimer's institute. In fact, Bateson developed a hyperorthodox version of Adorno's turn to identification of German propaganda and culture, its nonidentity. Kracauer must have appreciated that Bateson's obsession with the effectiveness of propaganda went so far as to view it as inducing a trance state in personal media,[113] and thereby challenging the theory of technical media as external tools of a mass culture.[114] In that way Bateson turned the institute's orthodoxy against itself, a move condensed in the translation of German "flattert" with "billows."

6

Germany as a Conceptual Scheme

In December 1944, three months after the taking of the first German city, Monschau, located in the Western German Eifel region, the social scientist Talcott Parsons contacted William L. Langer, his former colleague at Harvard University, now head of the Research and Analysis Branch of the Office of Strategic Services (OSS), inquiring about the next tasks at hand.[1] In his letter, sent from Cambridge, Massachusetts, to Washington, DC, Parsons writes: "Dear Dr. Langer, Carl Friedrich has told me of his discussions with you about the possibility of some of us going abroad as regular members of your O.S.S. staff in connection with German problems."[2] Parsons instigates this communication, since he apparently finds the once-in-a-lifetime opportunity, for a tenured professor to be dispatched across the Atlantic to work for the OSS in Europe, worthy of further exploration and serious consideration. After all, it appears like the right thing to do, the logical next step, and a culmination both of his activism and of various intellectual projects on the German problem since 1938, a timespan during which he has managed to develop a unique social scientific expertise on the National Socialist enemy. Before writing this letter, he had spent the early part of 1944 in collaboration with Margaret Mead and others intensely analyzing Nazi German culture patterns and imagining the concrete outlines of a "goodenough" Germany, as showcased in his seminal article "The Problem of Controlled Institutional Change"[3] (1945) but also in "Germany after the War" (1945), in which he helped shape the early American discussion about reeducation.[4] In his contributions to the discussion of Germany after the war, Parsons combines American cultural anthropological conceptions with a highly informed analysis of the sources of German power in the military, business, politics, and bureaucracy. He proposes to control the post-war "situation"[5] in Germany through "controlled institutional change."[6] While keeping close tabs on revolutionary tendencies of German authoritarianism and charismatic leadership, the militarist *Junker* class,[7] and explicit National Socialist Party ideology, the future Allied Military Government should primarily act indirectly as a sort of holding environment, in which, according to Parsons, the German government then in effect will do the right thing, but according to its own dualistic culture patterns. This leaves the arduous work of renegotiating "vested interests,"[8] largely invisible to the outsider, and the exposure to potentially averse moral sentiments to "'allies' within the social system."[9] Parsons therefore advocates to refrain from the urge to exert direct influence on the German population through social engineering measures[10] and recommends considering the interplay and consequences of calculated actions, that is, taking a systemic approach. One should "[u]tilize every opening for control which is practicable and can be shown to influence the system in the right direction, *but* / Analyze the repercussions of such change throughout the system as carefully as possible." The proposed analysis of such control measures enacted by the Allied Military Government would indeed require the enrolment of advisors – such as himself – with a high level of social scientific expertise on Germany.

In his letter to Langer, Parsons continues accordingly: "I have so much concerned [sic] with problems of Germany in a variety of professional connections that I should be enormously interested in having an opportunity for the kind of first-hand observations which such an assignment would make possible."[11] Parsons emphasizes here his scholarly interests. His studies of Nazi Germany conducted "at a distance" could finally be substantiated with fresh qualitative research and first-hand empirical data. He does not mention that he would also have the political opportunity, as part of the occupation power, to act as a radical reformer and to implement his vision for a postwar German society. Thanks to his close ties to the personnel he trained at Harvard's School of Overseas Administration to direct the future military government, he could reasonably expect to take up a role as one of the main advisors to remake the German economy, the German educational system, the German state administration, the German public sphere, as well as to shape various types of legislation, for example, in order to protect the rights of religious and racial minorities. Nevertheless, despite the lure of such a powerful position, to help initiate real-world changes after the catastrophic years of World War II, he expresses in the same letter his serious doubts about fulfilling his responsibility in service of the military government, because a medium or even long-term engagement in Europe would mean to leave behind his academic duties. "My situation here at Harvard is not, however, such as to make it easy to arrange to get away. [...] I have assumed considerable responsibility in the field of planning for the postwar development of my field [sic]. I have only very recently assumed the chairmanship of the Department and barely begun to get started on working out important plans."[12] His newly acquired academic role at Harvard University has put Parsons in a special position to take on a reform on a much smaller scale than the German nation-state – local academic reorganization in the field of the social sciences.

Soon after Parsons sent his ambivalent letter with a request for more information, especially about the expected timeline of such a commitment, he came to a final decision regarding his future employment. In another letter in January 1945, he declares his definite unavailability to Langer: "I am afraid I shall have to withdraw from any further consideration for an appointment in O.S.S. [sic] since the conditions are as you described them."[13] Again, Parsons reasons that he finds himself "in the middle of a piece of work in the field of planning and negotiation," sparing, however, the specifics. The timing is just not right: "Had this opportunity arisen a year ago, I think I should have felt quite differently about it."[14] And indeed, Parsons stayed, while Carl J. Friedrich, mentioned in the first letter, but also his former student, junior colleague, and close collaborator Edward Y. Hartshorne[15] went on to help reshape the institutional fundaments of the German nation and its role in Europe. Parsons instead participated in founding Harvard's Department of Social Relations, where he implemented a new model of interdisciplinarity in the social sciences, while institutionalizing the revolutionary concept of an autonomous sphere of human relations in modern society: the social system.[16] The decision to further pursue his local entanglements in Cambridge instead of following up on his wartime foreign politics-initiatives, therefore, were hardly a sign of modesty, but rather indicate that Germany was for Parsons no longer "enough," and his ambition had turned from a regional to a global scale.

Parsons' systems theory, as developed in the following years and outlined in his magisterial study *The Social System* (1951), arguably "the" classic of postwar sociology, is today considered one of the major intellectual sources of "modernization" during the Cold War that helped reimagine and shape societies around the world as liberal democracies.[17] This ascent from local hustle and bustle to having a world-wide impact, however, happened at such a breakneck pace during and after World War

II, that it is crucial to carefully trace some of the early steps of the actors as they scaled up the local debates on social theory into a universalized scheme used to develop the entire world in terms of social systems.

This chapter will turn back to the crossroads of Parsons' difficult career decision during the grueling winter of 1944/45, and explore how the apparently radically divergent options – should he stay or should he go? – are in fact intimately linked, and may not be fully grasped individually, but only in their interrelation. Parsons' engagement in the American memorandum culture of the 1940s provides a new key to understanding his work as a theorist[18] as connected with both his political activism[19] and his cunning maneuvering in the "interstitial academy" at Harvard University.[20] Situating Parsons' various wartime memoranda and related materials in the context of his concepts and practices, which include his group-based project work, his participation in private, semipublic, and public debates – all shaping his intellectual engagement with the German enemy – one finds, slowly emerging, the main ingredients of his postwar social theory presented in *The Social System*, albeit developed to various degrees. In order to describe the creation of his classic study as a result of his wartime work, I intend to scrutinize Parsons' reliance on culture patterns, his development of what he calls a conceptual scheme, his intervention in the discussion of antisemitism, and his foundation of social theory on the notion of double contingency. I will approach these questions, however, with special attention to the practices of gray literature, which means, in Parsons' case, his strategic use of citation and footnotes to ultimately generate a model of the social system.

6.1 HOW GERMAN IS IT?

At the heart of Parsons' wartime work is his close collaboration with Friedrich, a fellow Harvard professor. Friedrich not only played, as mentioned above, a crucial role as chief legal adviser to General Lucius Clay, the military governor of Germany,[21] but also acted in various positions in the memorandum culture before and during World War II as initiator and organizer of several short-lived groups and committees. Despite the renewed attention his work has recently attracted, Friedrich is still underappreciated in his role as a crucial intermediary figure between Germany and the United States during World War II.[22] Already in 1938, he had started serving as acting chairman to the "American Committee for the Guidance of Professional Personnel" that provided refugee lawyers with fellowships and training to help them adopt to the new legal system. Starting in 1940, he functioned as chairman of the executive committee and coordinator of the "Committee of Correspondence" for the "Council for Democracy," mobilizing academic expertise about Nazi Germany for the American public, and in 1943 as director of the short-lived "School of Overseas Administration" at Harvard University which trained, among others, future diplomats and military government officials to be sent to Nazi Germany.

By chance, Friedrich and Parsons had met early in their careers at Amherst College in Massachusetts in 1922, where Parsons studied as an undergraduate and Friedrich as a German exchange student.[23] The inconsequential first meeting in the historically Puritan culture of Amherst is more than just a curious anecdote with regard to the collaborative work between European émigrés and American intellectuals, as it points to a distinct and often downplayed factor. At least in the case of Friedrich and Parsons, their joint efforts were facilitated, both practically and conceptually, by their perceived common religious background. While the aspect of religious belief and practice has received sustained attention in the study of non-Christian, non-White, non-male intellectuals, it is notoriously neglected by intellectual historians of the twentieth century, especially when it comes to the study of homosocial interactions within secular Christian contexts, which often appear as unmarked, at least at first sight.[24] The collaboration between Parsons and Friedrich, from Amherst to Harvard, needs to be considered a "Calvinist collaboration," in light of both Friedrich's German theories of the United States and Parsons' American views on Germany and its "pathologies." The evidence is hiding in plain sight. Friedrich based his concept of democracy on a reading of the Early Modern Calvinist state theorist Johannes Althusius, originally an attempt to provide the Weimar Republic with a traditional Christian model of government.[25] This model, rediscovered and developed during Friedrich's time studying with Alfred Weber in Heidelberg, is clearly associated with the latter's brother, Max Weber, and his study of the Calvinist foundations of American politics and economy in his famous *Protestant Ethic and the Spirit of Capitalism*, originally published in German in 1905 and first translated into English by none other than Parsons in 1930.

Parsons had studied in the same circles in Heidelberg (1925–1926) and had written his German doctoral thesis on a comparative study of Werner Sombart's and Weber's theory of capitalism, entitled "Der Kapitalismus bei Sombart und Weber."[26] Parsons, though cultivating a secular public persona, never made a secret of the fact that he was born into a prominent Calvinist family that traced its genealogy to the early period of Protestant settler colonialism in North America.[27] His father, a trained minister, was affiliated with the Social Gospel movement,[28] a heterogenous group widely acknowledged for its influence on American society around 1900, serving as a conduit of social scientific thought into the public debate.[29]

In private, Parsons became even more assertive regarding his religion. In 1941, on occasion of a brief but intense exchange of letters with political philosopher Eric Voegelin, to which I will return later in more detail, he acknowledges in a discussion of his academic role that "by cultural heritage I am a Calvinist"[30] – strongly self-identifying with American Protestantism as described by Weber. During the 1940s, the German liberal sociologist Weber, who had died in 1920, indeed served as the invisible yet ever-present authority to find common ground among European émigrés and American social scientists, but also as an "in-group marker" for different schools of sociology within the United States.[31] Equally, Friedrich and Parsons heavily relied in their academic work as "Weberians" on Weber's reputation. In very disparate ways, however, especially during World War II, both their reputations depended on the general perception of Weber as a supposedly "good German." Intriguingly, their opposite reactions to this constellation both help explain Friedrich's and Parsons' self-positioning in the American public, directly affecting their project work, and, for Parsons, the very architecture of his *Social System*. Their main point of disagreement, which despite its fundamental significance never led to serious conflict, lay in the assessment of the implications of a term such as "good German." Friedrich, whom Parsons addressed with his idiomatically abbreviated middle name, including a distinct German fricative, "Achim," was socially marked, through his name and his biographical background, as a first generation German-American. Facing a choice of either embracing his ascribed identity or working against the identification of his "traits" with the enemy, he took a strong stance against the concept of "national character." In a speech on "Morale: An Essential of National Defense," held as Chairman of the Executive Committee for the Council for Democracy on September 13, 1940 in front of a regional association of businesspeople, he made this point clear. In his address, he forcefully asserts that international differences in morale cannot be explained by "difference in the races." He stresses that "[w]e do not know what national character is" and that employing this concept would lead to a logical fallacy. One should not, he argues, take national character as a cause to explain international politics, because "we are explaining what we know by what we don't know, and I don't care for that sort of thing."[32] He then calls attention to a nation's "historical tradition" as a factor of difference and redirects the audience's attention from social psychology to politics. Friedrich points to American democracy as central for American morale while clearly acknowledging the positionality and self-implication of his argument: "Now I still believe – that may seem very strange to you out of the mouth of a fellow with a German background – I still believe that the last war was fought to make the world safe for democracy."[33]

Within the memorandum culture and with regard to the range of analyses of Nazi Germany, Friedrich is clearly positioned against a significant group of people who either take the concept of national character for granted or consciously use it as a highly effective tool for translating their analyses into terms that can be easily linked to general social psychological arguments – and arguably to widespread forms of stereotyping.[34] Throughout the 1930s, Parsons ignored the so-called "culture of the Thirties"[35] and the powerful intellectual alliances made possible by this concept connecting to the intricate interdisciplinary network in which also Margaret Mead held a prominent place. Nevertheless, he eventually went on – against the stance of his close collaborator Friedrich – to embrace national psychology as an *explanans*, most conspicuously by introducing, via cultural anthropology, the notion of "culture pattern" into his writing on National Socialism.[36]

This transition, rather inconspicuous, can be found in a text written for the aforementioned Council for Democracy in 1940, his "Memorandum: The Development of Groups and Organizations Amenable to Use Against American Institutions and Foreign Policy and Possible Measures of Prevention."[37] Parsons here analyzes whether National Socialist propaganda poses a threat for the American society, and cites – without reference – Friedrich's emphasis on "historical tradition," associating it, with a skillful rhetorical move, to what he calls "culture elements": "National Socialism [...] does not come out of the blue, without, in the content of its developing *tradition* [emphasis added], continuity with that of the society out of which it has grown. It has, rather, developed by a process of gradual shift in certain culture elements."[38] He then goes on to point out five principal features of German National Socialism, "nationalism, including race, socialism, anti-intellectualism, militarism and what may be called particularism."[39] Parsons finds the first three of these cultural elements present in the United States, but, in 1940, does not see a strong American military tradition that could be harnessed and misdirected. He also argues that the German principle of unrestricted leadership with "unlimited powers with no legal definition"[40] goes against American values. Ultimately, however, there is a strong American "social tradition"[41] that protects the United States against fascism and should be reinforced through domestic initiatives (such as the work of Friedrich's Council for Democracy). Delicately pushing – and moving – Friedrich's notion of "historical tradition" from "political" to "social," he arrives at the most general, but also concrete of these initiatives, which can rely on American social traditions. It is the "Puritan conception of the 'Kingdom of God on Earth,'"[42] which in Parsons' view lies at the core of what "in a very rough way [...] may be called 'activism'"[43] (such as the work of Friedrich's Council for Democracy). Following this point, in effect declaring American political activism in 1940 explicitly a collaboration of Calvinists, he inconspicuously achieves the task of building a bridge – or rather spanning a tightrope – from Friedrich's ostensive refusal of national character-studies to the field's main concept. Parsons starts the conclusion of his memorandum: "This very sketchy outline of certain *elements* [emphasis added] of a basic desirable common orientation has been introduced because it seems to be the main focus of the morale problem."[44] Here Parsons refers to the notion of (cultural) "elements" and ties it directly to the "morale problem," which was also addressed in Friedrich's aforementioned speech. In the following sentence, however, Parsons adds the second part which, for the attentive reader, closes the circle: "The wars of promoting attachment to such a *pattern* [emphasis added] are many – but attempts to foster solidarity on a group level must all relate to some such pattern."[45] Parsons intertwines his focus on social tradition with the work on a (cultural) "pattern," implicitly referring to the aforementioned concept of culture patterns central to national character-studies, mainly produced by psychologists and cultural anthropologists. The fact that he does not spell out the full concept is a clear indication that Parsons, during this transitional moment in the elaboration of his social theory, tried to strike a delicate compromise between Friedrich, his most important addressee in the memorandum culture and his sense that it is culture-specific, if not relativistic, types of approaches, that provide the "energy" needed for the rapidly growing amount of gray literature on Nazi Germany.

Parsons' art of citation, here presented with a focus on what appears to be just a minor detail, seems to have been successful insofar as the intensity of Parsons' and Friedrich's collaboration only grew, not only in the Council for Democracy, but also in the American Defense, Harvard Group, and, between 1943–1945 in the aforementioned Harvard School of Overseas Administration. Nevertheless, the memorandum, written "at Friedrich's request,"[46] apparently never made it past its first reader into further digestion or circulation, and the difference in opinions apparently kept festering during the war years. As Uta Gerhardt has pointed out, Friedrich explicitly formulated his disapproval of Parsons' increasing embrace of national character studies only at a rather late stage, in a letter from April 16, 1945, reacting to Parsons' aforementioned seminal publication on "The Problem of Controlled Institutional Change" in *Psychiatry*, a journal founded in 1938 by psychiatrist Harry Stack Sullivan and others to study interpersonal processes, quickly becoming one of the strongholds of national character-studies.[47] The foundational intellectual disagreement on basic terms between Friedrich and Parsons was apparently held in suspense throughout the war years in favor of limited compromises and the displacement of potential epistemological and methodological conflicts into separate projects, such as Parsons' failed application for funding to initiate a "Research Project for the Study of the German and Italian Family Systems" based on a culture and personality-approach in 1943.[48] The common ground instead was negotiated in the administration of the rapid flow of communications, skillfully directed, among others, by Helen Walker Parsons, Parsons' wife, who worked congenially as a highly educated secretary,[49] which allowed for an intense collaboration in the memorandum culture, ultimately relying on their shared background in Calvinism.

Arguably, the difference between the political theorist and the social scientist could be finally made explicit, since Parsons had clearly, by that time, started to move on from his collaboration with Friedrich on Nazi Germany. His plan for the foundation of the Department of Social Relations in 1945/46, outlined in the "Confidential Memorandum on the Reorganization of the Social Sciences at Harvard," a text submitted to Dean Paul H. Buck by him and psychologists Gordon W. Allport, Henry A. Murray, O. Hobart Mowrer, and by anthropologist Clyde K. M. Kluckhohn, was the first important result of institutional reorganization initiated by the so-called Allport Committee in 1943.[50] From a Harvard-centric institutional perspective, it is right to point out that four of the five initiators of this project formed part of the "Levellers,"[51] an informal group of non-tenured faculty, growing out of the Pareto Circle gathering during the mid-1930s around one of Parsons' most important mentors, the biochemist and first chairperson of the prestigious Society of Fellows Lawrence J. Henderson. Indeed, as Parsons himself recounted later, some of them had already submitted in 1941 a report, "Toward a Common Language for the Area of Social Science," leading to the implementation of a "Basic Social Science" at Harvard.[52] The design presented in the "Confidential Memorandum," however, seems to be equally informed by its wider, national, and more urgent contemporary historical context, as it couches the social sciences within a framework of "culture and personality," to which most if not all of the committee members had independently subscribed during World War II. As a first suggestion, the plan of the "Confidential Memorandum" states that "[w]e recommend that the existent Departments of Anthropology, Sociology, and Psychology be dissolved," in order to build a new interdisciplinary department of "Basic Social Science."[53] The problems associated with this fusion of different disciplines and approaches led, after the implementation of the Department of Social Relations, to significant friction, and were never fully solved.[54] It is not for lack of trying, though. Indeed, the macro-architecture of Parsons' theory in *The Social System* cites the structure of the memorandum's vision for an institutionalized basic social science, and thus needs to be interpreted as an ambitious attempt to provide an operating system to run the recently implemented institutional hardware. The book was a major statement in mid-century social theory, and it was also gray literature addressed From: Parsons To: the Department of Social Relations.

The Social System, in its basic theoretical structure, interlocks three systems, the personality system, the culture system, and the social system, and treats all three of them, despite the suggestive title of the book, with equal attention. Parsons' World War II-focus on Nazi German culture patterns, social psychology, and national character clearly shapes his Cold War invention of a new set of disciplines constructed around his vision of systems theory.[55] For this invention's sake, however, he is forced to give up his focus on cultural specificity, ultimately following Friedrich, in order to be no longer identified with Germany, and to be able to make universal claims about the nature of modern sociality.

6.2 LESS-THAN-IDEAL CONCEPTUAL SCHEMES

If one compares Parsons' first book *The Structure of Social Action* (1937) with his second book fourteen years later, *The Social System*, one of the most striking differences lies in the latter's lack of almost any direct quotation and sparing use of footnotes, which, if added, largely refer either to the authority of Weber, Parsons' own work, the texts of close collaborators, or to unpublished manuscripts of dissertations at Harvard

University.[56] This "power move,"[57] wagering the self-sufficiency of Parsons' radiant academic charisma, contributes more than anything else to what became a decontextualization and universalization of his social theory after World War II. The methodical justification for this apparent lack of credit lies in Parsons' assertion that his actual work as theorist lies in the construction of "conceptual schemes" as tools for the social scientist.[58] But what strange tools these are. The reliance on conceptual schemes in the decades surrounding World War II was a marker of attachment to an American philosophy of science, as pursued by Charles S. Peirce, Alfred N. Whitehead, or Willard V. Quine, that was particularly *en vogue* at Harvard University. As Bernard Barber argues, Parsons' mentor Henderson was, more than anyone else, involved in the dissemination of the notion along with "dynamic" concepts of equilibrium among social scientists.[59] The success of the conceptual scheme needs to be understood within a climate of an increasing demand to present social research as scientific during the twentieth century, to receive recognition – and funding.[60]

The modern use of the notion goes back to philosopher Immanuel Kant and his *Critique of Pure Reason* (1781), which Parsons studied intensely during the 1920s.[61] The renaissance of the conceptual scheme on the American East Coast is all the more surprising in as much as post- and especially neo-Kantian philosophers in Europe had had significant troubles with the role of the *schema* – from the Greek for figure, order, structure – and its epistemology, and had tended to contain and sideline its systematic significance.[62] This in turn may have had to do with the scheme's ambivalent intermediary position as a "third" between perception and conception and its potential to wreak havoc, depending on the interpretation of its priority or secondary nature. The result of picking one side can be seen in Parsons' use of the term. The conceptual scheme, translated into a rule for a layout of tables and diagrams, takes precedence over perception and conception and therefore makes the quotation of empirical studies and social philosophies irrelevant.[63] Beyond that – and this is the consequence Kant-scholars might have dreaded the most, at least in Parsons' use of the notion, not much of Kant's intricate analysis of understanding or sensibility is left.

For better or worse, however, Parsons' diagrammatic art has undoubtedly played a part in his impact on the social sciences, and his diagrams, such as the AGIL-scheme, used as visual aids, determined his lasting didactic success. During World War II, Parsons' indebtedness to German idealism – together with the underlying entanglement of American academia with the German university system – was in no need of justification, despite the fact that even Parsons himself, following one of his tables (on the Types of Social Value-Orientation) in *The Social System*, identifies "the philosophy of 'idealism' and the German cultural ideal,"[64] leading to National Socialism. Parsons, however, met accusations of "idealism" only after World War II, and without being tied to the origins of National Socialist ideology.[65]

Still, the higher rationality of the conceptual scheme put the social scientist into a unique position of authority. For Parsons, his conceptual schemes turn all previous social scientific studies into "our knowledge,"[66] as he aptly puts it in the *Preface* to his work. This knowledge serves as a resource, a material, an "enormous reservoir"[67] that is freely available for the higher purpose of the "incurable theorist"[68] to choose, test, and adjust his main research instruments, which he calls "pattern variables."[69] The alleged autonomy of theory is reinforced by his very citation practice that cuts off any philological referentiality, a referentiality still practiced in his previous book *Structure of Social Action*. Curiously, in *The Social System*, Parsons' distilled text is nevertheless not entirely free of quotation marks. These mainly lift unspecific academic jargon, but also American colloquialisms and elements of every-day-speech into his writing and help demonstrate that his abstract language and terminological innovations are still founded on common sense. The process of purification therefore results in a mode of writing driven by brisk combinatorics and aphoristic clarity, leaving just as many open questions as it provides answers.

The synthetic style of Parsons' theory also reflects the training of writing gray literature "against the Nazis [...] pounding on the typewriter all day about it."[70] The problem-oriented study of Nazi Germany during World War II, after all, not only stirred up the boundaries between various fields of research setting a precedent for the kind of interdisciplinary collaboration that informed Parsons' reorganization of the American social sciences. It also established, at least in Parsons' case, the programmatic conflation of social scientific theory and applied studies practiced in wartime memoranda, a continuity which was obvious to most contemporary readers, but got forgotten or even rejected by the next generation of social scientists.[71]

Parsons himself states as much in his book regarding disciplinary and discursive boundaries: "Science, applied science, ideology, philosophy and religious beliefs are all necessarily articulated with one another, and in certain respects shade off into each other."[72] For him, there are no pure sciences, as they are always already woven into the fabric of the social system: "scientific investigation is itself a process of action."[73] Especially in modern societies, the social sciences form a crucial part of their ideological foundations: "In this perspective it becomes clear that the social sciences have a particularly crucial, and in certain respects precarious position relative to the ideological balance of the social system."[74] While traditional or authoritarian ideologies may use the social sciences for "non-rational mechanisms of stabilization,"[75] Parsons imagines that the best conditions are provided in societies with a "pattern of freedom of thought, which both permits ideological controversy and free interplay between the scientific and the ideological levels."[76] It comes less as a surprise that Parsons' view on the social sciences has a clear Americentric, liberal, and capitalist bent, than the fact that he freely admits so. "Ideology,"[77] for him, is not intrinsically problematic, but inevitable and indeed an important aspect for the integration of social systems. He even accepts ideology, alongside religion and magic, into the same category of what he terms "motivational orientation of action" together with science as "cognitive,"[78] as creating a "belief system."[79] In fact, Parsons uses the occasion in his elaboration on belief systems to affirm once more, implicitly, his religious background in relation to his academic work, as he claims that "the hospitality of science was greatly increased in the 'ascetic' branches of Protestantism [...] in England at the time of the great scientific developments of the 17th century."[80]

The cultural sociologist Jeffrey C. Alexander, in his comprehensive critical appreciation of Parsons' work, spends most of his book to disentangle the perceived confusion and conflation of these and further levels of analysis, ascribing them, however, not to Parsons but to the failure of his critics to fully appreciate the complex categorical order of his work.[81] As should have become clear in the description of the programmatic impurity of Parsons' work, this view does not live up to the evidence. From the careful study of Parsons' collaborative work during World War II, leading up to *The Social System*, a less clear and distinct – yet all the more intriguing – history of Parsons' systems theory emerges.

Put in terms of Parsons' analytic vocabulary ca. 1950, the question is whether it is more plausible to understand his theory of social systems starting with an "integrated" state of social equilibrium, or whether one should start with a dysfunctional state of "anomie," a notion coined by Émile Durkheim, which describes in Parsons' use a "lawless" system under stress, subject to trends of disintegration.

Considering the confusing jumble of unfinished studies and circulated manuscripts, which underly Parsons' publication strategy between the mid-1930s and the mid-1940s leading up to his second book, it seems just to point out "anomie" as the somewhat counterintuitive red thread leading through these years. Parsons, a sociologist trained in biology and economics, and supercharged, thanks to his years abroad in London and Heidelberg, by European social theory, first ventured to specialize in the field of medical sociology. There he tried, following an intuition in one of Henderson's idiosyncratic late papers, to understand the relationship between physician and patient as a social system, in which therapy helps reintegrate the deviant sick person to play their role again. Parsons' concept of therapy, at the beginning of World War II, shifts its social environment, but not its structure, and becomes (domestic) propaganda.[82] Toward the end of the war, projected on the enemy, it becomes social engineering, "controlled institutional change," or as he calls it in *The Social System* in its latest transformation, cut short following the latest cybernetic fashion, "control." For Parsons therefore, disease is not a specific metaphor for the general phenomenon of Nazism. Instead, for him Nazism is a particular instance of a basic concept of illness as social deviance. Parsons came from conducting interviews in hospitals to the study of propaganda and German institutions before he finally arrived at the idea of an integrated social system. Accordingly, the order of chapters in *The Social System* is genetically in reverse: Parsons starts with phenomena of deviant behavior, leading to a state of anomie and to processes of social change (discussed in chapters 6–11), before arriving at a classification of patterns in an integrated system modelled on his perception of contemporary (American) society, founded on the nuclear (suburban) family enacting (traditionally gendered White Christian) status roles (chapters 1–5). The latter chapters on contemporary society also form the part that despite its descriptive rather than normative character caused the fiercest objections, beginning almost immediately among his students with Harold Garfinkel's dissertation "The Perception of the Other: A Study in Social Order" in 1952.

6.3 ANTISEMITISM AS A PROBLEM FOR A SOCIOLOGIST

I want to point out one of these early objections, as it appears particularly helpful for the understanding of the relationship between *The Social System* and Parsons' wartime studies of Nazi Germany. Restaging the Schuetz-Parsons-controversy in 1940/41, to which I will come back later, Garfinkel analyzes in chapter 5 of his dissertation, "A Comparison of the Decisions of Parsons and Schuetz," the epistemological foundations of Parsons' work and scrutinizes his use of conceptual schemes and the assumption of differences in rationality between observer and actor. As an example, he imagines a "Parsonian" observer, who reacts to antisemitic "protestations of the actor that the Jews really have control of the country," simply dismissing the claim "with a quiet, 'Tush, *I* know better.'"[83] Considering this biting methodical critique of epistemological condescension among academics that guided much of Garfinkel's subsequent work in ethnomethodology, I'd like to ask back: Is that so? What does Parsons actually say about antisemitism, and how does this relate to his method?

In the following, I attempt to answer these questions, moving from *The Social System* back to Parsons' work on antisemitism during the World War, and contextualize it as part of a process of group-based writing within the memorandum culture, in particular with reference to a pamphlet titled *Nazi Poison*. In a next step, I will move to Parsons' correspondence with Eric Voegelin and their discussion about National Socialist antisemitism; to his controversy with Alfred Schuetz, a Jewish-Austrian social scientist; and return to the *The Social System* and its micro-architecture encapsulated in Parsons' notion of double contingency. These steps will help further elucidate the intricate relationship between the formation of Parsons' theory and his work in the memorandum culture.

Parsons in fact discusses antisemitism as an example in his *The Social System* in the chapter on patterns of deviant behavior. The antisemite belongs for him in the category of someone with "group prejudice."[84] He does not argue, as Garfinkel stages it in his imagined dialogue, that antisemites have a lack of proper knowledge, but rather that they articulate a "deviation from conformity." He then advances hesitantly a widespread psychological explanation "that the displacement of aggression against the Jew as a scapegoat object plays a part in anti-semitism." The particular mistreatment of the victims of antisemitism is in disagreement with a conflicting value pattern that demands "universalistically tolerant behavior," hence the antisemite is under "strong pressure to 'rationalize' his special treatment [by false] allegations."[85] These allegations help to create the false semblance of a sound integration of antisemitism into the universal value system, which, if not countered or even accepted, may create a deviant subgroup. Once such a subgroup has been established, the deviant behavior becomes sanctioned and enters a cycle of reinforcement,

6.3 Antisemitism as a Problem for a Sociologist

which then leads to negative sanctions for people opposing, rather than those ventilating antisemitic stereotypes.[86] Parsons describes here the broad outline of a process that questions the fundamental structures of systems (and of systems theory), that is, structures in which the hierarchical relationship between system and subsystem becomes subverted. At the core of this possibility of "tipping over" lies an "ambivalent motivational structure"[87] that is not stabilized invisibly through "vested interests."[88] Reenforcing one side of such an unacknowledged ambivalence leads to a "process of cumulative skewing" and provides "one very important possibility for social change."[89]

Identifying these ambivalent motivation structures seems to lie at the heart of Parsons' political activism, as it does in his view of social change, led by revolutionary movements in Early Christianity, France, Russia, China – and, significantly, the National Socialists in Germany.[90] The Nazi German "revolution" in fact is his most elaborately analyzed example of such a "deviant subculture becoming a movement."[91] According to Parsons, Nazi Germany stayed in a state of disintegration and actually never had the chance to face its necessary integration through consolidation of traditional German value patterns contradicting the movement's pure ideology, which made the Allied violent response provoked by the Nazis' aggressive militarism and the resulting defeat all the more decisive. Parsons therefore predicts in his *Social System* only six years after the end of World War II quite optimistically that "[w]hatever new combination of the ingredients which went into the Nazi movement may come about in the future, it is unlikely that just the same kind of movement will arise in Germany again."[92] Whatever one makes out of these compelling remarks about antisemitism and Nazi Germany, one cannot help but notice that they are heavily redacted and – at least at first glance – carelessly cut short to the point of parody, considering the intensity and depth of his occupation with these and related problems during eight of the thirteen years between his first and second book, that is, between 1938 and 1945.

While several prominent socialist intellectuals and artists such as Lillian Hellman and Ernest Hemingway were already drawn into the fight against fascist political movements in Europe during the Spanish Civil War starting in 1936, for Parsons, as for several other American intellectuals, the wake-up call to the dangers of Nazism came with the infamous antisemitic pogrom euphemistically called *Kristallnacht*. On November 9 and 10, 1938, German paramilitary groups together with regular citizens indeed shattered literal glass as they destroyed and plundered businesses and synagogues in coordinated attacks throughout Nazi Germany, but they also caused the deaths of an estimated 1000–2000 members of the Jewish-German community who were killed or died in the aftermath, about 30,000 people were deported to concentration camps.[93] In the United States, the pogrom quickly became a highly publicized "media event" that, despite the distance, created a brief wave of solidarity filled with anxiety about the increasing ruthlessness of National Socialist organizations toward its own population.[94] Previously, the coverage of Hitler's Germany and its rapid transformation into an authoritarian state had been decidedly mixed. Stark warnings like those of American foreign correspondent Dorothy Thompson,[95] which began to appear in the American news around the democratic election of the National Socialist Party (NSDAP) to a governing coalition in 1933, were largely met with disinterest by a self-absorbed American public struggling with domestic problems during the Great Depression. They were also drowned in the noise of an overall confusing coverage of events in Germany, caused in no small part by a concerted Nazi German publicity campaign including blunt propaganda lies and subtle attempts to instill doubt about the veracity of the news reporting.[96]

One can only speculate what exactly helped to finally strike a nerve among a group of socially liberal, anglophile, philosemitic intellectuals to go public, after a long succession of fateful domestic developments in Nazi Germany from the Enabling Act of 1933 and the Law for the Restoration of the Professional Civil Service, to the Nuremberg Laws in 1935 or the increasingly aggressive foreign politics leading to the *Anschluss* of Austria and the Sudeten crisis earlier in 1938. For Parsons, it seems quite clear that the large-scale domestic terrorism of the pogrom, criminal even according to applicable National Socialist law, delivered the model of the National Socialist society as lawless, that is, in a state of "anomie," a concept, as mentioned above, that would be the base of all his future analyses of National Socialism.[97]

On November 23, Parsons published his first public statement against Nazi Germany, "Nazis Destroy Learning, Challenge Religion," – a sort of test balloon for a local readership in *Radcliffe News*, the newspaper of Radcliffe College in Cambridge.[98] Parsons intertwines in his argument issues of freedom of religion with academic freedom, a line of reasoning that seems confusing in the context of National Socialist antisemitic violence, but makes all the more sense in a liberal arts college publication as an appeal to the First Amendment of the American constitution. From here, Parsons' preoccupation with academic freedom only grew, especially in collaboration with his junior colleague and expert on the topic Edward Y. Hartshorne, with whom he planned to write a book on "German Social Structure and National Psychology."[99] Similarly, the second aspect, the question of antisemitism not only concerned his own Christian sentiments of charity and religious toleration. Parsons, the career sociologist, might have also sensed that he was professionally vulnerable working in a discipline that antisemites frequently stigmatized as "Jewish." Even more importantly, Parsons realized that he had found a worthy "deadly enemy"[100] as object of social scientific study for his plans to reinvent his rather young discipline. He could take on the relatively recent arrival of the phenomenon of "anti-Semitism" in the public discourse and brand it into a genuine sociological problem. In 1941, the year Parsons entered the American debate on antisemitism, it was all but clear how to frame an academic conversation about antisemitism. The public discussion, it appears, almost exclusively centered around accusations and counteraccusations of libel.[101] In any way, it is clear that the American discourse was neither analytically nor ethically equipped to address the Holocaust as a new, hitherto unimaginable, phenomenon of genocidal industrial mass murder executed by Nazi Germany during World War II. The discussion was still in an exploratory phase and Parsons' analysis was indeed conducted, without taking notice, parallel to the horrific "mass murder"[102] resulting from a cumulative radicalization of Nazi antisemitic policy during World War II, briefly before the infamous plan to implement the Final Solution to the Jewish Question was discussed at the Wannsee Conference in Berlin on January 20, 1942.[103] Two years earlier, in late 1939, sociologist Isacque Graeber had contacted Parsons to solicit an article for an edited volume he was planning to publish on the problem of antisemitism, one of the first major academic publications on the topic. Even though Parsons had completed a first draft of his text in January or February 1940, the article did not come out until 1942, by then including unauthorized changes in his text.[104]

In the meanwhile, Parsons had collaborated as member of the Committee of Correspondence in a project organized by Friedrich, which was edited and printed as a pamphlet for the Council for Democracy in 1941. *Nazi Poison: How We Can Destroy Hitler's Propaganda against the Jews*, a 55-page booklet with an overly sensationalist title,[105] published as no. 8 in a series entitled "Democracy in Action," is easily overlooked in the vast amount of gray literature produced during World War II (Figure 6.1). Indeed, the text addresses with its accessible, at times didactical style, a general reader and purveys an abundance of facts, leaving however at times a sense of discursiveness and lack of analytic

FIGURE 6.1 A unique wartime collaboration, authored by the Committee of Correspondence of the Council for Democracy: *Nazi Poison* (1941).

clarity. After all, Friedrich took a pragmatic position toward the problem of propaganda, and argued quantitatively rather than qualitatively, albeit in private, that "the only cure for propaganda is more propaganda."[106]

The reading of the pamphlet, however, changes considerably if one studies its making. Looking at the pamphlet's underlying textual practices, it is not quite right to find in it primarily a testimony of a "debate," as Joseph W. Bendersky renders it, but of a collaboration.[107] As Bendersky himself describes it, the starting point of the text was a questionnaire that was drafted and then sent to various members of the aforementioned Committee of Correspondence of the Council for Democracy, but also to outsiders with a specialized expertise, who then mostly did not read each other's contributions. Instead, the answers, often to individual questions of the questionnaire that had previously been assigned to the respective expert, were then compiled, digested, and recomposed in a process of montage, first of all by Friedrich and his "special research writer" Harold Winkler, who then, again, organized a "peer-review" of *Nazi Poison* mainly by Jewish-American associations. The general process was established during the first year of the Committee's work, for which Friedrich had assembled an impressive network of experts who helped produce a series of widely circulated memoranda, reports, and pamphlets designed to influence opinions within specific organizations as well as the general American public about important current political and legal issues.[108]

What turned out to be indeed historic about it was the combination of contributors resulting in a unique publication. *Nazi Poison* was a singular meeting point of some of the most important members of the memorandum culture. Deeply buried in the piles of gray literature of World War II and so far unrecognized, Talcott Parsons collaborated with Friedrich, of course, but also for the first time with Margaret Mead and – even more astonishingly – Theodor W. Adorno, Max Horkheimer, Franz Neumann,[109] and David Riesman, Floyd H. Allport, as well as Reinhold Niebuhr, Miriam Beard Vagts, Max Radin, Salo Baron, again Isacque Graeber and others – toward one common text, the only literary collaboration of its kind.

In a particular irony of history, it was less the American public, which was propagandized by the pamphlet, but rather several of its consultants, such as those of the Institute of Social Research, and especially Neumann. Friedrich, rather carelessly, had chosen "Anti-Semitism – Spearhead of Nazism" as the working title for the pamphlet on top of the initial questionnaire, and phrased some of the questions accordingly. The underlying thesis amounted to the dubious claim that Nazi Germany consciously exported antisemitism as a propaganda tool of its foreign policy to the

United States in the hope of converting upright American Christians into National Socialists. Once the superficially added spearhead of antisemitism had pierced the American skin, the substance of the deadly weapon, the full-blown Nazi ideology, according to this oddly constructed metaphor, could penetrate and enter the American body. The actual title was later changed to *Nazi Poison*, still defining antisemitism as an invasive problem native to Europe, the "spearhead" survived as the first thematic subheading after the introduction. The theory, which was largely made-up ad-hoc and without any evidence to support its basic assumptions, strangely resonated with the Institute of Social Research, constituted by a group of Jewish-German scholars. Neumann, the group's most important analyst of Nazi Germany in the American memorandum culture, indeed enthusiastically appropriated the concept of the "spearhead" in Friedrich's questionnaire and used it for one of his intelligence reports written at the OSS, which then fed into the second edition of Franz Neumann's *Behemoth* in 1944.[110]

While the male correspondents and especially Radin provided the necessary abundance of authoritative facts cited to debunk antisemitic prejudices, the two female consultants contributed particularly insightful arguments, one of which Friedrich placed prominently at the beginning of the pamphlet, while he left out the second. Although much of her spirited response did not arrive in the pamphlet, it is Miriam Beard Vagts' line, anonymously quoted in the finished pamphlet, where one can read in italics: "As one of our consultants put it quite flatly: '*Anti-Semitism has precious little to do with Jews.*'"[111] Beard Vagts' forceful statement indeed establishes the baseline of the pamphlet, and arguably the epistemological ground for most future academic study of antisemitism. The second response, however, the memorandum "Anti Semitism – Spearhead of Nazism" by Margaret Mead, so far unknown, did not find its way into the pamphlet at all. This turns out to be even more consequential, as the piece of writing constitutes, on five brief pages, Mead's most extensive statement on antisemitism, a topic on which she otherwise refrained from publishing during World War II.[112] Mead acknowledges, as radically as no one else among the consultants was willing to, the pervasiveness of antisemitism in the United States, and its subtle persistence even in purportedly philosemitic speech. For this, the first of several examples she presents is particularly noteworthy: "A grandmother, deeply impressed with the Christian ethic and disapproving of alle race prejudice says to her five year old grandchild: 'Always remember, never forget that the Mother of Christ was a Jew.'" Mead introduces in what appears as an idyllic family portrait a supposedly benign dialogue between grandmother and grandson, free of hate speech or racial violence. Mead goes on to explain that "[o]n the surface this is not an anti-Semitic comment but a pro-Semitic." Yet, the grandmother's negation of antisemitism creates the same learning effect as affirmative antisemitism. Pushing Beard Vagts' statement – most likely unbeknown to Mead – one step further, Mead argues that "the day that grandmother said that to her grandchild, she taught that child, who had never seen a Jew, that Jews were people who were regarded with hostility, people for whom one had to find reasons for not hating [...]." Philosemitism in the grandmother's Christian interpretation still draws a line between "us" and a fictional out-group, "them." Once this separation is established, the philosemitic sentiment is held in its state of precarious balance only thanks to a restraining ethics. Once the child decides to unburden themselves of these restraining ethics, the implicit antisemitism taught by the grandmother comes to the fore. Mead finishes the long sentence accordingly, that the grandmother presents the "Jews" as "people who must be protected in the name of ethics because otherwise one – not remembering – would feel some unpleasant emotion or act in some unpleasant way towards them."[113] This leads Mead to conclude near the end of her memorandum that *"whenever Jews are mentioned in the terms traditional in our culture*, the groundwork for anti-semitism is laid." On the verge of entering World War II, Mead's diagnosis that American culture had a pervasive problem with antisemitism was apparently unpublishable.[114] To the credit of *Nazi Poison*, also those worries, explicitly uttered by representatives of the Jewish-American community themselves, about a possible backlash in the current heated climate, spoiling decades worth of work toward integration and acceptance, need to be factored into Friedrich's editing decisions.[115] Nevertheless, Mead's attack against "good Christians" certainly could have offended some of the philosemitic contributors to the pamphlet, and leaving it out certainly facilitated the publication. There are a few cases to be considered. Elton Mayo, the founder of industrial sociology and colleague of Parsons at Harvard, took the time to explain to Friedrich why he did not answer to the questionnaire and why, indeed, it was better to keep quiet entirely. He argues in a letter that the pamphlet will not be able to address the complexity of the problems it tries to solve, since "the real ill in our society is of the nature of stasis and anomie."[116] Instead, Mayo predicts a further polarization between philo- and antisemitism as the primary effect of the pamphlet, both underestimating the uncomfortable staying power of his cowardly letter in the Harvard archives, while probably overestimating the pamphlet's impact on the American readership.

As Bendersky has already pointed out in reference to Allport's response, Floyd – Gordon's brother – Allport had, despite his rejection of biologistic explanations, a history of reverting to scientific racism. In his memorandum, he explains that Orthodox Jews simply do not understand how to behave in the face of negative stereotypes, further contributing with their hostile reactions to the ongoing problem while at the same time holding back non-Orthodox, assimilated Jews.[117]

David Riesman, on the other hand, went to the other extreme, and wrote a thirty-seven-page memorandum, taking the opportunity to deal with some basic questions regarding his personal experience in responding to antisemitism – which seems to have had a cathartic effect on him. He, in turn, thanked his Christian collaborator Friedrich for his good deeds in a personal letter.[118]

Given the range of responses, Parsons' "Comments on Anti-Semitism" now occupy a precarious intermediary position, significant for the understanding of the pamphlet's main problem.[119] For a full appreciation of Parsons' statement on antisemitism in response toward Friedrich's questionnaire, however, one needs to glance beyond Parsons' Comments and their relationship to *Nazi Poison* and include his exchange of letters both with Voegelin and with Jewish-Austrian émigré sociologist Schuetz. This, in turn, will help to discover an important aspect of the microstructure of *The Social System* resulting from his collaboration in the memorandum culture during World War II.

Regarding the problem of antisemitism, Parsons, the Calvinist, clearly positions himself in the religious majority group, using an affirmative and exclusive "us" as in "our Christian tradition,"[120] criticized by Mead, indeed in the same August days that he declared his Calvinism in his letter to Voegelin on August 18, 1941. Parsons nevertheless pursues an argumentative strategy of partial inclusion, bringing together various strands of thought. Jewish "emancipation," according to his "Comments on Anti-Semitism," was a "consequence of what Max Weber called the 'process of rationalization.'" This process of rationalization, however, brought social change, causing a state of "disorganization," something "which Durkheim has classically called 'anomie.'" Therefore, "Anti-Semitism and Fascism are inherently linked together." The Fascist movement, for Parsons, is a counter-reaction to the process of rationalization, and antisemitism the misplaced object of projection of the negative sentiments created by these social changes in "fundamentalists."[121] This statement, it should be noted, is nothing less than the philosemitic foundation of Parsons' "smiley-faced reading of Weber"[122] that grounded the positive view of modernization in American Cold War social theory.[123]

In parts of his texts, however, Parsons uses the flawed strategy of meeting the "antisemite" half-way, as he repeats antisemitic stereotypes about "Jewish 'intellectualism,'" how "strikingly economically successful" the "Jewish group is"[124] and does not refrain from victim-blaming: "Hence the impressions of aggressiveness and oversensitiveness to questions of prestige on the part of Jews are not altogether mythical – all of us probably know how difficult it is, with the best of will, to deal with certain oversensitive Jews."[125]

It remains unclear what caused Parsons to verbalize this antisemitic prejudice. The statement was not made privately, but in a semi-public memorandum, after which it was largely beyond Parsons' control whether or not it could be included in the resulting pamphlet, without his name directly attached, but printed nonetheless.[126] Friedrich simply ignored this piece of text, and in fact, no antisemitic language ended up in the messaging of *Nazi Poison*, which in itself, absurdly, needs to be considered one of the achievements of the pamphlet against antisemitism. It remains nevertheless also the project's main flaw that this problem was simply brushed over and could not be addressed explicitly. Even within those academic circles where collaborations between intellectuals with Christian and Jewish backgrounds did occur frequently and intensely, and even if those Christian intellectuals went on to expose themselves in publications and public statements against antisemitism, as Parsons did consistently, the very antisemitic sentiments that they tried to fight were still a resource that could be activated especially in moments when conflicting perceptions clashed.

Even if it is impossible to trace the origin of Parsons' apparently strongly held view that certain "Jews" were hard to deal with – connecting them to older misogynist gender stereotypes about "oversensitive women" that are supposedly "hard to deal with" – this complex of affective refusal, tied-up within a precise intellectual argument, can be traced back to an instance from the same year the pamphlet was created.

6.4 MUTUAL MISAPPREHENSIONS

Parsons declared his being a Calvinist by cultural tradition in a specific setting: Parsons and Jewish-Austrian sociologist Schuetz had not been able to find common ground concerning their conflicting visions of social theory, and Voegelin, an acquaintance of both, had offered himself up as agent of a "mediation."[127] The conflict has already been dealt with extensively and, especially thanks to the recent publication of the Parsons-Voegelin exchange, has received insightful interpretations. For this chapter, one aspect of the conflict and its mediation appears particularly relevant because it allows to further grasp the reach of memorandum culture and how its practices of collaboration ended up shaping Parsons' *The Social System*.

Voegelin and Parsons had been in contact for a while and started in 1940 a discussion on the problems of antisemitism based on Parsons' manuscript that would lead to the aforementioned article published in 1942, which heavily drew from Weber's late work on the "Antike Judentum."[128] Voegelin, who already in 1938 had argued that National Socialism was a "political religion," broached the argument that National Socialist antisemitism may be less explained, as in the American case, from Christian-Jewish tensions, than from the identification of Christianity and Jewry as connected through their common monotheist, messianic heritage. National Socialist antisemitism for Voegelin channels "theogonic forces" directed against the Christian majority religion that first "wipes out the Jews incidentally to the attack against Christianity."[129]

In a letter sent on September 27, 1940 in response to the letter by Voegelin, Parsons, going beyond his manuscript from early 1940, shapes the argument that will return the next year in his memorandum for the pamphlet on *Nazi Poison*. In the letter, Parsons firmly establishes a connection between the "Jews" and the historical process of "rationalization": "There are reasons, of course, in the position of the Jews why, in the process of emancipation, they have been peculiarly susceptible to the tendency of rationalization and there is a real sense in which they form a quite reasonably appropriate symbol." National Socialism, for Parsons, following Voegelin, is at its core a religious movement, correspondingly antagonizing a religious target, the "Jews." "It seems to me that from this point of view National Socialism can be considered, as you say, an outburst of new religious force which centers about a re-orientation of precisely these fundamentalist sentiments."[130]

In a letter written one year later, on August 18, 1941, that is, during the time of his collaboration on *Nazi Poison*, Parsons picks up Voegelin's point once more and gives it a new twist: "In Nazi terms you might put it that the Anglo-Saxons, that is, the Calvinists, are really Jews (Perhaps the converse is also partly true – one source of Anti-Semitism in Germany lies in the feeling that the Jews are really Anglo-Saxons, that is, Calvinists. The two are identified.)"[131] The common enemy, following these logics,

6.4 Mutual Misapprehensions

might unite Calvinists and Jews in an anti-fascist alliance. In the same letter, however, Parsons introduces a distinction between rationalism and Calvinist theology, ascribing the emergence of scientific observation to the latter, as Calvinists were able to avoid the speculative tendencies of rationalists, "of getting bogged down in [...] philosophical problems."[132] It is exactly in this context, identifying Schuetz as a rationalist philosopher, that Parsons comes to his declaration of religious affiliation, quoted earlier out of context: "Possibly one of my troubles in my discussion with Schütz lies in the fact that by cultural heritage I am a Calvinist."[133] Parsons continues this projection of historical categories on his conflict with Schuetz: "I do not want to be a philosopher – I shy away from the philosophical problems underlying my scientific work."[134] This refusal of taking the same role as the other is, according to Parsons, mutual: "By the same token I don't think he wants to be a scientist as I understand the term until he has settled all the underlying philosophical difficulties."[135] Parsons leaves no doubt about which one of the two he finds more appropriate for the problems at hand: "If the physicists of the 17th century had been Schützes there might well have been no Newtonian system."[136] Parsons' polemics intricately constructs an image of himself as a Calvinist scientist against the backdrop of Schuetz's philosophy in the supposed tradition of rationalism, using his identification as Jewish as a foil, without, however, mentioning this aspect to Voegelin.[137]

Considering the succession of events, it seems just to point out that because Parsons' statement on the "rather extreme sensitiveness" of "Jews" relies on a stereotype that was firmly established in Parsons' world view in 1940, when he wrote his first manuscript on antisemitism, and it was therefore clearly active during his controversy with Schuetz. The conflict with Schuetz might even be considered the prime source of the intensification of the statement regarding "certain oversensitive Jews" in his response to Friedrich's questionnaire for *Nazi Poison*. While Voegelin did try to mediate and assuage Parsons in the conflict with Schuetz, he augmented it at the same time by connecting it to the analysis of National Socialism. Specifically, applying Nazi Germany as a conceptual scheme, they both built a flawed conceptual connection between "Jewry" and "rationalization," which led in the controversy between Parsons and Schuetz to even further mutual misapprehensions – and, as I will show, mimesis.[138]

The miscommunication between the two started with the very first surviving letter, sent by Parsons to Schuetz after their first encounter.[139] Here, Parsons invites Schuetz in the academic year of 1939/40 as a late addition to the roster of presentations to one of his seminars. Parsons' had started convening, together with Austrian economist Joseph A. Schumpeter, the interdisciplinary "Harvard Rationality Seminar," in a sense the culmination of Parsons' initial employment at Harvard as lecturer in economics, with his studies on Alfred Marshall and a spin-off of his book *The Structure of Social Action*, for which Schumpeter served as one of the reviewers.[140]

Along with the friendly invitation extended to the struggling social philosopher, who at the time worked as a "lawyer with extensive experience in international banking"[141] outside of academia in financial consulting, Parsons promises the arrival of a recent piece of writing: "Dear Doctor Schuetz: I am sending a copy of my manuscript under the title *Actor, Situation and Normative Pattern*, about which we have talked, to Mr. R. H. Williams. When he has read it, I have asked him to send it on to you, and I hope it reaches you before too long."[142] Richard H. Williams, a sociologist at the University of Buffalo, was present at Parsons' and Schuetz's first meeting, where they apparently discussed Parsons' recent work.[143] The manuscript "Actor, Situation and Normative Pattern," which in its posthumous first edition is dated around 1939,[144] has a curious status both as a "primer" on social theory, which Parsons apparently used for teaching purposes,[145] and as an intermediary step from *The Structure of Social Action* toward *The Social System*. To understand the dynamics of the controversy between Schuetz and Parsons, as well as Voegelin's role in it, the circulation of this piece of gray literature needs to take center stage, turning the study of the arguably somewhat lengthy exchange of arguments into a shell game.[146]

It is not clear, when exactly Schuetz received Parsons' manuscript, but when he did first receive it, most likely by April 1940, he clearly drew the wrong conclusions, as he seems to have ignored it entirely because of its unfinished and unpublished status. On the occasion of the seminar, Schuetz, who had managed to flee from Europe with his family arriving on June 22, 1939 in New York,[147] made in April 1940 his first appearance at Harvard with a paper on "The Problem of Rationality." Parsons himself had pragmatically recycled and condensed some of his earlier statements about rationality from *The Structure of Social Action* (1937) in his lecture "An Approach to the Analysis of the Role of Rationality in Social Action" held in late 1939, and even provided his notes to Schuetz. Schuetz, not fully understanding the casual nature of the seminar, delivered on April 13, 1940 by far the most elaborate paper of the seminar,

6.4 Mutual Misapprehensions

in which it is in fact him, who emphasized that "rationalization" is one of the meanings of what Max Weber famously calls "disenchantment of the world" ("Entzauberung der Welt").[148] Schuetz thus forges a connection from the seminars central notion to Weber, thereby historicizing the concept, which certainly was not an entirely original move, and was in fact also present in Parsons' reading of Weber in *The Structure of Social Action*. It was, however, with the exception of a passage in Wilbert E. Moore's paper, otherwise left out at the seminar, which applies also to Parsons' contribution to the seminar.[149] For the key argument of his paper, Schuetz takes up and develops, wrapped in polite remarks, a fundamental critique of his host's concept of rationality and explains that it is not suitable for the analysis of "everyday knowledge."[150] Contrary to what one might expect, the main problem at this point did not lie so much in the irreverent affront as such, but in his "citation practice," that is, a lack of philological reference: Schuetz did not refer to the present state of theoretical developments in Parsons' "Actor, Situation and Normative Pattern." Sharing his manuscript with Schuetz was a lose invitation into the emerging memorandum culture of the 1940s, and Parsons expected Schuetz's appreciation, thoughts, additions, references, objections, and maybe even critique, but in the spirit of collaboration.

Schuetz instead responded to Parsons' invitation to collaborate asymmetrically, with an ambivalent show of respect toward Parsons' scholarship according to the rules of behavior he arguably had learned in the European academic system of "mandarin" professors. The misapprehensions continued. Instead of following up with a quick reply, sharing his thoughts, Schuetz went silent and instead pulled out Parsons' 829-page book published in 1937, of which he undertook in the summer and fall of 1940 a thorough critical reading that he planned to publish as a review for the British journal *Economia*, edited by Friedrich A. Hayek. Parsons clearly felt betrayed in his trust, when Schuetz finally answered to his letter from October 30, in which Parsons asked Schuetz to forward his copy of "Actor, Situation and Normative Pattern" to Voegelin. After holding on to it for half a year, on November 15, 1940, Schuetz sent, instead of a friendly comment on his manuscript, a hefty, in fact unpublishable, 20,000-word review amounting to a thorough repudiation of Parsons' lauded first book.[151] The ensuing conflict shows that Schuetz was slow to adapt to the informal rules of gray literature production during World War II. Crucially, from the perspective of the memorandum culture, he initially refrained from turning his scholarly attention to National Socialism during the controversy.[152]

Parsons himself reacted to this denial of "cool collaboration" both with aggressivity and oversensitivity in three consecutive long letters from mid-January to early February 1941, pushing back defensively against some of Schuetz's points. Schuetz, who did not fully understand his mistake, replied apparently under the impression that Parsons had intellectually failed to grasp his comments. And again, despite Parsons repeated hints, he failed to look closer at Parsons' "Actor, Situation and Normative Pattern." There, he arguably could have found new aspects of Parsons' thought, deemphasizing, for example, the "unit act" as the atom of social action – one of the main targets of Schuetz's critique. The manuscript might have provided a common ground: the notion of "expectations," as held by what Parsons at that point called "Actor A" toward "Actor B." In "Actor, Situation and Normative Pattern," Parsons in fact argues with regard to the definition of roles in a social system, and loosely citing one of the classic notions of American social theory in 1902, Charles Cooley's "looking-glass self," regarding the definition of roles in a social system: "In one main aspect, this is a consequence of a fundamental phenomenon to which attention has been called several times, namely, the fact that, from the point of view of any given actor, there are 'expectations' relative to the behavior of others. Conversely, others build up expectations as to the actor's own behavior."[153] Parsons, however, does not really provide any new answers beyond Cooley's (or Herbert W. Mead's) interpretation of this problem. Schuetz instead picks up a central argument from his review and reemphasizes its importance in his letter from March 17, 1941, without linking it to Parsons' vocabulary. He refers instead of "Actor A" and "Actor B" to "actor" and "alter ego," a notion he had adopted prominently in his *Der sinnhafte Aufbau der sozialen Welt: Eine Einleitung in die Verstehende Soziologie* (1932) from philosopher Edmund Husserl and his late phenomenology. Schuetz argues that Parsons' social theory still lacks its centerpiece, the element that could explain the emergence of sociality, a fundamental attack against the core of the ambitious social theorist's project: "[N]owhere in your own theory do you deal with the specific *social* categories of acting and mutual interaction, with the problem of the frame of reference relative to the alter ego towards which the actor's own actions are oriented and within which the alter ego interprets the actor's action." Furthermore, Schuetz goes on to argue that Parsons' social theory faces the same problem on a macro scale as he does not explain the role of the social scientist within the social system and therefore takes the "social world [...] as given."

6.5 Parsons' Double Contingency: Tipping the Scales

You do not explain the specific attitude the social scientist has to adopt towards the social world, which is an attitude derived from that of the partner in the social world, but with quite other "operational signs" or "subscripts" which bestow in both cases a different meaning upon any interpretation of an alter ego's act; that hence your theory of values as well as the role you attribute to science *is* acceptable only if you forego the explanation of the problems of intersubjectivity involved in both and if you presuppose the whole social world with all its structural differentiations just as given [...][154]

At this point, Parsons was clearly exhausted by the lengthy exchange, and tries to invoke as a last resort the authority of Weber's study on Protestantism, which he had translated, against Schuetz, moving the discussion overtly to a central problem of sociology, but inconspicuously toward his earlier discussions about religion with Voegelin: "Even with regard to the things you mention toward the end of your letter about the role of the *alter ego* I cannot yet see the difference it would make if these considerations were taken into account with respect, for instance, to such a problem as that of the relations between Protestantism and the modern institutional order."[155]

Schuetz replied briefly on April 21, 1941, but more importantly, he had passed the copy of Parsons' manuscript "Actor, Situation and Normative Pattern," after stopping its circulation for an entire year, to Voegelin, on occasion of a meeting in Philadelphia on April 5, 1941, during which Schuetz had informed Voegelin about the "unpleasant [...] 'controversy.'"[156] Voegelin, who apparently understood the rules of collaboration, its pace, and style, had read the manuscript and replied to Parsons within two weeks. He drafted some polite remarks lifting Parsons' work on a level with Weber's, further igniting their exchange about religion during World War II.

Despite the failure to engage with Parsons, Schuetz apparently was convinced of the importance of his intervention for the American debate and immediately tried to "trademark" the notion of "alter ego," putting it prominently into the title of an article in the same year.[157] He did so, however, to little immediate effect during World War II.

6.5 PARSONS' DOUBLE CONTINGENCY: TIPPING THE SCALES

When Parsons chose in 1944/45 his path forward in the institutional reorganization of the social sciences at Harvard University, he soon left behind his hectic wartime engagements in the memorandum culture, among others his drafting of memoranda on German social structure, propaganda, and antisemitism for various wartime committees, councils, and government agencies, his radio speeches, his teaching at Harvard's School of Overseas Administration starting 1943, his participation in the Roundtable on Germany after the War in the spring of 1944, which shaped the outlines of reeducation policy, his participation in a conference on Japan after the war in December 1944, modeled on the Roundtable on Germany,[158] and finally, in 1945, his push in Washington, DC against the proposals of the Secretary of the Treasury, Henry Morgenthau.[159] However, his applied wartime work clearly stayed with him, and shaped his work as a postwar social theorist more profoundly than is apparent at first glance. This applies, as argued above, to the theory and practice of the interdisciplinary Department of Social Relations from the "Confidential Memorandum" to the macrostructure of his *Social System*, but also to its microstructure. As Parsons lays out the basic notions for his new conceptual scheme in the opening pages of his book, he largely abandons his previously central theoretical conceptualization of the "unit act" as the atom of social action and moves instead to what he calls the "double contingency"[160] at the core of his social theory. This is rather surprising, after his earlier mentioned last letter to Schuetz on March 28, 1941, in which he refused to accept the concept of alter ego into his theory to introduce "*social* categories of acting and interaction," saying that regarding the "role of the *alter ego* I cannot yet see the difference it would make if these considerations were taken into account." Parsons now cites the phenomenological conceptual scheme, without however acknowledging his debt to Schuetz, who, after thoroughly studying Parsons' work, first proposed it as a solution to the fundamental theoretical problem that Parsons had not managed to solve on his own. Thus, also Parsons' misapprehension of Schuetz is followed by mimesis:

It is a fundamental property of action [...] that the actor develops a *system* of "expectations" relative to the various objects of the situation [...] and [...] contingent on the various alternatives of action. [...] Part of ego's expectation [...] consists in the probable *re*action of *alter* [emphasis added] to ego's possible action, a reaction which comes to be anticipated in advance and thus to affect ego's own choices.[161]

This basic mechanism between ego and alter forming an "expectation system"[162] recurs time and again as a motif at all levels of abstraction in the construction of his *The Social System*, less for the reader's comprehension but almost like reminder to himself, which Parsons uses to ensure that his conceptual scheme serves to create a "social" theory.[163] Answering his own question regarding the value for the understanding of the "modern institutional order" posed to Schuetz ten years earlier, Parsons puts this mechanism at the center of his conception of the "institutional integration" of "action elements": "The starting point is the crucial significance of interaction and the corresponding complementarity of expectations. *What are expectations to ego are sanctions to alter and vice versa [...].*"[164]

Parsons presents the same theorem in his parallel contribution to *Towards a General Theory of Action* (1951), coauthored with Edward A. Shils, where he is even more straightforward in his definition, stating that "*social objects* or *alters*" interact with ego according to a "complementarity of expectations."[165] Parsons' thus coins, to define the mutual dependency on each other's expectations, in which the action of ego is dependent on the expectation of alter's reaction, the notion "double contingency." Double contingency creates the common ground, which serves as the condition of possibility of successful communication and interaction.

> Because of this double contingency, communication, which is the precondition of cultural patterns, could not exist without both generalization from the particularity of the specific situations (which are never identical for ego and alter) and stability of meaning which can only be assured by "conventions" observed by both parties.[166]

From a Parsonian point of view, it would indeed be suggestive to argue that Parsons' theoretical concept of double contingency emerges from a real wartime double contingency, in which the "specific situations" of him and the émigré Schuetz were in fact so different that a "stability of meaning" was rather difficult to establish.[167] It would, however, also mean taking sides in the controversy between Parsons and Schuetz. As Garfinkel was the first to hint at in his dissertation, Parsons' mimetic adaptation of Schuetz is in fact a creolization, and it transforms the German phenomenological conceptual pair of ego and alter ego into something else. As one of the few contemporary close readers of "Actor, Situation and Normative Pattern," Garfinkel must have realized that Parsons grafted Schuetz's terminology on his Actor A – Actor B-conception,[168] and concludes that rather than ego and alter, it would be more appropriate for Parsons to talk of "two Egos [...] Ego1 and Ego2."[169] Here, Garfinkel's assessment of Parsons' reliance on conceptual schemes, what he earlier calls the "'neo-Kantian' phenomenology [...] in the work of

Parsons"[170] is indeed correct: "Given the position of the observer, the alters for the observer are conceived as Egos. From an Ego's standpoint, the other person is an alter who the observer depicts in his Ego relevant terms for Ego1."[171]

As one of the few contemporary close readers of Schuetz's work, Garfinkel contends that for Schuetz, instead, "[t]he observer's Ego's alter is an object which is always empirically problematical [for] the observer [...]."[172] Schuetz accepts the "possibility of a community between the actor and the observer,"[173] and lets go of "the use of the rational man" as an analytical category. Turning Parsons (and with him the entire Harvard Rationality Seminar feeding into the Cold War discourse on rationality) from his "head onto his feet," Schuetz makes rationality an actor's category. "For Schuetz, unlike Parsons, the notion of rationality of the action [...] designates nothing else than the properties of the actor's model."[174] Nevertheless, as I have shown earlier, Garfinkel has it backward, when he synthesizes that "[l]ike Parsons, Schuetz achieves the notion of a social action by providing an other person as an object in the actor's order of actions."[175]

With the help of the alter as a "social" object, distinct from other types of objects, Parsons succeeds in scaling up double contingency as the nucleus of "social" action through its solidification in "institutions" progressively moving toward "rationality" on a national scale, determined by culture and personality. The new technical notions that in Parsons social theory gained prominence in describing these processes, notions such as "modernization," "development," "functional differentiation," "symbolic generalization of media," and "emergence of subsystems" were rather marginal during World War II. They helped moving from the largely national, culture and personality-bound framework, still active in *The Social System*,[176] to a universal scale, propagating systems theory under the unique conditions of economic growth during the "Trente Glorieuses,"[177] as the American ideological foundation for a liberal, capitalist world society, based on the idea of an autonomous social sphere. They also never fully lost their connection to Parsons' engagement with European and especially German social theory and his Calvinist collaboration on German problems and the question of reeducation during World War II, treated in more detail in the following chapter of this book. In fact, without explaining the conceptual shifts and adjustments elaborated collaboratively in wartime gray literature, the purpose of Parsons' book would not be understandable. Parsons, again, is quite explicit about his missionary ambition at the very end of his *The Social*

System. After linking the eschatological expectation of a new millennium to early Christian belief, still found in communist expectations of an egalitarian future, he reflects on the future of his own liberal, democratic, and capitalistic project of social theory: "When such a theory is available the millennium for social science will have arrived."[178] One is maybe too readily inclined to read into this statement of faith a touch of irony.

7

The Identity of the Enemy

The American reeducation of Germany has been one of the most controversial topics discussed in view of the aftermath of the collaborative study of Nazi Germany during World War II: Was it a dismal failure or an enormous success? Did a reeducation of the West German society by the occupying power according to US principles take place at all? If yes, were these principles consistently implemented? Were they subject to local appropriation or universal rejection? The nuanced scholarly debate on this brief episode, which coincided with the American occupation from 1945 to 1949, has largely revolved around these questions. Following the opening of the relevant archives in the 1970s and 1980s, this debate quickly brought rise to James F. Tent's (1982) standard work on reeducation. Tent's striking own view of Nazi Germany is succinctly formulated right at the outset of the book: "Following total defeat in 1945, German society underwent greater change under the four years of military occupation than it had under Hitler and the Nazis."[1] Thus downplaying the impact of the Nazi era on Germany and magnifying that of the years of US-American military occupation, however, Tent's study does not focus on Germany but rather on reeducation as part of the history of America and its involvement in Cold War Europe while considering the military government the most important actor or historical subject in this regard. As a "conquerors' catchword,"[2] according to him, reeducation signified the central instrument of American foreign policy. Nonetheless, rather than telling an American success story, Tent's account culminates in the defeat of US military officers by local "neoparticularist sentiment"[3] cultivated by educational institutions in Bavaria, Bremen, and elsewhere in western Germany. According to this account, it was not a German national interest that set itself against reeducation policies, but German provincialism.

In the past decade, however, Udi Greenberg has presented a thoughtful revision of certain aspects of this account. While Greenberg cautiously accepts Tent's claim that as a result of the American occupation, "Germany experienced one of the most dramatic intellectual, cultural, and educational transformations in history,"[4] he omits the comparison with the Nazi era. Greenberg instead presents another research direction, going beyond the aforementioned questions. In his research on German educational institutions in the postwar period, which gives special attention to, among others, the émigré Carl J. Friedrich, who was the chief legal adviser to the military governor Lucius D. Clay, Greenberg emphasizes the continuities of Weimar traditions, such as those of the Heidelberg Institut für Sozial- und Staatswissenschaften, in postwar Germany. What "the example of Friedrich demonstrates," according to Greenberg, is that "the Cold War indebtedness to Weimar intellectual structures went deeper and further back in time, and intellectual and educational life both in Germany and the United States was deeply influenced by the experiences of earlier periods."[5]

In a provocative generalization of his thesis regarding American domestic and foreign policy of the Cold War – in his book published three years later he speaks of a "Weimar Century" instead of an "American Century" – Greenberg emphasizes the role of German émigrés in the democratization of the occupation zone and thereby shifts the relationship between Americans and Germans once again: "It was the outcome of prolonged collaboration, in which both sides were crucial players. No group embodies this synergy better than the émigrés who returned to postwar Germany."[6] Rather than opting for a dominant national history, German or American, Greenberg emphasizes the role of intermediary figures and their work in transnational collaborative projects. Local and formerly marginal traditions and interests do not necessarily have to be at odds with the American project of democratizing and modernizing Germany or, as in Friedrich's case, may even be identical with it.

The conceptual history of reeducation presented here does not pursue a further revision of Tent's, Greenberg's, or comparable historical accounts. Instead, it is concerned with the question of how the American study of Nazi Germany in the memorandum culture relates to the history of reeducation. The American study of Nazi Germany had gained a renewed intensity after December 1941 and produced a spring tide of gray literature concerned with the enemy, which, as early as 1943, was also directed at the planning of a postwar order for Germany. The ensuing occupation policy of reeducation was accompanied by an expertise that was unique in this form, figuring, in a sense, as the most tangible immediate results of the study of Nazi Germany within the memorandum culture. This chapter will therefore highlight the collaboration between American cultural anthropologist Margaret Mead and the Danish-German-American developmental psychologist Erik (H. or Homburger) Erikson, both of whom played a determining role in this conjuncture between the analysis of Nazi Germany and the history of reeducation. In particular, a sustained examination will be carried out here for the first time of the reconstruction and reinterpretation of Erikson's contribution to the discussion of German reeducation with a focus on the still largely overlooked connection of his *magnum opus*, *Childhood and Society*, to the memorandum culture.

7.1 IDENTIFYING IDENTITY

Erikson's collaboration with Mead took place within the disciplinary framework of a (now largely forgotten) social scientific field, applied anthropology, first developed by the Bureau of Indian Affairs, and further institutionalized through the formation of the Society for Applied Anthropology in 1940, with Mead as one of the founding members and first president. Their collaboration between the late 1930s and the late 1940s in this field aided the coming together of two extremely momentous histories in the twentieth century: the aforementioned short history of reeducation and the long history of the concept of identity. Reinterpreting Erikson's *Childhood and Society*,[7] I present three historical corrections to the Erikson scholarship that will shed new light on his, at the time, extremely popular social psychological study. Aside from its reception in the social sciences,[8] the immense impact of *Childhood and Society*, first published as a book in 1950, had not least to do with life skill-problems of college students, for example, on the campus at Harvard University. Erikson's biographer Lawrence J. Friedman has shown that at the height of 1960s youth culture, his notion of "identity crisis" provided students in their senior year with a conceptual tool to rationalize their conflicting feelings and existential doubts before entering the adult world of the establishment.[9] The concept of identity spread from *Childhood and Society* via elite communication in very different directions, a process facilitated not by its clear meaning but precisely by its indeterminacy, which is also apparent in Erikson's own use of the concept. Consequently it reached various emancipatory political movements

7.1 Identifying Identity

in the form of "identity politics" being adopted, for example, as "gender identity," "racial identity," and, far less successfully, "class identity."[10] The concept of identity served as a model for real and imagined biographies or "life cycles" – another term Erikson coined – and had a transformative effect on contemporary American and Western culture, as seen, among other places, in film, television, and, mediated through the curricula of creative writing programs, literature.

Even at the times of the paperback revolution, the book's enormous success is at first glance surprising. In addition to chapters on Erikson's clinical work as a psychoanalyst, one finds in it analyses of two American "Indian tribes," the Sioux and the Yurok; an account of Erikson's method of using configurational play; his eight-stage model of child development; chapters on three industrialized nations, the United States, Nazi Germany, and the Soviet Union. Erikson's attempt to unify this patchwork[11] of evidently extremely diverse material and idiosyncratic topics finds expression in the first prominent use of the term "identity" in this book: "identity," Erikson said, "held them [the chapters] together."[12]

According to Erikson's autobiographical account of the development of his concept of identity, he began to use the term at the Mt. Zion Veterans Rehabilitation Clinic in San Francisco in the mid-1940s.[13] Erikson used "identity" in this context to diagnose returning war veterans who suffered from identity crisis due to the experience of violence during the conflict with the enemy. It thus designated here a psychosomatic disorder with obvious similarities to the symptomatology diagnosed in World War I as "shellshock" and today as "post-traumatic stress disorder" (PTSD). Erikson himself suggests that the term found its way from case discussions with colleagues into his published papers in 1946 through written conference remarks on clinical vignettes, presenting it as both a psychosomatic fact and an analytic concept; however, he fails to provide reliable information concerning the original use or coinage of the term.[14]

Nonetheless, the brief account sketching the prehistory of the concept of identity down to *Childhood and Society* does not stop there, making things even more complicated. In the intervening five years, Erikson carried the concept from project to project in various institutional contexts, modifying its meaning according to the situation with the help of new prefixes and compound formations. Given the apparent lack of a clear conceptualization, the question of original use or coinage cannot be simply treated as a lacuna that needs to be filled. Instead, I suggest, the term can be understood as tied to a long chain of translation. This chain must be reconstructed. For not only is the occasion of the publication of *Childhood and Society* in 1950 the first time that Erikson considers this chain, which, as will be shown, had actually evolved over a decade, in its entirety, but he also disregards on this occasion all intermediate steps, solely retaining thereby the apparently self-explanatory, universalized meaning of the term.

The description of the relationship between Erikson's early diagnostic use of identity and its use in *Childhood and Society* therefore requires a different approach. To understand both change and continuity in the evolving meaning of identity, it is necessary to consider it in the context of the development of Erikson's work, especially in that of his collaboration with Margaret Mead in the memorandum culture.

7.2 FATHER COMES HOME

Erikson and Mead first met in 1935 and quickly came to appreciate each other.[15] Mead helped Erikson shape his first publications in the United States and introduced him, together with the influential administrator of foundation funds Lawrence K. Frank, into the emerging memorandum culture. Mead's interest in Erikson, apart from his innovative methods and conceptions in the study of childhood and his stimulating perspective on her ethnographic research materials, was aroused by his psychoanalytic account of Adolf Hitler, based on Hitler's description of his childhood in *Mein Kampf*. Here Erikson skillfully interweaves psychoanalytic vignettes with social-psychological, cultural-historical, and domestic as well as foreign policy motifs while bringing into play the concept of "culture patterns."[16] In his analysis of the "imagery" of German childhood, Erikson interprets the attraction that National Socialists held for Germans with a special focus on Hitler's potential for identification. Hitler, on this account, is a character "that asks both fathers and sons to identify with the Führer; an adolescent who never gave in."[17] As an eternally adolescent rebel, the *Führer* breaks the father-mother-son schema of the German nuclear family by making the transitional phase between son and father, adolescence, a permanent condition.[18] In this limbo, he opens a new space of freedom like a gang leader who acts beyond the social constraints of bourgeois society. He presents both sons and fathers with the opportunity to leave behind the old family ties and join the Nazi gang. At the heart of Erikson's analysis of Germany is an imagined scene from the German "life with father" – *father comes home*:

A representative overt version of such a pattern is the following: When the father comes home from work, even the walls seem to pull themselves together. The mother – although often the unofficial master of the house – behaves differently enough to make a baby aware of it. She hurries to fulfill the father's whims and to avoid angering him.

The children hold their breath, for the father does not approve the "nonsense," that is, neither of mother's feminine moods nor of the children's playfulness. The mother is required to be at his disposal as long as he is at home; his behavior suggests that he looks with disfavor on that unity of mother and children in which they had indulged in his absence. He often speaks to the mother as he speaks to the children, expecting compliance and cutting off any answer. The little boy comes to feel that all the gratifying ties with his mother are a thorn in the father's side; and that her love and admiration – the model for so many later fulfillments and achievements – can be reached only without the father's knowledge, or against his explicit wishes. The mother increases this feeling by keeping some of the child's "nonsense" or badness from the father – if and when she pleases; while she expresses her disfavor by telling on the child when the father comes home, often making the father execute periodic – corporal – punishments for misdeeds, the details of which do not interest him. Sons are bad, and punishments always metaphysically justified. The mother's betrayal, of course, does not improve the boy's opinion of women; nor does his knowledge of the father's subservience to *his* superiors and that of his excessive sentimentality when drinking and singing with his equals strengthens the boy's belief in the dignity of the man. All this is often amply balanced by respect and love; during the storms of adolescence, however, it leads to a crisis with the alternatives of open rebellion, cynical deviousness, actual flight from home, or of a submissive type of obedience which breaks the boy's spirit, once and for all.[19]

It is no longer possible to ascertain when and on what basis Erikson wrote this literary scene, though the references to the motif of father-son conflicts in German expressionism are obvious. What is nonetheless certain is that the scene itself became the subject of conflict, namely between Erikson and Mead. Almost a year after the US entered the war, the first important American analyses of Germany had been written and some had already been published or at least widely circulated. The émigré Erikson had not yet been able to find a prominent publishing venue for his text, on which – unlike most of the other members of the memorandum culture, who joined much later – he had been working for almost 10 years.[20] In this tense situation and shortly before the publication of the text, it was precisely Erikson's above quoted and as of yet still uncredited description of German childhood that Mead and her husband Gregory Bateson used in October 1942 in a "Preliminary Memorandum on Problems of German Character Structure"[21] for the purpose of what they describe as a "diagrammatic" analysis of the "double father" and the "triple mother." Here they summarize Erikson's family play in a catchy way: One of the basic experiences of the German child is the "contrast between the father's dominance in the home, where he rules supreme over children and mother, and his compulsory and servile deference to superiors outside the home."[22] The mother reacts to this contrast between father at home and outside the home with a threefold transformation:

Diagrammatically stated, a German child has three mothers: – the mother who is loving companion and friend – while father is away; the mother who becomes father's ally and deserts and often even sacrifices her child to the father when he comes home; and the mother who, in spite of utmost docility, incurs father's disfavor and so, via suffering, turns back to the child when father has gone away. Playmate mother, betraying mother, suffering mother form a cycle.[23]

Erikson responded to this memorandum in an undated letter expressing extreme irritation with this schematic reduction of his analysis and disapproval of the appropriation and unauthorized development of his arguments. In particular, he vehemently criticized the subsequent "Propaganda Suggestions." They merely amounted to a "provocative construct which will antagonize everybody and leave the Germans icy cold."[24] Mead and Bateson had suggested that Hitler be understood as playing the role of the father and thereby invoked the notion of German longings for a bourgeois happy family. Through propaganda, the adolescent rebel is to be exposed as a "monster father" in order to shake confidence in the "Führer." "If it can be demonstrated that Hitler, who promised them that they need never grow up and surrender to their father's roles, [....] has actually betrayed them, robbed them of their future wives [...] and become a monster father who has seized all the women and left his sons neither their mothers nor future wives."[25] Expectedly, Erikson's decisive intervention brought about the temporary end of Mead and Bateson's "Preliminary Memorandum." Erikson's dismissive attitude toward Mead and Bateson was substantive in nature, but certainly also a defensive reaction to the constructive as well as deforming forces of the memorandum culture. Mead and Bateson, who had already made important contributions in discussions accompanying the creation of Erikson's text, were instrumental in the circulation of various versions of Erikson's Hitler memorandum in the American memorandum culture of the 1940s. Thanks to this circulation, Erikson's text not only assumed a central role in the history of identity, but was able to become one of the most influential American analyses of Germany during World War II and the period of reeducation.

The unusually long publication history of this memorandum, spanning the years from 1933 to 1950, presents considerable text genetic problems, not the least of which are related to Erikson's migration biography. Born in Denmark, Erikson grew up in the Jewish community of Karlsruhe, traveled Europe as an artist, and acquired education primarily as an autodidact before being accepted into the psychoanalytic circles of Vienna and completing a course of training analysis with Anna Freud. His early escape from Austria to the USA was possible thanks to his marriage to the Canadian Joan Serson. When he traveled from Vienna to the USA via Copenhagen in 1933, he wrote a draft of a psychoanalytic account of Hitler, both as a quintessence of his previous work and as a preparation for the challenges ahead. Like his later writings, this work was presumably coauthored with his wife, Joan, who, as a native speaker, contributed significantly to his texts. The Eriksons continued to work on his text over the next several years. Erik Erikson gathered additional material in the context of Mead and Bateson's activist work during World War II, especially in that of the Canadian Project, for which he interviewed German prisoners of war. His psychoanalysis of Hitler, originally titled "On Nazi Mentality," finally appeared in print in 1942 as "Hitler's Imagery and German Youth."[26] This article, the manuscript version of which Mead and Bateson had used for their "Preliminary Memorandum," was the basis of Erikson's first major public intellectual recognition in the United States, which eventually helped him to publish *Childhood and Society* in 1950. In between, the article was reprinted in 1949 in an anthology in a slightly different but therefore highly significant version, to which I will return later. Entitled "The Legend of Hitler's Childhood," the analysis then appeared in a completely different context when it was included as a chapter in *Childhood and Society*, functioning here as the fulcrum of the argument in a work devoted to the popularization of Erikson's concept of identity.

7.3 GERMAN FEAR OF LOSS OF IDENTITY

In the spring of 1944, Margaret Mead, together with the neurologist Richard Brickner, chairman of the "Sub-Committee on Problems of Rehabilitation set up by the New York City Committee for Mental Hygiene,"[27] prepared a working group in New York on "Germany after the War" called the "Joint Committee for Postwar Planning."[28] In Brickner[29] Mead had found a medical doctor capable of lending her cause the necessary scientific reputation and institutional support. Together with Geoffrey Gorer, she helped him in composing and publishing a book with the pointed title *Is Germany Incurable?* (1943), which was the psychiatric work constituting the starting point for the popularization of the term reeducation[30] – and which together with the conference, constitutes the high mark of the present investigation of Mead and Erikson's collaboration. In his work on reeducation quoted at the outset of this chapter, Tent, too, mentions Brickner's text in a brief remark on the conceptual history of the term, whose significance as the starting point of his historiography he nonetheless dismisses, thereby also overlooking Erikson's contribution: "The term, which had been borrowed from the jargon of psychiatrists, became a pet phrase of politicians and journalists during the war."[31] For the working group, an attempt had been made to assemble the "who is who" of the US social sciences, to combine social psychology, cultural anthropology, and sociology with psychiatry and neurology, but also to engage, among others, senators, ministers, and Eleanor Roosevelt, the activist and powerful first lady. While the political caste declined in unison in a friendly manner and with much interest in the topic, the organizers succeeded in assembling a working group that embodied a significant part of the scholarly expertise on Nazi Germany. This working group, which met irregularly from late April to June 1944, consolidated the knowledge that had emerged from the analyses of Germany in the 1940s.

However, the most important expert on Germany for Mead besides Bateson, Erikson, who was working on the West Coast of the USA at that time, could not personally participate in the working group. Instead, Erikson sent a memorandum that Margaret Mead introduced into the discussion referring to it as a "Letter from California."[32] This piece of gray literature served Mead in arguing for the approach she had developed based on her "culture and personality" research, whose purpose had been to analyze and treat the pathology of Nazi Germans by focusing, among other things, on family relationships. In particular, she used Erikson's text to mediate in the discussion about "hard" versus "soft" peace. This leads me to my first historical correction. In this letter, which has so far been misdated, dismissed as "clumsy and feeble" in terms of its vocabulary,[33] or altogether overlooked, one finds Erikson's first documented use of the notion of identity, aimed at addressing the problem of German reeducation. Because of the importance of the letter for what follows, I quote *in extenso*:

A few years ago, when H.S. Mekeel and I studied difficulties in the education of Sioux Indian children, we came to the conclusion that [American] governmental education failed [...]. Let us assume for a moment that Germany's reeducation is an *American* problem: He who wants to reeducate another nation or "change" another nation's "basic character structure" has to be part of an unequivocal historical force [...]. The general orientation of this committee is that of mental hygiene. Is mental hygiene an unequivocal force in the United States? Has it established a machinery of mutual collaboration with those who do the "dirty work" of history? If such machinery is not now established in this country, would it be sage to use defeated Germany as an experimental ground for psychiatric theories [...]? The fact that wars are becoming ever more intense and extensive probably is not so much the result of an insurmountable devilishness of human nature as rather of the fact that now and from now on, larger entities than ever before experience both the triumph of identification with one another and the *fear of loss of identity* [emphasis added]. The problem of Germany's reeducation seems to me neither a *national* nor an *individual* one. Maybe it ought to be *understood* as a *European* problem, and it ought to be *attacked* as a *regional* one. [...] I therefore hope that the problem will be attacked *region* by *region*, community by community [...]. I would suggest a panel on the status of women in Europe [...] in order to study the ways and means by which German woman [sic] can be approached by propaganda now, and in which the women of Europe might be trained to help prevent wars in the future. Who more than the women would have the right and the duty to form a permanent congress for the preservation of human resources? [...][34]

Regarding the problem of reeducation, Erikson proposes a regional approach to reeducation, but one taken from a European perspective rather than from an American one, in order to work against Germany's fear of loss of identity – a concern constituting the occasion for Erikson's first demonstrable use of the term identity. The most important measure against German paternalism, which in Erikson's analysis lacks true inner authority, is to establish a permanent women's congress for the peaceful government of Europe. This in itself is a remarkable turn of events, to which I will return later. Here, however, attention should first be directed to the sentence at the beginning of the letter: "Let us assume for a moment that Germany's reeducation is an American problem."[35] What does it mean if Germany's reeducation (contrary to Erikson's concluding assessment that it is a European and regional one) is an American problem?

Erikson considers "mental hygiene" the most obvious American agent for the task of reeducation.[36] But what was mental hygiene and what does it have to do with the anthropologist H. S. Mekeel, the educational difficulties of the Sioux, and German reeducation? As will be shown in the following, the terms "identity" and "reeducation" used here are the result and in some respects also the quintessence of the research practice of a now largely forgotten discipline, a discipline within the human sciences that lost much of its appeal in the turmoil of the transition from World War II to the Cold War – applied anthropology.

To classify applied anthropology, the general formula developed by the anthropologist of Germany John Borneman in an essay on the history of American anthropology will be taken up here: "American Anthropology as Foreign Policy." Borneman argues that the American history of anthropology can be most clearly summed up by viewing it as a continuous work on the question of foreign policy. Thus, it first dealt with the internal strangers, the Native Americans, for example in the works of Henry Lewis Morgan: "His books are not documents about American social structure but treatises on international order. They were attempts to deal with all peoples in a single, evolutionary framework – civilization measured by culture and state of polity."[37] During World War II, the United States turned its foreign policy toward the rest of the world to the effect that instead of the internal stranger, the external enemy became the object of study. After the victory over the Axis Powers, the word "foreign" was dropped altogether. Instead, during the Cold War, national interest was equated with global humanism as the project of American domestic policy. The field of applied anthropology, to which the study *Childhood and Society* belongs, is an expression of exactly this upheaval in the foreign policy of the long nineteenth century that took place in World War I and especially in World War II and during the subsequent transformation in the Cold War. Put schematically: *Long 19th c.: foreign policy (domestic) – WW2: foreign policy (foreign) – CW: domestic policy (foreign)*.

Considering Erikson's book in this light, one may make much better sense of its apparently strange chapter composition. Erikson composed *Childhood and Society* as a work of synthesis in applied anthropology in Berkeley, California having gone as a participant observer on a journey across the USA to the most important sites of its "foreign policy," real and imagined. Analogously to Borneman's formulation, the stages of his journey as related by Erikson can be described not as psychoanalytic case studies but as diplomatic accounts of different political orders with assessments of the stability of each political order in the face of the foreigner or enemy. Erikson's account is thus a travelogue that proceeds on a stage model from band (Sioux), that is, a nomadic group, through settled tribe (Yurok), to state: from liberal (USA) to fascist (Germany) and communist (Soviet Russia). Erikson's adventurous journey in *Childhood and Society* will now be traced following this scheme.

The task of taking apart and reconstructing the extremely heterogeneous patchwork of the aforementioned chapters of *Childhood and Society* admittedly demands patience. The path leads from Erikson's studies of child psychology among two American "Indian tribes," the Sioux and the Yurok, begun in 1937, through an analysis of American folklore, begun around 1948. This is then placed in relation to the chapter on the Cold War enemy, Soviet Russia. Finally, the path leads back to the incorporation of the Hitler chapter into the book. In this regard, one must also consider the outlines of an unwritten chapter on Jewish identity. Only then, through a complete reconstruction of all the links in the chain of translation, does one get a clear picture of the intersection of the two stories of reeducation and identity running through *Childhood and Society*.

7.4 INDIAN REEDUCATION

Friedman relates a telling anecdote about Erikson's first contact with applied anthropology. In the summer of 1937, after the linguist Edward Sapir had awakened in Erikson an initial interest in American cultural anthropology, he befriended the cultural anthropologist H. Scudder Mekeel, whom he had met at the Harvard Psychological Clinic and who now invited him to a "special summer institute" on the Pine Ridge Reservation of the Oglala Sioux in South Dakota: "Mekeel was aware that as a youngster, Erik had read the immensely popular novels by the German writer Karl May idealizing the Plains Indians for their noble and adventurous qualities. Without hesitation, Erik accepted Mekeel's invitation."[38] This decision, momentous for Erikson's work in child psychology – and thus for the history of reeducation – was also based on Erikson's own fascination with the real-life encounter with the novel characters of his own youth: "When I realized that Sioux is the name which we [in Germany] pronounced 'Seeux' and which for us was *the* American Indian, I could not resist."[39] Erikson's remark about his foolish identification of the Sioux as Seeux[40] is more than a joke here. It marks the positionality of his observations, his White gaze, and the epistemological violence that accompanies it. At the same time, it also points to one of the defining literary templates of the anthropological travelogue in *Childhood and Society*. It is, as will become apparent below, a comedy of errors, that is, the classic genre of identity confusion – initially in the triangle between Erikson, Mekeel, and the Sioux.

In the period before the war, the Indian Reorganization Act (IRA) of 1934, often referred to as the Indian New Deal, served as the most important institutional context for applied anthropology. The cultural anthropologists Clyde Kluckhohn and Robert Hackenberg noted in retrospect: "The IRA is a landmark not only for the American Indians but for the social scientists in the United States because it brought to Indian affairs and to the United States government, *for the first time, an explicit use of social science principles* [emphasis added]."[41]

Applied anthropology took a leadership role in introducing social science knowledge into the administrative practices of the US government in the early 1930s. During the implementation of the IRA, former New York social worker John Collier advocated the idea of American pluralism and relativism "as part of a clearly demarcated domestic policy."[42] That is, he suggested that the various Native American groupings should be seen as communities that had to be "organized," in a manner comparable to that of a community organizer in a migrant neighborhood in a big city. In 1935, Collier hired the young H. Scudder Mekeel as "field representative of the commissioner" and as head of the "Applied Anthropology Unit."[43] This appointment meant, in his case, that he acted for the government as a commissioner of the Indian Office and was to manage the affairs of Native Americans. This work was aimed at establishing the conditions for their economic independence and their "self-government."[44] Mekeel helped Collier steer the course of political action away from the previous "ethnocentrism" and attempts at "assimilation"[45] and toward the "pluralistic" program of "acculturation."[46]

In this process of coordinating "community," "tribe," and "culture," Mekeel called for "taking traditional social structure into account" and developed the "community plan" to create stable "bands,"[47] – following the Lakota concept of *tiyospaye*, which turned out to be a failure. When he also fell out with Collier, Mekeel's tenure ended abruptly at the end of 1937. As Mekeel put it in retrospect with a bitter pun: "In spite of strenuous efforts on my part the Applied Anthropology unit was dis*band*ed [emphasis added]."[48] Thus Erikson accompanied Mekeel to the Pine Ridge Reservation during the last summer of his work for Collier as an applied anthropologist. As might be expected from a comedy of errors, Erikson's presence was justified to the administration by professional role-playing. Erikson entered the reservation not as a psychoanalyst, but in professional disguise as a "mental hygienist."[49] And Erikson played the role surprisingly well. For it was precisely here, during this brief episode of speaking in character, that the term that would move from the periphery to the center of American discussion a few years later emerged. Having shown that Erikson's "Letter from California" is the first time he uses the term identity in direct connection with the reeducation of Germany, here is my second historical correction to the actual source of that reeducation. Erikson writes in the context of this visit to the reservation in a 1939 essay, speaking as a mental hygienist:

> [T]he administration is faced not only with the immense variety of unyielding ancient images and modern economic problems among the 300,000 people, called all too collectively American Indians but also with the historical peculiarities of the agency entrusted with *Indian re-education* [emphasis added], namey [sic] the Indian Service.[50]

Mekeel already used the term in a publication a year before Erikson's visit, in 1936: "Education of a native people by representatives of an alien culture is essentially a reeducation or a reconditioning process, regardless of how it may be considered or what may be attempted."[51] Erikson and Mekeel drew here on a vaguely defined term from a vocabulary that can be traced very precisely to a specific social group that had already fully developed the model for Erikson and Mekeel's collaboration as mental hygienist and social worker: the mental hygiene movement. Reeducation comes from the French *rééducation*, a medical term used in the nineteenth century in orthopedics to describe a therapeutic measure of muscular reconstruction. *Rééducation* was a practice for patients who had lost limbs and learned to integrate prostheses into their movements and body techniques. In particular, during World War I, American physicians in Europe took up the term "reeducation" when treating "crippled" and "disabled" soldiers. As part of the medical personnel, psychiatrists already affiliated with the emerging mental hygiene movement used the term equally for mental problems.[52] Reeducation thus became a central concept for the reintegration of a mentally ill individual into the community, according to Johannes C. Pols: "a social, optimistic, and environmental approach to mental problems, most aptly labeled reeducation."[53]

When Mekeel and Erikson used the term reeducation to restructure Native American group organization, Collier's background as a social worker continued to provide the reference point. As a result of the conceptualization of "Indian" groups as communities or "tribes," the Indian New Deal policies aimed – and here the crucial semantic leap occurs – at a unified "Indian" community of communities – the "Indians."[54] From this perspective, for the first time in the American history of the term, the community – not the individual – becomes the object of reeducation, that is, Indian reeducation. Although the term plays no role in the administrative documents of the IRA, Indian reeducation in Mekeel's coinage and Erikson's interpretation does correspond to the spirit of their work. Condensed in the mobile prefix "re" of the Indian Reorganization Act, New Deal legislators sought to institutionalize a specific historical model of constitutional democracy in Native American communities. In doing so, they worked to establish constitutions modeled after the *Constitution of the United States*. It was about self-government through progressive reform, which shifted the meaning of "re" from "back" to "new."[55] Controlling the immediate relationship between historical model and self-government was of particular significance for the US government since the last attempts on the part of Native Americans to establish an autonomous community of communities had resulted in messianic trance cults sweeping over large parts of Central and North America, which the US government viewed as an internal threat to the United States. The two waves of Ghost Dance in 1870 and 1890, and the Peyote Cult that spread shortly thereafter, were the first intertribal revitalization movements. These represented a direct response to the ethnic cleansing and deportation of Native Americans to reservations. Fear of a new "outbreak" was certainly still present among administrators, and the emancipatory "Indian" movements were also debated by anthropologists and served as a domestic model for the discussion of "nativist," "charismatic," "prophetic," "messianic," "chiliastic," or "apocalyptic" movements, such as the Nazi movement in Germany.[56]

7.5 SIOUX SOCIALISM, YUROK CAPITALISM

Erikson's discussion of Sioux childhood in *Childhood and Society* does not directly mention the "outbreak" of the Ghost Dance, but in his account, it is "history" as an actor itself that has become a central part of "Indian" identity. This is the "historical force" Erikson invokes in the "Letter from California," which must be understood in some proximity to the idea of a "mythologem," but which also encompasses the "dirty work" of history.[57] Erikson, however, draws on another trance phenomenon for his interpretation of historical change among the formerly nomadic Sioux – "these once proud people [...] beset by an apocalyptic sequence of catastrophes, as if nature and history had united for a total war on their too manly offspring"[58] – the famous Sun Dance.[59]

7.5 Sioux Socialism, Yurok Capitalism

As it turns out, "reeducation" remained part of Erikson's vocabulary not only until his 1944 "Letter from California" and with specific reference to American occupation policy, but it also plays a role in *Childhood and Society*, that is, already after the end of the occupation of Germany and also independently of it. Erikson still uses reeducation in 1950 under the auspices of the Cold War, as an echo of Indian reeducation and his analysis of Nazi Germany. Further pursuing the question of reeducation as an American problem in *Childhood and Society*, one may trace the final steps in the chain of translation under investigation all the way to the universalization of identity.

Erikson concludes that the aforementioned historical force creates an ambiguity among the Sioux, for "the administrator or teacher cannot possibly know when they are dealing with an old virtue, when with a new vice."[60] It is for this reason, according to Erikson in 1950, that "old virtues become stubborn and yet elusive obstacles to re-education."[61] In 1950, based on his studies, some of which date back more than 10 years, these "obstacles to reeducation" acquire a new relevance in the context of the Cold War, insofar as they take up the analysis of the East-West conflict of the two blocs. Namely, the values Erikson describes are the values of "Sioux socialism."[62] Sioux socialism is based on extreme cruelty against enemies and oneself as well as extreme generosity with one's own resources and those of others.[63] In Erikson's analysis, Sioux socialism stands in stark contrast with "Yurok capitalism."[64] Yurok capitalism, according to Erikson, is based on extreme simulation, both by affectation and hallucination, as well as extreme purification of moral and monetary values.[65] Erikson toured the Yurok in 1939 after the Sioux and following a similar model with the most important expert on the Native Americans of California, Alfred Kroeber. However, the Yurok were currently engaged in a land dispute with the US government, which meant the four-week fieldwork was limited to discussions with Kroeber's local informants. This of course did not prevent Erikson from writing a separate chapter on the Yurok and their Kepel Dam Dance, apparently primarily as a foil for contrast – a continuation of the comedy of mistaken identity not entirely free of slapstick elements.[66] Erikson again describes a professional role-playing game, this time in an encounter with a *doppelganger*, the shaman Fanny Flounders, an indigenous representative of his own specialization, child psychoanalysis.[67]

As in the case of the Sioux, the Yurok think Erikson is someone else, this time in terms that Erikson and the administration cannot agree on, but instead the Yurok and US government officials can. He is thought to be a secret agent: "They suspected me of being an agent come to investigate such matters as the property feuds brought about by the discussion of the Howard-Wheeler Act [sic, i.e., the Indian Reorganization Act]."[68] This incident, in turn, reveals his view on the historical situation of the Yurok, which Erikson otherwise only alludes to. The Yurok were among the few Native Americans who, according to Erikson, were not subjected to ethnic cleansing and deportation in comparable ways to the Sioux.[69] They retained a "sense of historical continuity" without an apocalyptic break with the past: "Thus, one has the impression that at least in some essentials the Yurok does not have to relearn the ABC of his ancient economic mind and whatever of the past is still a part of his child training."[70] In the case of disputes between the US government and the Yurok, as he experienced upon his arrival, it is a conflict between two American groups that escalates precisely because "Yurok and white man each understands too well what the other wants, namely, possessions."[71] It seems that a common political boundary object – possessions – established a symmetry that kept Yurok reeducation from becoming an American problem in Erikson's account. In this sense, the relevance of the Yurok to Indian reeducation lies in their status as the systematic opposite of the Sioux in Erikson's report.

7.6 COLD WAR PACIFISM

I continue to follow the chain of translation of identity in its intersection with reeducation as an American problem to the next link, which is also the next step in the stage model: the chapter on American identity. Little is known about the genesis of this chapter, not least because it is based primarily on book sources, especially folkloristics, enriched by observations from Erikson's psychoanalytic practice. It was probably written at Berkeley in the late 1940s and first published in *Childhood and Society*. Erikson suggests here that there is an interrelationship between Sioux, Yurok, and American settlers, at the "frontier"[72] and thus the boundary between Native Americans and American socialization, before Indian reeducation:

> We suggested that the mothers of the Sioux and of the Yurok were endowed with an indistinctive power of adaptation which permitted them to develop child-training methods appropriate for the production of hunters and hunters' wives in a nomadic society, and of fishermen and acorn gatherers in a sedentary valley society. The American mother, I believe, reacted to the historical situation on this continent with similar unconscious adjustment [...].[73]

7.6 Cold War Pacifism

Considering the question of the interrelationship between Native Americans and settler colonies, Erikson argues that on the one hand, American identity is grounded in Protestant rebellion against the British Empire and on the other, it is the result of a kind of "self-reeducation" in response to the aforementioned foreign policy idea of an "Indian" enemy waiting at the frontier that sends out a call. This leads in Erikson's comedy of errors to the appearance of the American child as split personality. The same person responds to the same call in two completely different ways: "In a world which developed the slogan, 'If you can see your neighbor's chimney, it is time to move on,' mothers had to raise sons and daughters who would be determined to ignore the call of the frontier – but who would go with equal determination once they were forced or chose to go."[74]

The transition from historical to contemporary analysis of American identity is particularly delicate. While Erikson was working on the chapter on American identity, as mentioned earlier, the omens of foreign policy had changed once more as the US had entered in a Cold War with the Soviet Union. Thus, Erikson also concludes the chapter with a question that brings the contemporary foreign policy relevance of his concept of identity to the fore. Identity itself becomes part of American identity; and the Americans are those who "have" an identity to offer: "The question of our time is, How can our sons preserve their freedom and share it with those whom, on the basis of a new technology and of a more universal identity, they must consider equals?"[75] A "more universal identity" becomes the means of an aggressive diplomacy, the meaning of which, however, only becomes apparent when the historically last element of the chain of translation, the analysis of the present enemy, is added.

In 1950, it is also no longer the chapter on Hitler and Nazi Germany that directly follows the analysis of American identity. Instead, the subsequent leg of the journey is the Russian Empire. At the same time, Erikson's chapter on Russian identity, written starting in 1948 on the basis of a film about the young Maxim Gorky, now leads back to Margaret Mead. New York's *Museum of Modern Art* had acquired a Soviet Russian propaganda film about the life of Maxim Gorky, *Detstvo Gorkogo* (1938), and loaned it to Mead's "Russian Project." Erikson, with Mead's help, analyzed the film along the lines of Bateson's analysis of *Hitlerjunge Quex* (1933), which, as discussed in Chapter 5, the latter had undertaken five years earlier.[76] Mead's Russian Project, funded by the RAND Corporation, turned the focus to the new Cold War enemy, continuing to rely on methods developed during World War II.[77] Erikson also emphasizes the importance of film as a counterpart to his Nazi analysis in the context of the nascent Sovietology.[78] However, the general atmosphere in applied research had become increasingly hostile to social psychological approaches originating from the Culture and Personality School, which eventually also led to the premature termination of Mead's Russian Project.[79]

To be sure, the demise of this type of research in the power struggles of the late 1940s appears to be a failure of applied anthropology. Here, however, it will be shown that it was rather the consequence of its success. Erikson's analysis of Russia, his "longest chapter so far,"[80] the last completed text for *Childhood and Society* before publication in 1950, is perhaps also the last attempt to bring applied anthropology to a synthesis. Discussing the Soviet Russian propaganda film, Erikson's central argument involves a character called "The Stranger" who teaches a life lesson to young Gorky, deeply alienated in his backward rural home: "one must learn to take life." He concludes: "As we shall see, this determined 'grasping,' paired with a resistance against sinking back into dependence, is of outstanding importance to Bolshevik psychology. [...] It later becomes apparent that the stranger was a revolutionary."[81] The structure Erikson imagines for Russian identity in relation to its enemy is a recombination of American foreign policy. In Erikson's historical, or rather mythological, analysis, Russian peasants, associated with Native Americans, also had to send out a call to their enemies, a cry for help. The identification of protector and enemy led to a rupture in which all the attributes of the enemy are projected onto the tyrant's intermediaries, while the tyrant himself acts as a protector in the constant struggle against enemies, internal and external.[82] In this structure, it is the new revolutionary elite, associated with the American rebels, who saw their mission in the "task of outer transformation and inner conversion of the masses of peasants"[83] and in their "re-orientation."[84] According to Erikson, this revolutionary reorientation must be understood as a Protestant rebellion led by an intelligentsia that "passionately wanted to be of the people and for the people; they once amplified and were amplified by a dark and illiterate tendency in the Russian masses [...] to find its national identity in a mystical international cause."[85] In this sense, Erikson ends with his own call from the imagined frontier between the US and the Soviet Union, this time referring to Protestantism as the boundary object common to both American and Russian identity: "We must succeed in convincing the Alyoshas [the revolutionary elite] – that from a very long-range point of view – their Protestantism is ours and ours, theirs."[86] As in the case of the Yurok,

Erikson avoids using the term "reeducation" for Soviet Russia and this time explicitly outlines an alternative in the form of a peace offering. Erikson proposes for the parties to the conflict to participate in his comedy of errors by following a common goal in foreign policy. Here Erikson attempts to transform the cultural relativism of applied anthropology into a political relativity. He concludes that, according to his analysis, both the American and the Russian intelligentsia concerned with foreign policy should recognize – in a form of anagnorisis, the dramatic re-recognition, of an orphan as a lost sibling – that they are as strange to each other as they are to their own populations. In their respective global policy, they are both internal strangers, acting simultaneously in their foreign policy as enemies as well as protectors of their populations, just as they are strangers to each other as citizens in a divided world. Along this path, the success of applied anthropology – a radical relativism – leads to a new imagined community of the United Nations via the domestication of the enemy. Conversely, however, the relativist questions of culture and personality-research in particular are replaced by a crystallized answer that is universalized and applicable to this new world of political relativity. The enemy becomes a question of domestic policy that spans the world: identity politics – Erikson's pacifist attempt to end the Cold War between the United States and Soviet Russia.

7.7 JEWISH IDENTITY

Looking at *Childhood and Society* as a whole, one understands the unifying power of identity only from this endpoint – and it is therefore perhaps no accident that Erikson's autobiographical writings obscure or forget its origins in reeducation as a problem of applied anthropology. Now, to properly string together all the links in the long chain of translation of identity requires another look at Erikson's Hitler chapter. Identity appears here not in its universalist usage but as a new import or substitute for the Nazis' domestic enemy. This is the 1942 version, still without identity:

In Hitler's world, however, the adolescent marches with his emancipated equals. Their leader has never sacrificed his will to any father. In fact, he says that conscience is a blemish like circumcision, and that both are Jewish blemishes. [...] One could go further and say that German anti-Semitism is the very projection of German weaknesses – projection meaning that one sees in others overclearly what one is unable to recognize in oneself.[87]

Friedman remarks on this anachronistically, but with the crucial association between the introduction of identity as a concept and the discussion of the role of Jewry:

> Most of the essential elements of the Hitler chapter in *Childhood and Society* originated in the 1942 article. The major deficiency in his concept was the absence, until the mid-1940s, of a clear idea of identity. But he was very close to that concept and only seemed to need the term itself, plus a few descriptive phrases, to make it gel. Another concern in the 1942 essay that was remedied in *Childhood and Society* was the fullness of the discussion of the Jew in German society.[88]

While it is debatable whether the four-page digression "A Note on Jewry" is indeed a comprehensive discussion of Jewish identity in the German context, it certainly did not receive an independent chapter in *Childhood and Society*. After the fact, the "missing" chapter cannot be fully reconstructed retrospectively since no coherent argument can be traced on the basis of the accessible materials, which are distributed mainly in further essays and case descriptions. What is striking, however, is that the observations on Jewish identity are – compared to the other chapters – emphatically focused on the body and appear to be superimposed by a presence of American antisemitism that inhibits closer analysis. For example, in *Childhood and Society*, in the first child psychology case study presented, Erikson explains "Sam's" epilepsy as a psychosomatic reaction to his Jewish family's relocation from a Russian ghetto to a "gentile" American living environment, generalizing this as a problem of "relativity in human existence."[89] In an earlier essay, Erikson analyzes a dancer, a "daughter of a second generation German-American."[90] He explains her postural problems, which originate from her spine, as the result of a "danger to her fragile ego-identity emanating from the association of her sexual conflicts with an unruly pair of historical prototypes, an *ideal* prototype (German, tall, phallic), and an *evil* prototype (Jewish, dwarfish, castrated, female)."[91] Erikson then connects this case study to an analysis of a ranch owner who conceals his Jewish origins.[92] Guided by phobias toward his fellow human beings, the patient enters into self-isolation because he has internalized the racist stereotypes of the "evil Jew." The patient fears that his nose will betray him and therefore lives just like a Jew in an antisemitic environment. In both cases, Erikson describes a bodily dissolution of ego identity in which individual body parts become associated with rival group identities. Thus, in reference to the ranch owner, Erikson notes, "the patient in question sincerely felt that the only true savior for the Jews would be a plastic surgeon."[93] In addition, there is another line that is already laid out in the 1942 text, associating Hitler with Sigmund Freud:

7.7 Jewish Identity

> The founder of psychoanalysis, Sigmund Freud was born within 250 miles of Hitler's birthplace, a member of the Jewish minority of the German-speaking part of the Austrian Empire. One wonders what common cultural determinants are responsible for the fact that the same sector on the fringe of German culture has produced the man who enlightened mankind in regard to the Œdipus conflict, and the man who advocates its universal solution by criminal action.[94]

Here, Erikson refers *en passant* to the trans-imperial periphery common to the Jewish population and Hitler, since the latter was born in the Bavarian-Austrian border region as a "member of the Austrian Empire's German [majority] minority."[95] This could have been the main motif of Erikson's analysis of Jewish identity, which might have guided all other motifs pursued here: the question of enmity, reeducation, and the stability of identity. This, however, did not happen, not least because the possible interchangeability of Hitler and Jew would have finally blown up the genre of the comedy of errors, or rather, this feat could not be repeated after Charlie Chaplin's *The Great Dictator* (1940).

For Erikson, the ultimate lack of engagement with the Jewish father figure or the father of psychoanalysis in a planned – but entirely left out – methodological chapter was the greatest shortcoming of his book. Erikson published the methodological statement, which he had first given as a lecture in a seminar on dream interpretation at the San Francisco Psychoanalytic Institute in 1949, separately in a later essay that marks his break, however, with the "mother," his teaching analyst Anna Freud. This text, too, still shows a connection between his analysis of Hitler and "Freud, the Jew,"[96] a connection that, as mentioned, no longer became relevant for an unwritten chapter on Jewish identity, but very much so for his chapter on Hitler's childhood.

Here, then, after proving the first use of identity and reeducation as Indian reeducation, is my third and last historical correction. The first introduction of identity into the chapter on Germany is not found in *Childhood and Society* of 1950, but happened a year earlier, in 1949, in the aforementioned "reprint" of the 1942 text, which has not yet received sustained treatment. In this text Erikson introduces – in a tacit revision – for the first time the concept of identity into his interpretation of Hitler, not universally as one might expect and especially not as German identity. Instead, it is about the identity of the enemy, Jewish identity: "Whoever and whatever can be identified today as Jewish contains in its *identity* [emphasis added] the extreme (but variably intense) opposition of two trends favored by centuries of dispersion, namely dogmatic orthodoxy vs. relativistic adaptability."[97] Thus, a formulation that had already been encapsulated in the 1942 analysis of Germany gains central importance in 1949, developed into a formula. It is the formula that best describes foreign policy at the time of the Cold War when recurring to the category of identity. It coincides with the antisemitic image of the enemy: "[T]here is the extreme role of the religiously dogmatic, culturally reactionary Jew, to whom change and time mean absolutely nothing: the Word is his reality. And there is his opposite, the Jew to whom geographic dispersion and cultural multiplicity have become second nature: relativity is his absolute."[98]

Identity is here, in 1949, with reference to Nazi Germany and Jewry, only once briefly appearing in this clarity, in fact, identification with the identity of the enemy, or rather the violent identification with the identity construction of one's own identity created by the enemy. This polemical interplay in the conception of identity is, even at the time of the Cold War, still the late consequence of the irreconcilable confrontation with the world war enemy.

A year later – in 1950 – in the pacifist synthesis of *Childhood and Society*, this identity is then universalized.[99] The intersection of the two stories of reeducation and identity first appearing in Erikson's "Letter from California" continues in Erikson's research until it fully merges in the publication of his anthropological travelogue *Childhood and Society* and thereby becomes invisible. What remains is a universalized notion of identity that only continues to gain momentum from its postwar history through the Cold War and into the new millennium.

7.8 ERIKSON'S CONTRIBUTION TO REEDUCATION

More directly, both Erikson's analysis of Hitler and his "Letter from California" migrated into the final report in which the group meeting around Mead and Brickner in 1944 summarized its findings, entitled "Germany after the War: Roundtable – 1945" and published in the *American Journal for Orthopsychiatry*.[100] After all, this publication figures as one of the central documents of reeducation and it is crucial to examine this text in order to understand the difficult transition between the gray literature of the memorandum culture analyzing Germany and the *Realpolitik* of the US occupation.[101] The report circulated, still unpublished, through the memorandum culture in 1944, reaching, among other places, the Psychological Warfare Division led by Supreme Allied Commander General Dwight D. Eisenhower,[102] the predecessor of the Information Control Division, shortly thereafter responsible for

7.8 Erikson's Contribution to Reeducation

the reeducation of Nazi German propagandists, that is, their transformation into democratic West German journalists. Sociologist Edward Y. Hartshorne, instrumental in reopening German universities, also helped the text to be distributed widely in British Government circles.[103] This anonymously published report, essentially written by Mead, Lawrence K. Frank, and possibly Talcott Parsons,[104] is also where Erikson's analysis of Germany – unmarked, mediated through Mead, and again diagrammatically restated against Erikson's will – becomes fully effective for the debate of reeducation. The analysis in Mead and Bateson's "Preliminary Memorandum," presented above thus comes to fruition after all, thanks to Mead's intervention. The double image of the father and the triple image of the mother, which lead to a dualism between "Type A" sentimental and "Type B" authoritarian behavior in the German character,[105] form the basic building block of the understanding of Germany elaborated upon in this text.[106] Mead deploys Erikson's argument adeptly against the distinction between "good" and "bad" Germans. There is no "other Germany" but only one – dualistic – German identity, which nonetheless may not directly be the object of reeducation, for otherwise the German fear of loss of status and identity would lead to rebellious counterreactions against the occupying power. This, however, would be detrimental to democratization or, as Erikson concluded from his experience with Indian reeducation, would lead to a failure and a relapse into old and undesirable patterns of behavior. This caution in Erikson's analysis leads to detailed policy recommendations, which, as he suggested in his letter, start primarily with the image of the mother and the emancipation of the German woman. New professions should be opened to women, hierarchies must be dismantled, and in the process the status of old male concepts of honor has to be reduced. The reeducation should not start at the national level but, in Erikson's "trans-imperial"[107] sense, regionally, province by province, provincialism by provincialism, with the purpose of provincializing Germany in Europe: "Advantage should be taken of whatever anti-centralization trends may occur as a reaction to Nazism; these should be used to decentralize education."[108] Here, too, it must be stated that the apparent failure of reeducation described by Tent at the beginning is possibly also the result of the success of its conception. Or, to quote Erikson's comment on Indian reeducation again, "the administrator or teacher cannot possibly know when they are dealing with an old virtue, when with a new vice."[109] The only way out seems to be to instruct Germans to reflect critically on the questions of reeducation in their own analyses of German identity: "The new system would aim to create Germans who could think with some objectivity and rationality about Germany or any other subject instead of centering upon the glorification of Germany."[110]

I have shown that the reconstruction of Erikson's contribution to reeducation in connection with the emergence of his concept of identity brings to light a hitherto unconsidered line in the history of American foreign policy that runs from the reform of the "Indian reservations" across the memorandum culture of the 1940s to the democratization of postwar Germany. At the center were Erikson's memoranda on Nazi Germany, the framework was provided by a forgotten social scientific discipline, applied anthropology, with Mead mediating in between. The resulting story could be traced to Erikson's sociopsychological classic *Childhood and Society*, first published in 1950, although a certain philological effort was necessary to be able to recognize it as a travelogue oscillating between real experience and imagination in a comedy of errors.

Unlike Friedrich's – mentioned initially –, Erikson's relationship to the real-world reeducation of Germany remained imaginary or limited to the analysis of imagery – even in his famous later book *Young Man Luther*,[111] which, from the perspective of *Childhood and Society*, is primarily a continuation of Erikson's studies of America and Soviet Russia's common – German? – Protestantism. Erikson was not one of the émigrés who returned to, say, Copenhagen, Vienna, or Karlsruhe. Instead, directly after the end of the war, in 1946, at the height of reeducation, he described from his own practice the case of a successful, actually American, alternative reeducation, which did not stop at the role of the mother, but, as in the "Preliminary Memorandum" by Mead and Bateson suggested, began with that of the father. It is the path from a "one-boy-Hitler-youth rebellion" to a "military school boy"; a path that still seems equally plausible in the immediate postwar period, thanks to Mead and Erikson *the road not taken*:

> In another case, the father is not an American soldier, of this war, but an ex-German soldier of the last war. He emigrated to this country because he could not accept Nazism or was unacceptable to it. His little son had hardly time to absorb Nazi indoctrination before he came to this country, where, like most children, he took to Americanization like a duck to water. Gradually, however, he developed a neurotic rebellion against all authority. What he said about the "older generation" and how he said it was clearly taken from Nazi leaves which he had never read; his behavior was an unconscious one-boy-Hitler-youth rebellion. A superficial analysis revealed that the boy in identifying with the slogans of the Hitler youths identified himself with his father's aggressors, according to the oedipus principle. At this point, the boy's parents decided to send him to a

7.8 Erikson's Contribution to Reeducation 195

military school. I expected him to rebel violently. Instead, something happened that I have since observed in other refugee children. A marked change came over the boy the moment he was handed a uniform with the promise of gold bars, stars and rank. It was as if these military symbols affected a sudden and decisive change in his inner economy. The boy was now an unconscious Hitler-youth wrapped up in an American prototype: the military school boy. The father, a mere civilian, now was neither dangerous nor important. Somewhere, however, it had been this same father and related father surrogates who with unconscious gestures (especially when speaking of military exploits during the last war) had helped establish in this boy the military prototype which is a part of every European's group identity, and in the German mind has the special significance of being one of the few thoroughly German and highly developed identities. As a historical focus of the family's general trend of identifications the military identity continues to exist unconsciously in those who are excluded from its consummation by political developments.[112]

8

Epilogue

To Whom It May Concern

Once gray literature has served its immediate purpose, most of it gets physically destroyed. Indeed, the texts considered most important are often those prepared for and "consumed" during meetings. Several of the most crucial memoranda, charts, reports, diagrams, minutes, papers, and drafts are likely prepared on a deadline, inconsistently edited, contain grammatical and orthographic mistakes, as well as last-minute handwritten corrections. Some are clipped, unclipped, stapled, unstapled, passed around from hand to hand, held up, pointed at, and damaged in the process. Individual pages may be singled out, removed from the entire body of text, read out loud, praised or criticized, and devalued. Summaries, passages, lines, or single words can be marked up or redacted. The text may be reshuffled, dog-eared, folded, water or coffee stained. When the meeting is finished and the collaborative "literary" work is done, the text gets ripped apart, shredded, crumpled, and habitually trashed on the way out of the room. As a rule of thumb, the more important gray literature, the less it remains in its original shape. Gray literature that distributes confidential information even comes with specific instructions to be physically destroyed to avoid further circulation, or even worse, publication: "burn after reading."

All these practices of discarding paper are a feature and not a bug. Without routines of clearing the desk, of making space, of moving on, that is, without processes of active "forgetting," gray literature quite quickly overwhelms the channels of communication. This holds also true – despite their name – for memoranda, and indeed applied to the gray literature produced by the memorandum culture during World War II. Most of the paper was simply discarded. The little remaining rest was kept for further reference and eventually stored away in private basements and attics, in office cabinets but also in special libraries, as well as in institutional archives. Some of these documents were even instantly chosen for long-term preservation on microfilm. Additionally, after the war's end, scholars immediately started to publish institutional histories with research based on first-hand information, interviews, as well as on the selectively surviving memoranda, reports, dossiers, protocols, and letters of the memorandum culture, mostly invisibilizing its material basis and instead bringing their achievements for the public interest into view. These studies, together with the ultimately published work of the memorandum culture, again, were put "on shelf" in American research libraries, often expertly organized together – and still may be accessed there by anyone, "to whom it may concern."

Not only the gray literature, but also the sociality of the collaborations of World War II, often bridging stark political contrasts, as well as fundamental intellectual disagreements, came to an end. Following Germany's unconditional surrender, alliances and enmities quickly shifted, as the Cold War gave rise to a wave of ideological purification during the Red Scare. Several of the intellectuals active in the study of Nazi Germany, especially those who had gone in the catastrophic first half of the twentieth century through multiple political conversions, were now suspected of Communist tendencies and of collaboration with Soviet spying rings. Most intellectuals, of course, were able to reaffirm themselves as staunch democrats and capitalists, with a surprising number abandoning their earlier socialist leanings and moving toward conservativism during midcentury. In this new era of suspicion, interdisciplinary collaborative ventures became, on the one hand, thanks to their apparent accomplishments during World War II part of the funding structures at universities, in "think tanks," as well as in military research and inspired several new developments to approach problem-oriented research projects in groups. They were, on the other hand, ideologically more exclusive. After the conservative backlash following twelve years of Roosevelt presidency, those unwilling to formally embrace the primacy of the politics over research, as for example famously enacted through loyalty oaths, were forced out or deliberately left the world of collaboration. Thomas Mann, the American, at that point in his late seventies, even left the United States after fourteen years utterly disappointed to return in 1952, not to Germany, but to the "neutral" grounds of Switzerland.

Gregory Bateson, the British social anthropologist turned secretary, film analyst, and colonial black propagandist is possibly, more than anyone else, indicative of the fate of the memorandum culture and its afterlife. Directly after the war, he strongly opposed the new American foreign politics of the Cold War, especially the proliferation of nuclear weapons and the escalating armament race, but he also participated in the famous interdisciplinary Macy Conferences, where mathematicians and physiologists worked with anthropologists and psychologists on "Constructing a Social Science for Postwar America."[1] He then moved to California and developed, collaborating with Juergen Ruesch, a theory of communication, following his theoretical engagement with cybernetics,[2] but also his study of propaganda as wartime administrator of gray literature and his experience as secretary in the memorandum culture. *Communication* (1951) theorizes the discipline of psychiatry based on Bateson's participant observation of the work of Californian psychiatrists and their "culture or habits of thought,"[3] building once again after World War II a bridge from social psychological national character studies to the analysis of mass communication and information theory. Bateson's postwar career vacillates between center (California) and periphery (Virgin Islands, Hawai'i) of American culture, between institutionalism (academia, federal grants, Rockefeller and Wenner-Gren Foundation) and anti-institutionalism (antipsychiatry movement, prophetic habitus), between theory (communication, epistemology, aesthetics) and practice (media experiments, letter writing, conference design), moving from memorandum culture (cultural anthropology) to counterculture (Hippie movement, environmentalism, syncretism) and cyberculture (Whole Earth network).[4] In particular, Bateson's "sociotechnological" path, sometimes alongside Margaret Mead, sometimes on parallel roads, from New York City and the analog, mimeograph-based memorandum culture of World War II to San Francisco and the computer-based digital cyberculture of the Cold War, is one of the most consequential extensions of wartime studies of Nazi Germany.

* * *

Immediately after World War II, the practice of using mimeograph machines for small-scale distribution of texts was put to a surprising new use. A young generation of authors with limited or no access to established publication venues started to make use of the cheap, accessible, and easy-to-use machines to anthologize their poetry in a new experimental format of distribution. The resulting ephemeral do-it-yourself journals, which started spreading in the 1940s and 1950s, before they took center stage between the 1960s and 1970s, are now often subsumed in the category of "little magazines."[5] These prints, together with newsletters, pamphlets, and fliers defined a subcultural literary space, variously called "clandestine," "revolutionary," "free," "independent," "radical," "anti-establishment," "dissident," or "underground," that allowed for media experimentation and new forms of political expression. Literary historians have started to call this recycling of wartime literary practices – largely unaware of the details of its prehistory in the memorandum culture during World War II – the "mimeograph revolution."[6] The mimeograph revolution happened in the United States, but similar techniques of distribution also created underground literature "transatlantically," such as the famous *samizdat* in the Soviet Union,[7] or, as Fatoumata Seck explores in her pioneering study of "écrits sous maquis," in the "underground of decolonization" in West African liberation movements.[8] The American mimeograph revolution, in the German case, took some years to be picked up, and fueled arguably as a hectograph or rotaprint revolution the reading circles of the 1960s with gray literature.[9] Horkheimer and Adorno's *Dialectic of Enlightenment* – to name one of the most prominent examples – thus had a first life in the memorandum culture as an edition mimeographed by the Institute of Social Research in 1944, before it was largely ignored in print only to have, in the 1960s, a second life as a pirated print. Their famous "message in a bottle" is a variation on the theme of "to whom it may concern."

In Germany, the translator, editor, and journalist Carl Weissner was in the 1960s one of the first to register the attraction of new modes of editing and constructing texts through techniques such as the "cut-up." Weissner understood quite early the immense literary potential of little magazines, and especially their significance for the circulation of texts. As Weissner repeated in several interviews, he gained access to the underground scene of American "beat literature" from Heidelberg, Germany, by relentless letter writing. For this purpose, Weissner emphasized in several interviews, he produced his first literary journal not so much to be read by a German audience, but as an object of barter.[10] He named the magazine in 1965 *Klactoveedsedsteen* (later *Klacto*). The enigmatic title references a piece by Charlie Parker, first recorded in 1947 alongside the young Miles Davis, "Klactoveedsedstene," possibly a phono-semantic riff on the German "*Klatscht, auf Wiedersehen*," "clap your hands, see you again," "thank you for listening, everybody."

Notes

I INTRODUCTION

1. For the American academic response to the Third Reich, and especially regarding the discipline of German Studies until World War II, see Norwood, *Third Reich*, 158–95. Catastrophically shrunk during and after World War I, German Departments by and large followed an ill-conceived defensive self-understanding as cheerful mediators of German language, literature, and culture. Many departments and German Clubs promoted after 1933 their sympathies for the aggressive and antisemitic ideology of the new German regime and sustained lively exchange programs. These activities lead historian Stephen H. Norwood to describe American German Departments between 1933 and 1941 wholesale as "Nazi nests." See Norwood, *Third Reich*, 169.
2. While most intellectuals diverted their attention away from Nazi Germany after its military aggression was finally contained, there are clear personal and institutional continuities that can be traced to the organization of Germany's military occupation, Operation Paperclip, the Nuremberg Trials, as well as to Cold War-era publications on "totalitarianism," such as George Orwell's novel *Nineteen Eighty-Four* (1949) and Hannah Arendt's *The Origins of Totalitarianism* (1951). With increasing historical distance, Nazi Germany slowly turned into the subject of specialized scholarship in various disciplines, in parts pioneered by former members of the memorandum culture.
3. Bateson to Erikson, "Letter, January 17, 1943," *Margaret Mead Papers and South Pacific Ethnographic Archives, 1838–1996* at Library of Congress, Washington, DC.
4. Mandler, *Return from the Natives*, 76.
5. Chambers, "Sin Rediscovered," 38.
6. American Friends of German Freedom, *In RE: Germany*.
7. Medawar and Pyke, *Hitler's Gift*.
8. Within intellectual history, H. Stuart Hughes' *Sea Change* is arguably the foundational work for the study of the intellectual migration around World

War II and has spurred a wealth of research in the following decades. Hughes collaborated with several other future influential intellectual historians as analyst at the OSS. See on his war years, Hughes, *Gentleman Rebel*, 117–79. Historian Tim B. Müller argues, relying on earlier statements by Hughes, by his OSS colleague Leonard Krieger and by Fritz Stern, a student of OSS colleague Franz Neumann, that the very discipline of intellectual history is tied to the wartime work of intellectuals analyzing Germany, such as Hughes, see Müller, *Krieger und Gelehrte*, 317–403.

9. Schreckenberger, *Alchemie des Exils*.
10. The writing of biographical accounts of course continues to this day and still provides important insights and framings. Compare inter alia on Hans Speier Bessner, *Democracy in Exile*; on Margaret Mead, Mandler, *Return from the Natives*; on Alain Locke, Stewart, *Alain Locke*.
11. The technical term emerged in the late 1960s or early 1970s, primarily in the British spelling "grey literature." I am using the American spelling.
12. See Auger, *Information Sources*, 1–17. In the last two decades, there has been a growing discussion about gray literature. For a survey, see Bonato, *Searching the Grey Literature*, 1–31. An authoritative history of gray literature in the twentieth century beyond the problems of library science is still a major *desideratum*. The British linguist Charles P. Auger pioneered the discussion of the term, which was originally a modification of notions such as "report" and "preprint literature." For a prominent use describing the new phenomenon in older terms with some alarm in 1963 – in a work of gray literature – by nuclear physicist Alvin M. Weinberg et al., the so-called "Weinberg-Report," see President's Science Advisory Committee, "The Emergence of the Report," 19–20. The report was published a few months later in a new journal edited by Edward Shils – without acknowledgment, in a highly edited form, cutting out the alarm, see NN. "Science, Government and Information." The term "gray literature" started only in the 1980s to enter the academic debate and has not been dealt with methodically in the context of intellectual history and related fields. More specific genres, however, that are part of gray literature such as memoranda, reports, and letters have their own trajectories and, in some cases, such as the letter, a long history of scholarship dedicated to understanding their development and impact on writing practices in general.
13. See Glissant, "Creolization in the Making of the Americas."
14. Galison takes the concept of the trading zone from linguistic anthropology and repurposes it for his study of interdisciplinary scientific collaborations, see Galison, *Image and Logic*, 770.
15. Gigerenzer, "From Tools to Theories."
16. Anderson to Horkheimer, "Letter, December 19, 1940," Nachlass Max Horkheimer, http://sammlungen.ub.uni-frankfurt.de/horkheimer/nav/index/all (August, 5, 2025).
17. See for the use of the term Appadurai, *Modernity at Large*.
18. Stanitzek, "Projektemacher."
19. See Koselleck, *The Practice of Conceptual History*.
20. Bourdieu, *Outline of a Theory of Practice*.

21. See Vismann, *Files*, 139.
22. See Krohn, *Intellectuals in Exile*, 95; 147.
23. See Rutkoff and Scott, *New School*. For his work in administrative reform in the United States, see Brecht, *Political Education*, and esp. Unger, "Berater der US-Regierung."
24. Fleck, *Transatlantic History*, 165–220.
25. Kohn, *Idea of Nationalism*, x.
26. Blackbourn, *Germany in the World*, 455–63.
27. The following description is based on the *Hans Kohn Collection* held by the *Leo-Baeck Institute New York*, https://archives.cjh.org/repositories/5/resources/16183 (August 5, 2025), his autobiography Kohn, *Living in a World Revolution*, and the biographies by Gordon, *Toward Nationalism's End* and Langeheine, *Von Prag nach New York*.
28. Kohn, *Vom Judentum*. See Kieval, *Making of Czech Jewry*, 148–53.
29. See Kohn, "Die Juden in Sibirien," 191–92.
30. Klausner, *Geschichte der Neuhebräischen Literatur*.
31. Kohn, *Nationalismus*.
32. Committee of Fifteen, *City of Man*, 101.
33. Gordon, "The Ideological Convert."
34. Compare for the crucial analysis of this complex, although revisionist and apologetic of German crimes, Boveri, *Verrat im 20. Jahrhundert*.
35. Kohn, *Idea of Nationalism*, 3.
36. Ibid.
37. Kohn, *Idea of Nationalism*, 4.
38. Ibid.
39. Kohn, *Idea of Nationalism*, 9.
40. Kohn, *Idea of Nationalism*, 10–11.
41. Kohn, *Idea of Nationalism*, 12.
42. Kohn, *Idea of Nationalism*, 15.
43. Kohn, *Idea of Nationalism*, 16.
44. Kohn, *Idea of Nationalism*, 20.
45. See chapter 4 "The Kohn Dichotomy. Fascism and German History" by Kenneth Wolf in his unpublished dissertation at University of Notre Dame, Wolf, *The Idea of Nationalism*, 120–73.
46. Compare, for example, Anderson, *Imagined Communities*.
47. The biographical information used here is largely based on interviews, private letters, and archival materials presented by Lewis' two main biographers Mark Schorer and Richard Lingeman, see Schorer, *Sinclair Lewis*; Lingeman, *Sinclair Lewis*.
48. Lingeman, *Sinclair Lewis*, 91. Riesman coins according to the same use of "dope" in *Lonely Crowd* the term "inside-dopester" for the paradigmatic other-directed type, who has exclusive knowledge, see Riesman, *Lonely Crowd*, 199–209.
49. The expression is used in a review of *Babbitt* by literary critic Henry Mencken, quoted in Lingeman, *Sinclair Lewis*, 210.
50. See Bender, *New York Intellect*, 207–62.
51. Lingeman, *Sinclair Lewis*, 101.

52. Lingeman, *Sinclair Lewis*, 126. The quotes are respectively by Lingeman and Harcourt.
53. Lingeman, *Sinclair Lewis*, 172. Riesman however mentions *Babbitt* only once in passing.
54. Richardson, "*Arrowsmith*: Genesis." See also Verhave, *Paul de Kruif*, 88–107.
55. See Lingeman, *Sinclair Lewis*, 208. Upton Sinclair had written his novel *King Coal* (1917) under the impression of the massacre.
56. Lingeman, *Sinclair Lewis*, 206.
57. Compare the antisemitic slurs against Flexner in his letters to Mencken, quoted in Verhave, "Mencken and de Kruif," 2.
58. See Grebstein, "Sinclair Lewis's Unwritten Novel." On the failed attempt to collaborate with activist and head of the Federated Press Carl Haessler, see Lingeman, *Sinclair Lewis*, 342–45.
59. On Thompson's leading role in the public debate on National Socialism, see Kurth, *American Cassandra*; see also Hoenicke Moore, *Know Your Enemy*, 52–58. Karina von Tippelskirch provides an account of Thompson's collaboration with German émigrés in the American Guild for German Cultural Freedom, the American Committee for Christian German Refugees, and the Emergency Rescue Committee. Tippelskirch, *Dorothy Thompson*.
60. Roosevelt survived an assassination attempt days before his inauguration in February 1933. The murder of Roosevelt in Miami is the counterfactual premise of Philip K. Dick's novel *Man in the High Castle* (1962) about a fascist American society.
61. Lingeman, *Sinclair Lewis*, 400–1.
62. Lingeman, *Sinclair Lewis*, 398.
63. Lingeman, *Sinclair Lewis*, 399.
64. On the collaboration between Thompson and Lewis, see Betz and Thunecke, "Sinclair Lewis's Cautionary Tale."
65. For responses to Lewis' early satirical depictions of service clubs, especially in *Babbitt*, see Charles, *Service Clubs*, 86–103. Charles points out that Lewis was far from alone in his debunking of service clubs. "In addition to Lewis and [Henry L.] Mencken, Dorothy Parker, Bruce Bliven, Clarence Darrow, Gilbert Seldes, and G. K. Chesterton" attacked the clubs. Charles, *Service Clubs*, 87. He ignores, however, like all research on service clubs so far, Lewis' *It Can't Happen Here*, as well as his *Gideon Planish*.
66. Lewis, *It Can't Happen Here*, 9.
67. On Elizabeth Dilling, arguably the real life-model of Gimmitch as female supporter and propagandist of the fascist dictator Windrip, see Erickson, "Elizabeth Dilling's Crusade."
68. Lewis, *It Can't Happen Here*, 98.
69. In his study of the Rotary Club, Brendan Goff points out that at least the international export of Rotary Clubs and their entanglement of Christian concepts of charity with capitalist business practices was actually not compatible with fascism, not even in its Christian version in Spain, see Goff, *Rotary International*, 43.

70. Roosevelt managed to pursue his close relationship to England against several initiatives by the America-First Committee. The defeat of Roosevelt by Charles Lindbergh in the 1940-election is the counterfactual premise of Philip M. Roth's *The Plot against America* (2004) about a fascist American society. For a general survey and analysis of the rich genre of "Hitler-Wins" counterfactual narratives before Roth, see Winthrop-Young, "Third Reich in Alternative History."
71. Lewis to Mencken, quoted in Schorer, *Sinclair Lewis*, 679.
72. Lewis, *Gideon Planish*, 15.
73. Lewis, *Gideon Planish*, 45.
74. Lewis, *Gideon Planish*, 76.
75. Lewis, *Gideon Planish*, 117.
76. Lewis, *Gideon Planish*, 166.
77. Lewis, *Gideon Planish*, 160. The quote is part of a three-page rant against the world of philanthropy, in which significant parts of the memorandum culture developed.
78. Lewis, *Gideon Planish*, 143.
79. Lewis, *Gideon Planish*, 181.
80. Lewis, *Gideon Planish*, 184.
81. Lewis, *Gideon Planish*, 185.
82. Lewis, *Gideon Planish*, 217.
83. Lewis, *Gideon Planish*, 350.
84. See Lewis, *Gideon Planish*, 392.
85. See Lewis, *Gideon Planish*, 350.
86. Lewis, *Gideon Planish*, 425.
87. Lewis, *Gideon Planish*, 426.
88. Lewis, *Gideon Planish*, 380–86.
89. Lewis, *Gideon Planish*, 387–88.
90. Lewis, *Gideon Planish*, 392.
91. Harry Maule, quoted in Lingeman, *Sinclair Lewis*, 470.
92. See Johnson, *George Sylvester Viereck*.
93. Lewis' inscription to the copy of *Gideon Planish* for the University of Minnesota, quoted in Schorer, *Sinclair Lewis*, 698–99.
94. Lewis, *Gideon Planish*, 222.
95. Thus, Thompson's nonresponse possibly prevented further damage, also to herself as a source.
96. Lewis, *Gideon Planish*, 364.
97. Herzstein, *Luce*, 83.
98. Herzstein, *Luce*, 223.
99. See Namikas, "The Committee to Defend America." While the CCCC in the novel is in fact not only alphabetically closer to the (CD)AAA, the DDD clearly resembles Luce's FFF.
100. Lewis, *Gideon Planish*, 375.
101. Lewis, *Gideon Planish*, 379.
102. Lewis, *Gideon Planish*, 375.
103. Lewis, *Gideon Planish*, 378.
104. Lewis, *Gideon Planish*, 379.

105. Lewis, *Gideon Planish*, 382.
106. Lewis' diary of the year 1942 is a remarkable document of his escapism and the minimal engagement with the news of the raging war, National Socialism, or the writing of his novel. "Perhaps first eve of July 4th, and 4th itself, in life, while in America, that didn't hear one firecracker explode, one toy pistol. Forbidden, re war. Many people on roads in another putative last fling before threatenied [sic] gas rationing. Egypt now menaced by Rommel – we talk mostly of that, if mention the war at all." Lewis, *Minnesota Diary*, 123.
107. "Proper Gander," a short story from 1935 constitutes in many ways the forgotten "bridge" between *It Can't Happen Here* and *Gideon Planish*. The protagonist T. Tilbury Plim, a lawyer and professional propagandist working in the world of Washington, DC-based politicians, pamphlets and action groups at one point realizes that he is lacking one crucial qualification to enter into the more powerful circles of the memorandum culture: He "found that these organizations were already heavily staffed with torch bearers and good-doers whom he could not match – thin ardent young men with intellectual little black mustaches, most of them Ph.D.'s." Lewis, "Proper Gander," 301.
108. See for the attempt to deconstruct American isolationism and for the important revision of the complexities of anti-interventionism in Doenecke, *Challenge to American Intervention*.
109. Johnstone, *Against Immediate Evil*, 4.
110. MacLeish to Frankfurter, "Letter, May 15, 1939," MacLeish, *Letters*, 299–301, 299.
111. MacLeish to Frankfurter, "Letter, May 15, 1939," MacLeish, *Letters*, 299–301, 299–300.
112. MacLeish to Roosevelt, "Letter, May 28, 1939," MacLeish, *Letters*, 301–2, 302.
113. Roosevelt to MacLeish, "Letter, June 1, 1939," MacLeish, *Letters*, 302–3, 302–3.
114. Benco, "Poet Librarian," 242.
115. MacLeish, "Librarian and Democratic Process," 388.
116. It is worth mentioning, however, that J. Edgar Hoover's Federal Bureau of Investigation (FBI) created – over time – a 600-page dossier on MacLeish. See Donaldson, *MacLeish*, xi.
117. Roosevelt, K., *War Report*, Vol. 1, 48–49.
118. The media historian Brett Gary provides some details, particularly regarding MacLeish's wartime activities at the Library of Congress, in a chapter of his book with focus on propaganda work. See Gary, "Intellectual Arsenal," 131–73. See also MacLeish's most comprehensive biography, Donaldson, *MacLeish*, esp. 220–395.
119. As Harold Garfinkel writes in a scathing review of a book on the administration of intelligence, it is precisely those moments when the actual rules of the game become visible: "Throughout, Mr. Hilsman is at long-winded pains to make ironic contrast between actual problem-solving methods and the methodological facts of life. In some interminable and homespun

reflections the author displays no better than commonplace knowledge of the nature of fact, theory, and the procedures of scientific inquiry. Without explicitly recognizing them as such, Mr. Hilsham lists many features of common-sense thinking in everyday canons of reasonable judgment in the activities of the functionaries. Whatever small value the book has for students of administrative science is found here." Garfinkel, "Review: Strategic Intelligence," 542–43.

120. For the history of this formula, see Shapin, "Problematic Identity."
121. See again Baltzell, *Protestant Establishment*. Confirming the commonplace, Baltzell points to the Ivy League universities of the East Coast as the central places, where these networks forged their lifelong personal bonds and ideology. MacLeish went to Yale, became member of the Skulls and Bones, and later went to Harvard Law School and became editor of the *Harvard Law Review*.
122. Goffman, "Cooling the Mark Out." The text performs a cunning transformation of underworld into sociological terminology, based on a study from the field of sociolinguistics, Maurer, *Big Con*. Particularly gangster language and African American sociolect such as "Harlem Jive" had become a source of fascination during mid-century, as they were adopted in various literary, artistic and musical circles, and on college campuses.
123. Latour, *Science in Action*, 78.
124. In his private response to MacLeish, Roosevelt argues: "It is one of those curious facts that when I got your first letter I took to my bed with a severe attack of indigestion – and that when your second letter came I found myself able to rise and resume my normal life. […] It is perfectly all right about your taking office after the Summer is over – say the end of September or the first of October. And I am also very clear that you will be able to take 'time off' for writing, especially if you like travel to distant parts where you could also improve your knowledge of ancient literature. For example, as Librarian of Congress, you should become thoroughly familiar with the inscriptions on the stone monuments of Easter Island – especially in their relationship to similar sign writing alleged to exist on ancient sheepskins in some of the remoter lamaseries of Tibet. If you go on such a trip I would like to go along as cabin boy and will guarantee that I will not interrupt the Muse when she is flirting with you!" Roosevelt to MacLeish, "Letter, June 6, 1939," cited in Benco, "Poet Librarian," 237.
125. "[D]uring the years he served as Librarian, MacLeish wrote only one poem. The frustration he frequently felt was expressed in his correspondence over the next five years. Nevertheless, he did write numerous speeches, articles, and radio scripts as Librarian." Benco, "Poet Librarian," 236.
126. Serge Guilbaut credits MacLeish's text as the first "attack on the silence of American intellectuals in the face of war in Europe [that] triggered a long series of polemics in which the *Nation*, the *New Republic*, and *Partisan Review* attempted to define the role of the artist and intellectual in wartime. The article also launched an anti-isolationist movement that culminated in 1943 in an internationalist policy." Guilbaut, *Modern Art*, 52.
127. MacLeish, "Irresponsibles," 618.

128. Ibid.
129. Luce introduced during the 1920s and 1930s with his weekly and monthly magazines *Time*, *Life*, and *Fortune* major changes in the very "practices of [...] relaying the news," resulting in a new narrative mode that conveyed "'omniscience,' an all-knowing point-of-view. [...] [H]is legacy thus concerns the transformation of American journalism from information to synthesis." Baughman, *Luce*, 5–6. In contrast to "new big-city tabloids [...] as well as the Associated Press," this new perspective developed for *Time* in an effort to create a recognizable "*Time* style" offered to a US-public for the first time what was considered a "national view" on the United States and international news. See Baughman, *Luce*, 46–55. This national view was equally a result of the unprecedentedly high circulation of Luce's magazines. "Even the *New York Times*, the great newspaper of record, had few outlets beyond the Greater New York area. Nonresidents received the *Times* in the mail several days later, and it was not sold outside New York except at the few newsstands displaying three-day-old out-of-town newspapers. So, the farther one traveled from New York, the more one saw and heard Times Inc.'s magazines." Herzstein, *Luce*, 148.
130. "'The American Century' provoked a heated controversy about America's role in the world. The essay elicited almost 5,000 letters, many of them thoughtful, even anguished. Some readers saw Luce's work as 'a light in the distance,' after years of stumbling about in the 'semi-darkness.' Businessman, federal regulators, editors, college presidents, engineers, and journalists raved about Luce's article. [...] The people who praised 'The American Century' were important men and women in their institutions and communities. Luce had given the more ardent interventionist minority (perhaps 20 percent of public opinion) a platform and a program." Herzstein, *Luce*, 181.
131. See Herzstein, *Luce*, 179. Billings noted that Luce was "so busy being a Great Personage that he has forgotten the source of his greatness – the magazines we put out for him." Herzstein, *Luce*, 179.
132. Herzstein, *Luce*, 179.
133. See Herzstein, *Luce*, 178.
134. See Brinkley, *Luce*, 261. For a detailed discussion of the various members of the Century Group formed in 1940 and its ambivalent anglophile political agenda, see the classic study Chadwin, *Hawks of World War II*.
135. Luce seems to have got his initial idea from Lippmann's 1939 article "The American Destiny" that indeed reads like a first draft of "The American Century," see also Brinkley, *Luce*, 265.
136. Luce asked MacLeish to write a memorandum that he received as "a series of drafts [...] of a 'Statement of Belief' [and from which Luce] borrowed passages [...] in his own later essay," Brinkley, *Luce*, 266.
137. For a more recent rendition of this conjecture compare Schivelbusch, *Entfernte Verwandtschaft*. For a thorough historical reevaluation of this complex, arguing that indeed only two nations, the USA and Weimar Germany, faced structurally the same economic problems after the world

depression of 1929, and indeed responded in similar fashion, see Patel, *Soldiers of Labor*.

138. "The President of the United States has continually reached for more and more power, and he owes his continuation in office today largely to the coming of the war. Thus, the fear that the United States will be driven to a national socialism as a result of cataclysmic circumstances and contrary to the free will of the American people, is an entirely justifiable fear." Luce, "American Century," 62–63. The text was in the same year published as a small book with comments by, among others, Dorothy Thompson.

139. "[W]e are in the war. The irony is that Hitler knows it – and most Americans don't." Luce, "American Century," 61.

140. Luce, "American Century," 64.

141. The dance historian Astrid Kusser interprets this list in the context of the mobilization of minorities for the war effort as an attempt to ease the racial tensions at the homefront ultimately resulting in the "Zoot Suit Riots" between soldiers, police, and members of a jazz-inspired youth movement consisting largely of African-Americans and second generation Hispanic and Filipino immigrants, see Kusser, *Schieflage*, 443–54.

142. Kusser, *Schieflage*, 65.

143. Kusser, *Schieflage*, 65. For the use of this "prestige" in American "jazz diplomacy" during the Cold War, see Davenport, *Jazz Diplomacy*, 25.

2 COOL COLLABORATION

1. Riesman, *Lonely Crowd*, 19. There lies a certain paranoid quality in the concept of other-direction – but also in researching the social world of its making in the American establishment. See Riesman's rendition of scholarly sociality in an early review: "For Professor Frankfurter had the leader's ability not only 'of piercing the future by knowing what questions to put and what direction to give to inquiry,' but also of winning attention to these questions in his students, colleagues, and friends. He succeeds by making his students into his colleagues and friends, and vice versa. The foreword by Mr. MacLeish, a former student, is in itself a single but appealing instance." Riesman, "Review: Frankfurter."
2. This is the plural form that Riesman uses.
3. Riesman, *Lonely Crowd*, 201.
4. Ibid.
5. Ibid.
6. Riesman, *Lonely Crowd*, 16.
7. Riesman, *Lonely Crowd*, 201.
8. The experience and sociality of Black Americans is considered by Riesman, but ventures mostly from racist stereotypes of the backward "Southern Negro," who is in Riesman's terminology "tradition-directed," while those who migrated to northern urban centers have developed to being "inner-directed." The interview material – despite its complications bound to the power asymmetries of researcher, local informant, interviewer, and

interviewee – yields more complicated results, see especially the interview with Mrs. Roberta Herderson, in Riesman, *Faces in the Crowd*, 81–151. On Riesman's methodology, see Lee, "Sociology of the Interview."

9. See Baltzell, *Protestant Establishment*.
10. Riesman himself gives one of the best examples in a reflection on his Jewish heritage and minority position within an American society dominated by antisemitic Protestantism. He proposes a "nerve of failure" as a reaction to othering, see Riesman, "Nerve of Failure." Autobiographically, this lesson seems to have been at the core of Riesman's psychoanalysis conducted by Erich Fromm, see Wilkinson, "Interview with Riesman," 159.
11. The memorandum is preserved in Papers of David Riesman, HUG(FP) 99.55 box 13. David Riesman, "XI. Inner-Direction and Other-Direction: Changes in the Agents of Character Formation," [1]. The early draft sheds an interesting light, especially thanks to its condensed form, on the hitherto insufficiently acknowledged importance of cultural anthropology and Margaret Mead's wartime work for Riesman's concept of other-direction. Furthermore, the draft is archived together with an unpublished and undated manuscript "The Individual in a World of Power," in which the phrasing receives an important twist, an aural and submissive semantic dimension absent in the later *Lonely Crowd*, when Riesman talks about feeling "obliged to listen to directions from others." Riesman, "The Individual in a World of Power," 3.
12. See Gans, "Best-Sellers." It is not clear from Gans' article, whether this number pertains to the American market or also to translations.
13. See Guillory, "Memo and Modernity."
14. Guillory, "Memo and Modernity," 117.
15. Guillory, "Memo and Modernity," 117–18.
16. Guillory, "Memo and Modernity," 125. These changes, one might add, coincided with significant gains in literacy rates in the 1870s and 1910s, see the data in Snyder, *120 Years*. The mid-century, of course, also saw a massive extension of college education, not least thanks to the G. I. Bill of Rights in 1944 to support the college education of returning World War II veterans. See Mettler, *Soldiers to Citizens*.
17. Yates, "Memo," 489. Yates relies here on the Oxford English Dictionary.
18. Yates, "Memo," 493.
19. Yates, "Memo," 489.
20. For "scientific management," that is Taylorism, as a "refinement and extension" of "systematic management," see Nelson, "Scientific Management," 479. See also the ground-breaking essay on "scientific management," Maier, "Between Taylorism and Technocracy"; as well as Anson Rabinbach's interpretation of the underlying utopia, a "vision of society, in which conflict was eliminated in favor of technological and scientific imperatives could embrace liberal, socialist, authoritarian, and even communist and fascist solutions. Productivism, in short, was politically promiscuous." Rabinbach, *Human Motor*, 272.
21. Yates, "Memo," 493.
22. See Yates, "Memo," 496.

23. Yates, "Memo," 504.
24. Yates, "Memo," 499.
25. Yates, "Memo," 506.
26. Ibid.
27. Guillory, "Memo and Modernity," 111.
28. Riesman, *Lonely Crowd*, 240. This quote belongs to a long series of ableist Roosevelt-critiques that allude to his paralytic illness, historically attributed to polio.
29. Riesman, *Lonely Crowd*, 26. The metaphors for inner-direction and other-direction in fact point quite directly to Riesman's World War II experience. Riesman worked during World War II in the legal profession, most importantly in the bureaucracy of the Sperry Gyroscope Company, despite its name responsible for the production of radar-technology.
30. The close connection between several of the postwar classics of sociology, *The Lonely Crowd* (1950), *The Authoritarian Personality* (1950), *White Collar* (1951), in an entanglement of "talented and underemployed social scientists," working between academic institutions such as Yale University, Columbia University, University of Chicago, as well as government funded social scientific research in the Bureau of Applied Social Research, the Eastern Office of the National Opinion Research Center, sometimes working with the same materials and the same methods, still warrant a thorough study. See for example the memorandum promoting Fromm's typology, where one may find other-direction and inner-direction as "Marketing Ethic" and "Protestant Ethic" not so much as theoretical concepts but – again "from tools to theories" – as keys for coding interviews, sent by Riesman to C. Wright Mills, published in Riesman, "Suggestion for Coding."
31. Riesman, "Becoming an Academic Man," 46. Riesman's father, however, was a Jewish-German émigré, born in 1867 – before the Proclamation of the German Empire in 1871 – in the *Großherzogtum Sachsen-Weimar-Eisenach*, and also his mother had a Jewish-German family background. See Riesman, "Memoir."
32. On Friedrich and his work, see also Chapter 6.
33. Quoted from the Finding Aid at *The New York Public Library Rare Books and Manuscripts Division*, www.nypl.org/sites/default/files/archivalcollections/pdf/americancommittee.pdf (August 5, 2025).
34. Among those lawyers were some who went on to work for the Office of Strategic Services (OSS) discussed in Chapter 3, most prominently Otto Kirchheimer and Franz Neumann. It is worth mentioning that at the same time, Riesman published a negative review of a book coauthored by Kirchheimer that received only a belated appreciation in the 1960s and in Michel Foucault's famous study of penal institutions in 1975. See Riesman, "Review Kirchheimer."
35. See on the Council for Democracy Chapter 1 and again Chapter 6.
36. Compare again Riesman's draft on "The Genesis of Marketers," quoted above. Regarding Erich Fromm, a German psychoanalyst associated to the Frankfurt school and his early influence on Riesman, see McLaughlin, "Riesman, Fromm," 10. As Raymond M. Lee points out, Riesman was not

only conceptually, but also methodically influenced by Fromm, especially with regard to his interview techniques developed for his *Arbeiter- und Angestellten-Erhebung* in 1929, working as the head of the branch for social psychology of the Institute of Social Research in Frankfurt. See again Lee, "Sociology of the Interview," 294.
37. See Stearns, *American Cool*.
38. Lethen, *Cool Conduct*. Lethen's congenial German translation of other-direction is *Außenlenkung*. Compare with a focus on female coolness, Stephan, *Eisige Helden*.
39. For the development of the concept in the context of international collaboration in twentieth-century physics, pivoting on the problem of radar and the atomic bomb in World War II, see Galison, *Image and Logic*. "To sail between the Scylla of exaggerated homogeneity and the Charybdis of mere aggregation, I repeatedly use the notion of a trading zone, an intermediate domain in which procedures could be coordinated locally even where broader meanings clashed." Galison, *Image and Logic*, 46.
40. The argument about national styles is complicated by the prominent role of "German" émigrés originating from the territories of the Austro-Hungarian Monarchy, as well as the importance of French "hypothermia" for the creolization of the cool, especially with regard to popular stylistic innovations expressed for example in "film noir," which, after all, is in English, albeit retrospectively, based on a Gallicism. Arguably, one might speak of a "European cool," which is based on the common experience of World War I.
41. "Attitude" here needs to be considered as the unity of attitude of mind and, in an older use of the word, attitude of the body, that is, posture.
42. Compare the work of the art historian Robert Farris Thompson, particularly his exhibition catalogue with a collection of essays *An Aesthetic of the Cool: Afro-Atlantic Music and Art* (2011); compare his *Flash of the Spirit: African and Afro-American Art and Philosophy* (1983); and *Tango: The Art History of Love* (2005).
43. Ecological historians, on the other hand, have already successfully started to "provincialize" the United States according to histories of economy, settler colonialism, and forced migration: "By 'Greater Caribbean' I mean the Atlantic coastal regions of South, Central, and North America, as well as the Caribbean islands themselves [...]." McNeill, *Mosquito Empires*, 2. The older concept is "Circum-Caribbean," developed, however, on findings mainly from the archaeology of pre-Colonial America in the 1940s.
44. I use the hyphenated spelling African-American following the model of German-American or Jewish-Austrian, as well as Black and White in capitalized form to mark central aspects of social identities important to the argument.
45. Besides the "Western Passage," there is of course also the possibility of an "Eastern Passage," (from Europe over Bali to the United States) that will be outlined in Chapter 5.
46. Arguably, anything may be viewed as an intermediary. The question is: for what? See for the Greek titan Atlas, eponym of the Atlantic, as a cultural and cosmological intermediary between earth and sky: "The signified of

Etruscan *aril* 'matchmaker' is backed up by the concurrence of two distinct pieces of data: one concerning Etruscan iconography, the other from Latin lexicology. Atlas was called *aril*, in the sense of a cosmological 'mediator' [...]." Martino, *Nome Etrusco di Atlante*, 46, my translation, FP.

47. Compare in this context particularly the chapter "'Cheer the weary traveler.' W. E. B. Du Bois, Germany, and the Politics of (Dis-)Placement," in: Gilroy, *Black Atlantic*. Gilroy refers here to Du Bois "Black Atlantic" point of view on the German unification in 1871 as paradigm for a Pan-African nationalism, praising in a commencement speech at Fisk University in 1888 the German chancellor Otto von Bismarck as a model, possibly for his own political persona. This was first highlighted in Marable, *Du Bois*, 12. In the meanwhile, Du Bois' studies abroad in Imperial Germany (1892–1894), but also his trip to Nazi Germany in 1936 supported by the Oberlaender Trust have received considerable attention. See for the latter especially Sollors, "Du Bois in Nazi Germany." For the development of Du Bois' social theory in dialogue with German scholars such as Adolph Wagner, Gustav von Schmoller, and Max Weber, see Morris, *Scholar Denied*. The Black Atlantic was also symbolically present in the 1930s and 1940s. The modern form of transatlantic travel for example was immediately appropriated by the Black community: The "Lindy Hop," a popular dance first developed in Harlem, was named in 1928 after the recent crossing of the Atlantic by aviator Charles A. Lindbergh in May 1927.

48. See on the importance of the category of Youth for the transfer of culture in the United States and between the US and Europe, the influential study by Savage, *Teenage*. Jazz as part of the entertainment complex arrived in Europe on a massive scale after World War I. "The Old World had been destroyed, and the New rushed in. With its doughboys, its movies, and its music, America had crossed the Atlantic and Europe would dance to a different piper." Savage, *Teenage*, 178. And regarding the late 1920s: "It did not go unnoticed that jazz had become the lingua franca of American youth. The popularity of the music provided a common ground among the races." Savage, *Teenage*, 230. But: "Despite the illusion of racial harmony, the reality of the Harlem Renaissance was barely ameliorated segregation." Savage, *Teenage*, 231.

49. "Jazz" became discursive in terms of "entertainment" for a largely White US-American public among other forms of appropriation, most notably "Negro folklore," "spirituals," and various forms of social dance developing from the "cakewalk."

50. Most of Adorno's knowledge of American jazz understood as African-American "folk music" goes back to his reading of two books he reviewed in 1941, see Adorno, "Review Jazz." See also his equally critical attitude toward state-directed support of folk music, for example, as directed by the Works Progress Administration (WPA), in an unpublished review, Adorno, "Review Music of the People."

51. Jay, *Dialectical Imagination*, 186. See also for alternative concepts of "culture industry" in Chapter 4 on folklore and Chapter 5 on propaganda.

52. On Adorno's place in the history of jazz criticism, see Harding, "Adorno, Ellison."
53. See the 1974 exhibition catalogue Thompson, R., *African Art in Motion*.
54. "The English emigrants to New England were the first Puritans to restrict membership in the church to visible saints, to persons, that is, who had felt the stirrings of grace in their souls, and who could demonstrate this fact to the satisfaction of other saints." Morgan, E., *Visible Saints*, 113.
55. See however Saidiya Hartman's "critical fabulation" in *Lose Your Mother* (2007), a narrative approach to the history of Atlantic slave trade.
56. Thompson, R., *Flash*, 12.
57. Thompson, R., *Flash*, 13.
58. Ibid.
59. Thompson, R., *Flash*, 13–15.
60. Thompson, R., *Flash*, 15.
61. Thompson, R., *Flash*, 16.
62. Ibid.
63. Ibid.
64. Thompson, R., *Flash*, 18.
65. Thompson, R., *Flash*, 19.
66. Ibid. Compare also on Eshu-Elegba: Wescott, "Eshu-Elegba."
67. Wescott, "Eshu-Elegba," 345.
68. See especially the first chapter of the book, "A Myth of Origins: Esu Elegbara and the Signifying Monkey" in Gates, *Signifying Monkey*, 3–48.
69. Gates, *Signifying Monkey*, 11.
70. Wescott, "Eshu-Elegba," 341.
71. Thompson, R., "Aesthetic of the Cool," 42.
72. Ibid.
73. Ibid.
74. Ibid.
75. Ibid.
76. The two essays by Alice Walker and Robert Hemenway initiating the revival of Hurston's work were published in 1975 and 1976. See Walker, "In Search" and Hemenway, "Folklore Field Notes."
77. On Hurston's childhood and youth between Notasulga, Alabama and Eatonville, Florida, a small, largely self-governed Black town see Boyd, *Wrapped in Rainbows*, 13–56.
78. Hurston, *Mules and Men*, 90. Even under the Nazi regime and its strict censorship, at least one print of the book traveled across the Atlantic to Germany and was apparently included in 1938 in the collection of the "Amerika-Abteilung des Englischen Seminars der Universität Berlin." In 2023, the copy is still in good condition and appears to be only lightly read. Friedrich Schönemann, nontenured and unsalaried professor for American culture in Berlin since 1930, delivered National Socialist propaganda lectures in the United States after 1933. In 1936, he was promoted to be the first full professor in American Literary and Cultural History in Germany, and he held a guest professorship at the University of Nebraska in Fall 1937/38. Schönemann possibly imported the book privately and then donated it to

the library. The copy is marked on a vacat page "Schö 1938. 70." It is now kept in the holdings of the Freie Universität Berlin. See on Schönemann's relationship to the United States, Hausmann, *Anglistik und Amerikanistik*, 190–206.
79. Hurston, *Spunk*, 261.
80. Hurston, "The Gilded Six-Bits," 90.
81. Hurston to Mason, "Letter, May 26, 1932," Hurston, *Life in Letters*, 257.
82. It is important to stress the role of regional differences and internal migration in the Greater Caribbean in the history of forced migration of enslaved people. Besides the Spanish, Portuguese and French colonial populations, the full picture also includes Native American enslaved people, Native American slavery, and people with mixed-race identities, variously categorized as "mulattos" or "mestizos." See Morgan, Ph., "Early Modern Atlantic World."
83. Dinerstein, *Origins of Cool*, 38–39.
84. Dinerstein, *Origins of Cool*, 57.
85. The term was used only later generally referring to the 1920s; the research on the dating of the "Harlem Renaissance" so far is inconclusive, see Fearnley, "Harlem Renaissance." The best one can say is that the Harlem Renaissance has repeated renaissances.
86. Locke, *New Negro*. Zora Neale Hurston was among the contributors. Parts of the group of writers introduced themselves to the public one year earlier – in a club meeting, with registered attendance and protocol. "Interest among the literati of New York in the emerging group of younger Negro writers found an expression in a recent meeting of the Writers' Guild, an informal group whose membership includes Countee Cullen, Eric Walrond, Langston Hughes, Jessie Fauset, Gwendolyn Bennett, Harold Jackman, Regina Anderson, and a few others. The occasion was a 'coming out party,' at the Civic Club, on March 21 – a date selected around the appearance of the novel 'There is Confusion' by Jessie Fauset. [...]" NN., "Debut," 144. For a detailed account of Locke's work as editor of a highly successful Harlem number of *Survey Graphic*, eventually growing into *The New Negro*, see Stewart, *Alain Locke*, 434–76.
87. Locke was "[b]orn and bred in Philadelphia's Black middle class, Anglophile in dress and class snobbishness, a man who seemed to represent in his learning and bearing an old world Black tradition that no one knew existed [...]." Stewart, *Alain Locke*, 7. Locke was also the first African-American Rhodes scholar, attending Oxford University. For Locke's remarkable biography, see Stewart, *Alain Locke*. Stewart characterizes Locke's upbringing as "Black Victorian," which is mixed with his experiences of European travel, counteracted by his queerness, all of which made Locke arguably cool before it was cool.
88. See Jackson, "Herskovits."
89. Herskovits, "The Negro's Americanism," 353.
90. Locke, "The New Negro," 6.
91. Locke, "The New Negro," 14.
92. Locke, "The New Negro," 14–15.

93. For the importance of French Caribbean literature, see his review two years earlier of René Maran's novel *Batouala* in Locke, "Colonial Literature of France." On the larger implications including the French reception, see the chapter "On Reciprocity: René Maran and Alain Locke" in Edwards, *Rise of Black Internationalism*, 69–118.
94. Locke, "Ancestral Arts," 254–55.
95. Compare the catalog presenting this collection: Clark, *Barnes Foundation*.
96. Stewart, *Alain Locke*, 421. Locke had been prior to the publication of *The New Negro* on a trip to Europe. In Paris, "he had met Albert Barnes and listened to his lectures on how Paul Guillaume and Guillaume Apollinaire had brought European aesthetic recognition to the genius of West African art." Stewart, *Alain Locke*, 403. On the difficult relationship between Locke and the Philadelphia millionaire chemist turned collector of African objects and art historical dilettante Barnes, see especially the chapter "Battling the Barnes" in Stewart, *Alain Locke*, 420–29.
97. See Locke, "Ancestral Arts," 264.
98. Locke, "Ancestral Arts," 262; 266. Locke accepted the suggestion by Paul Kellog, editor of *Survey Graphic*, to choose Winold Reiss as the illustrator for *New Negro*. Reiss, a German émigré artist, agreed to collaborate with Locke on the volume and created the celebrated portraits of Black artists and writers, as well as miniatures and decorative elements. See Stewart, *Alain Locke*, 438.
99. "Our poets have now stopped speaking for the Negro – they speak as Negroes. [...] The younger generation has thus achieved an *objective* [emphasis added] attitude toward life." Locke, "Negro Youth," 47. "[W]riters like Rudolph Fisher, Zora Hurston, Jean Toomer, Eric Warond, Willis Richardson, and Langston Hughes take their material *objectively* [emphasis added] with detached artistic vision; they have no thought of their racy folk types as typical of anything but themselves or of their being taken or mistaken as racially representative." Locke, "Negro Youth," 50.
100. See Schüttpelz, "Der Trickster," 224.
101. This moment is in effect the second creole invention of objectivity according to West African artistic practices. Compare William Pietz's work on the "problem of the fetish."
102. Gates, *Signifying Monkey*, 38.
103. Wescott, "Eshu-Elegba," 340–41.
104. Foster, "Creative Collaboration," 28. This movement, in turn, inherited forms of collaboration practiced in the New York-based *Freedom's Journal*, first published in 1827, bringing together people from "diverse areas, with diverse and sometimes divergent perspectives, and they intended to chronicle and to foment artistic and political change and racial self-esteem throughout the African Diaspora." Foster, "Creative Collaboration," 28.
105. One might argue that Thompson's entire research project on African "cool" in nonverbal arts started around 1966 precisely as a political attempt to address and possibly remedy the asymmetries engrained in Western imagination: "[W]hen an African, finding his security threatened, kills his neighbor, depressingly large segments of the Western world believe that he does so instinctively, without any moral check whatsoever. But an increasing

familiarity with the ideal of the cool, documented by the nonverbal 'texts' of dance, will reveal the fact of moral equality. Should Westerners, white and black alike, forsake comfort and estimate the meaning of the words that are made flesh in the dances of the Guinea Coast, they might find our double standards intolerable. [...] The time-resistant dances of the cool form a kind of prayer: May humanity be shielded from the consequences of arrogance and the penalties of impatience." Thompson, R., "West African Dance," 98–99. The formula he develops for the "symmetrical," "pluralistic" cool is "apart-playing." Thompson, R., "West African Dance," 93. See also for a useful discussion of artistic collaboration in West African drumming exemplifying this notion, Chernoff, "Rhythmic Medium."

106. Riesman acknowledges this asymmetry and its mimetic effects, and yet cannot help but describe the disadvantaged position as "pathetic": "The southern poor white or the poor Negro who moves North does not have to learn a new language, but he is usually about as deracinated as are the migrants from abroad. The costume and manners of the zoot-suiter were a pathetic example of the effort to combine smooth urban ways with a resentful refusal to be completely overwhelmed by the inner-directed norms that are still the official culture of the city public schools." Riesman, *Lonely Crowd*, 34.

107. See Ellison, "Change the Joke."

108. Stewart, *Alain Locke*, 903n31. As Stewart describes Locke's "bureaucratic" relationship to Mason: "After the contracts with Hughes and Hurston were finalized, Locke's role with Mason suddenly changed. Locke became overseer of the artists he had brought into her stable. A regular feature of her meetings with him would be answering her prepared questions about 'Langston's financial situation,' Zora's 'academic status,' their progress or lack of progress on their artistic and research projects, and any other personal item Mason thought crucial to their obligation to stay focused on the work for which they were being paid. Also, Locke was consistently recommending new protégés, such as Arthur Fauset and Aaron Douglas, and escorting Mason to exhibits, such as the Haiti pictures exhibit at the Ainslie Gallery in New York. For this he received sums of money as 'gifts.' Just as Locke was the first to be rewarded for his service to this system, he also was the first to feel the sting of Mason's condemnation and disapproval if he or they failed to follow all of her suggestions or keep her informed of all of their activities." Stewart, *Alain Locke*, 574–75.

109. Stewart, *Alain Locke*, 558.

110. Stewart, *Alain Locke*, 785. Stewart points out that Locke worked during this period consciously as a secretary: "His queerness shaped all aspects of this project, from the way that he moved secretly to garner the funding to finance the project, to his taking the title of 'secretary' rather than 'president' of the nonprofit organization, which allowed him to run it invisibly. Indeed the entire enterprise is largely invisible in American intellectual history and educational history, in part because he wanted it to be. It was radical knowledge in the closet. This critique of American and global White supremacy was hidden in an educational Trojan Horse – adult education – that would

transform what even Whites are able to read about the Negro if they went into a library and looked up 'Negro' in the finding aid." Stewart, *Alain Locke*, 759.
111. "An organization founded to defend the civil rights of the 'foreign born' was being steered by leftist Black intellectuals. That they had such a prominent role may explain why Locke was sent on this mission, but also why he was interested in going – to hear radical-thinking Black intellectuals direct an integrated radical organization that linked the issues of refugees fleeing fascism to Negroes fighting racism in America. [...] This meeting shows that Black intellectuals were using communist front organizations to advance a progressive agenda that made Negro civil rights an internationalist issue on the eve of US entry into World War II. They were suggesting that the foreign born, whether communist or not, had to be linked to the cause to eradicate racism in America if they wanted the support of Black thinkers to help eradicate xenophobia and anti-immigrant laws in America." Stewart, *Alain Locke*, 792–93.
112. Stewart, *Alain Locke*, 797.
113. A selection of Locke's writings, acknowledging the significance of his political writings of the late 1930s and 1940s, has been collected and edited in 2012 in Locke, *Works of Locke*. For a full bibliography including several important ephemeral publications, see Tidwell and Wright, "Locke Bibliography."
114. Molesworth, "Introduction," xxviii.
115. [Locke, Alain,] "The Universality of Cultural Interchange." Locke and Stern, *When Peoples Meet*, 31.
116. Locke, "Internationalism." The notion is further developed in Locke, "Contribution." For the religious background of Locke's social philosophy in his Bahá'í faith, see Locke, "Unity Through Diversity." The latter two articles were collected and reprinted in 1989 in Locke, *Philosophy of Locke*.
117. Kallen, "Locke and Cultural Pluralism," 125.
118. Gates, *Signifying Monkey*, 42.
119. On Bunche, first Black recipient of the Nobel Peace Prize in 1950, at the OSS and later at the State Department during World War II, See Henry, *Ralph Bunche*, 119–39.
120. Beier, *Yoruba Myths*, 55–56.
121. On the order of cloth colors used to dress some of Eshu's emblems: white, red, and black as third, see Gates, *Signifying Monkey*, 43.

3 THE INVENTION OF THE INTELLIGENCE REPORT

1. Neumann, *Behemoth* [1942].
2. For a biographical account and a thorough reading of *Behemoth*, see Kettler and Wheatland, *Learning from Neumann*, 249–327.
3. In fact, *Behemoth* has been largely overlooked for several decades in the debate on National Socialism among historians, especially in the German

language discussion. Even now, it is frequently referenced as a book describing "the theory of totalitarian monopoly capitalism," which may be considered a legitimate if necessarily reductionist summary. However, the repetition of this formula clearly neglects the actual wealth of description and analysis the book provides and leads to the false impression that Neumann gives a clear answer to the question of primacy – be it economic or political. Instead, the book is interested in the question of primacy in as much as it is relevant for the ideology or practice of National Socialism itself.

4. See the pioneering work in the media history of European bureaucracy in Vismann, *Files*. See also Siegert and Vogl, *Kultur der Sekretäre*. See for an anthropological study of Western bureaucracy in East Africa, Rottenburg, *Far-Fetched Facts*. The US-American revision of Vismann's project is a particularly urgent task since in the long history of "communication" (for the short history of communication studies see still Rogers, *History of Communication Study*), conditioned by the rules of membership authorization into the communities of communication, in which sanctioned exchange could happen, our present notion of communication depends precisely on the "Science of 'Muddling Through'" in which these American bureaucratic communities were organized. See Lindblom, "Muddling Through."

5. Politically speaking, this is a major task for today's study of literature. As Peter Galison estimates for the USA already in the year 2001 in terms of sheer numbers: "[T]he supervising agency, the Information Security Oversight Office (ISOO), reports a total expenditure in 2001 of $5.5 billion to keep classified documents secure. The Department of Energy costs are now about $0.30 per secure document per year. Estimating by this economic measure, we would figure that about 7.5 billion pages are being kept under wraps – *a classified Library of Congress* [emphasis added] [...]." Galison, "Removing Knowledge," 231.

6. Roosevelt, F., "Presidential Order," 112.

7. Together with William S. Stephenson, see Troy, *Donovan*.

8. Another useful comparison: "[T]hat's for the New Chaps with their little green antennas out for the usable emanations of power, versed in American politics (knowing the difference between the New Dealers of OWI and the eastern and moneyed Republicans behind OSS), keeping brain-dossiers on latencies, weaknesses, tea-taking habits, erogenous zones of all, all who might someday be useful." Pynchon, *Gravity's Rainbow*, 77.

9. Marcuse to Horkheimer, "Letter, April 18, 1943," Marcuse, *Technology, War and Fascism*, 243.

10. German "material," clippings, recordings, interviews, artefacts is a frequently used expression throughout the memorandum culture.

11. Former Department of Defense intelligence analyst Henry T. Nash describes the importance of the initial clearance that subsequently structures the internal hierarchy in intelligence work: "When I was denied access to special information I felt that I was not as fully informed as others and, because of this, I was not as fully a part of, or as responsible for, the ongoing work." Nash, "Bureaucratization of Homicide," 25.

12. "I am supposed to work in the Intelligence Bureau of the Office of War Information. My function would be to make suggestions on 'how to present the enemy to the American people,' in the press, movies, propaganda, etc. I would work directly with (or rather under) Leo Rosten. The job has to be done in Washington, because it requires material which is not available outside the government offices here (microfilms of European newspapers, short wave broadcasts, Consulate reports). The salary is $4600 – The appointment has been approved by all the chiefs, and although it has still to go through the routine of the Personnel Division and through the F.B.I., there seems unfortunately not the slightest doubt that it will go through. Probably within 10 days. As I told you, I would not accept it." Marcuse to Horkheimer, "Letter, November 11, 1942," Marcuse, *Technology, War and Fascism,* 234–35. Marcuse entered the OWI in December 1942 and transferred to the OSS in March 1943.
13. "Being cleared represented a flattering experience sharpened by the quality of selectivity, not unlike the feeling accompanying acceptance by a fraternity or country club." Nash, "Bureaucratization of Homicide," 24.
14. The best introduction to this complex with focus on R&A remains Söllner, "Forschungshypothese." Historians have produced a substantial amount of OSS-literature, gaining in range and depth since the declassification and public availability of most materials in the National Archives, starting in 1980. The most important institutional histories are Smith, R., *Secret History*; Smith, B., *Shadow Warriors*; Mauch, *Shadow War*; book-length studies regarding the R&A and its analysis of Germany may be found in Katz, *Foreign Intelligence*, Marquardt-Bigman, *Geheimdienstanalysen*; Müller, T., *Krieger und Gelehrte*.
15. Barnes, "Geographical Intelligence," 151. One may add that Bruno Latour himself originally developed the notion using an example from the history of geography, see Latour, *Science in Action*, 215–47.
16. Barnes, "Geographical Intelligence," 152.
17. Barnes, "Geographical Intelligence," 153.
18. For an account of the development of the Central Information Division, see Heaps, "Intelligence Information." See also Marquardt-Bigman, *Geheimdienstanalysen*, 60–61.
19. Barnes, "Geographical Intelligence," 153.
20. Ibid.
21. "R&A could, with microfilm and new techniques for photocopying and filing, hope to retain inert data across years, rather than playing the fool's game of 'relevance,' until such time as the data could prove their own relevance. R&A controlled the most powerful weapon in the OSS arsenal: the three-by-five index card." Winks, *Cloak & Gown*, 63. The indeterminacy of relevance and irrelevance repeats itself for the person studying the contents of materials of and about the OSS, as long as one does not insist on the fool's game theory as outlined in the previous chapter.
22. On the history of the index card in the USA, see Krajewski, *Paper Machines*, especially chapter 6.
23. Yee, "Attempts," 3.

24. Yee, "Attempts," 6.
25. For example: "If there are '57 varieties' of facsimile, they must all be differentiated. Some kinds would be called facsimiles on the catalog card and others would not. It would not matter if the word *facsim.* in the collation stood ambiguously for any of the valid kinds of facsimile. The decisions are not concerned with that kind of knowledge. The decision is simply to determine whether in this particular instance the general term *facsim.* has been used legitimately or not." Osborn, "Crisis," 397.
26. Yee, "Attempts," 7.
27. Osborn, "Crisis," 404.
28. Osborn, "Crisis," 397.
29. Heaps, "Intelligence Information," 290.
30. Heaps, "Intelligence Information," 294.
31. Meckler, *Micropublishing*, 25.
32. Meckler, *Micropublishing*, 30–31.
33. On the "Microfilm Mania" of the interwar period and especially on the role of microfilm in the "Operation Paperclip," transporting not only scientists, but also unprecedented amounts of (ultimately disappointing) information from Germany to the United States, see O'Reagan, *Taking Nazi Technology*, especially in chapter 6, 145–78. See also Crim, *Our Germans*.
34. [Moholy and] Moholy-Nagy, "Produktion – Reproduktion." On Lucia Moholy's coauthorship, and a discussion of the "problem 'production/reproduction,' which became [...] the starting point for our photogram-work," during a walk in the Rhön Mountains, see Moholy, "Das Bauhaus-Bild," 399; and Moholy, *Marginalien*. See also Valdivieso, "Arbeitsgemeinschaft," 68–9; and Sachsse, *Lucia Moholy*, 10–11. For an interpretation of the manifesto's role in the history of photography, see Jennings, "Photo-Essay."
35. See Richards, *Scientific Information*, 83.
36. Richards, *Scientific Information*, 84.
37. Moholy, "Aslib," 148.
38. Ibid. The article has an appendix with all scientific journals that the ASLIB Microfilm Service made available on microfilm.
39. Moholy, "Aslib," 151.
40. The OSRD was created in 1941, almost coincidentally with the COI. The "outsourcing" of microphotography matches the general trend: Vannevar Bush organized the OSRD by means of contracting and subcontracting that allowed for the unprecedented scaling of "Big Science," see Owens, "Vannevar Bush."
41. "Sometime in 1942, the German project was apparently abandoned as impractical, for a variety of reasons, one of which was that the Germans seem to have overestimated the amount of enriched uranium which would be necessary for the bomb's manufacture. In any case, the German government's conclusion about the impracticality of atomic fission for use in the war resulted in the release and publication in 1942 and 1943 of the results of the research bearing on the German atomic bomb project that had been done over the preceding two years. Eight papers in issues of the *Zeitschrift für Physik* in 1942 and 1943 and three papers of *Die Naturwissenschaften*

in 1943, written by Otto Hahn, Fritz Strassmann, H. J. Born, W. Seelmann-Eggert and their associates at the Kaiser Wilhelm Gesellschaft's Institut für Chemie and the Radiologische Abteilung der Auergesellschaft, gave detailed descriptions of experiments on the fission of the uranium atom, the gaseous and other by-products obtained, and the energy released. These papers, *all of which were microfilmed by the Aslib microfilm service* [emphasis added] and ultimately reprinted by the Americans, caused great excitement among the scientists at the Manhattan Project. At the end of the war a United States government report stated that they had been critical to the Allies' ability to have their bomb operational by the summer of 1945." Richards, *Scientific Information*, 90.

42. "Die Aufgabe ist, unter einer zentralen Verwaltung und auf der Basis eines gemeinsamen Vorgehens, Mikrofilm- und ähnliche Aktivitäten für die Zwecke allgemeinbildender Lehre, wissenschaftlicher Forschung, Erziehung und Umerziehung in der Nachkriegszeit zu organisieren." Moholy, "Microfilm Services," 84.

43. "Wenn meine These zutrifft und die Reprographie als Faktor in der Gesellschaftsbildung nicht nur rückblickende, sondern auch eine vorwärtsgerichtete Rolle spielt, so wären wir damit um einen kleinen Schritt näher einer Kulturgemeinschaft, die möglicherweise den Keim eines neuen Humanismus in sich trägt." Moholy, "Reprographie," 89.

44. See Moholy, "Co-Ordination"; see also Moholy, "Freeing the Mind."

45. Bush, "As We May Think [July]," Bush, "As We May Think [September]."

46. See Moholy, "Co-ordination," 176.

47. The interception of Nazi German signal intelligence played virtually no role in the OSS, since the US-military did not share the strategically extremely valuable secrets of the Polish and British successes in cryptology. See however for a curious case of other-directedness on the Atlantic, Rohwer, "Schlacht im Atlantik." Rohwer shows how thanks to intelligence arriving from Ultra, the enemy literally remote controlled the movements of the American fleet in 1941, not to win but to avoid military conflicts.

48. My translation, FP. "Nun, es begann mit den Quellen, die von Zeitungen, anderen Berichten und woher immer, besonders deutschen Zeitungen stammten – sie galt es zunächst zusammenzustellen und zu interpretieren. Wir saßen in einem großen L-förmigen Raum, in der Mitte stand ein großer runder Tisch, an dem wir diskutierten. Wir verständigten uns über einen bestimmten Gegenstand, sei es für einen einzelnen Report, sei es für den Weekly Report, wie er genannt wurde, und zwar jeweils in Reaktion auf die neuesten Ereignisse in Deutschland." Anderson, E., "Interview," 24. The interview was originally conducted in English by Alfons Söllner, who "directly translated from the recorder into German, the English audio tape is lost." Private Email-Correspondence, December 16, 2015. Eugene N. Anderson died briefly after the interview was conducted, in 1984.

49. Before arriving at the OSS, Eugene N. Anderson historian of American University of Washington was member of the "Sub-Committee on Studies of National Socialist Germany" in the "American Committee for International Studies," financed by the Rockefeller Foundation and headed by the

historian Edward Mead Earle. He was also designated codirector of the failed "German Project" of the Institute of Social Research.
50. See also the interviews in Erd, *Gespräche über Neumann*.
51. My translation, FP. "*Anderson*: Von den Emigranten war Neumann der wichtigste Mann, er leitete die Forschung an, aber auch er tat es auf kooperative Weise, wie all die anderen. An den round-table-discussions habe ich teilgenommen, aber die Forschung ließ ich in seiner Hand, obwohl ich natürlich immer informiert war. Franz ergriff die Initiative, aber er ließ sich auch etwas sagen, er konnte zuhören. Es galt nicht, Franz einfach zu folgen, sondern es war der kollektive Denkprozeß einer ganzen Gruppe. Mein Gott, diese Leute diskutierten ununterbrochen, beim Lunch oder am Abend, die waren doch versessen auf ihren Gegenstand, sie haben ihn gelebt. Ich muß ihnen sagen, ich hätte es nicht für möglich gehalten, daß es eine Emigrantengruppe geben könnte, die so objektiv, so cool, so leidenschaftslos bei der Sache war. Verstehen sie mich richtig. Ich selber kam oft viel mehr in Rage, muß ich gestehen, über das, was in Deutschland geschah, sie aber überließen sich nicht ihren Emotionen. Ihre Ansichten waren so gelehrt, so wissenschaftlich, wie man es nur wünschen konnte. Dieser Arbeitsprozeß war Ausdruck einer ganz neuen Denkweise. Im Institut für Sozialforschung war sie schon vorher praktiziert worden, doch jetzt in Amerika sahen sie, daß es wirklich so etwas gab wie die Sozialwissenschaften." Anderson, E., "Interview," 25.
52. "Friendly Enemy Alien" is the name of the legal status of émigrés allowed to work for the government.
53. Franz Neumann died in a car crash in 1954, and his papers appear to be lost. Neumann's success at the OSS cannot be properly understood without consideration of his first career as labor union- and SPD-lawyer in Berlin's legal scene and particularly in relation to Carl Schmitt's "Staatsrechtliches Seminar"; his second career as political leader of London's SPD group while at the same time pursuing a second PhD with political theorist Harold Laski in London; and his third career as administrator and legal consultant of the exiled Institute of Social Research in New York, while writing the book that got him, and arguably all other émigrés, a job at the OSS: *Behemoth*. Intelmann, "Franz L. Neumann." See also Kettler and Wheatland, *Learning from Neumann*.
54. Hayes, "Introduction," vii. If not indicated otherwise, all quotes from Neumann, *Behemoth*, refer to the second edition from 1944. Katz praises the R&A reports as a "unique running commentary on the world historical events of 1941–1945." Katz, *Foreign Intelligence*, 18.
55. On Max Weber see also Chapter 6.
56. On the considerable number of German Jewish émigrés who fled racial segregation, persecution and the threat of annihilation in Germany and who then found employment at historically Black colleges, subjected to racial segregation in the USA, see Edgcomb, *Black Colleges*.
57. My translation, FP. Herz, "Interview," 35.
58. My translation, FP. Herz, "Interview," 43.
59. For a critique of this framing, Kätz, "Frankfurt School Goes to War," 449n22.

60. My translation, FP. Söllner, "Forschungshypothese," 34.
61. This approach is rather close to Tim B. Müller's idea of a "contextual law" that, however, still refers to Marcuse's political thought. See Müller, T., *Krieger und Gelehrte*, 486.
62. See also Troy, *Donovan*, 26. Marquardt-Bigman remarks that R&A did not share the "trust-busting anti-cartel point of view" of the Foreign Economic Administration (FEA) when it came to the postwar reorganization of Germany. See Marquardt-Bigman, *Geheimdienstanalysen*, 127. This is, however, rather a problem of policy recommendation than of administrative practice.

    Franz Neumann had prior experience with the American legal system, as he remarks in an acknowledgment for his *Behemoth*: "The Honorable Thurman W. Arnold, Assistant Attorney General of the United States, kindly permitted me to use a memorandum originally prepared for him and the lectures on the German cartel system which I delivered before the members of the Anti-Trust division in 1938 and 1939." Neumann, *Behemoth*, xx.
63. See OSS memorandum "The Problem of Objectivity in R&A Reporting," RG 226, entry 1, box 9: Projects Committee Folder.
64. See OSS memorandum with the subject: "Footnote Security and Masking."
65. Marquardt-Bigman points to R&A 214 A, B "The German Economic and Military Position" from December 12, 1941 as the first report that produced a coherent "big picture" of Germany and was submitted to the President. After the reorganization of the COI into the OSS, the new "primary" addressees were the four Joint Chiefs of Staff, that is, the military.
66. Roosevelt, K., *War Report*, Vol. 1, 53.
67. Katz, *Foreign Intelligence*, 15–16.
68. Katz points to geographer Richard Hartshorne as the guardian of objectivity for the OSS, see again Katz, *Foreign Intelligence*, 15–16. If one looks at Richard Hartshorne's *The Nature of Geography* that was in the decades after its publication widely considered as having given American geography a scientific base, as well as at his work for the OSS, one may specify that Hartshorne's notion of objectivity is a perfect example for what Lorraine Daston and Peter Galison call "structural objectivity." See Daston and Galison, *Objectivity*, 253–307. It also becomes quite clear that Hartshorne must have thought that his structural perspective with a focus on "region" provided a privileged access to the object of study, as he implies – against his own rules of an objective style – in the following quote: "A sociologist, L. Gumplovicz, says: 'Ratzel's works contain more, and more important, knowledge concerning the state, than the entire theoretical political science literature of the last hundred years.'" Hartshorne, *Geography*, 121.
69. OSS Memorandum "Draft of proposed guide to preparation of political reports," National Archives at College Park/MD, RG 226, entry 37, box 5.
70. OSS Intelligence Report "German Morale after Tunisia," June 25, 1943, R&A 933. The report is, because of its internal success, compared to most (but not all) others, preserved in an easily legible form, as a microfiche copy

of an edited and typeset print, arranged in the style of a journal publication. Most reports remained in a typewritten draft status.
71. Neumann, "German Morale," 95. Laudani's edition has been justly criticized for normalizing the authorship of intelligence reports, and for a lack of contextualization, original footnotes are not clearly distinguished from editorial explanations, and the initial summary, according to Hartshorne's guide, quoted above, the nucleus of intelligence report writing (and reading), has been removed. As a historical source, Laudani's publication therefore has only limited use value.
72. This is the beginning of the initial summary that is not reproduced in Neumann, "German Morale."
73. See on this question also Kettler and Wheatland, *Learning from Neumann*, 343–47. Kettler and Wheatland also convincingly link this question to his contacts and limited collaboration as "Ruff" with two émigrés moving in the circles of the Institute of Social Research, Hede Massing and Paul Massing, who worked covertly as Soviet agents, see Kettler and Wheatland, *Learning from Neumann*, 347–50.
74. Marquardt-Bigman argues that the report constituted the conceptual missing link regarding the understanding of Nazi German anti-Semitism for the historically most important wartime study of Nazi Germany, Franz Neumann's *Behemoth*. Neumann published the book in 1942, started in 1943 to work for the OSS and added for the second edition in 1944 an appendix, where some arguments, circulated in R&A reports, are published in his name. See Marquardt-Bigman, *Geheimdienstanalysen*, 78. Marquardt-Bigman fails to point out that most passages of the appendix on anti-Semitism are verbatim reproductions of R&A 1113.9 "Anti-Semitism: Spearhead of Universal Terror."
75. Neumann, "German Morale," 95.
76. The report introduced the concept of totalitarianism into the supposedly theory-free cosmos of political intelligence writing in World War II. "What was new, however, about Neumann's analysis was its underlying postulate that the reports about the public mood and other dispatches from the Reich essentially had to be interpreted against the backdrop of the Hitler regime's totalitarian character." Mauch, *Shadow War*, 87–88.
77. This shift also happens to coincide with his scholarly practice while writing *Behemoth*, as well as with his theory of National Socialism. As Söllner points out in a recorded discussion: "Franz Neumann methodologically argued that National Socialism is not so much a system that disguises itself. If one analyzes the major German newspapers [...] then, he believed, all material could be taken from them that would reveal what kind of social order National Socialism was." Erd, *Gespräche über Neumann*, 120.
78. Tim B. Müller interprets "German Morale after Tunisia" within his history of intellectual history, according to which this report introduces a "functionalist frame of interpretation." Müller, T., *Krieger und Gelehrte*, 56.
79. Neumann, "German Morale," 96.
80. Neumann, "German Morale," 97.

81. Neumann, "German Morale," 98–99. Within intellectual history and Alfons Söllner's "archeology," intelligence report no. 933 should be appreciated for its attempt to translate the analysis of polycracy in Neumann's *Behemoth* relying on Max Weber's political theory based on the identification of "power," into Carl Schmitt's political theory based on the friend/enemy distinction.

82. See Katz, *Foreign Intelligence*, 9; 18.

83. Neumann, *Behemoth*, 464.

84. "The integration of rational and irrational activities which is peculiar to the Dual State – this rational core within an irrational shell – brings us to the culmination of our investigation. [...] The symbiosis of capitalism and National-Socialism finds its institutional form in the Dual State." Fraenkel, *Dual State*, 206–8. The distinction relies, again, on Carl Schmitt: "'The sovereign is he who has the legal power to command in an emergency' as Carl Schmitt has formulated in his book *Politische Theologie*. From this follows the principle that the presumption of jurisdiction rests with the Normative State. The jurisdiction over jurisdiction rests with the Prerogative State." Fraenkel, *Dual State*, 57. Neumann's *Behemoth* is unthinkable without the groundwork of Fraenkel's *Dual State*, and Neumann unfortunately dismisses the latter's work too easily on conceptual grounds without acknowledging his full debt, which is, in fact, more than anything: conceptual.

Fraenkel, a German Jew who had volunteered in World War I, remained in Berlin until September 20, 1938, where he wrote a first German version of *The Dual State*, directly experiencing the incremental change of the Nazi State. The first version of the English translation by Edward A. Shils is archived in the collection of the "American Committee for the Guidance of Professional Personnel," that is, David Riesman's committee. See Brünneck, "Urdoppelstaat," 31. Riesman's strong advocacy for Fraenkel secured him a grant to study at the University of Chicago Law School. See Ladwig-Winters, "Fraenkel," 58. See also for Ernst Fraenkel's biography and especially his later career in the United States, Greenberg, *Weimar Century*, 76–106.

85. Fraenkel argues that communities cannot be primary sources of law, since a preceding decision would be still necessary to determine the "community" bearing the concrete order, in order to avoid a relativism of various communities following their own laws. "Viewed in this light, the essence of Schmitt's theory may be summarized as follows: the National-Socialist legal system is embodied in concrete communities. The question as to which groups constitute concrete communities is decided politically, i.e., the decision is not made in accordance with pre-existent norms, but in accordance with the 'demands of the situation.'" Fraenkel, *Dual State*, 145.

86. The text was originally published in German as Schmitt, *Arten*. Schmitt strategically quotes Nazi Reich Minister of Justice Hans Frank's term "Sachgestaltung" and Neumann coins the composite term "Sachgestaltungsdenken" in *Behemoth*. In German legal discourse, the alternative term "konkretes Ordnungsdenken" prevailed – though tainted – after World War II. See Böckendörfer, "Ordnungsdenken, konkretes," 1313. Schmitt's original

reads: "Darum möchte ich als Bezeichnung [...] konkretes Ordnungs- und Gestaltungsdenken vorschlagen." Schmitt, *Arten*, 58.
87. Neumann, *Behemoth*, 451.
88. In a "Note on the Name Behemoth," the only part of the book that was not reprinted in the second edition, Neumann relates his interpretation of the two biblical monsters Behemoth and Leviathan and concludes that "we find it apt to call the National Socialist system The Behemoth." Neumann, *Behemoth* [1942], VI. For a contemporary reader, the book's title was a direct response to Schmitt, *Leviathan*.
89. See again Fraenkel's critique of the "concrete theory of order."
90. Fraenkel "credits" Best, mainly in his earlier role as legal counsel to the infamous secret state police Gestapo: "It is not by chance that the clearest analysis of the structure of the Third Reich available in National-Socialist juridical literature is the product of a man who, since he represents the Prerogative State (or rather its most powerful instrument, i.e., the Gestapo) need not fear its criticism." Fraenkel, *Dual State*, 62.
91. Herbert, *Best*, 24; 271–78. While initially insisting on the Nazi state instead of using "race" as the central concept, Schmitt accepts Best's point to speak of a "völkische Großraumordnung" within a large space, but not beyond, in Schmitt, "Großraum-Ordnung," see Herbert, *Best*, 277.
92. Neumann, *Behemoth*, 171.
93. "It is striking that Franz Neumann presents this article [on the administration of large spaces] in his famous 'Behemoth'-study from 1942 resp. 1944 [...] at length as foundational of a German theory of occupation, but omits in particular the passages presented above." Herbert, *Best*, 284, my translation. Those omitted passages in Best's theory of large space talk about the "total annihilation" or "expulsion" of certain foreign races, in order to keep the "master race" pure from mixing with "inferiors," clearly foreshadowing the coming genocide of European Jews and Sinti and Roma.

The same train of thought on the other hand leads Best to a rejection of slave work and an advocacy of "indirect" colonial rule over Western and Northern Europe, which put him in opposition to the Nazi Party line.
94. For Neumann's views on antisemitism, see Chapter 6.
95. Neumann, *Behemoth*, 551. See also Neumann, "Anti-Semitism," 30.
96. It is also Herbert, the biographer of Best, who coins the term "internal rationality" (Binnenrationalität) to describe Nazi rationality and describes Best as part of a "generation of objectivity" (Generation der Sachlichkeit), born around 1900 and slightly too young to fight in World War I. Herbert, *Best*, 12; 42–50.
97. Neumann's contact with Schmitt in 1930/31, together with Otto Kirchheimer and Ernst Fraenkel was mostly amicable. "Only after Neumann's emigration, one may see scathing criticism of Schmitt." See the chapter Breuer, "Dialog," 117, my translation, FP. Neumann's criticism of Schmitt's writing from the late 1930s strikingly matches Werner Best's.
98. Herbert, "Sachlichkeit." This connection may be part of the uncanny fascination for the "cool" SS officer in Hollywood film, shifting between hyper-rationality and murderous outbursts.

4 APPLIED GERMAN FOLKLORE

1. See however the series of articles by Hans R. Vaget for many important insights on the topic of "Thomas Mann's American exile," feeding into the standard work on the topic in Vaget, *Amerikaner*. An important source for Vaget's work is his edition of Thomas Mann's exchange of letters with his US-American patron Agnes E. Meyer. Mann and Meyer, *Briefwechsel*. For a recent reevaluation of Mann's exile in the United States, see Boes, *Mann's War*. The renewed interest in the topic is reflected in a volume accompanying an exhibition edited by Raulff and Strittmatter, *Thomas Mann in Amerika*, the special issue edited by Boes and Sina, *Thomas Manns transatlantische Autorschaft*, as well as Corngold, *Mann in Princeton*. See also Detering, *Manns amerikanische Religion*.
2. I follow here French anthropologist Louis Dumont in his study of German social philosophy. He emphatically describes Mann as "in his very being and activity, a *mediator*." Dumont, *German Ideology*, 28.
3. Boes, *Mann's War*, 15.
4. Ibid.
5. The title changed to "Fellow" after one year.
6. Donaldson, *MacLeish*, 323. The collection of American folklore in projects such as the folklore division of the Federal Writers' Project, the Federal Music Project, and the Archive of American Folk-Song at the Library of Congress predates Archibald MacLeish's tenure. See Retman, *Real Folks*, 7–14. The employment of MacLeish in 1939 at the Library of Congress helped to ensure the continuity of these projects at times of heightened political scrutiny and opposition to the projects' inclusive notion of "folk"; he had spoken in favor of the collection of American folklore in 1937. MacLeish argued for an enthusiastic extractivism and remarked that these collections provided "the kind of raw cultural material – the raw material of new creative work – which is so necessary to artists and particularly to artists in a new country." MacLeish quoted in Coyle, "Amassing American 'Stuff,'" 364.
7. Boes has pointed this out, see Boes, *Thomas Mann's War*, 154.
8. Wimmer, "Textlage," 91.
9. Mann to Evans, "Letter, June 15, 1947," Mann, *Dichter*, 92, original in English.
10. For a detailed reevaluation of the problems and merits of Lowe-Porter's translations, see Horton, *Mann in English*, 52–82.
11. Horton, *Mann in English*, 34.
12. Mann to Evans, "Letter, June 15, 1947," Mann, *Dichter*, 92. On the legal background of the problem, see Nawrocka, "Verlagssitz," 148–52. The arrangement continued for the rest of Mann's life. Mann's novel *Der Erwählte* in 1951 and his *Bekenntnisse des Hochstaplers Felix Krull* in 1954 were still first published as US-American mimeograph prints. See also the description of the problem in Boes, *Manns War*, 12.
13. Mann to Evans, "Letter, June 15, 1947," Mann, *Dichter*, 93.
14. And about three weeks later, on August 6, Mann notes in his diary: "Reply by Luther Evans, terribly disheartening in regard to copyright-situation and

Bermann's point of view." Mann, *Tagebücher 28.5.1946–31.12.1948*, 142. The exchange of letters between Mann and his editor Gottfried Bermann Fischer shows Thomas and Katia Mann's mercantile approach to the matter. See Mann, *Briefwechsel mit Bermann Fischer*.
15. One apparent reason that this argument has been so little explored lies in the historical reception of the novel: In the German debate during the post-war years, German authors used this claim as an accusation to discredit Thomas Mann's authority as German national author. These writers of the "Inner Emigration," often hiding their collaboration with the National Socialist regime, surprisingly agreed in this regard with parts of American literary criticism, for example, James Joyce-supporter Eugene Jolas, at the time editor of one of Germany's short-lived but highly influential post war newspapers *Die Neue Zeitung*. See Hajdu, *Kontroverse*, 291–95.
16. In a twist of fate, several of these low-grade prints survive. The mimeograph copies were rehashed in the manner of numbered and signed collectibles, a mode of publication well established in Mann's past for expensive special editions. See also Mendelssohn, "Vorwort," XXXI.
17. Horton, *Mann in English*, 3.
18. Aspects of this problem have been treated extensively in the study of "exile literature," see, for example, Spalek, *Deutsche Exilliteratur*. For an important work on the US-American perspective, see Turner, C., *Marketing Modernism*, on Mann esp. 81–110. The (few) notable examples of successful transitions to the United States – competing however with US-American authors of "German fiction" like Thomas Wolfe – are the Swiss Jewish émigré author of popular biographies Emil Ludwig, Austrian Jewish émigré Vicki Baum, famous for her best-selling novel *Grand Hotel*, Franz Werfel, whose books had been earlier translated into English, and Austrian Jewish émigré Lion Feuchtwanger, who had gained and maintained financial independence thanks to his novel *Jud Suess*. On the problem of nontransferable vs. transferable artistic skills, see Blackbourn, *Germany in the World*, 458. As Blackbourn points out, even transferable skills like musical composition could still prove not acceptable, as in the blacklisting of German composers on the BBC, instigated by composer Ralph Vaughan Williams and others.
19. For a summary of the discussion on the character Frau von Tolna, see Schneider, *Das literarische Porträt*, 140–42.
20. See Vaget, "Introduction," 55.
21. Parts of her World War II writing are collected in Meyer, *America's Home Front* (1943); Meyer, *Journey Through Chaos* (1944).
22. Mann to Meyer, "Letter, September 13, 1944," Mann and Meyer, *Briefwechsel*, 587.
23. See Berendsohn, *Die humanistische Front: Erster Teil*; see the second part for the war years, Berendsohn, *Die humanistische Front: Zweiter Teil*.
24. Propaganda was at that point arguably one of the most important contemporary genres of folk art, as discussed in further detail in Chapter 5.
25. The BBC was not the only institution for which he produced propaganda, Mann also prepared texts for the Office of War Information (OWI). See for Mann's definition of propaganda, demonstrating a clear grasp of both

the importance and the pitfalls of this notion in the United States, Mann, "Introduction." The *Free World Theatre*, produced by radio playwright Arch Oboler, was funded by the OWI. The genre of the US-American radio play flourished in World War II, see, for example, Oboler's "Persian Letter" "Memo to Berchtesgarden," in which the character Karl Smeckler types a memorandum about the United States to the Nazi leader. Oboler, "Memo to Berchtesgarden." See on the general phenomenon Blue, *Words at War*.
26. Peter de Mendelssohn, the editor of Mann's diaries for the years 1940–1943 observes this indirectly, when he states in the preface that Mann's notes differ significantly from the preceding, in as much as "America's 'challenges of the day'" (quoting Mann and Goethe) define his writing, Mann, *Tagebücher 1940–1943*, V.
27. See again the title of Vaget's book *Thomas Mann, der Amerikaner*.
28. Before making his final decision, Mann considered several first names, all starting with "A." See Mann, *Genesis*, 29.
29. Mann to Meyer, "Letter, June 7, 1943," Mann and Meyer, *Briefwechsel*, 496, my translation, FP.
30. Blöcker, "Amtsrichter Leverkühn," 583.
31. His role as a spy has been a long-standing topic in the intelligence service literature on the American OSS. See, for example, Cave Brown, *Wild Bill Donovan*, 127–48.
32. After the war, Leverkuehn published a detailed account of his work for the *Abwehr* that still serves as a standard source for historical research on the topic, see Leverkuehn, *German Military Intelligence*.
33. "'[M]ein Vertrauensmann' in Washington (das sind Sie) [...]." Mann to Meyer, "Letter, February 2, 1939," Mann and Meyer, *Briefwechsel*, 144, my translation, FP.
34. Mann, *Doctor Faustus*, 511; 513.
35. An earlier attempt to "pay back" Adorno for his help failed, when Mann unsuccessfully tried to convince his editor Bermann Fischer to publish Adorno's collection of aphorisms, written during wartime. Mann to Bermann Fischer, "Letter, August 27, 1946," Mann, *Briefwechsel Bermann Fischer*, 462–63, my translation, FP. Bermann Fischer finally turned down the manuscript of "Minima Moralia" two months later on November 27. Instead, Adorno went on to add to his aphorisms and published them as *Minima Moralia* only in 1951 with Suhrkamp. The intellectual historian Ulrich Raulff calls Adorno's belated bestseller, "presumably the last German philosophical Volksbuch," Raulff, "Nachwort," 123. The quote is printed as the blurb on the back of the edited volume.
36. Mann, *Genesis*, 42.
37. Mann, *Genesis*, 32. See also Mann to Adorno, "Letter, December 30, 1945," Adorno and Mann, *Correspondence*, 11. Mann first used the term without further elaboration in a letter to Adorno two years earlier. Thomas Mann to Theodor W. Adorno, "Letter, October 5, 1943," Adorno and Mann, *Correspondence*, 3–5, 3.
38. Meyer to MacLeish, "Letter, November 21, 1941," Mann and Meyer, *Briefwechsel*, 59.

39. See again Donaldson, *MacLeish*, 323–24.
40. Although the term gained prominence only decades later, Botkin developed the concept in 1939, see Hirsch, "Folklore in the Making," 24. For the larger context, see Hirsch, *Portrait of America*; Rodgers and Hirsch, *America's Folklorist*. For a detailed, neo-Marxist depiction of the political tradition of this project under the label not of a humanist, but the Popular Front, see Denning, *The Cultural Front*, 78–83.
41. Arlt and especially his collaborator Archer Taylor were instrumental in acquiring massive collections of "European folklore" for the emerging US-American research libraries. Together, they started in 1940 to edit *The California Folklore Quarterly*, see Arlt, "Archer Taylor." Not long before his exchange with Mann, Arlt published an essay on the history of the printing press and public libraries in the United States in which he anticipates some of Marshall McLuhan's arguments on the "Gutenberg Galaxy," see Arlt, "Printing." On the supposed "schism" in American folklore studies between "literary" and "anthropological" folklorists, see Zumwalt, *American Folklore Scholarship*.
42. Mann, *Tagebücher 1940–1943*, 550.
43. "Figur des syphilitischen Künstlers: als Doktor Faustus und dem Teufel Verschriebener. Das Gift wirkt als Rausch, Stimulans, Inspiration; er darf in entzückter Begeisterung geniale, wunderbare Werke schaffen, der Teufel führt ihm die Hand. Schließlich aber holt ihn der Teufel: die Paralyse. (Die Sache mit dem reinen jungen Mädchen, mit dem er es bis zur Hochzeit treibt, als Episode.)" Voss, *Entstehung*, 15, my translation, FP. The copied note from 1943 diverges slightly from the note in his notebook from 1904/05.
44. The notes are collected in the *Thomas-Mann-Archiv* of the ETH Zürich, A-II-Msv 33.
45. "Keimzelle," Voss, *Entstehung*, 15. Mann calls it a "three-line outline," Mann, *Genesis*, 17.
46. Mann misdates the note in his diary to the year 1901, see Mann, *Tagebücher 1940–1943*, 551.
47. At the turn of the century, the neurologist Paul Julius Möbius had introduced pathography, a biographical account of "great men" with regard to their medical records, as a popular genre. See Hilken, "Psychiatrische Anfänge der Pathographie," 12. Within this genre, Nietzsche's illness became the paradigmatic case. For the most recent pathographic reexamination of Nietzsche's life, diagnosing a genetic disease, cerebral autosomal-dominant arteriopathy with subcortical infarcts and leukoencephalopathy (CADASIL), an inherited, generalized small-artery disease caused by mutations in the Notch 3 gene on chromosome 19q12, instead of neurosyphilis as a cause for his illness, see Hemelsoet, "Illness of Nietzsche."
48. See Mann, *Genesis*, 20. In a second step, Mann updates the old note and adds words from his literary critical and political vocabulary in relation to what he outlines as the contemporary "explosion of the concept of the bourgeois" by means of "[...] fascism." See Voss, *Entstehung*, 16–17.
49. Mann takes this from an anecdote in Deussen, *Erinnerungen an Nietzsche*, 24.

50. See page 6 of Mann's preparatory notes, cited in Voss, *Entstehung*, 22. In the novel, the devil speculates indeed about a connection, based on the pun between flagellate and flagellant, between syphilis and witch-hunters, reformation, genius, and devilishness, giving the pathology of German history an ultimately physiological base, see Mann, *Doctor Faustus*, 247.
51. Most readings misuse the term, which is historically specific for the "humanist front" around 1940. At the time, Mann had been reading both the 1938-essay Auerbach, "Figura," and later, while writing *Doctor Faustus*, as a gift from Adorno, Benjamin's *Ursprung des deutschen Trauerspiels* (1928). The anachronistic reception of these texts makes it easy to overlook that Mann's novel therefore needs to be considered an effect or analysis of these works, rather than the other way around.
52. See Mann, *Doktor Faustus, Commentary*, 174.
53. Literary critic Thomas Schneider warns that in regard to characters, more conventional literary techniques like "portraying" are analytically better suited to describe Mann's work than "montage." See Schneider, *Das literarische Porträt*, 11.
54. For a description of the extensive documentation of this reading, see again Voss, *Entstehung*. "The excerpt from chapter 1 [...] shows, how Thomas Mann began, by means of transcription, to settle down [sich einzuleben] in the *Volksbuch*." Voss, *Entstehung*, esp. 24–34, 29, my translation, FP.
55. Petsch, *Volksbuch*.
56. Huszar Allen, "Montage," 111.
57. Huszar Allen, "Montage," 117.
58. Mann, "Goethe's Faust," 13. The text was first presented in English as a double-lecture on November 28/29, 1938, see Vaget, *Amerikaner*, 280.
59. Mann, "Kolleg über Faust," 597–98, the direct quotations are my translation, FP, with slight modification of Lowe-Porter's translation. See for a further qualification of De Huszar Allen's argument, however, the identical concepts used also in the description of the Joseph-novels, with Joseph practicing "mythical imatio" and as "religious conman," cited in Berger, *Motive*, 58–64.
60. Huszar Allen, "Montage," 117.
61. "Before long our German bourgeoisie knew *Faust* by heart. Scenes and images stamped themselves on the imagination of the people – one might almost say on the imagination of mankind; native and foreign artists were at once spurred on to illustrate the poem. The text, for German ears, seems to consist of quotations. I myself once heard, from a benighted soul in a theatre, the words: 'He makes it easy for himself; he just strings quotations together.'" Mann, "Goethe's Faust," 11.
62. Huszar Allen, "Montage," 111–12.
63. In the novel, the cyclical philosophy of history from cult to culture to cult is first introduced by Adrian Leverkühn's piano teacher Wendell Kretzschmar and later repeated by independent scholar Dr. Chaim Breisacher, both related to nationalist (völkisch) German Jewish philosopher of religion Oskar Goldberg and his *Die Wirklichkeit der Hebräer. Einleitung in das System des Pentateuch* from 1925 that Mann had already used in *Joseph and*

his Brothers. Taubes, "Cult to Culture." See also Voigts, *Goldberg*, 235–70 and Darmaun, *Mann et les Juifs*. In 1936, according to Goldberg, he was appointed by Mann for his journal *Mass und Wert* "as subject specialist for mythology and comparative religion," see Hülshörster, *Mann*, 102–17, my translation, FP.

64. Petsch had turned at the time of Mann's reading into a prominent and highly influential Nazi German scholar, and a declared enemy of Thomas Mann. See for Petsch's early career in folklore studies, working in Adolf Bastian's "Museum für Völkerkunde" in Berlin, as a successor to the chair of Keltologist Kuno Meyer in Liverpool, and as teacher of the above-mentioned Walter A. Berendsohn in Hamburg, Müller, H., "Petsch," 110–12.
65. Huszar Allen, "Montage," 110. A Latin original has never been found – it remains however vital for the *Volksbuch*'s historical reception.
66. Petsch, *Volksbuch*, XX.
67. Petsch, *Volksbuch*, XXXIX–XXXX.
68. Mann, *Story of a Novel*, 36–37.
69. Mann, *Genesis*, 121.
70. In the context of the Joseph tetralogy, the Egyptologist Jan Assmann refers in a similar vein as this chapter to "Thomas Mann's theory of a cultural memory." See Assmann, *Mann und Ägypten*, 70–71.
71. Hamacher, "Medien und Masken."
72. Mann, *Genesis*, 91.
73. See again Deussen, *Erinnerungen an Nietzsche*, 24. Another famous legend in Nietzsche's biography, "how Nietzsche embraced a beaten horse," was first published fully as an Italian newspaper article only in 1932, more than 40 years after the fact, by his Turino landlord Davide Fino.
74. See Bauman and Briggs, *Voices of Modernity*.
75. See Kreutzer, *Mythos vom Volksbuch*. Kreutzer also published in 1988 the currently authoritative edition of the text again with its historical genre – "Historia" – in the title: *Historia von D. Johann Fausten*.
76. Mann to Kerényi, "Letter, September 9, 1941," Mann and Kerényi, *Gespräch in Briefen*, 107, my translation, FP. "For the myth is the foundation of life," Mann writes in his essay on Freud, Mann, "Freud and the Future," 411.
77. Mann, *Tagebücher 1940–1943*, 552.
78. The use of the term in this chapter relies on the programmatic text by Bauman, "Philology of the Vernacular."
79. See the bibliography of printed sources in Mann, *Doktor Faustus, Commentary*, 1170–775, and for their appropriation the commentary, 170–901.
80. See Stocking, "Boasian Ethnography." Stocking describes the "Boasian goal of constituting the Kwakiutl equivalent of the remains of Sanskrit India." Stocking, "Boasian Ethnography," 5.
81. For the Nazification of German "Volkskunde" that has tainted the discipline, see the collaborative work of Hannsjost Lixfeld and James R. Dow in several publications, for example, Dow and Lixfeld, *Nazification*.

82. Bendix, *Authenticity*, 113–18. See for an attempt to revisit Naumann, Dow, "Kulturgut."
83. To assess this choice, a comparative study with Ernst Wiechert's anti-urban work, today largely forgotten, would be most appropriate. The national conservative Wiechert was among the best-selling novelists in the Third Reich, after choosing the flawed option to stay in Germany. Mann at least strategically considered returning to Germany between 1933 and 1935, before he was definitely declared an outcast, following the initiative of Reinhard Heydrich. Because of Wiechert's political statements – based on what he called Christian humanism – he spent in 1938 almost two months in the KZ Buchenwald, before compromising with the Nazi regime. See Niven, "Wiechert."
84. Literary critic T. J. Reed points to the "naïve" dialect-speaking farmer Else Schweigestill as the counter model to National Socialism as an urban phenomenon. See Reed, "Dialektik," 172–73.
85. See as a study contemporary to *Doctor Faustus*, McLuhan's *The Mechanical Bride: Folklore of Industrial Man* (1951).
86. Mann, "Humor und Ironie." For an audio recording of the entire discussion between present and future members of the newly founded "German Academy for Language and Literature" ("Deutsche Akademie für Sprache und Dichtung") Oskar Jancke, Werner Weber, literary critic Carl Helbling, and Thomas Mann, see www.srf.ch/audio/passage/thomas-mann-ueber-ironie-und-humor?id=bcf7f02e-7569-47c7-acf4-4cc7d1ca4de4 (August 5, 2025).
87. See Heller, *Ironic German*.
88. See Reed, *Uses of Tradition*.
89. See Dierks, *Mythos und Psychologie*.
90. See the classic text on this complex, convincingly situating the major boom of German (and European) inventions of tradition not in the era of Romanticism starting around 1800 – as most literary historians would agree – but largely in Thomas Mann's lifetime, starting much later in the 1870s, Hobsbawm "Mass-Producing Traditions." "The invention of the traditions of the German Empire is therefore primarily associated with the era of William II. [...] Since the 'German people' before 1871 had no political definition or unity, and its relation to the new Empire (which excluded large parts of it) was vague, symbolic or ideological, identification had to be more complex and – with the exception of the role of the Hohenzollern dynasty, army and state – less precise. Hence the multiplicity of reference, ranging from mythology and folklore (German oak, the Emperor Frederick Barbarossa) through the shorthand cartoon stereotypes to definition of the nation in terms of its enemies. Like many another liberated 'people,' 'Germany' was more easily defined by what it was against than in any other ways." Hobsbawm, "Mass-Producing Traditions," 274; 278.
91. Zimmer is therefore in a privileged position to comment on Mann's writing practices: "He took a thousand little details and profound thoughts from *Maya* and this Eranos lecture and simply, in part word for word, made a hash out of them [...]." Zimmer, quoted in Chapple, "Zimmer," 79n47.

92. Zimmer to Mellon, quoted in McGuire, "Zimmer," 40.
93. McGuire, "Zimmer," 41.
94. Campbell's biographers point to his reading of German anthropologist Leo Frobenius as the major reference for his approach, quoting from his "War Journal" that he kept during World War II: "I learned [from Frobenius] that the essential form of the myth is a cycle, and that this cycle is a symbolic representation of the form of the soul, and that in the dreams and fancies of modern individuals (who have been brought up along the lines of a rational, practical education) these myth-symbols actually reappear – giving testimony of a persistence, even into modern times, of the myth power. [...] With this [...] the emphasis of my studies shifted from the historical to the mythological. I began to read, with fresh understanding, the novels of Thomas Mann and the *Ulysses* of James Joyce. The role of the artist I now understood as that of revealing through the world-surfaces the implicit forms of the soul, and the great agent to assist the artist in this work was the myth." Larsen and Larsen, *Joseph Campbell*, 226.
95. See Campbell, *Hero*.
96. Campbell and Robinson, *Skeleton Key*.
97. Mann, *Tagebücher 1944–1.4.1946*, 85. This kinship between Mann and Joyce has since been treated extensively in secondary literature, for a helpful assessment see Schonfield, "Mann Re-Joyces"; see also for a study based on Mann's private library collected in the Thomas-Mann-Archiv of the ETH Zürich, Schmidt-Schütz, *Tradition und Moderne*. Campbell's assessment of kinship is based, however, on Mann's "unpolitical" work, see Larsen and Larsen, *Joseph Campbell*, 295–96. Campbell's and Mann's brief dispute about an American humanism in 1940/41 is a thinly veiled proxy conflict about the New Deal and Roosevelt, with Campbell backing down immediately, despite lingering reservations, see Larsen and Larsen, *Joseph Campbell*, 290. Campbell's postwar universal morphology nevertheless continues his positions developed as his – at the time aptly named – "Campbell's law" in 1937 and relies on the arguments developed in his speech "Permanent Human Values," criticized by Mann. The text of the speech is printed in Larsen and Larsen, *Joseph Campbell*, 287–90.
98. Levin, *James Joyce*. For example: "All of Joyce's books, like Thomas Mann's, fit into the broadening dialectical pattern of *Künstler* [artist] versus *Bürger* [citizen/bourgeois]." Levin, *James Joyce*, 66.
99. Levin, *James Joyce*, 66.
100. According to this hypothesis, the "missing link" between Mann's view on Joyce and the "montage of cultural products" expressed in the letter to Adorno or respectively in *The Genesis of Doctor Faustus*, may be found in a letter to Jacques Mercanton, a former collaborator of James Joyce, in a comparative description in terms of "products": "You reflect in one passage on the fact of the popularity of my books, which have however an uncanny quality [meiner doch niemals ganz geheuren Bücher], in opposition to those by Joyce. Of course, I have already thought about this phenomenon as well. It is probably largely based on a misunderstanding, but the readability for many readers of these *products* [emphasis added] may relate

to a complaisance and affability of their attitude that occludes many a contradiction, a traditionalism, the problems of which are accepted. These are coming to light ever more and my most recent book which you were unable to include in your reflection, the novel 'Dr. Faustus,' a pretty wild story, will leave little of the beautiful delusion of me as bourgeois-conservative Excellency and as ironically even-tempered mind." Mann to Mercanton, "Letter, January 21, 1948," Mann, *Dichter*, 127–28, my translation, FP.

101. Levin, *James Joyce*, 89.
102. Campbell's coauthor of the *Skeleton Key*, literary critic and freelance author Henry Morton Robinson worked as a Woodstock-based senior editor for *Reader's Digest*, see Larsen and Larsen, *Joseph Campbell*, 281.
103. Campbell and Robinson, *Skeleton Key*, 28.
104. "A few years after this time, Campbell would begin his annual entertainment for the Sarah Lawrence College community, the topic being James Joyce, by reciting that enigmatic first page from memory; he would then proceed over the next hour to reveal its mysteries to the wondering ears of students and faculty. It was to become one of his most popular lectures." Larsen and Larsen, *Joseph Campbell*, 280.
105. Campbell, "Reading." The recording also contains Joyce's famous historical reading of "Anna Livia Plurabelle."
106. See also McLuhan, "James Joyce."
107. Campbell and Robinson, *Skeleton Key*, 14.
108. Thompson, St., *Motif-Index*. See also Thompson, St., *Folklorist's Progress*.
109. According to folklore historian Mary E. Brown, Harvard University served in the United States since the late nineteenth century as the "headquarters for the study of the ballad and folksongs." Brown, M., *Child's Unfinished Masterpiece*, 227. Some of the most important early twentieth-century folklorists, among them the aforementioned Archer Taylor, and Stith Thompson, the "Linnaeus of folklore," were not only trained at Harvard, its reputation also allowed them consequently to become part of the European network of folklorists centered in Finland. See Brown, M., *Child's Unfinished Masterpiece*, 8.
110. Northrop Frye's systematic project needs to be considered, in this sense, one of its most important aftereffects in literary criticism.
111. The French reception as prompted by Maurice Blanchot – and drawing on similar theoretical sources – sees in Mann's work a "primordial narrative" ("narration primordiale") at work, see Blanchot, "Rencontre avec le Démon."
112. Mann, *Tagebücher 1940–1943*, 557.
113. See Mann, *Tagebücher 1940–1943*, 558. Officially, heroin was banned as a prescription drug since almost 20 years. See also the classic study McCoy, *Politics of Heroin*.
114. See Mann, *Tagebücher 1940–1943*, 562.
115. See Mann, *Tagebücher 1940–1943*, 564, 579.
116. Mann, *Tagebücher 1940–1943*, 572–573.
117. Mann, *Tagebücher 1940–1943*, 579.
118. Ibid.

119. See Mann to Meyer, "Letter, May 26, 1943," Mann and Meyer, *Briefwechsel*, 477–80.
120. See Berman, *Crisis and Charisma*, 54. This chapter in a way expands Berman's thesis of a bureaucratization of literary relations within the framework of late realism into the US-American memorandum culture. See also his chapter on *Doctor Faustus*, particularly insightful in its presentation of the "Italian hypnosis" in Mann's *Mario and the Sorcerer* in relation to concepts of alternative community, Bermann, *Crisis and Carisma*, 261–86, 265–68.
121. "Die Schweiz [...] verlangte Takt [...]." Mann, "Warum," 5, my translation, FP.
122. Despite his apparent linguistic problems, in regard to US-American sociality, the visit was a formative experience, as the editor Alfred A. Knopf introduced Mann into the rituals of New York's establishment culture.
123. Mann, *Tagebücher 1935–1936*, 86.
124. Mann, "Brief von Thomas Mann," *Neue Zürcher Zeitung*, February 3, https://kuenste-im-exil.de/KIE/Content/DE/Objekte/mann-thomas-offener-brief-nzz-1936.html (August 5, 2025).
125. For Mann's bureaucratic engagement in Swiss committee work at the predecessor-organization of the UNESCO, see his article Mann, "Geist in Gesellschaft." See also Renoliet, *L'Unesco oublieé*, 317–22.
126. Mann, *Listen, Germany* (1942); Mann, *Deutsche Hörer!* (2004). Several of the audio recordings of the speeches have been published, Mann, *Thomas Mann spricht*.
127. See "Layout of BBC broadcasts in German," printed in an abridged version in Valentin, *Steine in Hitlers Fenster*, 16–18.
128. Collected in Mann, *Addresses*.
129. Mills, *Power Elite*. Mills's notion of "power" relies on Franz Neumann's use of the term in *Behemoth*.
130. Mayer, *Thomas Mann*, 389–93.
131. Mann, "Brother." The long subtitle, a quote from the text, reads: "And if genius is madness tempered with discretion, this sly sadist and plotter of revenge is a genius."
132. Incidentally, Mann anticipates in his association of common elements Gregory Bateson's trance analysis of film, Balinese trance and Nazi German rituals, discussed in Chapter 5: "Lately, on the films, I saw a ritual dance of the Bali Islanders. It ended in the complete trance condition, with frightful twitchings of the bodies of the exhausted youths. Where is the difference between these practices and the procedure in the European mass meeting? [...] When I was still very young, I described in *Fiorenza* how the sway of beauty and culture was once broken by the religious and social fanaticism of a monk who heralded 'the miracle of regained detachment.'" Mann, "Brother," 133.
133. Mann portrays the Nazi leader as a relative following Mann's own character role of the artist – according to his theory of mythical reenactment. He thereby argues against the view held by a majority of European émigrés in the United States, to distinguish between two Germanys, Nazi Germany

and the "other Germany." For an extensive treatment of this topic, see Hoenicke Moore, *Know Your Enemy*.
134. Mann, "Germany and the Germans," 61.
135. Mann, "Germany and the Germans," 47.
136. Mann, "Germany and the Germans," 64–65.
137. See Bahr, "Kontroverse," 1500. See also Thyrnauer, "German Leaders-in-Exile."
138. Mann, "Germany and the Germans," 65–66.
139. Mann, "Germany and the Germans," 63.
140. See Mann, *Tagebücher 1940–1943*, 434. Dieter Borchmeyer contextualizes Mann's "most leftist" essay with regard to Mann's refusal, one month later, of the Free Germany Committee's exile politics, see Borchmeyer, *Thomas Mann*, 1095–97.
141. Mann, "War and Future," 32. The text was first titled in German as "Schicksal und Aufgabe" and later published in abbreviated form as Mann, "What Is German?" At the end of the novel, this passage reverberates in Mann's description of postwar Nazi German partisans, see Mann, *Doctor Faustus*, 505. See also Biddiscombe, *Werwolf*.
142. Mann, "Germany and the Germans," 51.
143. See again Mann to Evans, "Letter, June 15, 1947," Mann, *Dichter*, 93.
144. Mann, "Germany and the Germans," 66.
145. Kahler, "Säkularisierung des Teufels." The text is part of the intense interdisciplinary early discussion of the book at the English-speaking humanist front, see Fitzgerald, "Subjectivity Is Absolute"; See also for a curious theological response, as intriguing as perfidious, by politically compromised literary critic and poet Hans Egon Holthusen, as an *exemplum* for the mendacity and hypocrisy of the German post-war years, which Mann's novel nevertheless managed to address, Holthusen, "Welt ohne Transzendenz"; Holthusen, "Die Welt ohne Transzendenz (II)."
146. Mann to Meyer, "Letter, October 11, 1944," Mann and Meyer, *Briefwechsel*, 593, my translation, FP.
147. During the social inversions of carnival: "[F]inally, during carnival, at artists' galas in Schwabing, where acquaintances from all these other meeting places, whose circles of friends also overlapped, would meet again in topsy-turvy confusion." Mann, *Doctor Faustus*, 291.
148. See Wysling, "Maja-Projekt."
149. For Mann's usage of this obsolete term, also prominently employed in his *Magic Mountain*, see Mann, "Humaniora und Humanismus."
150. Mann, *Doctor Faustus*, 258. See Rieckmann, "Problem des Durchbruchs"; see also Mann, *Doktor Faustus*, *Commentary*, 572–73. Besides "breakthrough," "love" is the only rivaling category of sociality in the novel which is invoked by the narrator to describe his motivation to write the biographical account of the protagonist. At the same time, Adrian Leverkühn's devil-imposed inhibition to "love" leads to the "murder" of several characters culminating in the child sacrifice of the protagonist's nephew. See Mann, *Genesis*, 35, my translation of the German "Mord." See also Mann, *Doctor Faustus*, 525. Adrian Leverkühn's desire to love, however, ultimately

serves the purpose – through the loss of love – to achieve a breakthrough to "lament" ("Klage"). See Mann, *Doctor Faustus*, 509–10.
151. See again Taubes, "Cult to Culture."
152. See on the "Hungary-syndrome," in *Doctor Faustus*, Seidlin, "Hungarian Connection," 598.
153. The final chapter also echoes Clarissa Rodde's suicide in Pfeiffering in chapter 35 of *Doctor Faustus*, Clarissa Rodde poisons herself after publicly falling into disgrace due to a premarital affair. Her social death and suicide coincide.
154. Garfinkel, "Routine Grounds," 58. The sociologist Keith Doubt points to a short story about crossing the racial "color line" on a bus as another early literary illustration of Garfinkel's method of the ethnomethodological breaching experiment, see Doubt, "Garfinkel Before Ethnomethodology." See also Garfinkel, "Color Trouble."
155. Mann, *Doctor Faustus*, 521.
156. Ibid.
157. Mann, *Doctor Faustus*, 521–22.
158. Mann, *Doctor Faustus*, 522–23.
159. Mann, *Doctor Faustus*, 524–25.
160. Mann, *Doctor Faustus*, 525.
161. Mann, *Doctor Faustus*, 526.
162. Mann, *Doctor Faustus*, 527.
163. Ibid.

5 NAZI GERMAN MEDIA THEORY

1. See Wasson, *Museum Movies*. For the prehistory of the Film Library, see Polan, *Scenes of Instruction*. For the educational mission of the Film Library, see Wasson, "Studying Movies at the Museum."
2. Gary, Nervous Liberals, 12. See also Buxton, "John Marshall," 150; and Mueller, "Rockefeller Foundation."
3. See Moltke and Rawson, Siegfried Kracauer's *American Writings*, 242n25. See also Moltke, *Curious Humanist*, 20–21.
4. Gary, *Nervous Liberals*, 116.
5. Culbert, "Rockefeller Foundation," 510. For his views on Kracauer in the United States, see John Marshall's several diary entries between 1941 and 1942 in Rockefeller Foundation Records, Officers' Diaries, RG 12, Rockefeller Archive Center, Sleepy Hollow/NY, https://dimes.rockarch.org/collections/dCGwNLMdkwa8hU3QftoUbL (August 5, 2025).
6. It was difficult to translate their wartime work in collaborative projects into steady positions; see Kracauer to Bateson, "Letter, November 16, 1947," Siegfried Kracauer Nachlass.
7. See also Bryson, "Lawrence K. Frank"; Krige and Rausch, "Introduction"; and Link, "Sozialwissenschaften im Kalten Krieg."
8. See the assessment of the "Marseiller Entwurf" that Kracauer had pondered since 1937–1938 in Später, *Siegfried Kracauer*, 369–70; 476.

9. Elisabeth Kracauer, who used to work as a librarian, closely collaborated with Kracauer from 1930 on. She notes in an undated CV from the late 1940s that "from 1930 to 1945 I did extensive research for my husband," Zinfert, "Digression," 81.
10. For Kracauer's early mentorship, see Adorno and Kracauer, *Briefwechsel*.
11. Adorno, "Gutachten," 262. If not indicated otherwise, all translations from German are mine. See also Jay, "Extraterritorial Life."
12. Kracauer, *Totalitäre Propaganda*, 312.
13. At different stages of the application process referred to as "German Economy, Politics, and Culture 1900–1933" and "Cultural Aspects of National Socialism." For a description of the project's development, see Stackelberg, "Cultural Aspects." See also, for a brief mention, Jay, *Dialectical Imagination*, 169–70; Wiggershaus, *Frankfurt School*, 275; Wheatland, *Frankfurt School in Exile*, 220–21. Many of the archival materials are available at Universitätsbibliothek der Johann Wolfgang Goethe-Universität Frankfurt am Main, Archivzentrum, Nachlass Max Horkheimer, Archivzentrum shelf marks Na 1, 693 – Na 1, 699, sammlungen.ub.uni-frankfurt.de/horkheimer/nav/index/all (August 5, 2025).
14. Adorno to Horkheimer, "Letter, July 29, 1940," 76–77.
15. Quoted in Adorno and Horkheimer, *Briefwechsel*, 4.3,111. Original in English.
16. Susman, "Culture of the Thirties," 172. See also Hegeman, *Patterns for America*.
17. See also Turner, F., *Democratic Surround*.
18. On the early constitution of this circle, see Bryson, "Personality and Culture." Especially the month-long Seminar on Human Relations in Hanover, New Hampshire in the summer of 1934 proved pivotal for Mead, see Bryson, *Socializing the Young*, 137–86. In her autobiography, she calls it "the seminar at Dartmouth at which I began my interdisciplinary work." Mead, *Blackberry Winter*, 269.
19. All these initiatives are documented in Manuscript Division, Library of Congress in Washington/DC, Margaret Mead Papers and South Pacific Ethnographic Archives, 1838–1996, esp. boxes F1–6, M3–4, M29–35, O5–7, O9–10, O14–15. Regarding Mead's wartime collaborations, see Shankman, *Margaret Mead*, 86–97 and Mandler, *Return from the Natives*. See also Mead, *Selected Letters*; Bateson, *Daughter's Eye*; Howard, *Margaret Mead*.
20. For details on Bateson's work at the Film Library and especially his analysis of *Hitlerjunge Quex* as a pilot study for the (failed) establishment of a "Wartime Regional Materials Unit," see Brennan, "Cinema Intelligence Apparatus."
21. Faletti, "Reflections of Weimar Cinema," 11. Martin Loiperdinger describes *Hitlerjunge Quex* as part of a 1933 "Party film-trilogy," *Hans Westmar*, *Hitlerjunge Quex*, and *SA-Mann Fritz Brand*, all creating fascist martyr legends during the first year of the Nazi Party's rule in Germany, see Loiperdinger, *Märtyrerlegenden im NS-Film*, 159–72.
22. See Kreimeier, *Ufa Story*.
23. *Hitlerjunge Quex* (dir. Hans Steinhoff, 1933). In 1936 and 1937 the pioneering curator of the Film Library, Iris Barry, had traveled to Europe and the Soviet Union to obtain film reels from, among other institutions,

the *Reichsfilmkammer*. See Sitton, *Lady in the Dark*, 215–16. See also Decherney, *Hollywood and the Culture Elite*, 138.
24. Rentschler, *Ministry of Illusion*, 57.
25. The film's script was written by Karl Aloys Schenzinger, who the previous year had authored the novel *Der Hitlerjunge Quex*, loosely based on the stabbing death of Hitler Youth member Herbert Norkus in 1932. See Kater, *Hitler Youth*, 18–19; 33; see also Baird, *To Die for Germany*, 108–29. After *Der Hitlerjunge Quex*, Schenzinger published a far less successful novel, *Der Herrgottsbacher Schülermarsch* (1934), in which he sets up the conversion of Catholic boys into Hitler Youth members, identifying the "Leader" with the Christian god. See Stahl, "Literature and Propaganda," 138.
26. Baird, *To Die for Germany*, 109. Baird mimics here, without quotation marks, historical Nazi jargon according to his method of shifting focalization.
27. Price, *Anthropological Intelligence*.
28. The text survives in at least two versions from 1943 and 1945. One is kept at the Library of Congress in Washington, DC, Margaret Mead Papers, box K55 one in the Special Collections & Archives University of California Santa Cruz, Gregory Bateson Papers, box 95.
29. However, for a close reading of the memorandum, see Schüttpelz, "Vor der Re-Education (1943)." For a recent example of a prominent publication that does not consider the 1980 publication, see Baker, "Bateson Analysis."
30. Bateson, "Cultural and Thematic Analysis," 77.
31. Bateson, "Nazi Film," 344.
32. After a twenty- or, respectively, thirty-year gap, in 1974 "Bateson's analysis is used in Leiser, *Nazi Cinema* [...]; it has reappeared in almost every subsequent discussion of the film." Rentschler, *Ministry of Illusion*, 326n64.
33. Bateson, "Quex," 27. The identical quote appears also in Bateson, "Nazi Film," 306. In the following, I quote from Bateson's 1980 publication, even if identical passages also appear in the 1953 composite text, edited by Margaret Mead.
34. After a long and dramatic to and fro, Kracauer arrived with his wife in New York on April 25, 1941. See Später, *Siegfried Kracauer*, 384–409; see also Sitton, *Lady in the Dark*, 217–18.
35. After some years of consideration, Kracauer started writing his history of Weimar cinema in 1943 and finished the first manuscript, with the help of a two-year Guggenheim fellowship, in 1945–1946. Kracauer finally published his groundbreaking book in 1947. See Kracauer, *From Caligari to Hitler*. See also Gilloch, *Kracauer*, 123–41.
36. "Irretrievably sunk into retrogression, the bulk of the German people could not help submitting to Hitler. Since Germany thus carried out what had been anticipated by her cinema from its very beginning, conspicuous screen characters now came true in life itself." Kracauer, *From Caligari to Hitler*, 272.
37. The pad with Bateson's notes on *Hitlerjunge Quex* is preserved in the Margaret Mead Papers, box O6.
38. For the flag as a symbol in the National Socialist movement, see Behrenbeck, *Der Kult um die toten Helden*, 422–24. Behrenbeck relies on the study of flags in Nazi propaganda written by a former Hitler Youth

member, Hoffmann, *Triumph of Propaganda*; regarding *Hitlerjunge Quex*, see esp. 49–55.
39. Kracauer, "Propaganda and the Nazi War Film," 19–20.
40. Kracauer, *From Caligari to Hitler*, 262n17.
41. See Kracauer, *From Caligari to Hitler*, 262.
42. Erikson, "Hitler's Imagery," 480.
43. Kracauer, *From Caligari to Hitler*, 262.
44. Ibid.
45. See the typescript of Kracauer's English synopsis to "Hitlerjunge Quex, 30 September to 8 October, 1941, Library of Congress," reproduced in Culbert, "Rockefeller Foundation," 506–9. Both translations avoid the alliteration of the German "Fahne *f*lattert ... *v*oran" (e.g., "*f*lag *f*lutters" or, with less onomatopoetic effect, "*b*anner *b*illows *b*efore"). It is really about the "flag" that "billows."
46. Kracauer, *From Caligari to Hitler*, 262. At the time Bateson had published only his first brief article on *Hitlerjunge Quex*. As far as one can tell from the archived work preliminary to *From Caligari to Hitler*, Kracauer did not see the manuscript of Bateson's full analysis.
47. Bateson, "Letter," quoted in the pioneering study of the Culture and Personality School's war efforts by Yans-McLaughlin, "Science, Democracy, and Ethics," 202.
48. In his "Lay-out I" for *From Caligari to Hitler* from May 19–20, 1946, however, Kracauer distances himself from the Culture and Personality School: "This implies I am not stipulating a National Character. Against Anthropologists." Kracauer, "Layout I," in Von Caligari bis Hitler [Vorarbeiten], Ma 1, Siegfried Kracauer Nachlass. For a reading of the preliminary work to *From Caligari to Hitler* in general, and to this point in particular, see Quaresima, "Introduction to the 2004 Edition," xxvii.
49. Bateson, "Quex," 54n6.
50. Bateson probably worked initially with Kracauer's synopsis and deliberately changed the translation, see Bateson, "Quex," 27.
51. The standard biographical account of Bateson's life does not fully consider the importance of the "several short-term projects during the first years of the war." Lipset, *Gregory Bateson*, 166.
52. "Clonus," derived from Greek *klonos*, turmoil, is a medical concept originating in the early nineteenth century denoting a "muscular spasm involving repeated, often rhythmic, contractions." Stevenson and Lindberg, *New Oxford American Dictionary*, 327, lemma "clonus."
53. Bateson, "Birth of a Matrix," 200.
54. See Wiener, *Cybernetics*, 28. See also Rosenblueth, Wiener, and García Ramos, "Muscular Clonus"; Wiener, *I Am a Mathematician*, 254; and Kline, *Cybernetics Moment*, 76.
55. See for the term his collection of essays, Bateson, *Steps to an Ecology of Mind*.
56. Mead originally intended to use the photographs for a book titled *On the Karma Family*, see Sullivan, *Margaret Mead*, 18.
57. See Bateson and Mead, "For God's Sake, Margaret," 42. See also Jacknis, "Margaret Mead and Gregory Bateson in Bali."

58. See Heims, *Constructing a Social Science*, 14. Bateson's concern dates back at least to the meetings of Mead, Bateson, and Milton Erickson between November 1940 and January 1941. After a discussion of Balinese trance in November 1940, Mead writes in a follow-up letter to Erickson with reference to Bateson's ideas on trance posture in its relation to the contraction of individual muscles. See Mead to Erickson, "Letter, November 9, 1940," Margaret Mead Papers.
59. See Bateson and Mead, *Balinese Character*, 91.
60. Ibid. It is vital to the ritual that the men holding the stick do not go into trance themselves.
61. Bateson, "Some Components," 152.
62. Ibid.
63. Bateson, "Some Components," 153.
64. For a characterization of Bateson's trance model in the context of trance media research as one of the few attempts to give a systematic scientific understanding of the exceedingly incoherent states of trance often induced through shaking, see Schüttpelz, "Trance-Medien/Personale Medien," 228–29.
65. I use the term "teleology" here with reference to the historical cybernetic notion describing feedback processes. Bateson's article on trance may be read as a challenge to one of the proudest philosophical achievements of cybernetics, first discussed during the aforementioned "Cerebral Inhibition Meeting": Rosenblueth, Wiener, and Bigelow, "Behavior, Purpose, and Teleology."
66. See for photography, Chéroux, *Perfect Medium*; for the telegraph, Stolow, "Techno-religious Imaginaries"; and for the radio, Rowlands and Wilson, *Oliver Lodge and the Invention of Radio*.
67. Bateson could rely on the fact that to think of Nazi Germany as entranced was a trope introduced by the New York Times already in an article of 1933. Its subheading reads, "By a Vast Propaganda Aimed at Emotions, Germany's Trance Is Maintained." Stone, "Hitler's Showmen Weave a Magic Spell," 8.
68. Bateson, "Some Components," 152.
69. Bateson, "Some Components," 154.
70. See again Turner, F., *Democratic Surround*, 63–76. Turner takes this aspect of the trance ritual, the media surround, as the starting point of his book.
71. Bateson, "Some Components," 149. "In sum, the business of explanation and the business of socialization turn out to be the same. To make a premise 'self-evident' is the simplest way to make action based upon that premise seem 'natural.'" Bateson, "Some Components," 154–55.
72. Bateson, "Some Components," 153.
73. See Bateson, "Some Components," plate 20, unpaginated, between pages 154 and 155.
74. Bateson, "Letter," quoted in Yans-McLaughlin, "Science, Democracy, and Ethics," 202. See also again the use of "tick" in Bateson's didactic version of *Hitlerjunge Quex*.
75. The first prominent reference appears in precisely the text that codifies Bateson's theory of mass media: Ruesch and Bateson, *Communication*.
76. Bateson, "Quex," 21.

77. Adorno, "Psychological Technique," 25.
78. Bateson, "Some Components," 150.
79. Respectively learning 1, learning 2, and learning 3.
80. Bateson, "Some Components," 147; 145.
81. Bateson, "Quex," 27.
82. Bateson, "Age Conflicts and Radical Youth," 13. This twenty-two-page draft written in 1941 for the Committee for National Morale is preserved in the Margaret Mead Papers.
83. Bateson, "Quex," 27. See also Gregor Ziehen's influential report based on his early tour through Nazi German educational institutions. Ziehen both provides the model for interpreting songs and gives one of the earliest translations of the Hitler Youth song: "Our banners precede us, fluttering in the breeze." Ziehen, *Education for Death*, 136. Bateson seems to have ignored this rather free translation.
84. Bruns, *Kinomythen*, 43–76; Andriopoulos, *Possessed*.
85. Bateson, "Quex," 33. See Faletti, "Reflections of Weimar Cinema," 18.
86. Kracauer, "Conquest of Europe," 350.
87. Kracauer, "Conquest of Europe," 350–51. This passage echoes some motifs of Kracauer's essay on the "mass ornament," such as his remark on the "legs of the Tiller girls." Kracuer, "Mass Ornament," 79; 84.
88. The Frankfurt School's conception of mass hypnosis (as well as the Nazis', represented in Hitler's *Mein Kampf*) goes back to Gustave Le Bon's "Crowd Psychology," as rendered in his highly influential 1895 best seller *Psychologie des foules*. See, for the discursive context of the rise of crowd or mass psychology in France, Van Ginneken, *Crowds, Psychology, and Politics*.
89. Kracauer, "Newsreel," 354. See also Kracauer, "Propaganda and the Nazi War Film," 20.
90. Bateson, "Quex," 33.
91. Bateson, "Nazi Film," 344.
92. See Bosse, "Zur Sozialgeschichte des Wanderliedes."
93. See Bateson, "Quex," 43.
94. See Bateson, "Quex," 28.
95. The chart represents the result of a structural analysis of the film and indicates Bateson's original comparative effort: his notes show that he attempted to interpret Völker's becoming a Hitler Youth member as a process following Arnold van Gennep's model of rites of passage. (In *Balinese Character* Bateson and Mead title a whole section of photographs, plates 84–100, "Rites de Passage.") In the final version of his text, Bateson shrinks this initial intuition into a passing remark: "His [Heini's] first death by gas tells us that the entry into the age grade system is itself a passage rite, differing only from other passage rites and initiations in that Heini's mother, instead of mourning the loss of her boy when he leaves the family, is herself killed." Bateson, "Quex," 29.
96. Bateson, "Quex," 52.
97. Bateson, "Morale and National Character," 90.

98. Bateson, "Quex," 50. Plate 7 in Balinese Character (after the plates "Crowds" and "Industrialization" and before the plates "Official Trance" and "Sharing and Social Organization") depicts a state called "awayness" that Mead describes in the introduction as an "inverted" trance, a sort of inner emigration. See Bateson and Mead, *Balinese Character*, 4–5.
99. For the identification of command and "enemy Other," see Galison, "Ontology of the Enemy."
100. Bateson remarks about a difference to the novel, on which the film is based: "First there is a conversation between Stoppel [a communist] and the mother, in which the mother is described as hypnotized with fear in Stoppel's presence." Bateson, "Quex," 54n26.
101. See Bateson, "Quex," 53.
102. Ibid.
103. See Bateson, "Quex," 27.
104. It is this truncated version of the verse, spoken by the dying Heini, that Kracauer quotes from Bateson: "The flag billows ahead ... "
105. See Arnold, Schöning, and Schröter, *Hitlerjunge Quex*, 235–37.
106. Bateson, "Quex," 29.
107. See Behrenbeck, *Der Kult um die toten Helden*, 299–325.
108. Bateson, "Quex," 28. The Nazis appropriated the ritual structure from the Italian military, calling on fallen soldiers during World War I – a central context also in Germany – and answering for them "presente." Faust, "Trance und Trauma," 115. Behrenbeck further notices in her description of the November 9 rite that the thousand men were indeed Hitler Youth members who had been initiated in an "imitatio heroica" into the party, see Behrenbeck, *Der Kult um die toten Helden*, 311.
109. See Benedict, *Patterns of Culture*.
110. The notes documenting the drafting of these title links are preserved in the Margaret Mead Papers, box O6. During an interview with a former Hitler Youth member about his experience watching and rewatching *Hitlerjunge Quex*, Bateson comments on his work: "I have been working on this film in detail, picking it to pieces." Bateson, "Prediscussion and Discussion Following Showing 'Hitlerjunge Quex' May 12, 1943," 24, Margaret Mead Papers. This work of "picking it to pieces" and then creating a new version of the film needs to be understood as the most "engaged" aspect of Bateson's work on Nazi trance media.
111. Adorno, "Psychological Technique," 55.
112. Bateson, "Social Planning," 162. One may conclude from Bateson's diagrams that there is a direct, symmetrical, and therefore antagonistic relationship between Nazi media education and US reeducation. For the role of Bateson's memorandum in the discussion of reeducation policy proposals, see Füssl, "Fine-Tuning Utopia," 285–86.
113. In Bateson's notes on *Hitlerjunge Quex*, the only mention of trance is attributed to Kracauer, in a comparison with the film *Fährmann Maria* (1936): "F. Maria does *not* deceive death – walks? with her eyes shut, certainly not looking where she is walking – Kracauer thinks 'in trance.'" Margaret Mead Papers, box O6.

114. See the second draft of the famous "Culture Industry" chapter titled "Das Schema der Massenkultur," preserved in Nachlass Max Horkheimer, sammlungen.ub.uni-frankfurt.de/horkheimer/content/pageview/7316438 (August 5, 2025).

6 GERMANY AS A CONCEPTUAL SCHEME

1. On Harvard historian William L. Langer as head of the Research & Analysis Branch of the Office of Strategic Services and liaison to the Ivy League, see Katz, *Foreign Intelligence*, 5–7. For a pointed characterization of Langer, see Müller, *Krieger und Gelehrte*, 39–40.
2. Parsons to Langer, "Letter, December 19, 1944," Papers of Talcott Parsons, HUG(FP) 15.2, box 15.
3. Parsons, "Controlled Institutional Change." Before publication Mead commented on an earlier draft of the text. Here she strongly approves of Parsons' introduction of "a new ethical principle" not to act from a moral high ground according to American principles but to understand the role of the American military government in terms of German culture patterns. Parsons took Mead's remarks extremely seriously and included them, mostly without naming Mead, except for two cryptic references regarding civil service cited as Footnote 8 and regarding the lack of a reservoir of guilt as footnote 18 of the published article. See for Mead's comments Mead to Parsons, "Letter, October 30, 1944." Mead's comments continue a discussion that ensued during and after the conference on "Germany after the War" regarding Germany's flexibility or rigidity, where both attempt to reconcile cultural anthropological with sociological arguments. See Parsons to Mead, "Letter, May 5, 1944"; Mead to Parsons, "Letter, May 12, 1944"; Parsons to Mead, "Letter, May 19, 1944." Margaret Mead Papers, box C12. The immediate context of the final version of the article is, however, the news coverage of one of the most famous memoranda of World War II, the "Morgenthau-plan," see Parsons to Mead, "Letter, September 28, 1944." HUG(FP) 15.2, box 15. Parsons sent the completed draft of his article to Mead, and he waited politely for her late response – and approval – before publishing it.
4. On "Germany after the War" and reeducation, see Chapter 7.
5. Parsons, "Controlled Institutional Change," 84.
6. Ibid. See his earlier statement on the relationship of institutions and situation: "[T]he principal function of institutional patterns may, following W. I. Thomas, be said to be to 'define the situation.'" Parsons, "Propaganda and Social Control," 553.
7. Parsons had discussed the role of the Prussian *Junker* class, most famously represented by Otto von Bismarck and Paul von Hindenburg, in an article describing the problem of a Prussian, feudal, patriarchal, militaristic, authoritarian, Lutheran, romantic "formalism," see Parsons, "Democracy and Social Structure in Pre-Nazi Germany," 104.

8. Parsons, "Controlled Institutional Change," 81. Parsons problematized vested interests as a problem of institutionalization with regard to fascist movements in a 1942 article, see Parsons, "Fascist Movements," 145–46.
9. Parsons, "Controlled Institutional Change," 84.
10. See for a synthetic definition and critique of the political conception of the term, for example, in Popper's *Open Society and Its Enemies* (1945) in Etzemüller, "Verhaltenslehre des kühlen Kopfes," 20–31.
11. Parsons to Langer, "Letter, December 19, 1944," HUG(FP) 15.2, box 15.
12. Ibid.
13. Parsons to Langer, "Letter, January 8, 1945," HUG(FP) 15.2, box 15.
14. Ibid.
15. For Hartshorne's detailed diaries and letters 1945/46, see Tent, *Academic Proconsul*. See also Gerhardt, *Parsons: Intellectual Biography*, 65–68.
16. The analogy between a medical-biological organism and state administration underlying the concept of a social system was first established in post-revolutionary French physiology, see Pickstone, "Bureaucracy, Liberalism and the Body." See also on the nineteenth-century history of this complex, Rabinbach, *Human Motor*. Parsons receives the notion via Lawrence J. Henderson from Italian economist Vilfredo Pareto combined with a conservative ideal of equilibrium widely influential in 1930s physiology as introduced by Walter B. Cannon work on "homeostasis" in his *Wisdom of the Body*. On the "'soft' style" of a universal concept of equilibrium in social theory represented by Parsons, see Russett, *Equilibrium*, 143–52. See also Cross and Albury, "Organic Analogy."
17. See Gilman, *Mandarins of the Future*, 73–154. See also Janos, *Changing Theories of Change*, 60.
18. After decades of a vibrant discussion, elaboration, development, critique, and creative repurposing of Parsons's social theory, recent editions of manuscripts prepared by Helmut Staubmann and Victor Lidz such as Parsons's 1939 manuscript of *Actor, Situation and Normative Pattern* (2010), and the *Schumpeter-Parsons Seminar 1939–1940* on rationality (2018), his exchange of letters with Eric Voegelin (2013) edited by Peter Brickey Lequire and Daniel Silver, as well as the publication of his "lost" dissertation on *Capitalism according to Sombart and Max Weber* (2018) by Günter Stummvoll and Bruce C. Wearne have added significant layers to the discussion. Ironically, however, Parsons shares the fate of many American academics collaborating with émigré intellectuals that unlike for several of their German counterparts, and in Parsons's case, despite his vital importance for the twentieth century as a theorist, organizer and teacher, there is no critical edition of their collected works, unpublished manuscripts, and letters.
19. Uta Gerhardt first established Parsons's role as a political activist during World War II and has published widely on the topic, including her important edition of published and unpublished essays, reports, and memoranda in *Parsons on National Socialism*. See also Gerhardt, *Parsons: Intellectual Biography*. Her decades worth of work to reconstruct Parsons's intellectual project culminates in Gerhardt, *Social Thought of Parsons*. Gerhardt counts for the period from 1939 to 1945 in addition to seven war-related articles,

"three unpublished manuscripts, at least fourteen radio speeches, apart from the numerous ad-hoc memoranda, reports, minutes, or resolutions for various groups or agencies." Gerhardt, "Parsons and the War Effort," 268.
20. See for the term "interstitial academy" Isaac, *Working Knowledge*. Isaac's work on Parsons's synthesizes significant new trends to rewrite the historiography of the social sciences informed by methods developed in the field of history of science, intellectual history, and social history. See also the groundbreaking essay by Heyck, "Patrons of the Revolution" (2006) and the edited volume by Mark Solovey and Hamilton Cravens on *Cold War Social Science* (2012). Barbary Heyl's 1968-article on the "Pareto Circle" in Harvard first established this field of research, see Heyl, "Harvard." "Interstitial" is a concept taken from Parsons' own vocabulary to describe structures connecting sub-systems.
21. See Greenberg, "Reeducation."
22. Friedrich, the German born and Heidelberg trained founder of the predecessor organization of the German Academic Exchange Service (DAAD) had moved to the United States for professional and private reasons in the 1920s. He started to teach in 1926 at Harvard University as a lecturer and married the American (former exchange student in Heidelberg) Lenore Pelham. He was naturalized as an American citizen in 1938, the same year his American academic career reached its first peak, as he was introduced as member of the Harvard Graduate School of Public Administration. After taking an ambivalent position toward Germany and especially Italian fascism until the mid-1930s, he became an outspoken critic of National Socialism during World War II. Lietzman, in his useful biographical sketch, points to 1937 as the year of Friedrich's political turn against National Socialism, reaching ultimately in the time of the "Hitler – Stalin Pact" in 1939 his oppositional stance, that is, much later than argued in several retrospective accounts, see Lietzmann, *Politikwissenschaft*, 23.
23. Greenberg, "Reeducation," 18.
24. Greenberg convincingly argues in his *Weimar Century* that Calvinism played an important role for Friedrich's political theory. I want to emphasize that it also played an important role for his political practice.
25. See Lietzmann, *Politikwissenschaft*, 51–54. Lietzmann's study also contains the most comprehensive bibliography of published and unpublished texts by Friedrich so far. On Friedrich's activities in the memorandum culture in light of his views on propaganda, see Lietzmann, *Politikwissenschaft*, 47–117.
26. See Derman, *Weber in Politics*, 168–75. The text was considered lost during Parsons' lifetime. Victor Lidz, however, found Parsons' manuscript, see the recent edition in Parsons, *Kapitalismus*.
27. See Parsons, Ch., "Some Remarks." See also the diary entry by social scientist Anne Parsons, Talcott's first daughter, in 1963: "My name is Anne and I come from the best new England families Mayflower and all that [...]." Quoted in: Breines, "Anne Parsons," 831.
28. Talcott Parsons's father Edward S. Parsons, graduate of the Yale divinity school, is the author of *The Social Message of Jesus* (1912).

29. See Evans, Ch., *Social Gospel*. Parsons writes in his autobiographical essay about his father that Edward Parsons "had begun his career as Congregational minister and was very much involved with the then important 'social gospel' movement, which, it is now clear, had much to do with the origins of sociology in this country." Parsons, "Personal History," 877.
30. Parsons to Voegelin, "Letter, August 18, 1941," Parsons and Voegelin, "Correspondence," e36.
31. Bruce Wearne mentions in his early study of Parsons that – very plausibly, but without success – émigré philosopher Alfred Schutz "had suggested that Parsons should head up a Max Weber Society in the USA," see Wearne, *Parsons*, 190. References to Jewish-German founder of sociology Georg Simmel did not hold the same sway, despite his strong influence on early American sociology via Robert Ezra Parks. As William Buxton has shown, Parsons thought about introducing Simmel besides Alfred Marshall, Vilfredo Pareto, Émile Durkheim, and Max Weber as a fifth European founder of social thought in his first book *The Structure of Social Action* (1937), but ultimately did not include the fragment, see Buxton, "Reflections."
32. Friedrich, "Morale," 9. A typescript record of the address with annotations and revisions by Friedrich dated September 23, 1940, is held in Papers of Carl J. Friedrich, HUG(FP) 17.24, box 4.
33. Friedrich, "Morale," 10, HUG(FP) 17.24, box 4.
34. See for a general outline of national character-studies in the context of World War II psychology and anthropology, see especially Herman, *Age of Experts*, 32–81.
35. Susman, "Culture of the Thirties," 172. See also Chapter 5.
36. "Patterns" do already appear earlier in Parsons' work such as his first book *The Structure of Social Action* (1937) and even in the title of his unfinished manuscript "Actor, Situation and Normative Pattern." The term at this point, however, is not yet citing Ruth Benedict's *Patterns of Culture* (1934) and instead serves as a loosely defined notion to describe abstract structures in general.
37. The manuscript was first published in 1993 in Gerhardt, *Parsons on National Socialism*, 101–30.
38. Parsons, "Memorandum," 113.
39. Parsons, "Memorandum," 114. The early ad-hoc list still holds up quite well in the twenty-first century, see the list of sociologist Michael Mann in his comparative reevaluation of European fascist movements, which includes nationalism, statism, transcendence, cleansing and paramilitarism in Mann, M., *Fascists*, 13–17.
40. Parsons, "Memorandum," 119.
41. Parsons, "Memorandum," 120.
42. Parsons, "Memorandum," 124.
43. Parsons, "Memorandum," 123.
44. Parsons, "Memorandum," 124.
45. Ibid.
46. Parsons to Murray, "Letter, April 21, 1941," quoted in: Gerhardt, *Parsons: Intellectual Biography*, 75.

47. The paper is a longer version of his contribution to the discussion of German reeducation in "Germany After the War: Roundtable – 1945" in 1944, presented in more detail in Chapter 7. Parsons conference paper is preserved in Margaret Mead Papers.
48. HUG(FP) 15.2, box 10. See for this project also Gerhardt, *Parsons: Intellectual Biography*, 109–10.
49. Unfortunately, the collaboration between Parsons and his wife Helen Walker Parsons, whom he had met as a fellow student at the London School of Economics, has not yet been systematically researched. During the war years, she also worked as secretary for Friedrich and the Council for Democracy.
50. Allport et al., "Confidential Memorandum." Papers of Gordon W. Allport, HUG 4418.60, box 1.
51. See Isaac, *Working Knowledge*, 174–79.
52. See Isaac, *Working Knowledge*, 165.
53. Allport et al., "Confidential Memorandum," 6.
54. See again Isaac, *Working Knowledge*, 176–79.
55. See especially the last chapter of the book entitled "Conclusion: The Place of Sociological Theory Among the Analytical Sciences of Actions," in Parsons, *Social System*, 536–55.
56. The unfinished book-manuscript on "Actor, Situation and Normative Pattern" in this sense constitutes an intermediary step in between the first and the second book.
57. See for the local power struggles, first of all Parsons' alliance with students, fellow outsiders, and interstitial actors to "dethrone" the chair of Harvard's Department of Sociology Pitirim A. Sorokin, see Johnston, *Sorokin*, 93–102; 129–65. Sorokin later attacks Parsons' strategy of citation in *The Social System*, but also in *The Structure of Social Action* and accuses Parsons of plagiarism, lack of originality and scholarly erudition, see Sorokin, *Fads and Foibles*, 12–15; 323–24. Some of these accusations certainly had a point. Sorokin for example published *Society, Culture, and Personality: Their Structure and Dynamics. A System of General Sociology* in 1947, four years before Parsons' *The Social System*. Despite the fact, that Parsons' system has an identical structure, he omits any reference or comment on Sorokin's book.
58. The historical study of Parsons' work arguably only started with a challenge to this self-portrayal: "As can be learned from the material preserved in the Harvard Archives, however, [Parsons'] style of work when he familiarized himself with a topic was different from the procedure in the finished product. He studied historical records and empirical as well as analytical accounts characteristic of the phenomenon concerned, before giving it a tentative analytical shape in his lecture notes or draft paper(s), to be revised time and again. Working from the published texts only, as most secondary accounts have done, tends to de-emphasize the background and sometimes miss out on the baseline of his analyses." Gerhardt, *Parsons: Intellectual Biography*, X.
59. Barber, B., "Introduction," 5.
60. One of Parsons' major initiatives in the immediate aftermath of World War II connected to the foundation of the Department of Social Relations, to

have the National Science Foundation recognize social scientific research as worthy of funding, failed despite his best efforts, conveying the usefulness of social scientific research for the war effort, see Gerhardt, *Parsons: Intellectual Biography*, 150–67.
61. See Parsons, "Personal History," 826; 829; 876.
62. In 1914, Ernst R. Curtius calls the chapter on schematism in an article for the authoritative *Kant-Studien* "one of the most disreputable parts of the *Critique of Pure Reason*." Curtius, "Schematismuskapitel," 338, my translation, FP.
63. See Stegmaier "Schema, Schematismus," 1252.
64. Parsons, *Social System*, 111. Only Theodor W. Adorno seems to have noticed and immediately drawn his conclusions when he drafted his famous chapter on the "Culture Industry" in 1942. In this essay, which was initially entitled "Das *Schema* [emphasis added] der Massenkultur," he explains that – not American philosophy and the American social sciences but – American culture had appropriated and realized the Kantian scheme: "The active contribution which Kantian schematism still expected of subjects – that they should, from the first, relate sensuous multiplicity to fundamental concepts – is denied to the subject of industry. It purveys schematism as its first service to the customer. According to Kantian schematism, a secret mechanism within the psyche preformed immediate data to fit them into the system of pure reason. That secret has now been unraveled." Horkheimer and Adorno, *Dialectic of Enlightenment*, 98.
65. See Alexander, *Talcott Parsons*, 212–76. However, Jeffrey C. Alexander does caution in reference to Parsons' theory of generalized media (systematically developed after *The Social System*), that his overall mix of normative statements and theory could inadvertently be used to legitimize "religious fundamentalism, revolutionary socialism, exploitative capitalism – even fascism itself." Alexander, *Talcott Parsons*, 210.
66. Parsons, *Social System*, vii.
67. Parsons, *Social System*, 20.
68. Parsons, *Social System*, [v]. The self-description as "incurable theorist" stems from the book's dedication to his wife and collaborator, Helen Walker Parsons.
69. Parsons' use of pattern variables arguably finds an unacknowledged wartime precedent in Gregory Bateson und Margaret Mead's diagrammatic analysis of behavioral patterns in comparative national character-studies such as presented in Bateson, "Morale and National Character."
70. Breines, "Anne Parsons," 830.
71. See Staubmann "Conservative Grand Theorist," published in *American Sociologist*. *The American Sociologist*, it should be noted, has recently published a series of apologetic articles on Parsons, which have provided important historical revisions of his work.
72. Parsons, *Social System*, 366.
73. Parsons, *Social System*, 544.
74. Parsons, *Social System*, 358.
75. Ibid.

76. Parsons, *Social System*, 358–59.
77. Parsons, *Social System*, 331.
78. Parsons, *Social System*, 7.
79. Parsons, *Social System*, 327.
80. Parsons, *Social System*, 341.
81. See Alexander, *Talcott Parsons*, 119–20.
82. See Parsons, "Propaganda and Social Control."
83. Garfinkel, "Perception of the Other," 115.
84. Parsons, *Social System*, 290.
85. Ibid.
86. See Parsons, *Social System*, 290.
87. Parsons, *Social System*, 254.
88. Parsons, *Social System*, 491–93.
89. See Parsons, *Social System*, 291.
90. Parsons touches on this question on several occasions in his book and gives it a sustained treatment toward the end, see Parsons, *Social System*, 520–33.
91. Parsons, *Social System*, 523.
92. Parsons, *Social System*, 525.
93. Evans, R. J., *Third Reich in Power*, 590–91.
94. On the American Press coverage of the November pogrom, see Domeier, *Weltöffentlichkeit und Diktatur*, 519–24. See also the classic study Lipstadt, *Beyond Belief*, 98–111. For the immediate American Protestant response to the news, see Jantzen, "Mainline American Protestants." For the general response of American academia, see Norwood, *Third Reich*, 220–42.
95. Thompson was the first American foreign correspondent to be "expelled from the Third Reich on the personal order of Adolf Hitler." Kurth, *American Cassandra*, 198.
96. See again Lipstadt, *Beyond Belief*, 18–27.
97. It should be noted that this interpretation constitutes a striking misunderstanding of the pogrom as well as of the Nazi German system in general, considering the Nazis' – perfidious – use of German law throughout their twelve years in power, and after. For the rivalry and collaboration without consent between the responsible Nazi officials involved in the decision making around the pogrom leading to and amplifying the orchestrated event, especially between Joseph Goebbels, Heinrich Himmler, and Hermann Göring, see Kley, "Hitler and the Pogrom."
98. Uta Gerhardt has found and republished this short article as the first text in her edition *Talcott Parsons on National Socialism*, see Parsons, "Nazis Destroy Learning, Challenge Religion."
99. See Gerhardt, *Parsons: Intellectual Biography*, 93.
100. Parsons, "Nazis Destroy Learning, Challenge Religion," 83.
101. One immediate context of the pamphlet is the public debate around Charles Lindbergh's suspected Nazi-sympathies and antisemitic views. Especially his speech on an America First-Committee rally in Des Moines, Iowa on September 11, 1941, in which he accused the "Jews" of being warmongers unduly influencing the government, a widespread antisemitic stereotype at

the time. For an analysis of the context of Lindbergh's speech, following quarrels with Dorothy Thompson and Harold L. Ickes, arguing against widespread suspicions of collaboration that Lindbergh did not directly work with the Nazi regime or indirectly with their American supporters during World War II, see Berg, *Lindbergh*, 384–432. Berg's interpretation of Lindbergh's antisemitism presents it correctly as nonviolent and clearly differing from German annihilatory antisemitism. His treatment, however, of Lindbergh's views as based on factual misunderstanding is not entirely convincing.

102. Friedländer, *Years of Extermination*, 197–328.
103. The authoritative study of Christopher Browning argues against prior assessments that the American entry into the war (after the completion of the galley proofs but briefly before the publication of the pamphlet *Nazi Poison* in December 1941) played no significant role in this radicalization, see Browning, *Origins of the Final Solution*, 321.
104. Parsons, "Sociology of Modern Anti-Semitism" [1942]. Uta Gerhardt reconstructs the conflict between Graeber and Parsons in Gerhardt, *Parsons: Intellectual Biography*, 83–84. She has also published Parsons' unabridged and unrevised manuscript, see Parsons "The Sociology of Modern Anti-Semitism" [1993] in *Talcott Parsons on National Socialism*. Gerhardt's argument regarding the decision not to republish neither the article nor his manuscript in his collections of articles after World War II might be reevaluated in light of this chapter.
105. The title remained a problem throughout, see Friedrich to Jackson, "Letter, October 8, 1941," HUG(FP) 17.24, box 15.
106. Friedrich quoted in Lietzmann, *Politikwissenschaft*, 93.
107. Bendersky, "Debate over Antisemitism."
108. Friedrich placed the "Committee of Correspondence" in the tradition of the eponymous prerevolutionary Calvinist institution that produced political pamphlets starting in 1772, see Brown, R., *Revolutionary Politics in Massachussetts*. The first memorandum produced for the Council for Democracy was on the topic of freedom of assembly, "Shall Nazis, Communists and Other Anti-Democratic Groups in the United States Be Allowed to Meet?," completed in December 1940. Already on this occasion, Margaret Mead and David Riesman were among those who provided their expertise, see for a draft of Riesman's response, Papers of David Riesman, HUG(FP) 99.55, box 14.
109. The collaboration of the Institute of Social Research goes back to an important meeting of Friedrich with Neumann in New York on August 12, 1941, during which they discussed the late entry into the editing-process of what Neumann calls a "memorandum" on antisemitism. They also talked about the chances of the Institute's German Project-application at the Rockefeller Foundation and Friedrich's skepticism regarding the Institute's relationship to Marxism. The meeting is recorded in a letter by Neumann sent to Horkheimer in California. See Neumann to Horkheimer, "Letter, August 13, 1941," Horkheimer, *Briefwechsel 1941–1948*, 130–32. The letter also shows the urgency with which Neumann tried to associate himself and the

Institute with the American memorandum culture, and the fascination of Neumann especially for the work of the Council for Democracy and the Committee for National Morale.

110. It should be noted that some criticism of the Institute's position on antisemitism conflates the critique of Horkheimer and Adorno's position with that of Neumann. See for the beginning of the resounding critique of Horkheimer and Adorno's position in Bahr, "Failure of Critical Theory." Neumann provides a thorough and largely convincing ideological analysis of why "Anti-Semitism, which is the German form of racism, is accepted not merely as a device for persecution but as a genuine philosophy of life pervading the whole National Socialist outlook." Neumann, *Behemoth*, 99. However, contradicting himself, he distinguishes later in his text between the National Socialist movement's antisemitism and "spontaneous, popular Anti-Semitism [which is] still weak in Germany. This assertion cannot be proved directly [...]." He even concludes, surprisingly, that it is "[t]he writer's personal conviction, paradoxical as it may seem, [...] that the German people are the least Anti-Semitic of all." Neumann, *Behemoth*, 121. The theory of antisemitism as a "spearhead," as he lays it out in his 1944 appendix, adds another self-contradiction that in "Anti-Semitic ideology and practice the extermination of the Jews is only the means to the attainment of the ultimate objective, namely the destruction of free institutions, beliefs, and groups." Neumann, *Behemoth*, 551. See also Chapter 3.

111. Committee of Correspondence, *Nazi Poison*, 5.

112. Mead, however, oversaw together with Ruth Benedict starting in 1947 the Columbia University Research in Contemporary Cultures-project funded by the Office of Naval Research. See Mandler, *Return from the Natives*, 193–201. For this project, the Jewish-Ukrainian researcher and former Soviet spy Mark Zborowski worked on *Life Is with People* (1952), a book about the culture of Eastern European Jewry, supplanting to great effect antisemitic stereotypes with largely philosemitic stereotypes. See Zipperstein, "Underground Man."

113. Mead, "Anti Semitism – Spearhead of Nazism." Margaret Mead Papers, box E60.

114. The classic historical study on American antisemitism, largely confirms Mead's position, diagnosing a pervasive Christian fundament for American antisemitism. Dinnerstein finds a high-tide of antisemitism starting during the Great Depression of the 1930s and into World War II, see Dinnerstein, *Anti-Semitism in America*, 128–49. He quotes a striking survey, according to which in June 1944, scrutinizing the nationalities, religious and racial groups living in America "24 percent now identified the Jews as the greatest menace, with the Japanese at 9 percent and Germans reduced to 6 percent." Dinnerstein, *Anti-Semitism in America*, 131.

115. Interesting is here especially the response by Richard Rothschild, director of public education and information of the influential American Jewish Committee's, who does not want to make the American public "Jew-conscious," as elucidated and contextualized in Bendersky, "Debate over Antisemitism," 104–5.

116. Mayo to Friedrich, "Letter, August 25, 1941," HUG(FP) 17.24, box 2.
117. See Bendersky, "Debate over Antisemitism," 92–93.
118. "Dear Achim, Just a little while ago, I finished the Anti-Semitism memo, now grown to thirty-seven pages. In the course of it, I have thought several times how much my attitude toward what is also a personal problem had become 'straight' and unafraid during the last years, when indeed there were external reasons for an increase in personal insecurity. There is no doubt in my mind that you were responsible for changing my attitude. Your profound respect for me, for other Jews such as Winkler and Herzog, your interest in and respect for a Jewish tradition from which my parents, and other relatives (numbers of them intermarried and aggressively detached from Jewish roots) drew no visible sustenance, your realization of how important it was for me to come clean with myself on this issue – long before I realized its importance, having either fled from it unconsciously or been unaware of it – for these I am glad and grateful. Here you were a teacher, the only one I had in fact, in the highest sense, and a friend." Riesman to Friedrich, "Letter, September 1, 1941," HUG(FP) 17.24, box 9. Riesman published his views on antisemitism, also referring to the "spearhead"-theory in Riesman, "Politics of Persecution," 53.
119. Parsons, "Comments on Anti-Semitism" [not dated, ca. August 1941], HUG(FP) 17.24, box 2.
120. Parsons, "Comments on Anti-Semitism," 1.
121. Parsons, "Comments on Anti-Semitism," 3.
122. Gilman, *Mandarins of the Future*, 93.
123. Parsons further elaborates on the idea in part two of his article on Weber in 1942, diluting however its philosemitic origin: "This, undoubtedly, is a most prominent aspect of National Socialism, as is shown by the fact that most of its negative symbols are chosen to represent the phenomena and groups of emancipation, the capitalist, the internationalist, the Jew (not the 'orthodox,' but the metropolitan emancipated Jew), the political radical." Parsons, "Max Weber II," 161.
124. Parsons, "Comments on Anti-Semitism," 2.
125. Parsons, "Comments on Anti-Semitism," 5.
126. In his published text from 1942, the theme (unchanged from the original manuscript) is indeed present but less conspicuous and moderated in a sociological argument: "Indeed, the pride and honor of being a Jew were in a sense the principal source of self-respect; but this self-respect could never be clothed in the accepted symbols of glory and greatness, as in the case of other peoples. It is not surprising, therefore, that the Jews have often displayed a rather extreme sensitiveness in matters touching self-respect and status." Parsons, "Sociology of Modern Anti-Semitism" [1942], 107. This problem was noticed early on. Parsons' former student Ben Halpern, then working for the Institute of Jewish Affairs in New York, criticized in 1942 several of Parsons' theses as antisemitic in their tendency, both in a private letter and in a review for *Jewish Frontier*, see Gerhardt, "Faschismustheorie von Talcott Parsons," 258. For a critique of Gerhardt's position on Parsons' "The Sociology of Modern

Anti-Semitism" that, however, does not consider Parsons' "Comments on Anti-Semitism," see Judaken, "Anti-Antisemitism."
127. The original spelling for Alfred Schuetz's last name is Schütz. In the United States, he dropped the *Umlaut* that could not be produced without manual correction on American typewriters and mainly used the German-style historically correct transliteration Schuetz; after World War II, Garfinkel and others quote him as Schutz. I use the spelling Schuetz in the main text, but I quote the name according to the respective publication's spelling.
128. "I have re-read his *Antike Judentum* three or four times and, I think, am more impressed with it each time." Parsons to Voegelin, "Letter, September 27, 1940," Parsons and Voegelin, "Correspondence," e11.
129. Voegelin to Parsons, "Letter, September 11, 1940," Parsons and Voegelin, "Correspondence," e9–e10.
130. Parsons to Voegelin, "Letter, September 27, 1940," Parsons and Voegelin, "Correspondence," e14. It should be noted that Parsons applies the same strategy in *The Social System*, where he treats Communism throughout as a secularized religious movement.
131. Parsons to Voegelin, "Letter, August 18, 1941," Parsons and Voegelin, "Correspondence," e34.
132. Parsons to Voegelin, "Letter, August 18, 1941," Parsons and Voegelin, "Correspondence," e35.
133. Parsons to Voegelin, "Letter, August 18, 1941," Parsons and Voegelin, "Correspondence," e36.
134. Ibid.
135. Ibid.
136. Ibid. The letter is in a way echoed by anthropologist Clifford Geertz and his often-quoted statement that Parsons "sometimes spoke of [his project] as the sociological equivalent of the Newtonian system." Geertz, *After the Facts*, 100.
137. In his autobiographical statements, Voegelin clouded his religious background and views in mystery. He was born to a Lutheran father and Catholic mother – at the turn of the century in Germany socially a highly problematic union – in Cologne and grew up Lutheran in Vienna, both majority Catholic cities.
138. The first part has been recognized early on while the second is still in need of elucidation. See the review of the letters in Ortiz and Hedwig, "Austausch von Missverständnissen."
139. The letter (and Schuetz's reply) is unfortunately not printed in several English and German-language editions of their exchange of letters, which so far has made it difficult to fully understand the Schuetz-Parsons-controversy.
140. In his review, Schumpeter strongly associates Parsons' early work with Weber and the German tradition of sociology: "The author has in fact so deeply penetrated into the German thicket as to lose in some places the faculty of writing in English about it and some turns of phrase become fully understandable only if translated into German." Schumpeter to Conant, "Letter, November 17, 1936," quoted in Johnston, *Sorokin*, 99. For further details on the background of the collaboration with Schumpeter, who

in May 1940 was strongly considering leaving Harvard, while also working on the manuscript of his famous *Capitalism, Socialism and Democracy* (1942), see McCraw, *Prophet of Innovation*. See Straubmann and Lidz, "Editor's Introduction." The edition by Lidz and Straubmann also prints for the first time the first two letters from Parsons to Schuetz, without however explaining their relationship to the later controversy.

141. Barber, M., *Participating Citizen*, 84. In spring 1943, Schuetz started to teach an evening class in sociology at the New School for Social Research in New York.
142. Parsons to Schuetz, "Letter, January 10, 1940," HUG(FP) 42.8.2.
143. Parsons in fact sent a parallel letter to Williams instructing him to forward the manuscript after his reading to Schuetz, see Parsons to Williams, "Letter, January 10, 1940," HUG(FP) 42.8.2.
144. Parsons himself suggests that he completed the manuscript in September or October 1939, as he writes in a letter to Voegelin that he "might perhaps, though not very soon, ask your permission to send you a manuscript of my own which I completed early in the fall," referring to "a draft of a restatement of the generalized theory of action in a somewhat different form from that in my book." Parsons to Voegelin, "Letter, February 8, 1940," Parsons and Voegelin, "Correspondence," e5.
145. Lidz and Staubmann, "Introduction," 5.
146. For an introduction to the controversy, see Jules-Rosette, "Parsons and the Phenomenological Tradition."
147. Barber, M., *Participating Citizen*, 85.
148. See Schütz, "Rationality" [2018], 90.
149. Regarding the change of the concept of rationality in Parsons' work, one also must consider his long-running translation project, resulting in Weber, *Theory of Social and Economic Organization*, published in 1947. In *The Social System* Parsons uses prominently – without clear distinction from what he calls "sociological" uses – the "psychological" notion of rationalization, that is, justifying inappropriate or unexpected behavior. He does so, however, especially in the context of ideology, delinquent behavior, and, as quoted earlier, it comes inevitably to his mind, when he analyzes antisemitism. See again Parsons, *Social System*, 290. Building on his earlier views on Weber's understanding of the "process of rationalization," he goes on to declare rationalization one of the fundamental laws of social systems, equating it with entropy according to the laws of thermodynamics in classical mechanics, in that it has an "inherent trend of change." Parsons, *Social System*, 501.
150. Schütz, "Rationality" [2018], 91. The publication is based on the manuscript preserved in the Talcott Parsons Papers at Harvard University Archives. Schuetz himself published a shorter version of the paper in *Economica* in 1943.
151. Already here, his main attack against Parsons' central concept of the "unit act" is phrased with regard to the "alter ego": "Let us start with the principal question. Is it logically possible to break down an action system into unit acts as its last available elements? We wish to defend the thesis that this 'breaking down' will and must lead to radically different results according

to whether it is performed by the actor or by the observer. This difference is not accidental; it is essentially determined by the logical structure peculiar to the understanding of the alter ego. The very terms 'system of actions' and even 'action' itself are equivocal in so far as they require a subscript, indicating for *whom* the concrete occurrence under consideration presents itself as an 'action' or as a 'system of actions.'" Schutz "Parsons' Theory of Social Action," 26.

152. In 1943, however, Schuetz took on the role as "senior consultant of the Board of Economic Warfare" in Washington, DC, to provide "analyses useful for the occupation of Germany and Austria at the end of the war," by 1944, he started working with "culture patterns" in his teaching and writing. Barber, M., *Participating Citizen*, 99–100. See Schuetz, "The Stranger," 499.
153. Parsons, *Actor, Situation and Normative Pattern*, 129.
154. Schuetz to Parsons, "Letter, March 17, 1941," Schutz, *Collected Papers V*, 65.
155. Parsons to Schuetz, "Letter, March 29, 1941," Schutz, *Collected Papers V*, 67.
156. Voegelin to Schütz, "Letter, May 28, 1941," Schütz and Voegelin, *Briefwechsel*, 77. My translation from German.
157. Schuetz wrote the article in 1941, it appeared in the following year, see Schuetz, "General Thesis of the Alter Ego."
158. See Buxton and Nichols, "Talcott Parsons and the 'Far East,'" 10.
159. "To practice what he preached, [Parsons] took his only position ever in Washington, DC. Between March and October 1945, he held a part-time advisory function in the Foreign Economic Administration Agency, Enemy Branch (FEA), whose task was to draft disarmament and deindustrialization measures for Germany." Gerhardt, *Parsons: Intellectual Biography*, 121. For a summary of his several memoranda written on this occasion, see Gerhardt, *Parsons: Intellectual Biography*, 121–26.
160. Parsons, *Social System*, 10.
161. Parsons, *Social System*, 5.
162. Ibid.
163. While it is true that Parsons came into close contact with psychoanalysis during World War II and adapted especially the ideas of projection, transference, and cathexis, the terms ego and alter are not psychoanalytically but phenomenologically grounded. However, it should be noted that Freud and Husserl both attended the lectures of philosopher Franz Brentano at the University of Vienna.
164. Parsons, *Social System*, 50.
165. Parsons and Shils, *General Theory*, 15.
166. Parsons and Shils, *General Theory*, 16.
167. Robert F. Bales, like Garfinkel one of Parsons' students and arguably one of the "model" social scientists of his vision of future studies in "Social Relations" at Harvard started the experimentalization of the "situation" by constructing special rooms equipped with microphones suspended from the

ceiling and other methods of observation in 1946, see Erickson et al., "The Situation."
168. See Garfinkel, *Perception of the Other*, 120.
169. Garfinkel, *Perception of the Other*, 128.
170. Garfinkel, *Perception of the Other*, 110.
171. Garfinkel, *Perception of the Other*, 128.
172. Garfinkel, *Perception of the Other*, 127–28.
173. Garfinkel, *Perception of the Other*, 112.
174. Garfinkel, *Perception of the Other*, 117.
175. Garfinkel, *Perception of the Other*, 126.
176. The main reference points for Parsons in *The Social System* are: Classical China, India, and the Western World starting with Ancient Greece, Early Christianity, Medieval Christianity, Early Modern Europe, Revolutionary France, America, Nazi Germany – and Soviet Russia.
177. See Fourastié, *Les trente glorieuses*. Fourastié's term describes the unprecedented continuous economic growth during the decades following World War II.
178. Parsons, *Social System*, 534.

7 THE IDENTITY OF THE ENEMY

1. Tent, *Reeducation*, 1.
2. Ibid.
3. Tent, *Reeducation*, 251.
4. Greenberg, "Reeducation," 11.
5. Greenberg, "Reeducation," 31.
6. Greenberg, *Weimar Century*, 7.
7. Erikson, *Childhood and Society*.
8. Gleason, "Identifying Identity."
9. Friedman, *Identity's Architect*, 309–23.
10. For the antecedents of this development in relation to gender, race, and class, see Eder, "Volatility of Sex"; Rose, "Region and Race"; Mann, M., *Globalizations*, 67. A prehistory of the concept of identity itself in the context of the history of American social psychology can be found in part in already established and widely used terms such as personality and character.
11. In an autobiographical interview, Erikson describes the compilation of the chapters as a mere "accident." Evans, R. I., *Erik Erikson*, 60.
12. Erikson, cited in Evans, R. I., *Erik Erikson*, 234.
13. Erikson, *Identity*, 16–17.
14. See also on the conceptual history of identity again Gleason "Identifying Identity," who takes Erikson "Ego Development" and thus its ego-psychological version as the starting point of identity. I would like to contradict this in terms of conceptual history. The editor of Erikson's writings, Stephen Schlein, following Erikson's self-representation, also refers to a short text from 1945 about the "rehabilitat[ion]" of veterans, some of whom were diagnosed with "psychoneurosis," as "his first published statement about the

problem of ego identity confusion/diffusion." Erikson, "Returning Veteran," 118; Schlein, *Clinical Erik Erikson*, 18. However, the term identity does not appear in this text.

15. On their attendance of the meeting of the Topology Group around émigré psychologist Kurt Lewin at Bryn Mawr College in late 1935, see Marrow, *Practical Theorist*, 112. On their relationship during the 1930s, initially facilitated by Lawrence K. Frank, see Friedman, *Identity's Architect*, 135–39. "By 1939," Friedman points out regarding the growing intensity of their collaboration, "Erik Homburger found himself as dependent on Mead as she was on him." Friedman, *Identity's Architect*, 137. Friedman locates their first meeting at an unspecified conference in Cincinnati, citing a passage from Jane Howard's Mead biography, which does not support this statement. The first surviving letter from Erikson to Mead, dated January 7, 1936, refers to preceding in-person meetings and their recent encounter at Bryn Mawr College. It is unclear, whether Erikson met Mead in 1935 through Frank or in the context of a seminar held by Caroline Zachary, head of the Bureau of Child Guidance of the New York City Board of Education, where Erikson presented his research on his method focused on play, later published in Homburger, "Configurations in Play."
16. Benedict, *Patterns of Culture*.
17. Erikson, "Hitler's Imagery," 480.
18. In *Childhood and Society*, this corresponds, to proceed for once ahistorically and associatively, to a state of permanent identity crisis.
19. Erikson, "Hitler's Imagery," 478.
20. In addition, there may have been a conflict over unpaid consultant fees and expenses, see Hoffman, "Erikson on Hitler," 82.
21. The memorandum is preserved with other sources used for this essay in Margaret Mead Papers.
22. Bateson and Mead, "Preliminary Memorandum," 2, Margaret Mead Papers.
23. Bateson and Mead, "Preliminary Memorandum," 3, Margaret Mead Papers.
24. Erik [Homburger Erikson] to Gregory [Bateson], "Letter, ca. October 1942" Margaret Mead Papers.
25. Bateson and Mead, "Preliminary Memorandum," 12–13, Margaret Mead Papers.
26. Erikson produced three versions of the 1942 text: one for Meads and Bateson's Committee for National Morale, a second as a report for the COI resp. OSS, the foreign intelligence service, and, apparently without OSS approval, a third version for the November issue of the journal *Psychiatry*. On the structural differences between the published and unpublished versions, see Hoffman, "Erikson on Hitler," 77. The COI had commissioned two more psychoanalytic studies of Adolf Hitler, one by Walter C. Langer, the other by Henry A. Murray.
27. Arrington and Grossmann, "Psychiatric Social Worker," 610.

28. See Olick, *House of the Hangman*, 58–64; Füssl, "Fine-Tuning Utopia," 290–93; Mandler, *Return from the Natives*, 148–55; Heims, *Constructing a Social Science*, 172.
29. Mead had become aware of Brickner thanks to a previous analysis of Germany in which Brickner attested to a paranoid trend in German culture. See the two-part publication Brickner, "Paranoid Trend" and Brickner and Vosburgh Lyons, "Treatment of Germany."
30. Curiously, the term "reeducation" is virtually absent as it appears only once and in the context of psychiatric care of individuals in the main text of the book, Brickner, *Is Germany Incurable*, 103. Instead, "rehabilitation" appears three times, directly referring to the treatment of Germany, Brickner, *Is Germany Incurable*, 299–302. Mead does not use the concept in her "Introduction" to the book. In the second "Introduction," Edward Strecker, however, employs the term prominently in the last sentence: "Its cure might stem from a better use of the human brain by all of us, though a well-thought-out, thorough plan of reëducation, of reculturing, such as Dr. Brickner suggests." Strecker, "Introduction," 18. The concept of a "German reeducation" only gained prominence in the reception of the book.
31. Tent, *Reeducation*, 1. Most of the later work follows this assessment. The best work on the conceptual history of reeducation is by Uta Gerhardt, but she overlooks Erikson's role. See Gerhardt, "Hidden Agenda"; Gerhardt, "Re-Education-Politik"; and Gerhardt, *Talcott Parsons*. The only acknowledgement of Erikson's importance that I am aware of can be found in Schüttpelz, *Moderne*, 235–40; 249.
32. Mead had Erikson's memorandum mimeographed in the Mimeographic Department of the Greater New York American Women's Voluntary Service and then circulated as reading. Since the text arrived late, it was distributed in preparation for the second weekend-session. The copy of the letter may be found in the Margaret Mead Papers. It is, except for the paratextual framing and pagination, largely identical to Erikson's selected papers, see Erikson, "Memorandum." For the sake of accessibility, the published text will be cited in the following.
33. Mandler, *Return from the Natives*, 149.
34. Erikson, "Memorandum," 367–73.
35. Erikson, "Memorandum," 368.
36. The call for papers to the Roundtable was signed by a group of officials from influential psychiatric associations, among others by Lawrence K. Frank in his role as Chairman of the National Committee for Mental Hygiene, see Lawrence K. Frank et al., "Conference on Germany after the War," 3, Margaret Mead Papers.
37. Borneman, "Foreign Policy," 668.
38. Friedman, *Identity's Architect*, 133–34.
39. Friedman, *Identity's Architect*, 134.
40. With respect to Karl May's "foreign policy," the situation is somewhat more complicated than Friedman presents it: In most of May's adventure stories, the Sioux play the role of the "evil" arch-enemies of the "noble"

Apache tribe and its hero Winnetou, the most popular of all May's characters. May's first Winnetou character from 1875, however, was In-nu-who, the chief of the Sioux, who only changed his name and tribal affiliation in a new version three years later. Nevertheless, it is conceivable that especially the reading public of the politically unified Germany after 1871, which May entertained with his texts, in the tradition of the reception and popularization of Tacitus *Germania*, could secretly or in some cases openly identify not with the civilized hero, but with the barbarian antagonist. Thus, it is probably no coincidence that the *Winnetou* trilogy was also initially published with the subtitle *Der Rote Gentleman*, the hero was thus identified with "civilized" England, after 1871 the strongest European rival of the German Empire. "Their names were Parranoh and Riccarroh, Matto Sih and Ma-ti-ru, Ka-wo-mien and Ko-itse, Hong-peh-te-keh and Oihtka-petay, Schi-tscha-pah-tah, Langer Leib and Kiktahan Schonka. They all had great things in common. They all belonged to the great Sioux tribe, in the vast majority of cases the Oglala Sioux. And all of them were ... the villains, always portrayed negatively by Karl May ... Coincidence? Hardly." Grießbach, "Karl May und die Sioux," 31, my translation, FP.
41. Kluckhohn and Hackenberg, "Indian Reorganization Act," 29.
42. Borneman, "Foreign Policy," 666.
43. Kelly, "Indian New Deal," 9–10.
44. Taylor, "Indian New Deal," 156.
45. Taylor, "Indian New Deal," 154.
46. See Redfield, Linton, and Herskovits, "Memorandum"; Kelly, "Applied Anthropology," 128–29.
47. Biolsi, "Mekeel," 149.
48. Mekeel, "Appraisal," 212.
49. Erikson, "Sioux Education," 101.
50. Ibid.
51. Mekeel, "Indian Education," 156.
52. For such a translation between orthopedic and (ortho-)psychiatric reeducation in 1923, see Franz, *Reeducation*. Four years earlier, Franz had still advocated using the term rehabilitation instead of reeducation: "Rehabilitation includes all of the processes that are used and the actual result of these processes, for the functional restoration of an individual who has become unable to hold his place in the social life of his community." Franz, "Rehabilitation and Reeducation," 33. Rehabilitation and reeducation remain interchangeable in their usage even in the context of the later mental hygiene movement.
53. Pols, "Managing the Mind," 211. The role of the mental hygiene movement and its connection especially to the Rockefeller Foundation in the history of "mental health" in the United States during the 1930s and 1940s is treated in Ridenour, *Mental Health*, and for the role of the mental hygiene movement in the war effort, see Schwartz Greene, *Breaking Point*. See also Anderson, R. et al., *Neuropsychiatry in World War II*.

54. On the invention of a comprehensive concept of "tribe" to unify the highly diverse organization of "Indian" cultures of North America, see Cornell, "Transformations of Tribe," 36.
55. Note, however, the resonance of reorganization and reform with the notion of a retreat, the reservation. Reform of reservations is the bitter political compromise that endures to this day.
56. See Barber, B., "Peyote Cult"; Barber, B., "Messianic Movements."
57. Erikson, "Memorandum," 368. An important part of Erikson's later academic success is based on the combination of historiography and psychological interpretation under the concept of psychohistory.
58. Erikson, *Childhood and Society*, 116.
59. Erikson, "Sioux Education," 140; Erikson, "Observations on the Yurok," 291–92; Erikson, *Childhood and Society*, 147–49.
60. Erikson, *Childhood and Society*, 129.
61. Ibid.
62. This is Mekeel's term, which Erikson himself does not use: "Whatever money does come into the community is quite evenly divided by the functioning of many customs, which, in their totality, virtually prescribe a state of socialism." Mekeel, "Economy," 11.
63. See Erikson, "Observations on the Yurok," 291; Erikson, *Childhood and Society*, 191.
64. See Erikson, "Childhood and Tradition," 327. Erikson sent his article on Sioux education to Mead. He also announced his trip to the Yurok in a letter to Mead: "It seems that I am [...] going to the Klamath River to see some fishing Indians who love property." Homburger Erikson to Mead, "Letter, June 6, 1939," Margaret Mead Papers.
65. See Erikson, *Childhood and Society*, 176–82.
66. Kroeber does not describe the Yurok so much as capitalists, but instead notes that "the Yurok are an anarchic people." Kroeber, "The Yurok," 3. In an earlier text, Kroeber writes: "I cannot name a single strictly 'social' aspect of their culture [...]." Kroeber, "California Kinship Systems," 383. Erikson, despite these fundamental differences in conceptualizing the social psychology of the Yurok, invokes Kroeber, using a misquote. "The dam building is 'the largest mechanical enterprise undertaken by the Yurok, or, for that matter, by any California Indians, and the most communal attempt' (Kroeber)." Erikson, *Childhood and Society*, 168. Here is the – unreferenced – original quote: "The Sa'a-Kepel dam ritual is of interest in several ways. First, as Waterman says, it represents the largest mechanical enterprise undertaken by the Yurok, or for that matter by any *northwest* California Indians, and the most *nearly* [emphases added] communal attempt." Waterman and Kroeber, "Kepel Fish Dam," 78. Now for the slapstick: a text coauthored by Kroeber published ten years after *Childhood and Society* again responds to Erikson's erroneous citation with a critique of Erikson's quote now fully attributed to his authorship: "Yet the sweeping statement that this is the most pretentious

communal undertaking among any of the California Indians might be challenged when we consider the building of one of the large ceremonial dance houses in the Central California area." Kroeber and Barett, "Fishing," 12.
67. For a reassessment of their relationship that reconstructs the context of the Yurok's healing practices and Fanny Flounder's perspective in particular, see Buckley, *Standing Ground*, 127–244.
68. Erikson, *Childhood and Society*, 169–70.
69. See, however, the clearly contradicting statement on the official website of the Yurok: "The gold mining expeditions resulted in the destruction of villages, loss of life and a culture severely fragmented. By the end of the gold rush era at least 75% of the Yurok people died due to massacres and disease, while other tribes in California saw a 95% loss of life." www.yuroktribe.org/gold-rush-in-yurok-country (August 5, 2025).
70. Erikson, *Childhood and Society*, 178–79.
71. Erikson, "Observations on the Yurok," 258.
72. Turner, F., *Frontier in American History*.
73. Erikson, *Childhood and Society*, 293.
74. Ibid. In Turner's classic study of the frontier, this call also has a concrete background, the "frontier appeals for garrison aid." Turner, F., *Frontier in American History*, 47.
75. Erikson, *Childhood and Society*, 324.
76. Friedman, *Identity's Architect*, 192.
77. See Bessner, "Organizing Complexity," 35.
78. Engerman, *Know Your Enemy*.
79. On the relationship between American World War II and Cold War scholarship, see Herman, "Project Camelot," again Bessner, "Organizing Complexity," and Crowther-Heyck, "Patrons of the Revolution."
80. Erikson to Mead, cited in Friedman, *Identity's Architect*, 192.
81. Erikson, *Childhood and Society*, 385.
82. For Erikson, this is a genuine longue durée from Rurik, the Viking, to Stalin, and probably beyond, see Erikson, *Childhood and Society*, 373; 401.
83. Erikson, *Childhood and Society*, 377.
84. Erikson, *Childhood and Society*, 400.
85. Erikson, *Childhood and Society*, 399.
86. Erikson, *Childhood and Society*, 402.
87. Erikson, "Hitler's Imagery," 487.
88. Friedman, *Identity's Architect*, 171.
89. Erikson, *Childhood and Society*, 37.
90. Erikson, "Ego Development," 371.
91. Ibid.; emphases in original.
92. See Erikson, "Ego Development," 373.
93. Erikson, "Ego Development," 373.
94. Erikson, "Hitler's Imagery," 481n5.
95. Erikson, "Hitler's Imagery," 476.
96. Erikson, "Dream Specimen," 43.
97. Erikson, "Hitler's Imagery [1949]," 503.

98. Ibid.
99. An important shortcoming for applied anthropology and its historicization was that Mead – as one of its central actors – did not present a synthesis of her own. The attempt that came closest was her book project *Learning to Live in One World*, on which she worked until she abandoned it in 1945, see Mandler, *Return from the Natives*, 188–90.
100. NN, "Roundtable – 1945."
101. Michaela Hoenicke Moore's historical study largely rejects the existence of such a transition as well as the overestimation of the role of the émigrés and focuses on the small-scale political processes that led to the reeducation of Germany, which can be directly traced in the archives. Thus, she also considers the final report with a realistic view at least of Brickner's minor role to be a sideshow, see Hoenicke Moore, *Know Your Enemy*, 220–32.
102. Mandler, *Return from the Natives*, 150.
103. Hartshorne to Parsons, "Letter, April 10, 1945," Tent, *Academic Proconsul*, 274.
104. Mandler, *Return from the Natives*, 151.
105. NN, "Roundtable – 1945," 392.
106. Erhard Schüttpelz has already pointedly demonstrated this for the first part of the final report, NN, "Roundtable – 1945," 390–93, see again Schüttpelz, *Moderne*, 236.
107. See Høgel, "World Literature."
108. NN, "Roundtable – 1945," 415.
109. Erikson, *Childhood and Society*, 129.
110. NN, "Roundtable – 1945," 415.
111. Erikson, *Young Man Luther*.
112. Erikson, "Ego Development," 368–69.

8 EPILOGUE: TO WHOM IT MAY CONCERN

1. Heims, *Constructing a Social Science*.
2. Ruesch and Bateson, *Communication*, 168.
3. Ruesch and Bateson, *Communication*, 257.
4. For the latter, see Turner, F., *Counterculture to Cyberculture*. For Bateson's work with film, especially with Weldon Kees, and other media, see Geoghegan, *Code*, 60–84.
5. This categorization arguably ties them to the publication practices of the early avantgarde, Knight, "Little Magazines," 43.
6. See Clay and Philipps, "Mimeograph Revolution." The catalogue is based on an exhibition from January 24–July 25, 1998, in the New York Public Library. Despite the title of the book and the undeniable importance of its scene, the catalogue shows that little magazines were pervasive and not confined to New York City.

7. Pospielovsky, "Samizdat," 44. Soviet underground literature, however, relied since the 1970s largely on photography-based techniques of reproduction and on manual typing, see Zitzewitz, *Culture of Samizdat*, 47; 59.
8. Seck, "Underground of Decolonization," 289.
9. Felsch, *Sommer der Theorie*, 76
10. See Dougherty, "Translating Bukowski," 70–71. On Weissner, see Sahner, *Der Wirklichkeit verfallen*, 245–91.

Bibliography

ARCHIVES

Deutsches Literaturarchiv, Marbach am Neckar, Siegfried Kracauer Nachlass.
ETH Bibliothek Zürich, Thomas Mann Archiv.
Harvard University Archives, Cambridge, MA.
    Papers of Carl J. Friedrich, HUG(FP) 17.
    Papers of David Riesman, HUG(FP) 99.
    Papers of Gordon W. Allport, HUG 4118.
    Papers of Talcott Parsons, HUG(FP) 15 and 42.
Johann Wolfgang Goethe-Universität Frankfurt am Main, Archivzentrum, Nachlass Max Horkheimer.
Leo Baeck Institute, New York, Hans Kohn Collection.
Manuscript Division, Library of Congress in Washington, DC, Margaret Mead Papers and South Pacific Ethnographic Archives, 1838–1996.
Rockefeller Archive Center, Sleepy Hollow, NY, Rockefeller Foundation Records, Officers' Diaries, RG 12, M–R, 1911–1992, Marshall, John (1911–2005).
Special Collections & Archives University of California Santa Cruz, Gregory Bateson Papers.
The National Archives at College Park, MD.

BIBLIOGRAPHY

Adorno, Theodor W. "Review: Wilder Hobson's *American Jazz Music* and Winthrop Sargeant's *Jazz Hot and Hybrid*," written with the assistance of Eunice Cooper. *Studies in Philosophy and Social Science* 9, no. 1 (1941): 177–78.
Adorno, Theodor W. "The Psychological Technique of Martin Luther Thomas' Radio Addresses." In *Soziologische Schriften II: Erste Hälfte*, edited by Susan Buck-Morss and Rolf Tiedemann. Frankfurt am Main: Suhrkamp, 1975, 7–141.

Adorno, Theodor W. "Review: W. van de Wall, The Music of the People, New York: American Association for Adult Education 1938." In *Musikalische Schriften VI: Opern- und Konzertkritiken. Kompositionskritiken. Buchrezensionen. Zur Praxis des Musiklebens*, edited by Rolf Tiedemann in collaboration with Gretel Adorno et al. Frankfurt am Main: Suhrkamp, 1984 [1939], 373–74.

Adorno, Theodor W. "Gutachten über die Arbeit 'Die totalitäre Propaganda Deutschlands und Italiens,' S.1 bis 106, von Siegfried Kracauer." In Siegfried Kracauer. *Totalitäre Propaganda*, edited by Bernd Stiegler. Berlin: Suhrkamp, 2013 [1938], 262–65.

Adorno, Theodor W. and Max Horkheimer. *Briefwechsel 1927–1969*. Vol. 4, pts. 2–3, edited by Christoph Gödde and Henri Lonitz. Frankfurt am Main: Suhrkamp, 2005–2006.

Adorno, Theodor W. and Siegfried Kracauer. *Briefwechsel 1923–1966*, edited by Wolfgang Schopf. Frankfurt am Main: Suhrkamp, 2008.

Adorno, Theodor W. and Thomas Mann. *Theodor W. Adorno and Thomas Mann: Correspondence 1943–1955*, edited by Christoph Gödde and Thomas Sprecher, translated by Nicholas Walker. Cambridge, MA: Polity, 2006 [2002].

Alexander, Jeffrey C. *Theoretical Logic in Sociology*. Vol. 4: *The Modern Reconstruction of Classical Thought: Talcott Parsons*. Berkeley: University of California Press, 1983.

American Friends of German Freedom. eds. *In Re: Germany*, 4 Vols., 1941–1944.

Anderson, Benedict. *Imagined Communities: Reflections on the Origin and Spread of Nationalism*, revised edition. London: Verso, 2006 [1983].

Anderson, Eugene. "'Ich habe eigentlich gar nicht gemerkt, daß es sich um Marxisten handelt.' Interview mit Prof. Eugene N. Anderson am 10. Dezember 1983 in Santa Barbara/Californien." In *Zur Archäologie der Demokratie in Deutschland*. Vol. 2, edited by Alfons Söllner. Frankfurt am Main: Fischer, 1986 [1983], 22–34.

Anderson, Robert S., Albert J. Glass, and Robert J. Bernucci eds. *Neuropsychiatry in World War II*. Vol. 1: *Zone of Interior*. Washington, DC: Office of the Surgeon, 1966.

Andriopoulos, Stefan. *Possessed: Hypnotic Crimes, Corporate Fiction, and the Invention of Cinema*. Chicago, IL: University of Chicago Press, 2008.

Appadurai, Arjun. *Modernity at Large: Cultural Dimensions of Globalization*. Minneapolis: University of Minnesota Press, 1996.

Arlt, Gustave O. "Printing and the Democratic Movement in the Western World." In *Printing and Progress, two lectures by Archer Taylor and Gustave O. Arlt*. Berkeley: University of California Press, 1941, 37–67.

Arlt, Gustave O. "Archer Taylor." In *Humaniora: Essays in Literature, Folklore, Bibliography*, edited by Wayland D. Hand and Gustave O. Arlt. Locust Valley, NY: Augustin, 1960, 1–7.

Arnold, Thomas, Jutta Schöning, and Ulrich Schröter. *Hitlerjunge Quex: Einstellungsprotokoll*. Munich: Filmland-Presse, 1980.

Arrington, Winifred W. and Grace Grossmann. "Potential Functions of the Psychiatric Social Worker under the Selective Service Act." *American Journal of Orthopsychiatry* 12 (1942): 603–10.

Assmann, Jan. *Thomas Mann und Ägypten: Mythos und Monotheismus in den Josephsromanen*. Munich: C.H. Beck, 2006.

Auerbach, Erich. "Figura." *Archivum Romanicum* 22 (1938): 436–89.
Auger, Charles P. *Information Sources in Grey Literature*, fourth edition. London: Bowker Saur, 1998.
Bahr, Ehrhard. "The Anti-Semitism Studies of the Frankfurt School: The Failure of Critical Theory." *German Studies Review* 1, no. 2 (1978): 125–38.
Bahr, Ehrhard. "Die Kontroverse um 'Das andere Deutschland'." In *Deutschsprachige Exilliteratur seit 1933*. Vol. 2: *New York*, pt. 2, edited by John M. Spalek and Joseph Strelka. Bern: Francke, 1989, 1493–513.
Baird, Jay W. *To Die for Germany: Heroes in the Nazi Pantheon*. Bloomington: Indiana University Press, 1990.
Baker, Gary L. "18 January 1943: Bateson Analysis of Hitlerjunge Quex Stresses Value of Film as Key to National Culture." In *A New History of German Cinema*, edited by Jennifer M. Kapczynski and Michael D. Richardson. Rochester, NY: Camden House, 2012, 300–4.
Baltzell, E. Digby. *The Protestant Establishment: Aristocracy and Caste in America*. New Haven, CT: Yale University Press, 1987 [1964].
Barber, Bernard. "A Socio-Cultural Interpretation of the Peyote Cult." *American Anthropologist* 43, no. 4 (1941a): 673–75.
Barber, Bernard. "Acculturation and Messianic Movements." *American Sociological Review* 6, no. 5 (1941b): 663–69.
Barber, Bernhard. "Introduction." In *L.J. Henderson on the Social System: Selected Writings*, edited by Bernhard Barber. Chicago, IL: University of Chicago Press, 1970.
Barber, Michael D. *The Participating Citizen: A Biography of Alfred Schuetz*. Albany, NY: State University of New York Press, 2004.
Barnes, Trevor J. "Geographical Intelligence: American Geographers and Research and Analysis in the Office of Strategic Services 1941–1945." *Journal of Historical Geography* 32 (2006): 149–68.
Bateson, Gregory. "Cultural and Thematic Analysis of Fictional Films." *Transactions of the New York Academy of Sciences* Series 2, no. 5 (1943): 72–78.
Bateson, Gregory. "An Analysis of the Nazi Film Hitlerjunge Quex." In *The Study of Culture at a Distance*, edited by Margaret Mead and Rhoda Métraux. Chicago, IL: University of Chicago Press, 1953, 331–47.
Bateson, Gregory. "Morale and National Character." In *Steps to an Ecology of Mind*. New York: Ballantine, 1972a, 82–93.
Bateson, Gregory. "Social Planning and the Concept of Deutero-Learning." In *Steps to an Ecology of Mind*. New York: Ballantine, 1972b, 159–76.
Bateson, Gregory. *Steps to an Ecology of Mind: Collected Essays in Anthropology, Psychiatry, Evolution and Epistemology*. New York: Ballantine, 1972c.
Bateson, Gregory. "Some Components of Socialization for Trance." *Ethos* 3, no. 2 (1975): 143–55.
Bateson, Gregory. "An Analysis of 'Hitlerjunge Quex.'" *Studies in Visual Communication* 6, no. 3 (1980): 20–55.
Bateson, Gregory. "The Birth of a Matrix, or Double Bind and Epistemology." In *A Sacred Unity: Further Steps to an Ecology of Mind*, edited by Rodney E. Donaldson. San Francisco, CA: HarperCollins, 1991, 191–213.
Bateson, Gregory and Margaret Mead. *Balinese Character: A Photographic Analysis*. New York: Academy of Sciences, 1942.

Bateson, Gregory and Margaret Mead. "For God's Sake, Margaret." *CoEvolution Quarterly* no. 10 (1976): 32–44.

Bateson, Mary C. *With a Daughter's Eye: A Memoir of Margaret Mead and Gregory Bateson*. New York: Morrow, 1984.

Baughman, James L. *Henry R. Luce and the Rise of the American News Media*. Boston, MA: Twayne Publishers, 1987.

Bauman, Richard. "Philology of the Vernacular." *Journal of Folklore Research* 45, no. 1 (2008): 29–36.

Bauman, Richard and Charles L. Briggs. *Voices of Modernity: Language Ideologies and the Politics of Inequality*. Cambridge, GB: Cambridge University Press, 2003.

Behrenbeck, Sabine. *Der Kult um die toten Helden: Nationalsozialistische Mythen, Riten und Symbole 1923 bis 1945*. Vierow: SH-Verlag, 1996.

Beier, Ulli ed. *Yoruba Myths*. Cambridge, GB: Cambridge University Press, 1980.

Benco, Nancy. "Archibald MacLeish: The Poet Librarian." *The Quarterly Journal of the Library of Congress* 33, no. 3 (1976): 232–49.

Bender, Thomas. *New York Intellect: A History of Intellectual Life in New York City, From 1750 to the Beginnings of Our Own Time*. Baltimore, MD: Johns Hopkins University Press, 1987.

Bendersky, Joseph W. "Dissension in the Face of the Holocaust: The 1941 American Debate over Antisemitism." *Holocaust and Genocide Studies* 24, no. 1 (2010): 85–116.

Bendix, Regina. *In Search of Authenticity: The Formation of Folklore Studies*. Madison: University of Wisconsin Press, 1997.

Benedict, Ruth. *Patterns of Culture*. Boston, MA: Houghton Mifflin, 1934.

Benjamin, Walter. *Ursprung des deutschen Trauerspiels*. Berlin: Rowohlt, 1928.

Berendsohn, Walter A. *Die humanistische Front: Einführung in die deutsche Emigranten- Literatur. Erster Teil: Von 1933 bis zum Kriegsausbruch 1939*. Zurich: Europa, 1946.

Berendsohn, Walter A. *Die humanistische Front: Einführung in die deutsche Emigranten-Literatur. Zweiter Teil: Vom Kriegsausbruch 1939 bis Ende 1946*. Worms: G. Heintz, 1976.

Berg, A. Scott. *Lindbergh*. New York: Putnam, 1998.

Berger, Willy R. *Die mythologischen Motive in Thomas Manns Roman 'Joseph und seine Brüder.'* Cologne: Böhlau, 1971.

Berman, Russell A. *The Rise of the Modern German Novel: Crisis and Charisma*. Cambridge, MA: Harvard University Press, 1986.

Bessner, Daniel. "Organizing Complexity: The Hopeful Dreams and Harsh Realities of Interdisciplinary Collaboration at the RAND Corporation in the Early Cold War." *Journal of the History of the Behavioral Sciences* 51, no. 1 (2015): 31–51.

Bessner, Daniel. *Democracy in Exile: Hans Speier and the Rise of the Defense Intellectual*. Ithaca, NY: Cornell University Press, 2018.

Betz, Frederick and Jörg Thunecke. "Sinclair Lewis's Cautionary Tale *It Can't Happen Here* (1935)." *Orbis Litterarum* 52 (1997): 35–53.

Biddiscombe, A. Perry. *Werwolf! The History of the National Socialist Guerila Movement, 1944–1946*. Toronto: University of Toronto Press, 1998.

Biolsi, Thomas. "The Anthropological Construction of 'Indians': Haviland Scudder Mekeel and the Search for the Primitive in Lakota Country." In *Indians and Anthropologists: Vine Deloria, Jr., and the Critique of Anthropology*, edited by Thomas Biolsi and Larry J. Zimmerman. Tucson: University of Arizona Press, 1997, 133–59.

Blackbourn, David. *Germany in the World: A Global History 1500–2000*. New York: Norton and Company, 2023.

Blanchot, Maurice. "La Rencontre avec le demon." In *Hommage de la France à Thomas Mann: À l'occasion de son quatre-vingtième anniversaire*, edited by Karl Flinker. Paris: Flinker, 1955, 83–103.

Blöcker, Karsten. "Der Lübecksche Amtsrichter Dr. August Leverkühn und Thomas Manns Roman 'Doktor Faustus: Das Leben des deutschen Tonsetzers Adrian Leverkühn, erzählt von einem Freunde.'" *Neue Juristische Wochenschrift* 55, no. 8 (2002): 581–83.

Blue, Howard. *Words at War: World War II Era Radio Drama and the Postwar Broadcasting Industry Blacklist*. Lanham, MD: Scarecrow Press, 2002.

Böckendörfer, Ernst-Wolfgang. "Ordnungsdenken, konkretes." In *Historisches Wörterbuch der Philosophie*. Vol. 6, edited by Joachim Ritter and Karlfried Gründer. Basel: Schwabe, 1984, 1312–15.

Boes, Tobias. *Thomas Mann's War: Literature, Politics and the World Republic of Letters*. Ithaca, NY: Cornell University Press, 2019.

Boes, Tobias and Kai Sina eds. *Literatur für Leser:innen* 43, no. 3 *Thomas Manns transatlantische Autorschaft* (2023).

Bonato, Sarah. *Searching the Grey Literature: A Handbook for Searching Reports, Working Papers, and Other Unpublished Research*. Lanham, MD: Rowman and Littlefield, 2018.

Borchmeyer, Dieter. *Thomas Mann: Werk und Zeit*. Frankfurt am Main: Insel, 2022.

Borneman, John. "American Anthropology as Foreign Policy." *American Anthropologist* 97, no. 4 (1995): 663–72.

Bosse, Heinrich. "Zur Sozialgeschichte des Wanderliedes." In *Wanderzwang – Wanderlust: Formen der Raum- und Sozialerfahrung zwischen Aufklärung und Frühindustrialisierung*, edited by Wolfgang Albrecht and Hans-Joachim Kertscher. Tübingen: Niemeyer, 1999, 135–57.

Bourdieu, Pierre. *Outline of a Theory of Practice*, translated by Richard Nice. Cambridge, GB: Cambridge University Press, 1977 [1972].

Boveri, Margret. *Der Verrat im 20. Jahrhundert*. 4 Vols. Reinbek: Rowohlt, 1956–60.

Boyd, Valerie. *Wrapped in Rainbows: The Life of Zora Neale Hurston*. New York: Scribner, 2003.

Brecht, Arnold. *The Political Education of Arnold Brecht: An Autobiography, 1884–1970*. Princeton, NJ: Princeton University Press, 1970.

Breines, Winifred. "Alone in the 1950s: Anne Parsons and the Feminine Mystique." *Theory and Society* 15, no. 6 (1986): 805–43.

Brennan, Nathaniel. "The Cinema Intelligence Apparatus: Gregory Bateson, the Museum of Modern Art Film Library, and the Intelligence Work of Film Studies during World War II." In *Cinema's Military Industrial Complex*, edited by Heidi Wasson and Lee Grieveson. Oakland: University of California Press, 2018, 137–56.

Breuer, Stefan. "Den Adler des Zeus nähren: Carl Schmitt im Dialog mit Otto Kirchheimer, Ernst Fraenkel und Franz Neumann." In *Carl Schmitt im Kontext: Intellektuellenpolitik in der Weimarer Republik*. Berlin: Akademie Verlag, 2012, 111–41.

Brickner, Richard. "The German Cultural Paranoid Trend." *American Journal of Orthopsychiatry* 12, no. 3 (1942a): 544–45.

Brickner, Richard. "The German Cultural Paranoid Trend." *American Journal of Orthopsychiatry* 12, no. 4 (1942b): 611–32.

Brickner, Richard. *Is Germany Incurable?* Philadelphia, PA: Lippincott, 1943.

Brickner, Richard and Lawrence Vosburgh Lyons. "A Neuropsychiatric View of German Culture and the Treatment of Germany." *Journal of Nervous and Mental Disease* 98, no. 3 (1943): 281–93.

Brinkley, Alan. *The Publisher Henry Luce and His American Century*. New York: Knopf, 2010.

Brown, Mary E. *Child's Unfinished Masterpiece: The English and Scottish Popular Ballads*. Urbana: University of Illinois Press, 2011.

Brown, Richard D. *Revolutionary Politics in Massachusetts: The Boston Committee of Correspondence and the Towns, 1772–1774*. Cambridge, MA: Harvard University Press, 1970.

Browning, Christopher R. *The Origins of the Final Solution: The Evolution of Nazi Jewish Policy, September 1939–March 1942*. Lincoln and Jerusalem: University of Nebrasksa Press and Yad Vashem, 2005.

Brünneck, Alexander von. "Ernst Fraenkels Urdoppelstaat von 1938 und der Doppelstaat von 1941/1974." In *Vom Sozialismus zum Pluralismus. Beiträge zu Werk und Leben Ernst Fraenkels*, edited by Hubertus Buchstein and Gerhard Göhler. Baden-Baden: Nomos, 2000, 29–42.

Bruns, Karin. *Kinomythen 1920–1945: Die Filmentwürfe der Thea von Harbou*. Stuttgart: Metzler, 1995.

Bryson, Dennis R. "Lawrence K. Frank, Knowledge, and the Production of the 'Social.'" *Poetics Today* 19, no. 3 (1998): 401–21.

Bryson, Dennis R. *Socializing the Youth: The Role of Foundations, 1923–1941*. Westport, CT: Bergin and Garvey, 2002.

Bryson, Dennis R. "Personality and Culture, the Social Science Research Council, and Liberal Social Engineering: The Advisory Committee on Personality and Culture, 1930–1934." *Journal of the History of the Behavioral Sciences* 45, no. 4 (2008): 355–86.

Buckley, Thomas. *Standing Ground: Yurok Indian Spirituality, 1850–1990*. Berkeley, CA: University of California Press, 2002.

Bush, Vannevar. "As We May Think." *Atlantic Monthly*, July (1945a): 101–8.

Bush, Vannevar. "As We May Think." *Life*, September 10 (1945b): 112–24.

Buxton, William J. "From the 'Missing Fragment' to the 'Lost Manuscript': Reflections on Parsons's Engagement with Simmel." *American Sociologist* 29 (1998): 57–76.

Buxton, William J. "John Marshall and the Humanities in Europe: Shifting Patterns of Rockefeller Foundation Support." *Minerva* 41, no. 2 (2003): 133–53.

Buxton, William J. and Lawrence T. Nichols. "Talcott Parsons and the 'Far East' at Harvard, 1941–48: Comparative Institutions and National Policy." *American Sociologist* 31, no. 2 (2000): 5–17.

Campbell, Joseph. *The Hero with a Thousand Faces*. New York: Pantheon Books, 1949.

Campbell, Joseph. "Reading of and Comments on Page 1." *Meeting of James Joyce Society, October 23, 1951*. Vinyl LP, Folkway Records, 1951, Track A2.

Campbell, Joseph and Henry Morton Robinson. *A Skeleton Key to Finnegans Wake*. New York: Penguin Books, 1944.

Cave Brown, Anthony. *The Last Hero: Wild Bill Donovan*. New York: Times, 1982.

Chadwin, Mark L. *The Hawks of World War II*. Chapel Hill: University of North Carolina Press, 1968.

Chambers, Whittacker. "Sin Rediscovered." *Time*, March 24 (1941): 38–40.

Chapple, Gerald. "Heinrich and Henry R. Zimmer: The Translator Translated." *Heinrich Zimmer: Coming into His Own*, edited by Margaret H. Case. Princeton, NJ: Princeton University Press, 1994, 61–85.

Charles, Jeffrey A. *Service Clubs in American Society: Rotary, Kiwians, and Lions*. Urbana: University of Illinois Press, 1993.

Chernoff, John F. "The Rhythmic Medium in African Music." *New Literary History* 22, no. 4 (1991): 1093–102.

Chéroux, Clément. *The Perfect Medium: Photography and the Occult*. New Haven, CT: Yale University Press, 2005.

Clark, Christa. *African Art in the Barnes Foundation: The Triumph of L'Art nègre and the Harlem Renaissance*. New York: Skira Rizzoli, 2015.

Clay, Steven and Rodney Philipps. "A Little History of the Mimeograph Revolution." *A Secret Location on the Lower East Side: Adventures in Writing, 1960–1980*, edited by Steven Clay and Rodney Philipps. New York: New York Public Library and Granary Books, 1998, 12–54.

Committee of Correspondence. *Nazi Poison: How We Can Destroy Hitler's Propaganda Against the Jews*. New York: Council for Democracy, 1941.

Committee of Fifteen. *City of Man: A Declaration on World Democracy*. New York: Viking, 1940.

Cornell, Stephen. "The Transformations of Tribe: Organization and Self-Concept in Native American Ethnicities." *Ethnic and Racial Studies* 11, no. 1 (1988): 27–47.

Corngold, Stanley. *The Mind in Exile: Thomas Mann in Princeton*. Princeton, NJ: Princeton University Press, 2022.

Coyle, John Y. "Amassing American 'Stuff': The Library of Congress and the Federal Arts Projects of the 1930s." *Quarterly of the Library of Congress* 40, no. 4 (1983): 356–89.

Crim, Brian E. *Our Germans: Project Paperclip and the National Security State*. Baltimore/MD: Johns Hopkins University, 2018.

Cross, Stephen J. and William R. Albury, "Walter B. Cannon, L. J. Henderson, and the Organic Analogy." *Osiris* 3 (1987): 165–92; 183–85.

Crowther-Heyck, Hunter. "Patrons of the Revolution: Ideals and Institutions in Postwar Behavioral Science." *Isis* 97, no. 3 (2006): 420–46.

Culbert, David. "The Rockefeller Foundation, the Museum of Modern Art Film Library, and Siegfried Kracauer, 1941." *Historical Journal of Film, Radio and Television* 13, no. 4 (1993): 495–511.

Curtius, Ernst R. "Das Schematismuskapitel in der Kritik der reinen Vernunft. Philologische Untersuchung." *Kant-Studien* 19, nos. 1–3 (1914): 338–66.

Darmaun, Jacques. *Thomas Mann et les Juifs*. Bern: Lang, 1995.

Daston, Lorraine and Peter Galison. *Objectivity*. New York: Zone Books, 2007.

Davenport, Lisa E. *Jazz Diplomacy: Promoting America in the Cold War Era*. Jackson: University Press of Mississippi, 2009.

Decherney, Peter. *Hollywood and the Culture Elite: How the Movies Became American*. New York: Columbia University Press, 2005.

Denning, Michael. *The Cultural Front: The Laboring of American Culture in the Twentieth Century*. London: Verso, 1997.

Derman, Joshua. *Max Weber in Politics and Social Thought: From Charisma to Canonization*. Cambridge, GB: Cambridge University Press, 2012.

Detering, Heinrich. *Thomas Manns amerikanische Religion: Theologie, Politik und Literatur im amerikanischen Exil*. Frankfurt am Main: Fischer, 2012.

Deussen, Paul. *Erinnerungen an Friedrich Nietzsche*. Leipzig: F.A. Brockhaus, 1901.

Dierks, Manfred. *Studien zu Mythos und Psychologie bei Thomas Mann: An dem Nachlaß orientierte Untersuchungen zum "Tod in Venedig," zum "Zauberberg" und zur "Joseph"-Tetralogie*. Bern: Francke, 1972.

Dinerstein, Joel. *The Origins of Cool in Postwar America*. Chicago, IL: University of Chicago Press, 2017.

Dinnerstein, Leonard. *Anti-Semitism in America*. Oxford: Oxford University Press, 1994.

Doenecke, Justus D. *Storm on the Horizon: The Challenge to American Intervention, 1939–1941*. Lanham, MD: Rowman and Littlefield, 2000.

Domeier, Norman. *Weltöffentlichkeit und Diktatur. Die amerikanischen Auslandskorrespondenten im "Dritten Reich."* Göttingen: Wallstein, 2021.

Donaldson, Scott. *Archibald MacLeish: An American Life*. Boston, MA: Houghton Mifflin, 1992.

Doubt, Keith. "Garfinkel Before Ethnomethodology." *American Sociologist* 20, no. 3 (1989): 252–62.

Dougherty, Jay. "Translating Bukowski and the Beats: An Interview with Carl Weissner." *Gargoyle* 35 (1988): 66–87.

Dow, James R. "Hans Naumann's *gesunkenes Kulturgut* and *primitive Gemeinschaftskultur*." *Journal of Folklore Research* 51, no. 1 (2014): 49–100.

Dow, James R. and Hannsjost Lixfeld. *The Nazification of an Academic Discipline: Folklore in the Third Reich*. Bloomington: Indiana University Press, 1986.

Dumont, Louis. *German Ideology: From France to Germany and Back*. Chicago, IL: University of Chicago Press, 1994 [1991].

Eder, Sandra. "The Volatility of Sex: Intersexuality, Gender and Clinical Practice in the 1950s." *Gender & History* 22, no. 3 (2010): 692–707.

Edgcomb, Gabrielle S. *From Swastika to Jim Crow: Refugee Scholars at Black Colleges*. Malabar/FL: Krieger, 1993.
Edwards, Brent H. *The Practice of Diaspora: Literature, Translation, and the Rise of Black Internationalism*. Cambridge, MA: Harvard University Press, 2003.
Ellison, Ralph. "Change the Joke and Slip the Yoke." In *Shadow and Act*. New York: Random House, 1964 [1958], 45–59.
Engerman, David C. *Know Your Enemy: The Rise and Fall of America's Soviet Experts*. Oxford: Oxford University Press, 2009.
Erd, Rainer ed. *Reform und Resignation: Gespräche über Franz L. Neumann*. Frankfurt am Main: Suhrkamp, 1985.
Erickson, Christine K. "'I have not had One Fact Disproven': Elizabeth Dilling's Crusade Against Communism in the 1930s." *Journal of American Studies* 36, no. 3 (2002): 473–89.
Erickson, Paul et al. "'The Situation' in the Cold War Behavioral Sciences." In *How Reason Almost Lost its Mind: The Strange Career of Cold War Rationality*. Chicago, IL: University of Chicago Press, 2013, 115–31.
Erikson, Erik Homburger. "Observations on Sioux Education." *The Journal of Psychology* 7, no. 1 (1939): 101–56.
Erikson, Erik Homburger. "Hitler's Imagery and German Youth." *Psychiatry* 5, no. 4 (1942): 475–93.
Erikson, Erik Homburger. "Observations on the Yurok: Childhood and World Image." *University of California Publications in American Archeology and Ethnology* 35, no. 10 (1943): i–v; 257–301.
Erikson, Erik Homburger. "Plans for the Returning Veteran." In *Community Planning for Peacetime Living: Report of the 1945 Stanford Workshop on Community Leadership*, edited by Louis Wirth, Ernest R. Hilgard and I. James Quillen. Stanford, CA: Stanford University Press, 1945, 116–21.
Erikson, Erik Homburger. "Childhood and Tradition in Two American Tribes – A Comparative Abstract, with Conclusion." *Psychoanalytic Study of the Child* 1 (1945): 319–50.
Erikson, Erik Homburger. "Ego Development and Historical Change–*Clinical Notes*." *Psychoanalytic Study of the Child* 2 (1946): 359–96.
Erikson, Erik Homburger. "Hitler's Imagery and German Youth." In *Personality: In Nature, Society, and Culture*, edited by Clyde Kluckhohn. New York: Knopf, 1949, 485–510.
Erikson, Erik Homburger. "The Dream Specimen of Psychoanalysis." *Journal of the American Academy of Psychoanalysis* 2 (1954): 5–56.
Erikson, Erik Homburger. *Young Man Luther: A Study in Psychoanalysis and History*. New York: Norton, 1958.
Erikson, Erik Homburger. *Identity: Youth and Crisis*. New York: Norton, 1968.
Erikson, Erik Homburger. "A Memorandum to the Joint Committee on Post War Planning (1945)." In *A Way of Looking at Things: Selected Papers from 1930 to 1980 Erik H. Erikson*, edited by Stephen Schlein. New York: Norton, 1987 [1944], 366–74.
Erikson, Erik Homburger. *Childhood and Society*. New York: Norton, 1993 [1950].

Etzemüller, Thomas. "*Social engineering* als Verhaltenslehre des kühlen Kopfes: Eine einleitende Skizze." In *Die Ordnung der Moderne: Social Engineering im 20. Jahrhundert*, edited by Thomas Etzemüller. Bielefeld: Transcript, 2009, 11–39.

Evans, Christopher H. *The Social Gospel in American Religion: A History*. New York: New York University Press, 2017.

Evans, Richard I. *Dialogue with Erik Erikson: A World-Famous Psychoanalyst Expounds on his Life's Work*. New York: Harper and Row, 1969 [1967].

Evans, Richard J. *The Third Reich in Power: 1933–1939*. New York: Penguin, 2005.

Faletti, Heidi E. "Reflections of Weimar Cinema in the Nazi Propaganda Films SA-Mann Brand, Hitlerjunge Quex, and Hans Westmar." In *Cultural History through a National Socialist Lens: Essays on the Cinema of the Third Reich*, edited by Robert C. Reimer. Rochester, NY: Camden House, 2000, 11–36.

Faust, Lene. "Trance und Trauma: Totenkult im neofaschistischen ambiente." *Zeitschrift für Kulturwissenschaften* 9 no. 2 (2015): 113–20.

Fearnley, Andrew M. "When the Harlem Renaissance Became Vogue: Periodization and the Organization of Postwar American Historiography." *Modern Intellectual History* 11, no. 1 (2014): 59–87.

Felsch, Philipp. *Der lange Sommer der Theorie: Geschichte einer Revolte 1960–1990*. Munich: C.H. Beck, 2015.

Fitzgerald, Robert. "Subjectivity is Absolute: Erich Kahler, David Sachs, E. B. O. Borgerhoff, Joseph Kerman, Edmund King and Francis Ferguson on Mann's Doctor Faustus." In *Enlarging the Change: The Princeton Seminars in Literary Criticism, 1949–1951*. Boston, MA: Northeastern University Press, 1985, 175–208.

Foster, Frances S. "Creative Collaboration: As African American as Sweet Potato Pie." In *Post-Bellum, Pre-Harlem: African American Literature and Culture, 1877–1919*, edited by Barbara McCaskill and Caroline Gebhard. New York: New York University Press, 2006, 17–33.

Fourastié, Jean. *Les trente glorieuses ou la Révolution invisible de 1946 à 1975*. Paris: Fayard, 1979.

Fraenkel, Ernst. *The Dual State: A Contribution to the Theory of Dictatorship*, translated by E. A. Shils, in collaboration with Edith Lowenstein and Klaus Knorr, New York: Oxford University Press, 1941.

Franz, Shepherd Ivory. "Rehabilitation and Reeducation–Physical, Mental and Social." *Mental Hygiene* 3, no. 1 (1919): 33–47.

Franz, Shepherd Ivory. *Nervous and Mental Reeducation*. New York: Macmillan, 1923.

Friedländer, Saul. *The Years of Extermination: Nazi Germany and the Jews, 1939–1945*. New York: HarperCollins, 2007.

Friedman, Lawrence J. *Identity's Architect: A Biography of Erik H. Erikson*. Cambridge, MA: Harvard University Press, 1999.

Füssl, Karl-H. "Fine-Tuning Utopia: American Social Sciences, European Émigrés, and U.S. Policy towards Germany, 1942–1945." In *Weltanschauliche Orientierungsversuche im Exil/New Orientations of Worldview in Exile*, edited

by Reinhard G. Andress, Evelyn Meyer, and Gregory Divers. Amsterdam: Rodopi, 2010, 283–97.
Galison, Peter. "The Ontology of the Enemy: Norbert Wiener and the Cybernetic Vision." *Critical Inquiry* 21, no. 1 (1994): 228–66.
Galison, Peter. *Image and Logic: A Material Culture of Microphysics*. Chicago, IL: University of Chicago Press, 1997.
Galison, Peter. "Removing Knowledge." *Critical Inquiry* 31, no. 1 (2004): 229–43.
Gans, Herbert J. "Best-Sellers by American Sociologists: An Exploratory Study." In *Required Reading: Sociology's Most Influential Books*, edited by Dan Clawson. Amherst: University of Massachusetts Press, 1998, 19–27.
Garfinkel, Harold. "Color Trouble." In *The Best Short Stories 1941*, edited by Edward J. O'Brien. Boston, MA: Houghton Mifflin, 1941 [1940], 97–119.
Garfinkel, Harold. "The Perception of the Other: A Study in Social Order." PhD Dissertation, Harvard University, 1952.
Garfinkel, Harold. "Review: Strategic Intelligence and National Decisions. By Roger Hilsman." *Administrative Science Quarterly* 1, no. 4 (1957): 541–43.
Garfinkel, Harold. "Studies of the Routine Grounds of Everyday Activities." In *Studies in Ethnomethodology*. Englewood Cliffs, NJ: Prentice-Hall, 1967, 35–75.
Gary, Brett. "Mobilizing the Intellectual Arsenal of Democracy: Archibald MacLeish and the Library of Congress." In *The Nervous Liberals: Propaganda Anxieties From World War I to the Cold War*. New York: Columbia University Press, 1999a, 131–73.
Gary, Brett. *The Nervous Liberals: Propaganda Anxieties from World War I to the Cold War*. New York: Columbia University Press, 1999b.
Gates, Henry Louis, Jr. *The Signifying Monkey: A Theory of African-American Literary Criticism*. Oxford: Oxford University Press, 1988.
Geertz, Clifford. *After the Facts: Two Countries, Four Decades, One Anthropologist*. Cambridge, MA: Harvard University Press, 1995.
Geoghegan, Bernard D. *Code: From Information Theory to French Theory*. Durham, NC: Duke University Press, 2023.
Gerhardt, Uta. "Die soziologische Erklärung des nationalsozialistischen Antisemitismus während des Zweiten Weltkriegs in den USA: Zur Faschismustheorie von Talcott Parsons." *Jahrbuch für Antisemitismusforschung* 1 (1992): 253–73.
Gerhardt, Uta. "A Hidden Agenda of Recovery: The Psychiatric Conceptualization of Re-education for Germany in the United States during World War II." *German History* 14, no. 3 (1996): 297–324.
Gerhardt, Uta. "Talcott Parsons und die Re-Education-Politik der amerikanischen Besatzungsmacht." *Schweizerische Zeitschrift für Soziologie* 24, no. 1 (1998): 121–51.
Gerhardt, Uta. "A World From Brave to New: Talcott Parsons and the War Effort at Harvard University." *Journal of the History of the Behavioral Sciences* 35, no. 3 (1999): 257–89.
Gerhardt, Uta. *Talcott Parsons: An Intellectual Biography*. Cambridge, GB: Cambridge University Press, 2002.

Gerhardt, Uta. *The Social Thought of Parsons: Methodology and American Ethos*. Surrey: Ashgate, 2011.
Gigerenzer, Gerd. "From Tools to Theories: A Heuristic of Discovery in Cognitive Psychology." *Psychological Review* 98, no. 2 (1991): 254–67.
Gilloch, Graeme. *Siegfried Kracauer: Our Companion in Misfortune*. Cambridge, GB: Polity, 2015.
Gilman, Nils. *Mandarins of the Future: Modernization Theory in Cold War America*. Baltimore, MD: Johns Hopkins University Press, 2003.
Gilroy, Paul. *The Black Atlantic: Modernity and Double Consciousness*. London: Verso, 1993.
Gleason, Philip. "Identifying Identity: A Semantic History." *Journal of American History* 69, no. 4 (1983): 910–31.
Glissant, Éduoard. "Creolization in the Making of the Americas." In *Race Discourse, and the Origin of the Americas: A New World View*, edited by Vera Lawrence Hyatt and Rex Nettleford. Washington, DC: Smithsonian Institution Press, 1995, 268–75.
Goff, Brendan. *Rotary International and the Selling of American Capitalism*. Cambridge, MA: Harvard University Press, 2021.
Goffman, Erving. "Cooling the Mark Out: Some Aspects of Adaptation to Failure." *Psychiatry* 15, no. 4 (1952): 451–63.
Gordon, Adi. "The Ideological Convert and the 'Mythology of Coherence': The Contradictory Hans Kohn and his Multiple Metamorphoses." *Leo Baeck Institute Year Book* 55 (2010): 273–93.
Gordon, Adi. *Toward Nationalism's End: An Intellectual Biography of Hans Kohn*. Waltham, MA: Brandeis University Press, 2017.
Grebstein, Sheldon. "Sinclair Lewis's Unwritten Novel." *Philological Quarterly* 37, no. 4 (1958): 400–9.
Greenberg, Udi. "Germany's Postwar Re-education and Its Weimar Intellectual Roots." *Journal of Contemporary History* 46, no. 10 (2011): 10–32.
Greenberg, Udi. *The Weimar Century: German Émigrés and the Ideological Foundations of the Cold War*. Princeton, NJ: Princeton University Press, 2014.
Griessbach, René. "Karl May und die Sioux." *Mitteilungen der Karl-May-Gesellschaft* 39, no. 151 (2007): 31–41.
Guilbaut, Serge. *How New York Stole the Idea of Modern Art: Abstract Expressionism, Freedom, and the Cold War*, translated by Arthur Goldhammer. Chicago, IL: University of Chicago Press, 1983.
Guillory, John. "Memo and Modernity." *Critical Inquiry* 31, no. 1 (2004): 108–32.
Hajdu, Marcus. *"Du hast einen anderen Geist als wir!" Die "große Kontroverse" um Thomas Mann 1945–1949*. PhD Dissertation Justus-Liebig-Universität Gießen, 2002.
Hamacher, Bernd. "Thomas Manns Medientheologie: Medien und Masken." In *Autorinszenierungen: Autorschaft und literarisches Werk im Kontext der Medien*, edited by Christine Künzel and Jörg Schönert. Würzburg: Königshausen und Neumann, 2007, 59–78.
Harding, James M. "Adorno, Ellison, and the Critique of Jazz." *Cultural Critique*, no. 31 (1995): 129–58.

Hartman, Saidiya. *Lose Your Mother: A Journey Along the Atlantic Slave Route.* New York: Farrar, Straus and Giroux, 2007.
Hartshorne, Richard. *The Nature of Geography: A Critical Survey of Current Thought in the Light of the Past.* Lancaster, PA: Association of American Geography, 1939.
Hayes, Peter. "Introduction." In Franz Neumann. *Behemoth: The Structure and Practice of National Socialism 1933–1944.* Chicago, IL: Ivan R. Dee, 2009, vii–xxii.
Heaps, Jennifer Davis. "Tracking Intelligence Information: The Office of Strategic Services." *American Archivist* 61, no. 2 (1998): 287–308.
Hegeman, Susan. *Patterns for America: Modernism and the Concept of Culture.* Princeton, NJ: Princeton University Press, 1999.
Heims, Steve J. *Constructing a Social Science for Postwar America: The Cybernetics Group, 1946–1953.* Cambridge, MA: MIT Press, 1993 [1991].
Heller, Erich. *The Ironic German: A Study of Thomas Mann.* Boston, MA: Little, Brown, 1958.
Hemelsoet, Dimitri et al. "The Neurological Illness of Friedrich Nietzsche." *Acta Neurologica Belgica* 108, no. 1 (2006): 9–16.
Hemenway, Robert. "Folklore Field Notes from Zora Neale Hurston." *Black Scholar* 7, no. 7 (1976): 39–47.
Henry, Charles P. *Ralph Bunche: Model Negro or American Other?* New York: New York University Press, 1999.
Herbert, Ulrich. "'Generation der Sachlichkeit': Die völkische Studentenbewegung der frühen zwanziger Jahre in Deutschland." In *Zivilisation und Barbarei: Die widersprüchlichen Potentiale der Moderne. Detlev Peukert zum Gedenken,* edited by Frank Bajorh et al. Hamburg: Christians, 1991, 115–44.
Herbert, Ulrich. *Best: Biographische Studien über Radikalismus, Weltanschauung und Vernunft, 1903–1989.* Bonn: Dietz, 1996.
Herman, Ellen. "Project Camelot and the Career of Cold War Psychology." In *Universities and Empire: Money and Politics in the Social Sciences During the Cold War,* edited by Christopher Simpson. New York: New Press, 1988, 97–134.
Herman, Ellen. *The Romance of American Psychology: Political Culture in the Age of Experts, 1940–1970.* Berkeley: University of California Press, 1995.
Herskovits, Melville J. "The Negro's Americanism." In *The New Negro: An Interpretation,* edited by Alain Locke. New York: A. and C. Boni, 1925, 353–60.
Herz, John H. "'Forced to be free!' – dieser Widerspruch war uns allen klar: Interview mit Prof. John Herz am 30. November 1983 in New York." In *Zur Archäologie der Demokratie in Deutschland.* Vol. 2, edited by Alfons Söllner. Frankfurt am Main: Fischer, 1986 [1983], 34–46.
Herzstein, Robert E. *Henry E. Luce: A Political Portrait of the Man Who Created the American Century.* New York: Scribner, 1994.
Heyl, Barbara S. "'The Harvard 'Pareto Circle.'" *History of the Behavioral Sciences* 4, no. 4 (1968): 316–34.
Hilken, Susanne et al. "Psychiatrische Anfänge der Pathographie." In *Kunst und Krankheit. Studien zur Pathographie,* edited by Matthias Bormuth et al. Göttingen: Wallstein, 2007, 11–26.

Hirsch, Jerrold. "Folklore in the Making: B.A. Botkin." *Journal of American Folklore* 100, no. 395 (1987): 3–38.
Hirsch, Jerrold. *Portrait of America: A Cultural History of the Federal Writers' Project*. Chapel Hill: University of North Carolina Press, 2003.
Hobsbawm, Eric. "Mass-Producing Traditions: Europe, 1870–1914." In *The Invention of Tradition*, edited by Eric Hobsbawm and Terence Ranger. Cambridge, GB: Cambridge University Press, 1983, 263–307.
Hoenicke Moore, Michaela. *Know Your Enemy: The American Debate on Nazism, 1933–1945*. Cambridge, GB: Cambridge University Press, 2010.
Hoffman, Louise E. "Erikson on Hitler: The Origins of 'Hitler's Imagery and German Youth.'" *Psychohistory Review* 22, no. 1 (1993): 69–86.
Hoffmann, Hilmar. *The Triumph of Propaganda: Film and National Socialism, 1933–1945*, translated by John A. Broadwin and Volker R. Berghahn. Providence, RI: Berghahn, 1996.
Høgel, Christian. "World Literature is Trans-Imperial: A Medieval and a Modern Approach." *Medieval Worlds*, no. 8 (2018): 3–21.
Holthusen, Hans E. "Die Welt ohne Transzendenz: Eine Studie zu Thomas Manns 'Dr. Faustus' und seinen Nebenschriften." *Merkur* 3, no. 11 (1949a): 38–58.
Holthusen, Hans E. "Die Welt ohne Transzendenz (II): Eine Studie zu Thomas Manns 'Dr. Faustus' und seinen Nebenschriften." *Merkur* 3, no. 12 (1949b): 161–80.
Homburger, Erik. "Configurations in Play: Clinical Notes." *Psychoanalytic Quarterly* 6 (1937): 139–212.
Horkheimer, Max. *Gesammelte Schriften*. Vol. 17: *Briefwechsel 1941–1948*, edited by Gunzelin Schmid Noerr. Frankfurt am Main: Suhrkamp, 1996.
Horkheimer, Max and Theodor W. Adorno. *Dialectic of Enlightenment: Philosophical Fragments*, edited by Gunzelin Schmid Noerr, translated by Edmund Jephcott. Stanford, CA: Stanford University Press, 2002.
Horton, David. *Thomas Mann in English: A Study in Literary Translation*. London: Bloomsbury, 2013.
Howard, Jane. *Margaret Mead: A Life*. New York: Simon & Schuster, 1984.
Hughes, H. Stuart. *The Sea Change: The Migration of Social Thought, 1930–1965*. New York: Harper and Row, 1975.
Hughes, H. Stuart. *Gentleman Rebel: The Memoires of H. Stuart Hughes*. New York: Ticknor and Fields, 1990.
Hülshörster, Christian. *Thomas Mann und Oskar Goldbergs 'Wirklichkeit der Hebräer.'* Frankfurt am Main: Klostermann, 1999.
Hurston, Zora N. *Mules and Men*. Philadelphia, PA: Lippincott, 1935.
Hurston, Zora N. "The Gilded Six-Bits." In *The Complete Stories*. New York: Harper, 1995, 86–98.
Hurston, Zora N. *A Life in Letters*, edited by Carla Kaplan. New York: Anchor Book, 2003.
Hurston, Zora N. Spunk. In *Collected Plays*, edited by Jean L. Cole and Charles Mitchell. New Brunswick, NJ: Rutgers University Press, 2008, 227–68.
Huszar Allen, Marguerite de. "Montage and the Faust Theme: The Influence of the 1587 *Faustbuch* on Thomas Mann's Technique in *Doktor Faustus*." *Journal of European Studies* 13, nos. 49–50 (1983): 109–21.

Intelmann, Peter. "Zur Biographie von Franz L. Neumann." *1999. Zeitschrift für Sozialgeschichte des 20. und 21. Jahrhunderts* 5, no. 2 (1990): 14–52.
Isaac, Joel. *Working Knowledge: Making the Human Sciences from Parsons to Kuhn*. Cambridge, MA: Harvard University Press, 2012.
Jacknis, Ira. "Margaret Mead and Gregory Bateson in Bali: Their Use of Photography and Film." *Cultural Anthropology* 3, no. 2 (1988): 160–77.
Jackson, Walter. "Melville Herskovits and the Search for Afro-American Culture." In *Malinowski, Rivers, Benedict and Others: Essays on Culture and Personality*, edited by George W. Stocking. Madison, WI: University of Wisconsin Press, 1988, 96–126.
Janos, Andrew C. *Politics and Paradigms: Changing Theories of Change in Social Science*. Stanford, CA: Stanford University Press, 1986.
Jantzen, Kyle. "'The Fatherhood and Brotherhood of Man': Mainline American Protestants and the Kristallnacht Pogrom." In *American Religious Responses to Kristallnacht*, edited by Maria Mazzenga. New York: Palgrave Macmillan, 2009, 31–55.
Jay, Martin. *The Dialectical Imagination: A History of the Frankfurt School and the Institute of Social Research, 1923–1950*. London: Heinemann, 1973.
Jay, Martin. "The Extraterritorial Life of Siegfried Kracauer." *Salmagundi* 31–32 (1975–1976): 49–106.
Jennings, Michael. "Agriculture, Industry, and the Birth of the Photo-Essay in the Late Weimar Republic." *October* 93 (2000): 23–56.
Johnson, Niel M. *George Sylvester Viereck: German-American Propagandist*. Urbana, IL: University of Illinois Press, 1972.
Johnston, Barry V. *Pitirim A. Sorokin: An Intellectual Biography*. Lawrence: University Press of Kansas, 1995.
Johnstone, Andrew. *Against Immediate Evil: American Internationalists and the Four Freedoms on the Eve of World War II*. Ithaca, NY: Cornell University Press, 2014.
Judaken, Jonathan. "Talcott Parsons's 'The Sociology of Modern Anti-Semitism': Anti-antisemitism, Ambivalent Liberalism, and the Sociological Imagination." In *Antisemitism and the Constitution of Sociology*, edited by Marcel Stoetzler. Lincoln: University of Nebraska Press, 2014, 249–73.
Jules-Rosette, Bennetta. "Talcott Parsons and the Phenomenological Tradition in Sociology: An Unresolved Debate." *Human Studies* 3, no. 4 (1980): 311–20.
Kahler, Erich von. "Die Säkularisierung des Teufels." *Neue Rundschau* 59, no. 2 (1948): 185–203.
Kallen, Horace M. "Alain Locke and Cultural Pluralism." *Journal of Philosophy* 54, no. 5 (1957): 119–27.
Kater, Michael H. *Hitler Youth*. Cambridge, MA: Harvard University Press, 2004.
Kātz, Barry M. "The Criticism of Arms: The Frankfurt School Goes to War." *Journal of Modern History* 59, no. 3 (1987): 439–78.
Katz, Barry M. *Foreign Intelligence: Research and Analysis in the Office of Strategic Services 1942–1945*. Cambridge, MA: Harvard University Press, 1989.
Kelly, Lawrence C. "Anthropology and Anthropologists in the Indian New Deal." *Journal of the History of Behavioral Sciences* 16, no. 1 (1980): 6–24.

Kelly, Lawrence C. "Why Applied Anthropology Developed When it Did: A Commentary on People, Money, and Changing Times, 1930–1945." In *Social Contexts of American Ethnology, 1840–1984*, edited by June Helm. Washington, DC: American Ethnological Society, 1984, 122–38.

Kettler, David and Thomas Wheatland. *Learning from Franz L. Neumann: Law, Theory, and the Brute Facts of Political Life*. London: Anthem Press, 2019.

Kieval, Hillel J. *The Making of Czech Jewry: National Conflict and Jewish Society in Bohemia, 1870–1918*. Oxford: Oxford University Press, 1988.

Klausner, Joseph. *Geschichte der Neuhebräischen Literatur*, translated from Russian and Hebrew by Hans Kohn. Berlin: Jüdischer Verlag, 1921.

Kley, Stefan. "Hitler and the Pogrom of November 9/10, 1938," translated by William Templer. *Yad Vashem Studies* 28 (2000): 87–112.

Kline, Ronald D. *The Cybernetics Moment; or, Why We Call Our Age the Information Age*. Baltimore, MD: Johns Hopkins University Press, 2015.

Kluckhohn, Clyde and Robert A. Hackenberg. "Social Science Principles and the Indian Reorganization Act." In *Indian Affairs and the Indian Reorganization Act: The Twenty Year Record*, edited by William H. Kelly. Tucson: University of Arizona Press, 1954, 29–34.

Knight, Melinda. "Little Magazines and the Emergence of Modernism in the 'Fin de Siècle.'" *American Periodicals* 6 (1996): 29–45.

Kohn, Hans ed. *Vom Judentum: Ein Sammelbuch*. Leipzig: Kurt Wolff, 1913.

Kohn, Hans. "Die Juden in Sibirien." *Der Jude* 5, no. 3 (1921): 185–92.

Kohn, Hans. *Nationalismus: Über die Bedeutung des Nationalismus im Judentum und in der Gegenwart*. Vienna: R. Löwit, 1922.

Kohn, Hans. *The Idea of Nationalism: A Study in Its Origins and Background*. New York: Macmillan, 1944.

Kohn, Hans. *Living in a World Revolution: My Encounters with History*. New York: Trident, 1964.

Koselleck, Reinhart. *The Practice of Conceptual History: Timing History, Spacing Concepts*, translated by Todd Samuel Presner et al. Stanford, CA: Stanford University Press, 2002.

Kracauer, Siegfried. "Propaganda and the Nazi War Film." *Film Library*, Museum of Modern Art: New York, 1942.

Kracauer, Siegfried. "The Conquest of Europe on the Screen: The Nazi Newsreel, 1939–1940." *Social Research* 10, no. 3 (1943): 337–57.

Kracauer, Siegfried. *From Caligari to Hitler: A Psychological History of the German Film*. Princeton, NJ: Princeton University Press, 1947.

Kracauer, Siegfried. *The Mass Ornament: Weimar Essays*, edited and translated by Thomas Y. Levin. Cambridge, MA: Harvard University Press, 1995.

Krajewski, Markus. *Paper Machines: About Cards & Catalogs, 1548–1929*, translated by Peter Krapp. Cambridge, MA: MIT Press, 2011.

Kreimeier, Klaus. *The Ufa Story: A History of Germany's Greatest Film Company, 1918–1945*, translated by Robert Kimber and Rita Kimber. New York: Hill and Wang, 1996.

Kreutzer, Hans J. *Der Mythos vom Volksbuch: Studien zur Wirkungsgeschichte des frühen deutschen Romans seit der Romantik*. Stuttgart: Metzler, 1977.

Krige, John and Helke Rausch. "Introduction – Tracing the Knowledge: Power Nexus of American Philanthropy." In *American Foundations and the Coproduction of World Order in the Twentieth Century*, edited by John Krige and Helke Rausch. Göttingen: Vandenhoeck und Ruprecht, 2012, 7–34.

Kroeber, Alfred L. "California Kinship Systems." *University of California Publications in American Archaeology and Ethnology* 12, no. 9 (1917): 339–96.

Kroeber, Alfred L. "The Yurok." In *Handbook of the Indians of California*. Washington, DC: Government Print Office, 1925, 1–97.

Kroeber, Alfred L. and Samuel A. Barett. "Fishing Among the Indians of Northwestern California." *Anthropological Records* 21, no. 1 (1960): 1–210.

Krohn, Claus-Dieter. *Intellectuals in Exile: Refugee Scholars and the New School for Social Research*, translated by Rita and Robert Kimber. Amherst: University of Massachusetts Press, 1993.

Kurth, Peter. *American Cassandra: The Life of Dorothy Thompson*. Boston, MA: Little, Brown and Company, 1990.

Kusser, Astrid. *Körper in Schieflage: Tanzen im Strudel des Black Atlantic um 1900*. Bielefeld: Transcript, 2013.

Ladwig-Winters, Simone. "Ernst Fraenkel als Stipendiat des American Committee in Chicago." In *Vom Sozialismus zum Pluralismus: Beiträge zu Werk und Leben Ernst Fraenkels*, edited by Hubertus Buchstein and Gerhard Göhler. Baden-Baden: Nomos, 2000, 43–61.

Langeheine, Romy. *Von Prag nach New York. Hans Kohn: Eine intellektuelle Biographie*. Göttingen: Wallstein, 2014.

Larsen, Stephen and Robin Larsen. *A Fire in the Mind: The Life of Joseph Campbell*. New York: Doubleday, 1991.

Latour, Bruno. *Science in Action*. Cambridge, MA: Harvard University Press, 1987.

Lee, Raymond M. "David Riesman and the Sociology of the Interview." *Sociological Quarterly* 49, no. 2 (2008): 285–307.

Lethen, Helmut. *Cool Conduct: The Culture of Distance in Weimar Germany*, translated by Don Reneau. Berkeley: University of California Press, 2002 [1994].

Leverkuehn, Paul. *German Military Intelligence*, translated by R.H. Stevens and Constantine FitzGibbon. London: Weidenfeld and Nicolson, 1954.

Levin, Harry. *James Joyce: A Critical Introduction*. Norfolk, CN: New Directions Books, 1941.

Lewis, Sinclair. *It Can't Happen Here*. London: Cape, 1935.

Lewis, Sinclair. *Gideon Planish*. New York: Random House, 1943.

Lewis, Sinclair. *Minnesota Diary, 1942–1946*, edited by George Killough. Moscow: University of Idaho Press, 2000.

Lewis, Sinclair. "Proper Gander." In *The Short Stories of Sinclair Lewis (1904–1949). Vol. 6: June 1931–March 1941*, edited by Samuel J. Rogal, Lewiston: Edwin Mellen Press, 2007 [1935], 287–312.

Lidz, Victor and Helmut Staubmann. "Introduction." In Talcott Parsons. *Actor, Situation and Normative Pattern: An Essay in the Theory of Social Action*, edited by Victor Lidz and Helmut Staubmann. Münster: Lit, 2010, 5–29.

Lietzmann, Hans J. *Politikwissenschaft im "Zeitalter der Diktaturen": Die Entwicklung der Totalitarismustheorie Carl Joachim Friedrichs*. Opladen: Leske and Budrich, 1999.
Lindblom, Charles E. "The Science of 'Muddling Through.'" *Public Administration Review* 19, no. 2 (1959): 79–88.
Lingeman, Richard. *Sinclair Lewis: Rebel from Main Street*. New York: Random House, 2002.
Link, Fabian. "Sozialwissenschaften im Kalten Krieg: Mathematisierung, Demokratisierung und Politikberatung." *H-Soz-Kult Literature Reviews*, May 15, 2018. www.hsozkult.de/literaturereview/id/forschungsberichte-3095 (30/11/2023).
Lipset, David. *Gregory Bateson: The Legacy of a Scientist*. Englewood Cliffs, NJ: Prentice-Hall, 1980.
Lipstadt, Deborah E. *Beyond Belief: The American Press and the Coming of the Holocaust, 1933–1945*. New York: Free Press, 1986.
Locke, Alain. "The Colonial Literature of France." *Opportunity* 1, no. 11 (1923): 331–35.
Locke, Alain. "Internationalism – Friend or Foe of Art." *World Tomorrow* 8, no. 3 (1925a): 75–76.
Locke, Alain ed. *The New Negro: An Interpretation*. New York: A. and C. Boni, 1925b.
Locke, Alain. "The New Negro." In *The New Negro: An Interpretation*, edited by Alain Locke. New York: A. and C. Boni, 1925c, 3–16.
Locke, Alain. "Negro Youth Speaks." In *The New Negro: An Interpretation*, edited by Alain Locke. New York: A. and C. Boni, 1925d, 47–53.
Locke, Alain. "The Legacy of the Ancestral Arts." In *The New Negro: An Interpretation*, edited by Alain Locke. New York: A. and C. Boni, 1925e, 254–67.
Locke, Alain. "The Contribution of Race to Culture." *The Student World* 23, no. 4 (1930): 349–53.
Locke, Alain. "Unity Through Diversity: A Bahá'í Principle." *Bahá'í World* 4, no. 4 (1930–1932): 372–74.
Locke, Alain. *The Philosophy of Alain Locke: Harlem Renaissance and Beyond*, edited by Leonard Harris. Philadelphia, PA: Temple University Press, 1989.
Locke, Alain. *The Works of Alain Locke*, edited by Charles Molesworth. Oxford: Oxford University Press, 2012.
Locke, Alain and Bernhard J. Stern eds. *When Peoples Meet: A Study in Race and Culture Contacts*, revised edition. New York: Hinds, Hayden and Eldridge, 1946 [1942].
Loiperdinger, Martin ed. *Märtyrerlegenden im NS-Film*. Opladen: Leske und Budrich, 1991.
Luce, Henry R. "The American Century." *Life*, February 17 (1941): 61–65.
MacLeish, Archibald. "The Irresponsibles." *The Nation*, May 18 (1940a): 618–23.
MacLeish, Archibald. "The Librarian and the Democratic Process." *American Library Association Bulletin* 34, no. 6 (1940b): 385–88; 421–22.
MacLeish, Archibald. *Letters of Archibald MacLeish 1907 to 1982*, edited by Roy H. Winnick. New York: Houghton Mifflin, 1983.

Maier, Charles S. "Between Taylorism and Technocracy: European Ideologies and the Vision of Industrial Productivity in the 1920s." *Journal of Contemporary History* 5, no. 2 (1970): 27–61.

Mandler, Peter. *Return from the Natives: How Margaret Mead Won the Second World War and Lost the Cold War*. New Haven, CT: Yale University Press, 2013.

Mann, Michael. *Fascists*. Cambridge, GB: Cambridge University Press, 2004.

Mann, Michael. *The Sources of Power*. Vol. 4: *Globalizations, 1945–2011*. Cambridge, GB: Cambridge University Press, 2013.

Mann, Thomas. "Der Geist in Gesellschaft: Das 'Comité Permanent des Lettres et des Artes.'" *Neue Zürcher Zeitung*, October 9 and 10 (1932).

Mann, Thomas. "Humaniora und Humanismus." *Pester Lloyd, Morgenblatt*, June 11 (1936): 2–3.

Mann, Thomas. "Aus dem Princetoner Kolleg über Faust." *Mass und Wert* 2, no. 5 (1939a): 590–612.

Mann, Thomas. "That Man Is My Brother." *Esquire* 11, no. 3 (1939b): 31; 132–3.

Mann, Thomas. *Listen, Germany! Twenty-five Radio Messages to the German People over BBC*. New York: Knopf, 1942.

Mann, Thomas. "Introduction." *Free World Theatre: Nineteen New Radio Plays*, edited by Arch Oboler and Stephen Longstreet. New York: Random House, 1944a, ix–xi.

Mann, Thomas. "What Is German?" *Atlantic Monthly* 173, no. 5 (1944b): 78–85.

Mann, Thomas. "Warum ich nicht nach Deutschland zurückgehe: Antwort auf einen Brief Walter von Meles in der deutschen Presse." *Aufbau* 11, no. 39 (1945): 5–6.

Mann, Thomas. "Freud and the Future." In *Essays of Three Decades*, translated by Helen T. Lowe-Porter. New York: Knopf, 1947 [1936], 411–28.

Mann, Thomas. "Goethe's Faust." In *Essays of Three Decades*, translated by Helen T. Lowe-Porter. New York: Knopf, 1947 [1938], 3–42.

Mann, Thomas. "Humor und Ironie: Beitrag zu einer Rundfunkdiskussion." In *Nachlese: Prosa 1951–1955*. Berlin: Fischer, 1956 [1953], 166–69.

Mann, Thomas. *The Story of a Novel: The Genesis of Doctor Faustus*, translated by Richard Winston and Clara Winston. New York: Knopf, 1961 [1949].

Mann, Thomas. *Addresses Delivered at the Library of Congress, 1942–1949*, edited by Don H. Tolzmann. Oxford: Lang, 1963a.

Mann, Thomas. "The War and the Future." In *Addresses Delivered at the Library of Congress, 1942–1949*, edited by Don H. Tolzmann. Oxford: Lang, 1963b [1943], 21–43.

Mann, Thomas. "Germany and the Germans." In *Addresses Delivered at the Library of Congress, 1942–1949*, edited by Don H. Tolzmann. Oxford: Lang, 1963c [1945], 47–66.

Mann, Thomas. *Briefwechsel mit seinem Verleger Gottfried Bermann Fischer 1932–1955*, edited by Peter de Mendelssohn. Frankfurt am Main: Fischer, 1973.

Mann, Thomas. *Tagebücher 1935–1936*, edited by Peter de Mendelssohn. Frankfurt am Main: Fischer, 1978.

Mann, Thomas. *Dichter über ihre Dichtungen*. Vol. 14: *Thomas Mann*, pt. III: *1945–1955*, edited by Hans Wysling, in collaboration with Marianne Fischer. Munich: Heimeran, 1981.

Mann, Thomas. *Tagebücher 1940–1943*, edited by Peter de Mendelssohn. Frankfurt am Main: Fischer, 1982.

Mann, Thomas. *Tagebücher 1944–1.4.1946*, edited by Inge Jens. Frankfurt am Main: Fischer, 1986.

Mann, Thomas. *Tagebücher 28.5.1946–31.12.1948*, edited by Inge Jens. Frankfurt am Main: Fischer, 1989.

Mann, Thomas. *Doctor Faustus: The Life of the German Composer Adrian Leverkühn as Told by a Friend*, translated by John E. Woods. New York: Vintage International, 1997 [1947].

Mann, Thomas. *Deutsche Hörer! Radiosendungen nach Deutschland aus den Jahren 1940–1945*, fourth, rev. and ext. edition. Frankfurt am Main: Fischer, 2004a.

Mann, Thomas. *Thomas Mann spricht Deutsche Hörer! BBC Reden 1941–1945*. Bayerischer Rundfunk and British Broadcasting Corporation, Audio CD, 2004b.

Mann, Thomas and Karl Kerényi. *Gespräch in Briefen*, edited by Karl Kerényi. Zürich: Rhein Verlag, 1960.

Mann, Thomas and Agnes E. Meyer. *Briefwechsel, 1937–1955: Thomas Mann, Agnes E. Meyer*, edited by Hans R. Vaget. Frankfurt am Main: Fischer, 1992.

Marable, Manning. *W.E.B. Du Bois: Black Radical Democrat*. Boston, MA: Twayne, 1986.

Marcuse, Herbert. *Technology, War and Fascism: Collected Papers of Herbert Marcuse*, Vol. 1, edited by Douglas Keller, translated by Benjamin Gregg. London: Routledge, 1998.

Marquardt-Bigman, Petra. *Amerikanische Geheimdienstanalysen über Deutschland 1942–1949*. München: R. Oldenbourg, 1995.

Marrow, Alfred J. *The Practical Theorist: The Life and Work of Kurt Lewin*. New York: Basic Books, 1969.

Martino, Paolo. *Il Nome Etrusco di Atlante*. Rome: Dipartimento di Studi Glottoantropologici dell'Universitá di Roma 'La Sapienzia', 1987.

Mauch, Christoph. *Shadow War against Hitler: The Covert Operations of America's Wartime Secret Intelligence Service*. New York: Columbia University Press, 2003 [1999].

Mayer, Hans. *Thomas Mann: Werk und Entwicklung*. Berlin: Volk und Welt, 1950.

McCraw, Thomas K. *Prophet of Innovation: Joseph Schumpeter and Creative Destruction*. Cambridge, MA: Harvard University Press, 2007.

McGuire, William. "Zimmer and the Mellons." In *Heinrich Zimmer: Coming into His Own*, edited by Margaret H. Case. Princeton, NJ: Princeton University Press, 31–42.

McLaughlin, Neil. "Critical Theory Meets America: Riesman, Fromm, and *The Lonely Crowd*." *American Sociologist* 32, no. 1 (2001): 5–26.

McLuhan, Marshall. *The Mechanical Bride: Folklore of Industrial Man*. New York: Vanguard, 1951.

McLuhan, Marshall. "James Joyce: Trivial and Quadrivial." *Thought* 28, no. 1 (1953): 75–98.

McNeill, John R. *Mosquito Empires: Ecology and War in the Greater Caribbean, 1620–1914*. Cambridge, GB: Cambridge University Press, 2010.

Mead, Margaret. *Blackberry Winter: My Early Years.* Morrow: New York, 1972.
Mead, Margaret. *To Cherish the Life of the World: Selected Letters of Margaret Mead*, edited by Margaret M. Caffrey and Patricia A. Francis. New York: Basic, 2006.
Meckler, Alan M. *Micropublishing: A History of Scholarly Micropublishing in America, 1938–1980.* Westport, CN: Greenwood Press, 1982.
Medawar, Jean and David Pyke. *Hitler's Gift: The True Story of the Scientists Expelled by the Nazi Regime.* New York: Arcade, 2000.
Mekeel, H. Scudder. "An Anthropologist's Observations on Indian Education." *Progressive Education* 13, no. 3 (1936a): 151–59.
Mekeel, H. Scudder. "The Economy of a Modern Teton Dakota Community." *Yale University Publications in Anthropology* 6 (1936b): 3–13.
Mekeel, H. Scudder. "An Appraisal of the Indian Reorganization Act." *American Anthropologist* 46, no. 2 (1944): 209–17.
Mendelssohn, Peter de. "Vorwort." In Thomas Mann. *Briefwechsel mit seinem Verleger Gottfried Bermann Fischer 1932–1955*, edited by Peter de Mendelssohn. Frankfurt am Main: Fischer, 1973, V–XXXV.
Mettler, Suzanne. *Soldiers to Citizens: The G.I. Bill and the Making of the Greatest Generation.* Oxford: Oxford University Press, 2005.
Meyer, Agnes E. *America's Home Front.* Washington, DC: Washington Post, 1943.
Meyer, Agnes E. *Journey Through Chaos.* New York: Harcourt Brace, 1944.
Mills, C. Wright. *The Power Elite.* New York: Oxford University Press, 1956.
Moholy, Lucia. "The Aslib Microfilm Service: The Story of its Wartime Activities." *Journal of Documentation* 2, no. 3 (1946): 147–73.
Moholy, Lucia. "Co-Ordination of Scientific Information." *Research* 1, no. 4 (1948): 173–76.
Moholy, Lucia. "'Freeing the Mind.' Entlastung des Gehirns: Befreiung des Geistes?" *Du* 24, no. 8 (1964): 66–67.
Moholy, Lucia. "Das Bauhaus-Bild." *Werk* 55, no. 6 (1968): 397–402.
Moholy, Lucia. *Marginalien zu Moholy-Nagy, Dokumentarische Ungereimtheiten.* Krefeld: Scherpe, 1972.
Moholy, Lucia. "Microfilm Services and Their Application to Scholarly Study, Scientific Research, Education and Re-Education in the Post-War Period, A Suggestion with 5 Appendices, UNESCO Preparatory Commission 1945, through Alfred Zimmer," excerpt of manuscript printed in *Lucia Moholy: Bauhaus Fotografin*, edited by Rolf Sachsse. Berlin: Museumspädagogischer Dienst, Bauhaus-Archiv Berlin, 1995a [1945], 84–85.
Moholy, Lucia. "Die Reprographie als Faktor in der Gesellschaftsbildung," excerpt of manuscript printed in *Lucia Moholy: Bauhaus Fotografin*, edited by Rolf Sachsse. Berlin: Museumspädagogischer Dienst, Bauhaus-Archiv Berlin, 1995b [1964], 89.
[Moholy, Lucia] and Moholy-Nagy, László. "Produktion – Reproduktion." *De Stijl* 5, no. 7 (1922): 98–100.
Molesworth, Charles. "Introduction." In Alain Locke. *The Works of Alain Locke*, edited by Charles Molesworth. Oxford: Oxford University Press, 2012, xi–xxxvi.
Moltke, Johannes von. *The Curious Humanist: Siegfried Kracauer in America.* Oakland, CA: University of California Press, 2016.

Moltke, Johannes von and Kristy Rawson eds. *Siegfried Kracauer's American Writings: Essays on Film and Popular Culture*. Berkeley: University of California Press, 2012.

Morgan, Edmund S. *Visible Saints: The History of a Puritan Idea*. New York: New York University Press, 1963.

Morgan, Philip D. "Lowcountry Georgia and the Early Modern Atlantic World, 1733–ca. 1820." In *African American Life in the Georgia Lowcountry: The Atlantic World and the Gullah Geechee*, edited by Philip D. Morgan. Athens: The University of Georgia Press, 2010, 13–47.

Morris, Aldon D. *The Scholar Denied: W.E.B. Du Bois and the Birth of Modern Sociology*. Oakland: University of California Press, 2015.

Müller, Hans-Harald. "Robert Petsch: Sein akademischer Werdegang und die Begründung der Allgemeinen Literaturwissenschaft in Hamburg." In *100 Jahre Germanistik in Hamburg: Traditionen und Perspektiven*, edited by Myriam Richter and Mirko Nottscheid. Berlin: Reimer, 2011, 107–24.

Müller, Tim B. *Krieger und Gelehrte: Herbert Marcuse und die Denksysteme im Kalten Krieg*, Hamburg: Hamburger Edition, 2010.

Mueller, Tim B. "The Rockefeller Foundation, the Social Sciences, and the Humanities in the Cold War." *Journal of Cold War Studies* 15, no. 3 (2013): 108–35.

Namikas, Lise. "The Committee to Defend America and the Debate between Internationalists and Interventionists, 1939–1941." *Historian* 61, no. 4 (1999): 843–63.

Nash, Henry T. "The Bureaucratization of Homicide." *The Bulletin of the Atomic Scientists* 36, no. 4 (1980): 22–27.

Nawrocka, Irene. *Verlagssitz: Wien, Stockholm, New York, Amsterdam. Der Bermann-Fischer Verlag im Exil (1933–1950): Ein Abschnitt aus der Geschichte des S. Fischer Verlages. Archiv für Geschichte des Buchwesens* 53 (2000): 1–216.

Nelson, Daniel. "Scientific Management, Systematic Management, and Labor, 1880–1915." *Business History Review* 48, no. 4 (1974): 479–500.

Neumann, Franz. *Behemoth: The Structure and Practice of National Socialism*. New York: Oxford University Press, 1942.

Neumann, Franz. *Behemoth: The Structure and Practice of National Socialism 1933–1944*, second, ext. edition. New York: Oxford University Press, 1944.

Neumann, Franz. "Anti-Semitism: Spearhead of Universal Terror." In *Secret Reports on Nazi Germany: The Frankfurt School Contribution to the War Effort*, edited by Raffaele Laudani. Princeton, NJ: Princeton University Press, 2013a [1943], 27–30.

Neumann, Franz. "German Morale After Tunisia." In *Secret Reports on Nazi Germany: The Frankfurt School Contribution to the War Effort*, edited by Raffaele Laudani. Princeton, NJ: Princeton University Press, 2013b [1943], 95–99.

Niven, Bill, "Ernst Wiechert and his Role Between 1933 and 1945." *New German Studies* 16, no. 1 (1990–1): 1–20.

NN. "The Debut of the Younger School of Negro Writers." *Opportunity* 2, no. 17 (1925): 143–44.

NN. "Germany after the War: Roundtable-1945." *American Journal of Orthopsychiatry* 15, no. 3 (1945): 381–441.
NN. "Science, Government and Information: The Responsibilities of the Technical Community and the Government in the Transfer of Information." *Minerva* 2, no. 1 (1963): 91–117.
Norwood, Stephen H. *The Third Reich in the Ivory Tower: Complicity and Conflict on American Campuses.* Cambridge, GB: Cambridge University Press, 2009.
Oboler, Arch. "Memo to Berchtesgarden." *The Best One-Act-Plays of 1942*, edited by Margaret Mayorga. New York: Dodd Mead, 1943 [1942], 189–208.
Olick, Jeffrey K. *In the House of the Hangman: The Agonies of German Defeat, 1943–1949.* Chicago, IL: University of Chicago Press, 2005.
O'Reagan, Douglas M. *Taking Nazi Technology: Allied Exploitation of German Science After the Second World War.* Baltimore, MD: Johns Hopkins University Press, 2019.
Ortiz, Maria and Klaus Hedwig. "Über den Austausch von Missverständnissen: Briefwechsel Schütz-Parsons." *Philosophische Rundschau* 27, no. 3/4 (1980): 259–64.
Osborn, Andrew D. "The Crisis in Cataloging." *Library Quarterly* 11, no. 4 (1941): 393–411.
Owens, Larry. "The Counterproductive Management of Science in the Second World War: Vannevar Bush and the Office of Scientific Research and Development." *Business History Review* 68, no. 4 (1994): 515–76.
Parsons, Charles. "Some Remarks on Talcott Parsons's Family." *American Sociologist* 35, no. 3 (2004): 4–22.
Parsons, Talcott. *The Structure of Social Action: A Study in Social Theory with Special Reference to a Group of Recent European Writers.* New York: McGraw Hill, 1937.
Parsons, Talcott. "The Sociology of Modern Anti-Semitism." In *Jews in a Gentile World: The Problem of Anti-Semitism*, edited by Isacque Graeber and Steuart Henderson Britt. Westport, CT: Greenwood Press, 1942a, 101–22.
Parsons, Talcott. "Max Weber and the Contemporary Political Crisis: II." *Review of Politics* 4, no. 2 (1942b): 155–72.
Parsons, Talcott. "Some Sociological Aspects of the Fascist Movements." *Social Forces* 21, no. 2 (1942c): 138–47.
Parsons, Talcott. "Democracy and Social Structure in Pre-Nazi Germany." *Journal of Legal and Political Sociology* 1, nos. 1–2 (1942d): 96–114.
Parsons, Talcott. "Propaganda and Social Control." *Psychiatry* 5, no. 4 (1942e): 551–72.
Parsons, Talcott. "The Problem of Controlled Institutional Change." *Psychiatry* 8, no. 1 (1945): 79–101.
Parsons, Talcott. *The Social System.* New York: Free Press, 1951.
Parsons, Talcott. "On Building Social System Theory: A Personal History." *Daedalus* 99, no. 4 *The Making of Modern Science: Biographical Studies* (1970): 826–81.
Parsons, Talcott. *Talcott Parsons on National Socialism*, edited by Uta Gerhardt. New York: De Gruyter, 1993a.

Parsons, Talcott. "Nazis Destroy Learning, Challenge Religion." In *Talcott Parsons on National Socialism*, edited by Uta Gerhardt. New York: De Gruyter, 1993b, 81–83.

Parsons, Talcott. "The Sociology of Modern Anti-Semitism." In *Talcott Parsons on National Socialism*, edited by Uta Gerhardt. New York: De Gruyter, 1993c, 243–74.

Parsons, Talcott. *Actor, Situation and Normative Pattern: An Essay in the Theory of Social Action*, edited by Victor Lidz and Helmut Staubmann. Münster: Lit, 2010 [1939].

Parsons, Talcott. *Der Kapitalismus bei Sombart und Max Weber. Capitalism according to Sombart and Max Weber: Talcott Parsons' Dr. Phil Dissertation in German and English*, edited and translated by Günter Stummvoll and Bruce C. Wearne. Münster: Lit, 2018.

Parsons, Talcott and Edward H. Shils. *Towards a General Theory of Action*. Cambridge, MA: Harvard University Press, 1951.

Parsons, Talcott and Eric Voegelin. "Correspondence, 1940–1944," edited by Peter Brickey Lequire and Daniel Silver. *European Journal of Sociology* 54, no. 2 (2013): e1–e64.

Patel, Kiran K. *Soldiers of Labor: Labor Service in Nazi Germany and New Deal America, 1933–1945*. Cambridge, GB: Cambridge University Press, 2005 [2003].

Petsch, Robert ed. *Das Volksbuch vom Doctor Faust*, second edition. Halle an der Saale: Niemeyer, 1911 [1587].

Pickstone, John V. "Bureaucracy, Liberalism and the Body in Post-Revolutionary France: Bichat's Physiology and the Paris School of Medicine." *History of Science* 19, no. 2 (1981): 115–42.

Polan, Dana. *Scenes of Instruction: The Beginning of the U.S. Study of Film*. Berkeley: University of California Press, 2007.

Pols, Johannes C. "Managing the Mind: The Culture of American Mental Hygiene, 1910–1950." PhD Dissertation, University of Pennsylvania, 1997.

Pospielovsky, Dimitry. "From *Gosizdat* to *Samizdat* and *Tamizdat*." *Canadian Slavonic Papers* 20, no. 1 (1978): 44–62.

President's Science Advisory Committee. "The Emergence of the Report and Preprint Literature." In *"Science, Government, and Information: The Responsibilities of the Technical Community and the Government in the Transfer of Information."* Washington/DC: Superintendent of Documents, U.S. Government Printing Office, 1963, 19–20, https://files.eric.ed.gov/fulltext/ED048894.pdf (August 5, 2025).

Price, David H. *Anthropological Intelligence: The Deployment and Neglect of American Anthropology in the Second World War*. Durham, NC: Duke University Press, 2008.

Pynchon, Thomas. *Gravity's Rainbow*. New York: Viking, 1995 [1973].

Quaresima, Leonardo. "Introduction to the 2004 Edition: Rereading Kracauer." In Siegfried Kracauer. *From Caligari to Hitler: A Psychological History of the German Film*, translated by Michael F. Moore, xv–xlix. Princeton, NJ: Princeton University Press, 2004.

Rabinbach, Anson. *The Human Motor: Energy, Fatigue, and the Origins of Modernity*. New York: Basic Books, 1990.

Raulff, Ulrich. "Nachwort: Die Minima Moralia nach fünfzig Jahren: Ein philosophisches Volksbuch im Spiegel seiner frühen Kritik." In *Theodor W. Adorno: "Minima Moralia" neu gelesen*, edited by Andreas Bernard and Ulrich Raulff. Frankfurt am Main: Suhrkamp, 2003, 123–31.
Raulff, Ulrich and Ellen Strittmatter eds. *Marbacher Magazin 163–4, Thomas Mann in Amerika*. Marbach am Neckar: Deutsche Schillergesellschaft, 2018.
Redfield, Robert, Ralph Linton, and Melville J. Herskovits. "Memorandum for the Study of Acculturation." *American Anthropologist* 38, no. 1 (1936): 149–52.
Reed, Terence J. *Thomas Mann: The Uses of Tradition*. Oxford: Clarendon Press, 1974.
Reed, Terence J. "'... dass alles verstehen alles verzeihen heisse...': Zur Dialektik zwischen Literatur und Gesellschaft bei Thomas Mann." In *Internationales Thomas-Mann-Kolloquium 1986 in Lübeck*. Bern: Francke, 1986, 159–73.
Renoliet, Jean-Jacques. *L'Unesco oublieé: La Société des Nations et la coopération intellectuelle (1919–1946)*. Paris: Publications de la Sorbonne, 1999.
Rentschler, Eric. *The Ministry of Illusion: Nazi Cinema and Its Afterlife*. Cambridge, MA: Harvard University Press, 1996.
Retman, Sonnet. *Real Folks: Race and Genre in the Great Depression*. Durham, NC: Duke University Press, 2011.
Richards, Pamela Spence. *Scientific Information in Wartime: The Allied-German Rivalry, 1939–1945*. Westport, CT: Greenwood Press, 1994.
Richardson, Lyon N. "*Arrowsmith*: Genesis, Development, Versions." *American Literature* 27, no. 2 (1955): 225–44.
Ridenour, Nina. *Mental Health in the United States: A Fifty-Year History*. Cambridge, MA: Harvard University Press, 1961.
Rieckmann, Jens. "Zum Problem des 'Durchbruchs' in Thomas Manns *Doktor Faustus*." *Wirkendes Wort* 29, no. 2 (1979): 114–28.
Riesman, David. "Review: 'Law and Politics. Occasional Papers of Felix Frankfurter, 1913–1938,' Edited by Archibald MacLeish and E.F. Pritchard Jr." *Washington University Law Review* 25, no. 2 (1940a): 299–301.
Riesman, David. "Review: Punishment and Social Structure. By Georg Rusche and Otto Kirchheimer." *Columbia Law Review* 40, no. 7 (1940b): 1297–301.
Riesman, David. "The Politics of Persecution." *Public Opinion Quarterly* 6, no. 1 (1942): 41–56.
Riesman, David. "A Philosophy for 'Minority' Living: The Jewish Situation and the 'Nerve of Failure.'" *Commentary* 6 (1948): 413–22.
Riesman, David. *The Lonely Crowd: A Study of the Changing American Character, in Collaboration with Reuel Denney and Nathan Glazer*. New Haven, CT: Yale University Press, 1950.
Riesman, David. *Faces in the Crowd: Individual Studies in Character and Politics, in Collaboration with Nathan Glazer*. New Haven, CT: Yale University Press, 1952.
Riesman, David. "On Discovering and Teaching Sociology: A Memoir." *Annual Review of Sociology* 14 (1988): 1–25.
Riesman, David. "Becoming an Academic Man." In *Authors of Their Own Lives: Intellectual Autobiographies by Twenty American Sociologists*, edited by Bennett M. Berger. Berkeley: University of California Press, 1990, 22–74.

Riesman, David. "A Suggestion for Coding the Intensive *White Collar* Interviews." In *David Riesman's Unpublished Writings and Continuing Legacy*, edited by Keith Kerr, B. Garrick Harden, and Marcus Aldredge. London: Routledge, 2015 [1948], 105–8.

Rodgers, Lawrence and Jerold Hirsch. *America's Folklorist: Benjamin A. Botkin and American Culture*. Norman: University of Oklahoma Press, 2010.

Rogers, Everett M. *A History of Communication Study: A Biographical Approach*. New York: Free Press, 1994.

Rohwer, Jürgen. "Die USA und die Schlacht im Atlantik." In *Kriegswende Dezember 1941: Referate und Diskussionsbeiträge des internationalen historischen Symposiums in Stuttgart vom 17. bis 19. September 1981*, edited by Jürgen Rohwer and Eberhard Jäckel. Koblenz: Bernard & Graefe, 1984, 81–103.

Rose, Anne C. "Putting the South on the Psychological Map: The Impact of Region and Race on the Human Sciences during the 1930s." *Journal of Southern History* 71, no. 2 (2005): 321–56.

Rosenblueth, Arturo, Norbert Wiener, and Julian Bigelow. "Behavior, Purpose, and Teleology." *Philosophy of Science* 10, no. 1 (1943): 18–24.

Rosenblueth, Arturo, Norbert Wiener, and Juan García Ramos. "Muscular Clonus: Cybernetics and Physiology." In Norbert Wiener. *Collected Works with Commentaries*. Vol. 4, edited by Pesi Masani. Cambridge, MA: MIT Press, 1985, 466–510.

Roosevelt, Franklin D. "Presidential Order Establishing a Coordinator of Information (COI) on 11 July 1941." *Studies in Intelligence* 37, no. 5 (1994 [1941]): 112–13.

Roosevelt, Kermit ed. *War Report of the OSS*. Vol. 1. New York: Walker, 1976 [1949].

Rottenburg, Richard. *Far-Fetched Facts: A Parable of Development Aid*, translated by Allison Brown and Tom Lampert. Cambridge, MA: MIT Press, 2009 [2002].

Rowlands, Peter and J. Patrick Wilson eds. *Oliver Lodge and the Invention of Radio*. Liverpool: PD, 1994.

Ruesch, Jurgen and Gregory Bateson. *Communication: The Social Matrix of Psychiatry*. New York: Norton, 1951.

Russett, Cynthia E. *The Concept of Equilibrium in American Social Thought*. New Haven, CT: Yale University Press, 1966.

Rutkoff, Peter M. and William B. Scott. *New School: A History of The New School for Social Research*. New York: Free Press, 1986.

Sachsse, Rolf. *Lucia Moholy*. Düsseldorf: Marzona, 1985.

Sahner, Simon. *Der Wirklichkeit verfallen: Deutsche Beat- und Undergroundliteratur 1960–1980*. Bielefeld: Transcript, 2022.

Savage, Jon. *Teenage: The Creation of Youth Culture*. New York: Viking, 2007.

Schivelbusch, Wolfgang. *Entfernte Verwandtschaft – Faschismus, Nationalsozialismus, New Deal*. Munich: Hanser, 2005.

Schlein, Stephen. *The Clinical Erik Erikson: A Psychoanalytic Method of Engagement and Activation*. London: Routledge, 2016.

Schmidt-Schütz, Eva. *Doktor Faustus zwischen Tradition und Moderne: Eine quellenkritische und rezeptionsgeschichtliche Untersuchung zu Thomas Manns literarischem Selbstbild*. Frankfurt am Main: Klostermann, 2003.
Schmitt, Carl. *Über die drei Arten des rechtswissenschaftlichen Denkens*. Hamburg: Hanseatische Verlagsanstalt, 1934.
Schmitt, Carl. *Der Leviathan in der Staatslehre des Thomas Hobbes: Sinn und Fehlschlag eines politischen Symbols*. Hamburg: Hanseatische Verlagsanstalt, 1938.
Schmitt, Carl. *Völkerrechtliche Großraum-Ordnung mit Interventionsverbot für raumfremde Mächte*, third, extended edition. Berlin: Deutscher Rechtsverlag, 1941 [1939].
Schneider, Thomas. *Das literarische Porträt: Quellen, Vorbilder und Modelle in Thomas Manns Doktor Faustus*. Berlin: Frank und Timme, 2005.
Schonfield, Ernest. "Mann Re-Joyces: The Dissemination of Myth in *Ulysses* and *Joseph*, *Finnegans Wake* and *Doctor Faustus*." *Comparative Critical Studies* 3, no. 3 (2006): 259–90.
Schorer, Mark. *Sinclair Lewis: An American Life*. New York: McGraw-Hill, 1961.
Schreckenberger, Helga ed. *Die Alchemie des Exils: Exil als schöpferischer Impuls*. Vienna: Edition Praesens, 2005.
Schüttpelz, Erhard. "Trance-Medien / Personale Medien." In *Handbuch Medienwissenschaft*, edited by Jens Schröter in collaboration with Simon Ruschmeyer and Elisabeth Walke. Stuttgart: Metzler, 2013, 227–33.
Schüttpelz, Erhard. "Vor der Re-Education (1943)." In *Die Moderne im Spiegel des Primitiven: Weltliteratur und Ethnologie (1870–1960)*. Munich: Fink, 2005a, 225–50.
Schüttpelz, Erhard. *Die Moderne im Spiegel des Primitiven: Weltliteratur und Ethnologie (1870–1960)*. Munich: Fink, 2005b.
Schüttpelz, Erhard. "Der Trickster." In *Die Figur des Dritten: Ein kulturwissenschaftliches Paradigma*, edited by Eva Esslinger et al., Frankfurt am Main: Suhrkamp, 2010, 208–24.
Schuetz, Alfred. "Scheler's Theory of Intersubjectivity and the General Thesis of the Alter Ego." *Philosophy and Phenomenological Research* 2, no. 3 (1942): 323–47.
Schuetz, Alfred. "The Problem of Rationality in the Social World." *Economica* NS 10, no. 38 (1943): 130–49.
Schuetz, Alfred. "The Stranger: An Essay in Social Psychology." *American Journal of Sociology* 49, no. 6 (1944): 499–507.
Schutz, Alfred. *Collected Papers V: Phenomenology and the Social Sciences*, edited by Lester Embree. Dordrecht: Springer, 2011a.
Schutz, Alfred. "Parsons' Theory of Social Action." In Alfred Schutz. *Collected Papers V: Phenomenology and the Social Sciences*, edited by Lester Embree. Dordrecht: Springer, 2011b, 8–41.
Schütz, Alfred. "The Problem of Rationality in the Social World." In *Rationality in the Social Sciences: The Schumpeter-Parsons Seminar 1939–40 and Current Perspectives*, edited by Helmut Straubmann and Victor Lidz. Cham, CH: Springer, 2018, 85–102.

Schütz, Alfred and Eric Voegelin. *Eine Freundschaft, die ein Leben ausgehalten hat: Briefwechsel 1938–1959*, edited by Gerhard Wagner and Gilbert Weiss. Konstanz: UVK, 2004.

Schwartz Greene, Rebecca. *Breaking Point: The Ironic Evolution of Psychiatry During World War II*. New York: Fordham University Press, 2023.

Seck, Fatoumata. "The Cultural Underground of Decolonization." *Cambridge Journal of Postcolonial Literary Inquiry* 10, no. 3 (2023): 287–309.

Seidlin, Oskar. "Doctor Faustus: The Hungarian Connection." *German Quarterly* 56, no. 4 (1983): 594–607.

Shankman, Paul. *Margaret Mead*. New York: Berghahn, 2021.

Shapin, Steven. "'A Scholar and a Gentleman': The Problematic Identity of the Scientific Practitioner in Early Modern England." *History of Science* 29, no. 3 (1991): 279–327.

Siegert, Bernhard and Joseph Vogl eds. *Europa: Kultur der Sekretäre*. Zurich: Diaphanes, 2003.

Sitton, Robert. *Lady in the Dark: Iris Barry and the Art of Film*. New York: Columbia University Press, 2014.

Smith, Bradley F. *The Shadow Warriors: O.S.S. and the Origins of the C.I.A.* New York: Basic Books, 1983.

Smith, R. Harris. *OSS: The Secret History of America's First Central Intelligence*. Berkeley: University of California Press, 1972.

Snyder, Thomas D. ed. *120 Years of American Education: A Statistical Portrait*. Washington, DC: U.S. Department of Education, Office of Educational Research and Improvement, National Center for Education Statistics, 1993.

Söllner, Alfons. "Archäologie der deutschen Demokratie: Eine Forschungshypothese zur theoretischen Praxis der Kritischen Theorie im amerikanischen Geheimdienst." In *Zur Archäologie der Demokratie in Deutschland*. Vol. 1, edited by Alfons Söllner. Frankfurt am Main: Fischer, 1986, 7–40.

Sollors, Werner. "W.E.B. Du Bois in Nazi Germany, 1936." *Amerikastudien / American Studies* 44, no. 2 (1999): 207–22.

Solovey, Mark and Hamilton Cravens eds. *Cold War Social Science: Knowledge Production, Liberal Democracy, and Human Nature*. New York: Palgrave Macmillan, 2012.

Spalek, John M. et al. eds. *Deutsche Exilliteratur seit 1933*, 4 Vols. Bern: Francke, 1976–2010.

Später, Jörg. *Siegfried Kracauer: Eine Biographie*. Berlin: Suhrkamp, 2016.

Stackelberg, Roderick. "'Cultural Aspects of National Socialism': An Unfinished Project of the Frankfurt School." *Dialectical Anthropology* 12, no. 2 (1987): 253–60.

Stahl, John D. "Literature and Propaganda: The Structure of Conversion in Schenzinger's Hitlerjunge Quex." *Studies in Twentieth Century Literature* 12, no. 2 (1988): 129–47.

Stanitzek, Georg. "Der Projektemacher: Projektionen auf eine unmögliche Kategorie." *Ästhetik und Kommunikation* 17, nos. 65–66 (1987): 135–46.

Staubmann, Helmut. "C. Wright Mills' *The Sociological Imagination* and the Construction of Talcott Parsons as a Conservative Grand Theorist." *American Sociologist* 52 (2021): 178–93.

Stearns, Peter N. *American Cool: Constructing a Twentieth-Century Emotional Style*. New York: New York University Press, 1994.
Stegmaier, Werner. "Schema, Schematismus." In *Historisches Wörterbuch der Philosophie*. Vol. 8: *R–Sc*, edited by Joachim Ritter and Karlfried Gründer. Darmstadt: Wissenschaftliche Buchgesellschaft, 1992, 1246–63.
Stephan, Inge. *Eisige Helden: Kälte, Emotionen und Geschlecht in Literatur und Kunst vom 19. Jahrhundert bis in die Gegenwart*. Bielefeld: Transcript, 2019.
Stevenson, Angus and Christine A. Lindberg eds. *New Oxford American Dictionary*, third edition. Oxford: Oxford University Press, 2010.
Stewart, Jeffrey C. *The New Negro: The Life of Alain Locke*. Oxford: Oxford University Press, 2018.
Stocking, George W. "The Aims of Boasian Ethnography: Crafting Materials for Traditional Humanistic Scholarship." *History of Anthropology Newsletter* 4, no. 2 (1977): 4–5.
Stolow, Jeremy. "Techno-religious Imaginaries: On the Spiritual Telegraph and the Circum-Atlantic World of the Nineteenth Century." *Globalization Working Papers* 6, no. 1 (2006): 1–32.
Stone, Shepard. "Hitler's Showmen Weave a Magic Spell." *New York Times*, December 3, 1933.
Straubmann, Helmut and Victor Lidz. "Editor's Introduction: The Harvard Rationality Seminar." In *Rationality in the Social Sciences: The Schumpeter-Parsons Seminar 1939–40 and Current Perspectives*, edited by Helmut Straubmann and Victor Lidz. Cham, CH: Springer, 2018, 1–25.
Strecker, Edward. "Introduction." In Richard Brickner. *Is Germany Incurable?* Philadelphia, PA: Lippincott, 1943, 15–18.
Sullivan, Gerald. *Margaret Mead, Gregory Bateson, and Highland Bali: Fieldwork Photographs of Bayung Gedé, 1936–1939*. Chicago, IL: University of Chicago Press, 1999.
Susman, Warren I. "The Culture of the Thirties." In *Culture as History: The Transformation of American Society in the Twentieth Century*. New York: Pantheon, 1984, 150–83.
Taubes, Jacob. "From Cult to Culture." *Partisan Review* 21 (1954): 387–400.
Taylor, Graham D. "Anthropologists, Reformers, and the Indian New Deal." *Prologue* 7, no. 3 (1975): 151–62.
Tent, James F. *Mission on the Rhine: 'Reeducation' and Denazification in American Occupied Germany*. Chicago, IL: University of Chicago Press, 1982.
Tent, James F. *Academic Proconsul: Harvard Sociologist Edward Y. Hartshorne and the Reopening of German Universities 1945–1946. His Personal Account*. Trier: Wissenschaftlicher Verlag, 1998.
Thompson, Robert F. "An Aesthetic of the Cool: West African Dance." *African Forum* 2 (1966): 85–102.
Thompson, Robert F. "An Aesthetic of the Cool." *African Arts* 7, no. 1 (1973): 40–43; 64–67; 89–91.
Thompson, Robert F. *African Art in Motion: Icon and Act*. Los Angeles: University of California Press, 1974.
Thompson, Robert F. *Flash of the Spirit: African and Afro-American Art and Philosophy*. New York: Random House, 1983.

Thompson, Robert F. *Tango: The Art History of Love*. New York: Pantheon, 2005.

Thompson, Robert F. *An Aesthetic of the Cool: Afro-Atlantic Music and Art*. Pittsburgh, PA: Periscope Publishing, 2011.

Thompson, Stith ed. *Motif-Index of Folk-Literature, a Classification of Narrative Elements in Folk-Tales, Ballads, Myths, Fables, Mediaeval Romances, Exempla, Fabliaux, Jest-Books, and Local Legends*, 6 Vols. Bloomington: Indiana University Press, 1932–1936.

Thompson, Stith. *A Folklorist's Progress: Reflections of a Scholar's Life*. Bloomington: Indiana University Press, 1996.

Thyrnauer, Alfred. "German Leaders-in-Exile Ponder Country's Postwar Fate: Thomas Mann Highly Regarded for President – Democratic Revolution Favored by Many." Washington Post, July 4, 1943.

Tidwell, Edgar and John Wright. "Alain Locke: A Comprehensive Bibliography of His Published Writings." *Callaloo*, nos. 11–13 (1981): 175–92.

Tippelskirch, Karina von. *Dorothy Thompson and German Writers in Defense of Democracy*. Berlin: Peter Lang, 2018.

Troy, Thomas F. *Wild Bill and Intrepid: Donovan, Stephenson and the Origin of CIA*. New Haven, CT: Yale University Press, 1996.

Turner, Frederick Jackson. *The Frontier in American History*. New York: Henry Holt and Company, 1920.

Turner, Catherine. *Marketing Modernism Between the Two World Wars*. Amherst: University of Massachusetts Press, 2003.

Turner, Fred. *From Counterculture to Cyberculture: Stewart Brand, the Whole Earth Network, and the Rise of Digital Utopianism*. Chicago, IL: University of Chicago Press, 2006.

Turner, Fred. *The Democratic Surround: Multimedia and American Liberalism from World War II to the Psychedelic Sixties*. Chicago, IL: University of Chicago Press, 2013.

Unger, Corinna R. "Wissenschaftlicher und politischer Berater der US-Regierung im und nach dem Zweiten Weltkrieg." In *Arnold Brecht 1884–1977: Demokratischer Beamter und politischer Wissenschaftler in Berlin und New York*, edited by Claus-Dieter Krohn and Corinna R. Unger. Stuttgart: Steiner, 2006, 129–50.

Vaget, Hans R. "Einleitung." In Thomas Mann and Agnes E. Meyer. *Briefwechsel, 1937–1955*, edited by Hans R. Vaget. Frankfurt am Main: Fischer, 1992, 5–71.

Vaget, Hans R. *Thomas Mann, der Amerikaner: Leben und Werk im amerikanischen Exil, 1938–1952*. Frankfurt am Main: Fischer, 2011.

Valdivieso, Mercedes. "Eine 'symbiotische Arbeitsgemeinschaft': Lucia und László Moholy-Nagy." In *Liebe Macht Kunst: Künstlerpaare im 20. Jahrhundert*, edited by Renate Berger. Köln: Böhlau, 2000, 65–85.

Valentin, Sonja. *"Steine in Hitlers Fenster": Thomas Manns Radiosendungen Deutsche Hörer! 1940–1945*. Göttingen: Wallstein, 2015.

Van Ginneken, Jaap. *Crowds, Psychology, and Politics, 1871–1899*. Cambridge, GB: Cambridge University Press, 1992.

Verhave, Jan P. "Henry Mencken and Paul de Kruif, a Writer's Friendship." *Menckeniana*, no. 210 (2015): 1–10.

Verhave, Jan P. *A Constant State of Emergency: Paul de Kruif Microbe Hunter and Health Activist*. Holland, MI: Van Raalte Press, 2020.
Vismann, Cornelia. *Files: Law and Media Technology*, translated by Geoffrey Winthrop-Young. Stanford, CA: Stanford University Press, 2008 [2000].
Voigts, Manfred. *Oskar Goldberg: Der mythische Experimentalwissenschaftler – Ein verdrängtes Kapitel jüdischer Geschichte*. Berlin: Agora, 1992.
Voss, Lieselotte. *Die Entstehung von Thomas Manns Roman "Doktor Faustus": Dargestellt anhand von unveröffentlichten Vorarbeiten*. Tübingen: Niemeyer, 1975.
Walker, Alice. "In Search of Nora Zeale Hurston." *Ms.* (March 1975): 74–89.
Wasson, Haidee. *Museum Movies: The Museum of Modern Art and the Birth of Art Cinema*. Berkeley, CA: University of California Press, 2005.
Wasson, Haidee. "Studying Movies at the Museum: The Museum of Modern Art and Cinema's Changing Object." In *Inventing Film Studies*, edited by Lee Grieveson and Haidee Wasson. Durham, NC: Duke University Press, 2008, 121–48.
Waterman, Thomas T. and Alfred L. Kroeber. "The Kepel Fish Dam." *University of California Publications American Archeology and Ethnology* 35, no. 6, (1938): 49–80.
Wearne, Bruce C. *The Theory and Scholarship of Talcott Parsons to 1951: A Critical Commentary*, Cambridge, GB: Cambridge University Press, 1989.
Weber, Max. *The Theory of Social and Economic Organization*, translated by A.M. Henderson and Talcott Parsons. Glencoe, IL: Free Press, 1947.
Wescott, Joan. "The Sculpture and Myths of Eshu-Elegba, the Yoruba Trickster: Definition and Interpretation in Yoruba Iconography." *Africa: Journal of the International African Institute* 32, no. 4 (1962): 336–54.
Wheatland, Thomas. *The Frankfurt School in Exile*. Minneapolis: University of Minnesota Press, 2009.
Wiener, Norbert. *Cybernetics; or, Control and Communication in the Animal and the Machine*. New York: Wiley and Sons, 1948.
Wiener, Norbert. *I Am a Mathematician: The Later Life of a Prodigy*. Garden City, NY: Doubleday, 1956.
Wiggershaus, Rolf. *The Frankfurt School: Its History, Theories, and Political Significance*, translated by Michael Robertson. Cambridge, MA: MIT Press, 1995.
Wilkinson, Rupert. "Toward the Lonely Crowd: A Report on an Interview with David Riesman." In *David Riesman's Unpublished Writings and Continuing Legacy*, edited by Keith Kerr, B. Garrick Harden, and Marcus Aldredge. London: Routledge, 2015, 154–80.
Wimmer, Ruprecht. "Textlage." In Thomas Mann. *Doktor Faustus: Das Leben des Deutschen Tonsetzers Adrian Leverkühn, erzählt von einem Freunde. Commentary*, edited by Ruprecht Wimmer in collaboration with Stephan Stachorski. Frankfurt am Main: Fischer, 2007, 84–99.
Winks, Robin W. *Cloak & Gown: Scholars in the Secret War, 1939–1961*, second edition. New Haven, CT: Yale University Press, 1996 [1987].
Winthrop-Young, Geoffrey. "The Third Reich in Alternative History: Aspects of a Genre-Specific Depiction of Nazi Culture." *Journal of Popular Culture* 39, no. 5 (2006): 878–96.

Wolf, Kenneth H. *The Idea of Nationalism: The Intellectual Development and Historiographical Contribution of Hans Kohn*. PhD dissertation, University of Notre Dame, 1972.

Wysling, Hans. "Zu Thomas Manns 'Maja'-Projekt." In *Quellenkritische Studien zum Werk Thomas Manns*, edited by Paul Scherrer and Hans Wysling. Bern: Francke, 1967.

Yans-McLaughlin, Virginia. "Science, Democracy, and Ethics: Mobilizing Culture and Personality for World War II." In *Malinowski, Rivers, Benedict, and Others: Essays on Culture and Personality*, edited by George W. Stocking. Madison: University of Wisconsin Press, 1988, 184–217.

Yates, JoAnne. "The Emergence of the Memo as a Genre." *Management Communication Quarterly* 2, no. 4 (1989): 485–510.

Yee, Martha M. "Attempts to Deal With the 'Crisis in Cataloging' at the Library of Congress in the 1940s." *Library Quarterly* 57, no. 1 (1987): 1–31.

Yurok Tribe Website. www.yuroktribe.org/gold-rush-in-yurok-country (August 5, 2025).

Ziehen, Gregor. *Education for Death: The Making of the Nazi*. London: Oxford University Press, 1941.

Zinfert, Maria. "Digression: Lili Kracauer; A Biographical Sketch," translated by Michael Turnbull. In *Kracauer Fotografic Archive*, edited by Maria Zinfert. Zurich: Diaphanes, 2014, 79–86.

Zipperstein, Steven J. "Underground Man: The Curious Case of Mark Zborowski and the Writing of a Modern Jewish Classic." *Jewish Review of Books*, no. 2 (2010): 38–42.

Zitzewitz, Josephine von. *Culture of Samizdat: Literature and Underground Networks in the Late Soviet Union*. London: Bloomsbury, 2021.

Zumwalt, Rosemary L. *American Folklore Scholarship: A Dialogue of Dissent*. Bloomington: University of Indiana Press, 1988.

Index

Aarne-Thompson-Index, 106
"Actor, Situation and Normative Pattern" (Parsons), 162–68
Adejumo, J. K., 52
adolescence, 120, 174
Adorno, Theodor W., 21, 50, 86, 88, 95, 98, 115, 132, 155, 251
  Dialectic of Enlightenment (with Horkheimer), 51, 86, 95
Afghanistan, 14
Alexander, Jeffrey C., 148
Allport, Floyd H., 155, 158
Allport, Gordon W., 144
  Allport Committee, 144
Althusius, Johannes, 140
America First Committee, 26, 31
"American Century" (Luce), 37–40
American Committee for the Guidance of Professional Personnel, 47, 139, 226
American Committee for the Protection of Foreign Born, 62
American Friends of German Freedom, 7
American Museum of Natural History, 116
American University (Washington, DC), 11
Amherst College, 140
"An Analysis of the Nazi Film, Hitlerjunge Quex, (1933)" (Bateson), 114, 118–35
Andersen, Hans Christian, 102
Anderson, Eugene N., 11, 74
Ann Arbor, MI, 72
anti-interventionism, 206

antisemitism, 24, 26, 83–84, 110, 139, 149–60, 190–92
apart-playing, 217
Apollinaire, Guillaume, 216
Archive of American Folk-Song, 228
Arendt, Hannah, 201
Arlt, Gustave O., 21, 88, 96, 231
ars tradiendi, 44
ASLIB Microfilm Service, 72, 82
Assmann, Jan, 233
Atlantic Ocean, 49
Atlas, 212
Auerbach, Erich, 232
Auger, Charles P., 202

Bacon, Francis, 44
Bahia, 53
Bales, Robert F., 259
Bali, 121–32, 212, 237
Balinese Character (Mead and Bateson), 122–25
Bar Kochba, 14
Barber, Bernard, 146
Barnes, Albert C., 60
Barnes, Trevor J., 69
Barnes Foundation Collection, 59, 62
Baron, Salo, 155
Bastian, Adolf, 233
Bateson, Gregory, 6, 21, 114–35, 175–78, 187, 193–94, 197–98, 237, 251
  "An Analysis of the Nazi Film, Hitlerjunge Quex, (1933)", 114, 118–35
  Balinese Character (with Mead), 125

Baum, Vicki, 229
Behemoth (Neumann), 6, 66–67, 82–84
Bendersky, Joseph W., 155
Benedict, Ruth, 63
Benjamin, Walter, 232
Berendsohn, Walter A., 233
Bergmann, Hugo, 14
Bergson, Henri, 105
Berkeley, CA, 6, 186
Bermann Fischer, Gottfried, 230
Best, Werner, 83
Binkley, Robert C., 71
Binnenrationalität, 227
Birkhead, Leon M., 24, 26
birth of cool, 57, 60
Bismarck, Otto von, 213, 246
Black Atlantic, 49–51
Black Legion, 25
Blackbourn, David, 14
Blanchot, Maurice, 236
Bliven, Bruce, 204
Boas, Franz, 56–57, 63, 103
Boes, Tobias, 87
Book-of-the-Month Club, 93
Borgese, Giuseppe, 16
Botkin, Benjamin A., 96, 109, 231
Brandeis, Louis, 47
Brazil, 53, 60
Brecht, Arnold, 12
Brentano, Franz, 259
Brickner, Richard M., 177, 192, 261, 265
Brit Shalom, 15
British Broadcasting Corporation (BBC), 94, 107–8
Broch, Hermann, 16
Buck, Paul H., 144
Bunche, Ralph, 64
Bureau of Applied Social Research, 211
Bureau of Indian Affairs, 172
Bush, Vannevar, 73

cakewalk, 213
Calvinism, 20, 140–41, 143–44, 158–61, 168, 248, 253
Cambridge, MA, 136, 138
Cambridge University, 72
Campbell, Joseph, 21, 88, 104, 105
Cannon, Walter B., 247
Carnegie Foundation, 4, 13, 24, 30
Carpathian Mountains, 14
Central Intelligence Agency (CIA), 4

Century Group, 38, 208
Chapin, Katherine G., 62
Chaplin, Charlie, 191
Chesterton, Gilbert K., 204
Childhood and Society (Erikson), 6, 172–77, 180–92
China, 151
circulation, 2, 5, 7–8, 33, 38, 78, 80, 90, 117, 144, 149, 155, 162, 165, 175–76, 192, 196, 199
Citizen Kane, 32
Clay, Lucius D., 139, 171
clearance, 69, 219
clonus, 115, 121–26, 131, 242
collaboration, 2–6, 8–13, 16–17, 19–25, 33, 37, 40–65, 70, 74–77, 80, 84, 88, 90, 95, 104, 106, 114, 119, 124, 127, 132, 136, 138–40, 143–45, 147, 152–55, 158–60, 163–65, 168, 170–74, 178–79, 183, 196–98
Collier, John, 182–83
Columbia University, 104, 211
Comité des Délégations Juives, 15
Committee for National Morale, 6, 116, 254, 261
Committee on Food Habits, 4
Committee to Defend America by Aiding the Allies (CDAAA), 32, 34
Communist Front, 62
conceptual scheme, 139, 145–47, 150, 161, 166–68
Cooley, Charles, 164
Coordinator of information (COI), 68, 261
Copenhagen, 194
Council for a Democratic Germany, 109
Council for Democracy, 13, 38, 47, 140–42, 153, 155, 250, 253–54
  Committee of Correspondence, 140
  Nazi Poison, 150–61
Council on Intercultural Relations, 6, 116
coup d'état, 79, 81
covert identity, 95
creole, 48, 57–58
creolization, 10, 47, 52–54, 59, 63–65, 76, 167
critical fabulation, 214
critical theory, 47, 84, 125
Cuba, 53, 60
cultural pluralism, 63, 182
culture pattern, 59, 133, 136, 139, 142–43, 145, 167, 174, 246, 258

cybernetics, 122
Czechoslovak Republic, 15

Darrow, Clarence, 204
Davis, Miles, 57, 199
Dawes Commission, 72
de Huszar Allen, Marguerite, 98–100
dementia praecox, 123
democracy, 1, 26, 29, 31–32, 117, 140, 142, 184
Denmark, 177
Dialectic of Enlightenment (Horkheimer & Adorno), 51, 86, 95
Dilling, Elizabeth, 204
Doctor Faustus (Mann), 6, 86–113
Donovan, William J., 68, 95
Donovan Leisure Newton & Lumbard, 68
dope, 23
double contingency, 165–68
Douglas, Aaron, 217
Dow, James R., 233
Du Bois, W. E. B., 16, 213
Dürer, Albrecht, 102
Durkheim, Émile, 148, 158

Earle, Edward Mead, 223
Easter Island, 207
Eastern Office of the National Opinion Research Center, 211
Eatonville, FL, 214
ecstasy, 111
Eisenhower, Dwight D., 192
Eliot, Charles William, 44
Ellison, Ralph, 51
England, 4, 39, 68, 72, 148, 205
entropy, 258
equilibrium, 146
Erickson, Milton H., 243
Erikson, Erik H. (also Erik Homburger), 6–7, 21, 120, 172–95
    Childhood and Society, 6, 172–77, 180–92
Erikson, Joan, 177
Eshu-Elegba, 54, 58, 60, 63–64
    Esu-'tufunaalo, 55
Evans, Luther, 90–91
exile literature, 20, 86–87, 92, 229
expectancy breaching procedure, 111

Fabian Society, 15
fascism, 3, 11, 18, 25, 31, 102, 143, 158

Father Coughlin, 25
Fauset, Arthur, 217
Faustian pact, 86, 95, 97, 103, 111, 112
Federal Bureau of Investigation (FBI), 206
Federal Writers' Project (FWP), 96, 228
    Federal Music Project, 228
Feuchtwanger, Lion, 229
Fight for Freedom Committee (FFF), 32, 38
Film Library of the New York Museum of Modern Art, 114, 116–17, 119, 121–22, 127
Fischer, Gottfried Bermann, 88
Fisher, Rudolph, 216
flag, 27, 115, 117, 119–21, 128–30, 133, 241
Flexner, Abraham, 24
Flexner, Simon, 24
Flexner Report, 24
Florida, 55–56
Flounders, Fanny, 185
folklore, 17, 49–50, 56, 88, 96–106, 109–13, 181, 186, 213, 228, 236
Foreign Economic Administration (FEA), 224, 258
Foreign Policy Association, 62
Fortress Europe, 86, 106
Foster, Frances S., 61
Fraenkel, Ernst, 82
France, 3, 151
Franco, Francisco (Franco), 31
Frank, Hans, 226
Frank, Lawrence K., 128, 174, 193, 260, 262
Frankfurter, Felix, 34, 209
Franz, Shepherd I., 262
Freedom's Journal, 216
Freud, Anna, 191
Freud, Sigmund, 190
Friedrich, Carl J., 16, 21, 47, 136, 139–45, 153–59, 171, 194
friendly enemy alien, 2, 50, 74, 84, 119, 223
Friends of Democracy, 26
Frobenius, Leo V., 235
From Caligari to Hitler (Kracauer), 6, 120–21
Fromm, Erich, 47–48, 210–11
Frye, H. Northrop, 236

G. I. Bill of Rights, 210
Gadamer, Hans-Georg, 54

Galison, Peter, 10
Garfinkel, Harold, 149–50, 167–68, 206
　"Perception of the Other", 149–50, 167–68
Garvey, Marcus, 59
Gates, Jr., Henry L., 54
Geertz, Clifford, 256
General Education Board, 62
Geneva, 62
Gerhardt, Uta, 144
German Academic Exchange Service (DAAD), 248
German catastrophe, 97, 110, 113
"German Morale after Tunisia" (OSS), 20, 79–82
German-American Bund, 25
Gideon Planish (Lewis), 23, 26–34
Glazer, Nathan, 43
Glissant, Édouard, 10
Goebbels, Joseph, 252
Goethe, Johann Wolfgang von, 99
Goff, Brendan, 204
Goldberg, Oskar, 232
Gorer, Geoffrey, 114, 178
Göring, Hermann, 252
Gorky, Maxim, 187
Graeber, Isacque, 153, 155
gray literature, 5, 7–12, 19, 22, 33–34, 38, 45, 48, 63, 65, 67, 114, 117, 139, 143, 145, 155, 162–63, 168, 178, 196–97
Great Dictator, 191
Great Migration, 50, 57, 59
Greater Caribbean, 49, 57, 212
Grimmelshausen, Hans Jakob Christoffel von, 102
Guggenheim Foundation, 4, 13, 241
Guillaume, Paul, 216
Gultscha, 14

Habsburg Monarchy, 14
Hahn, Otto, 72
Hamacher, Bernd, 102
Hamburg, 39
Harcourt, Alfred, 23
Harlem, 56–61
Harlem Renaissance, 49, 56, 58, 61, 65
Hart, James, 26
Hartshorne, Edward Y., 138, 153, 193
Hartshorne, Richard, 77, 224
Harvard University, 47, 58, 139, 165, 236
　American Defense, Harvard Group, 143
　Bureau of International Research, 13
　Department of Social Relations, 138, 144
　Graduate School of Public Administration, 248
　Harvard Law School, 47
　Harvard Rationality Seminar, 162
　Harvard Summer School, 16
　Pareto Circle, 144, 248
　School of Overseas Administration, 13, 137, 140, 144, 166
Havana, 53
Hayek, Friedrich A., 163
Hearst, William R., 32
Heidelberg, 140
Heidelberg University
　Institut für Sozial- und Staatswissenschaften, 171
Hellman, Lillian, 151
Helmstätter, Georg, 98
Hemingway, Ernest, 151
Henderson, Lawrence J., 144, 146, 149
Herbert, Ulrich, 83
Hermann, Eva, 106
Hermes, 54
Herskovits, Melville J., 57–58
Herz, John H., 74
Heydrich, Reinhard, 234
Himmler, Heinrich, 252
Hindenburg, Paul von, 246
Hitler Youth, 117, 119–20, 127–33, 195
Hitler, Adolf, 21, 24, 26, 31, 108, 189–92
Hitlerjunge Quex, 21, 114–35
Hollywood, 39, 104, 227
Holthusen, Hans Egon, 238
homoeroticism, 118
Hoover, J. Edgar, 206
Horkheimer, Max, 11, 51, 69, 86, 115, 135, 155
　Dialectic of Enlightenment (with Adorno), 51, 86, 95
Howard University, 75
Hughes, H. Stuart, 201
Hughes, Langston, 216
humaniora, 110
Hurston, Zora Neale, 20, 56–58, 62, 64, 216
　Mules and Men, 56–57
Husserl, Edmund, 164

Ickes, Harold L., 253
identity, 2, 22, 65, 99, 141, 172–74, 176, 178–95
Indian New Deal, 182–83
Indian Reorganization Act (IRA), 182
Inner Emigration, 86, 245
Institute of Child Guidance, 6
Institute of International Education, 15–16
Institute of Social Research, 11, 69, 84, 115, 156, 199, 212, 253
  German Project, 115, 127, 132
intelligence, 20
intelligence report, 2, 9, 67–68, 71–73, 76–84
internationalism, 39, 59, 63
interventionism, 34
Iowa, 27
Ipokia, 52
Irkutsk, 14
isolationism, 34, 206
It Can't Happen Here (Lewis), 24–25
itutu, 52, 57, 65

Jay, Martin, 50
jazz, 39, 50–51, 61
jazz diplomacy, 209
Jerusalem, 15
Johnstone, Andrew, 33
Joint Committee for Postwar Planning, 177
Jolas, Eugene, 229
Josiah Macy Jr. Foundation, 121
Joyce, James, 104–5
Jung, Carl G., 105

Kafka, Franz, 14
Kansas City, MO, 26
Kant, Immanuel, 146
Karlsruhe, 177, 194
Katz, Barry M., 76
Kees, Weldon, 266
Kellog, Paul, 216
Kepel Dam Dance, 185
Keren Hajessod, 15
Kerényi, Karl, 102
Keynes, J. Maynard, 23
Khabarovsk, 14–15
Kirchheimer, Otto, 75, 211
Klausner, Joseph, 15
Kluckhohn, Clyde K. M., 144
Knopf, Alfred A., 90, 237

Kohn, Hans, 13–19, 63
Korzybski, Alfred, 126
Kracauer, Elisabeth, 115
Kracauer, Siegfried, 6, 21, 114–16, 119–21, 128–29, 132, 135
  From Caligari to Hitler, 6, 120–21
Krasnoyarsk, 14
Kreutzer, Hans J., 233
Krieger, Leonard, 202
Kristallnacht (antisemitic pogrom), 47, 151
Kruif, Paul de, 24

Langer, Walter C., 261
Langer, William L., 136, 246
Laudani, Raffaele, 80
Laura Spelman Rockefeller Memorial Fund, 13
Lazarsfeld, Paul F., 13
League of Nations, 62
Lee, Robert E., 27
Lethen, Helmut, 48–49, 64
Leverkuehn, Paul, 94, 95
Leverkühn, August Otto, 94
Levin, Harry, 104
Lewin, Kurt, 128
  Topology Group, 260
Lewis, Sinclair, 23–37, 39, 56
  Gideon Planish, 23, 26–34
  It Can't Happen Here, 24–25
Lewis, Wilmarth S., 71
Library of Congress (LOC), 3–4, 21, 36, 67, 70, 88, 92, 94, 96–97, 106, 108–9
Licklider, J. C. R., 73
Lindbergh, Charles A., 26, 205, 213, 253
Lindy Hop, 213
Lippmann, Walter, 38
Lixfeld, Hannsjost, 233
Locke, Alain LeRoy, 16, 20, 58–64, 74
  When Peoples Meet, 62–63
Lomax, Allan, 96
Lomax, John A., 96
Lonely Crowd (Riesman), 6, 24, 41–44, 46–47
Long, Huey, 25
Los Angeles, CA, 87
Louisiana, 25
Lowe-Porter, Helen T., 90, 228
Lübeck, 107
Lucas, George, 104

Luce, Henry R., 31–32, 34, 37–40, 47
  "American Century", 37–40
  Fortune, 31
  Life, 31, 37
  Time, 31
  Times Inc., 31
Ludlow Massacre, 24
Ludwig, Emil, 229
Luther, Martin, 102

MacLeish, Archibald, 3–4, 32–38,
  70, 88, 90, 96, 107, 206,
  209, 228
Macy Conferences, 198
Magus, Simon, 99
Manhattan Project, 222
Mann, Erika, 87
Mann, Heinrich, 87
Mann, Katia, 92
Mann, Klaus, 87, 106
Mann, Michael, 249
Mann, Thomas, 4, 6, 16, 21, 23,
  85–113, 197
  Doctor Faustus, 6, 86–113
Marcuse, Herbert, 68, 75
Marseille, 15
Marshall, Alfred, 162
Marshall, John, 114
Mason, Charlotte O., 56, 62
Matanzas, 53
material, 4, 23, 26, 36, 67–73, 78, 81, 98,
  102, 103, 110, 147, 177
May, Karl, 262
Mayflower, 248
Mayo, Elton, 157
McCarthyism, 108
Mead, Herbert W., 164
Mead, Margaret, 3–5, 21–22, 63,
  116–17, 120–23, 136, 142,
  155–57, 172, 174–78, 187,
  192–94, 246, 251
  Balinese Character (with Bateson),
    122–25
media, 3, 5–6, 9, 32, 67, 73, 90, 115,
  123–28, 130, 132, 135, 152, 168,
  198–99
mediator, 57, 85–88, 92–94, 107–9, 201,
  213, 228
Mekeel, H. Scudder, 179, 181–84
Mellon, Mary, 104
Memex, 73

memorandum culture, 5, 7, 9, 6–13, 19,
  21–22, 27, 33–34, 47, 49–50, 62,
  67, 92, 95, 107, 116, 118, 139,
  142–44, 150, 155–56, 158, 160,
  163, 165, 171, 196
Mencken, Henry L., 204
mental health, 263
mental hygiene, 179
mental hygiene movement, 183, 263
Mercanton, Jacques, 235
Meyer, Agnes E., 21, 88, 90, 92–97, 107
Meyer, Eugene I., 93
Meyer, Hans, 98
Miami, FL, 53
microfilm, 71–74, 197, 221
microphotography, 67, 71–74
Middle Passage, 51, 53, 60
migration, 8, 12, 14, 17, 20, 54, 57–58, 63,
  110, 177
Mimeographic Department of the Greater
  New York American Women's
  Voluntary Service, 261
mimeography, 2, 7, 29–30, 89, 92, 117,
  198–99
Minnesota, 33
Möbius, Paul J., 103, 231
Moholy, Lucia, 72–73, 84
Moholy-Nagy, László, 72
Monschau, 136
Moore, Wilbert E., 163
morale, 9, 79–82, 116, 141–43
Morgan, Edmund S., 51
Morgenthau, Henry, 166
Mowrer, O. Hobart, 144
Mt. Zion Veterans Rehabilitation Clinic,
  173
Mules and Men (Hurston), 56–57
Mumford, Lewis, 16
Munich, 87, 103, 107, 110
Murray, Henry A., 144, 261
Mussolini, Benito, 31, 94

narcissism, 65, 130–31
Nash, Henry T., 219
national character, 127, 141–45, 198
  American, 41
  Balinese, 126
  German, 6, 91, 103, 109, 117,
    126, 193
National Committee for Mental
  Hygiene, 262

national literature, 17, 19–20, 71, 88, 93, 96, 103, 107, 109
National Research Council (NRC), 4
national security, 67–68, 71, 73, 79, 91
National Socialism, 1–2, 11, 19, 24, 26, 32, 39, 51, 64, 66, 76, 81–82, 87, 95, 108–10, 116, 118, 127, 132–37, 142–43, 147, 150–53, 156, 160–61, 163, 174–76, 219
National Socialist Party (NSDAP), 72, 87, 133, 137, 152
nationalism, 13–19, 59, 86, 142
Nazi Poison (Committee of Correspondence), 150–61
Neilson, William A., 16
Neumann, Franz L., 6, 20, 66, 79–84, 109, 155, 202, 211, 223, 237
  Behemoth, 6, 66–67, 82–84
New Deal, 5, 16, 68, 75, 96, 106, 182, 184
New Guinea, 121, 126
New Negro (Locke), 58–61
New Objectivity, 48, 76
New Orleans, 57
New School for Social Research, 15–16, 257
  University in Exile, 12
New York, 4, 7, 11, 21, 23, 26–27, 29–31, 38, 53, 57, 59, 68, 104, 114–15, 117, 122–23, 162, 177, 182, 198
New York City Board of Education, 45
  Bureau of Child Guidance, 260
New York Evening Post, 24
Niebuhr, Reinhold, 7, 155
Nietzsche, Friedrich, 94, 97, 101, 108
Nigeria, 52, 60
Nobel Prize, 4, 23–24, 88, 218
nonidentity, 125, 127, 135
noninterventionism, 34
Norkus, Herbert, 117
Normative State, 226
Northampton, MA, 13, 15
Notasulga, AL, 214
Novosibirsk, 14

objectivity, 17, 37, 40, 42, 48, 60–61, 64–65, 76–78, 84, 107, 216, 227
Oboler, Arch, 230
Office Facts and Figures (OFF), 36
Office of Naval Research (ONR), 254
Office of Scientific Research and Development (OSRD), 72

Office of Strategic Services (OSS), 4, 10–11, 64, 67, 69, 72, 79, 82, 84, 117, 202, 211, 261
  Central European Section, 11, 74
  Central Information Division (CID), 69
  Research and Analysis Branch (R&A), 20, 67–84, 136
Office of War Information (OWI), 13, 68, 220, 229
Officer Candidate School in Salzburg, 14
Ohio, 27
Old Boys Network, 36
Olden, Georg, 64
Operation Paperclip, 201, 221
Orwell, George, 201
other-direction, 20, 41–50, 55, 59–63, 84, 210
Otlet, Paul, 73

Pacific Palisades, CA, 21, 93, 106
Palestine, 15, 17
Pareto, Vilfredo, 247
Paris, 15, 24, 115, 216
Parker, Charlie, 57, 199
Parker, Dorothy, 204
Parks, Robert Ezra, 249
Parsons, Edward S., 249
Parsons, Helen Walker, 144
Parsons, Talcott, 6, 21, 135–55, 158–69, 193
  "Actor, Situation and Normative Pattern", 162–68
  Social System, 6, 145–51, 158, 160, 166–67
Pasadena, CA, 38
Pearl Harbor, 29, 32
Peirce, Charles S., 146
"Perception of the Other" (Garfinkel), 150, 167–68
Petsch, Robert, 96, 98, 99
Philadelphia Public Ledger, 24
Philadelphia, PA, 47, 215–16
philanthropy, 4–5, 11, 27–30, 33
  critique of, 29
Pine Ridge Reservation, 20, 181–82
Pittsburgh, PA, 38
Poland, 3, 222
polycracy, 66
Popular Front, 231
Powers, Eugene, 72
Prague, 14–15

Prerogative State, 226
Princeton Radio Research Project, 13
print culture, 9, 99, 100
prisoner of war (POW), 6, 14, 177
Project A, 71
propaganda, 3, 9, 13, 20–21, 25, 32, 50, 67–68, 81–82, 94, 103, 107–8, 113–22, 124, 127, 130, 132–35, 152, 155, 206, 220
Putnam, Herbert, 35

Quine, Willard V., 146

radar-type, 46
Radin, Max, 155
RAND Corporation, 187
rationalization, 158, 160–61, 163, 257
Raulff, Ulrich, 230
Recife, 53
reciprocity, 10, 63
Reed, T. Jim, 234
reeducation, 2–4, 20, 22, 91, 109, 136, 166, 168, 170–72, 176–95, 245
Reichsfilmkammer, 240
Reiss, Winold, 216
Richardson, Willis, 216
Riesman, David, 6, 20, 41–49, 59, 65, 76, 155, 158, 209, 226
  Lonely Crowd, 6, 24, 41–44, 46–47
Rio de Janeiro, 53
Robinson, Henry Morton, 104
Rockefeller, John D., 24, 71
Rockefeller Foundation, 4, 12, 24, 98, 114, 117, 223, 263
  Rockefeller Institute for Medical Research, 24
Rommel, Erwin, 206
Roosevelt, Eleanor, 178
Roosevelt, Franklin D., 31, 35–37, 39, 46, 68, 106, 197
Rotary Club, 25, 27, 204
Russia, 14, 151, 180, 187–90, 194

Sachgestaltungsdenken, 83–84, 226
Salvation Army, 27
Samara, 14
Samarkand, 14
Sauk Centre, MN, 23
Scheible, Johann, 102
schizophrenia, 121, 123
Schmitt, Carl, 82–84

Schmoller, Gustav von, 213
Schoenberg, Arnold, 106
Schönemann, Friedrich, 214
Schuetz, Alfred, 21, 149–50, 158–68, 256
Schumann, Robert, 97
Schumpeter, Joseph A., 162
Seldes, Gilbert, 204
Seminar on Human Relations in Hanover, NH, 240
Serres, Michel, 54
Shakespeare, William, 102
Shils, Edward A., 167, 202
Siberia, 14
Silver Shirts, 25
Simmel, Georg, 249
Sinclair, Upton, 25
situation, 42, 83, 137–38, 162, 166–67, 186, 246, 259
Smith, Adam, 44
Smith, Al, 25
Smith College, 13, 15
Social Gospel movement, 141
Social Science Research Council (SSRC), 13
Social System (Parsons), 6, 145–51, 158, 160, 166–67
socialization, 123–30, 132
Society for Applied Anthropology, 172
Söllner, Alfons, 75
Sombart, Werner, 140
Sorokin, Pitirim A., 250
Soviet Union, 3, 173, 187–88, 199, 240
Sovietology, 188
Spanish Civil War, 31, 151
Speier, Hans, 202
Sperry Gyroscope Company, 211
Stearns, Peter N., 48–49, 64
Stern, Fritz, 202
Still, William G., 62
Stocking, George W., 233
Strecker, Edward, 261
Strunk, William, 44
study of culture at a distance, 116–17
Sullivan, Harry Stack, 144
Sun Dance, 184
Surinam, 58
Switzerland, 15, 62, 88, 107, 197

Tacitus, Publius Cornelius, 262
Taylor, Archer, 231
Taylorism, 210

teleology, 123, 126, 243
Thompson, Dorothy, 24–26, 30, 152, 253
Thompson, Robert F., 52–57, 59, 65, 212
Tokyo, 15
Toomer, Jean, 216
Townsend, Francis E., 25
trading zone, 10, 48, 75–76
trance, 111, 115, 121–35, 184, 237, 243, 245
translation, 119–21, 129, 135, 165, 199
Trenker, Luis, 120
Tulsa, OK, 38
Turkestan, 14

understanding, 67, 73, 78, 82–84, 113, 116, 126, 146
UNESCO, 73
University of Chicago, 211
University of Vienna, 259
Universum-Film AG, 117

Vaget, Hans R., 92
Vagts, Miriam Beard, 155–56
van Gennep, Arnold, 244
Vienna, 177, 194
Viereck, George S., 30
Vismann, Cornelia, 219
Voegelin, Eric, 21, 150, 158–65
Voss, Lieselotte, 97

Wagner, Adolph, 213
Wagner, Richard, 50
Wandervögel, 129
War Department, 13
Warond, Eric D., 216
Washington, DC, 4, 7, 11, 21, 27, 29, 68, 78, 87–88, 94, 116, 136, 166, 206
Weber, Alfred, 140
Weber, Max, 74, 140–41, 145, 158, 160, 163, 165, 213
Weinberg-Report, 202
Weissner, Carl, 199

Werfel, Franz, 229
When Peoples Meet (Locke), 62–63
White, William A., 32
Whitehead, Alfred N., 105, 146
Wiechert, Ernst, 234
Wiener, Norbert, 122
Williams, Ralph Vaughan, 229
Williams, Richard H., 162
Willkie, Wendell, 31, 38
Winkler, Harold, 155, 255
Winterthur, 88
Wise, Stephen S. (Rabbi Wise), 27
Wittfogel, Karl A., 46
Wolf, Hugo, 97
Wolfe, Thomas, 229
Wolff, Kurt, 104
Wolof language, 57
Wood, Robert E., 26
Works Progress Administration (WPA), 96, 213
World Zionist Organisation, 15
Wysling, Hans, 98

Yale University, 26, 211
    Committee on National Policy, 43
Yates, JoAnne, 44–45
YMCA., 27
Yokohama, 15
Yoruba, 48–65
Yoruba diaspora, 48, 53
Young, Lester, 57
youth, 55, 117–18, 128–29, 172, 181, 213, 237

Zachary, Caroline, 260
Zanzibar, 39
Zborowski, Mark, 254
Ziehen, Gregor, 244
Zimmer, Henry R., 104
Zionism, 14–16, 59
Zoot Suit Riots, 93, 209
Zurich, 105

For EU product safety concerns, contact us at Calle de José Abascal, 56–1°, 28003 Madrid, Spain or eugpsr@cambridge.org.